SPECIAL ATMOSPHERE THEMES FOR FOODSERVICE

by
Jule Wilkinson
assisted by
Audrey Garvey, Madelin Schneider,
and the staff of
Institutions/Volume Feeding Magazine

Published by
INSTITUTIONS/VOLUME FEEDING MAGAZINE
5 S. Wabash Ave., Chicago, Ill. 60603

Distributed to the book trade by:
Cahners Books, 89 Franklin St., Boston, Mass. 02110

Copyright © 1972 by Cahners Publishing Co., Inc. All rights reserved. This book or parts thereof may not be reproduced in any form without permission of the publisher.

Library of Congress Catalog Card No. 78-184740

ISBN 0-8436-0536-7

Printed in the United States of America

History of
INSTITUTIONS/VFM Award Programs

The need in the foodservice/lodging industry for benchmarks to be used in evaluating foodservice and interior design was recognized many years ago. To answer the need, INSTITUTIONS/VFM Magazine launched two award programs; The Foodservice Award Program and The Interior Design Program.

- The Foodservice Award Program was designed to honor operators who recognized that sound planning would increase productivity and that innovative solutions and flexibility were essential to continuing success in foodservice operation.

- The Interiors Design Award Program was initiated to honor the operations that complement their good food and service with exceptional surroundings.

Entries for the Foodservice Award Program are judged in the spring with Awards presented during the National Restaurant Association's annual convention. The Interior Design Award entries are judged in the fall and Awards are presented at the National Hotel Exposition.

Panels of highly qualified experts review entries individually. Each aspect of the material submitted is carefully scrutinized and evaluated. In Foodservice Award entries, judges check on such factors as the efficiency of the use of space, equipment and employee input; indications of good employee morale; marketing techniques that accurately profile patrons. In Interior Design Award entries, judges determine how well form and function relate; how the design selected enhances the operation; whether the elements combined in the interiors attract a predetermined clientele.

Not only does such careful critiquing honor individual operations, there is an added value. Those ideas that are rated exceptional are disseminated to the entire industry both through INSTITUTIONS/VFM Magazine and through many of the books now being published by I/VFM, and distributed through Cahners Books.

Much of the material presented in this book comes from Award winners in the two programs who have submitted their entries in recent years. For many years, the entries have been an invaluable source of statistics and data made available to qualified operators and designers seeking to clarify special areas of foodservice or interiors.

Operators of foodservice/lodging establishments interested in submitting entries can get full details on entering either of the programs—The Foodservice Award Program or The Interior Design Award Program—from the Awards Program Director, INSTITUTIONS/VFM, 5 S. Wabash, Chicago 60603.

TABLE OF CONTENTS

OLE—SPANISH, MEXICAN, LATIN AND SOUTH AMERICAN

Introduction	6
Creating an Ole Atmosphere	27
Foods to Feature on Ole Menus	31
Serving Ole Foods	34
Ole Food Preparation	40
Menus	43
Promoting Ole Foodservice	54
Appetizers	59
Soups	61
Entrees	62
Salads	74
Sauces	76
Desserts	77
Beverages	78

THE NAUTICAL WAY—SEAFOOD THEMES

Introduction	82
Elements of a Sea-Going Setting	99
Purchasing Fish, Seafood	102
Preparing Fish, Seafood	107
Secrets of Seafood Success	112
Sauces for Seafood	113
Merchandising Seafood	117
Seafood Recipes	122
Crab	123
Fish Portions	125
Flounder	127
Halibut	129
Lobster	131
Oysters	133
Salmon	135
Scallops	136
Shrimp	138
Sole	142
Pike	142
Tuna	143
Seafood Species Charts	145

COUNTRY/COLONIAL—FARM STYLE AND EARLY AMERICAN THEMES

Introduction	*152*
Succeeding with Country/Colonial Themes	*170*
Historic Appeals for Modern Diners	*172*
Keep Patrons Coming Back to the Farm	*179*
Old Country Customs Add to Rural Charm	*187*
Design Approach to Country/Colonial	*191*
Menus that Meld with Country/Colonial Interiors	*206*
Appetizers	*213*
Soups	*213*
Entrees	*215*
Vegetables	*221*
Salads	*223*
Breadstuff	*226*
Cakes	*227*
Puddings	*228*
Pies	*231*
Cookies	*232*

BIBLIOGRAPHY *235*

INDEX TO RECIPES *237*

ABOUT THIS BOOK

People eating out today go in search of something new—an experience not ordinarily encountered, one that will take them away from their usual routine. They want a mini-respite from the "daily."

To make eating out this kind of escape event may require the creation of a special environment, whether permanently or for a day. Themes that can be developed to provide a unique setting and foodservice are numerous; the problem is in deciding which one to follow. This book tells how operators have made effective and successful use of four such special themes: OLE (Spanish, Mexican, South American); NAUTICAL (Seafood); COUNTRY (Farm Style) and COLONIAL (Early American).

How successful operators have adapted these themes both for commercial and noncommercial foodservice is spelled out in detail. Although a total package is presented for each theme, the basic theme ideas can also be adapted for a once-a-week or once-a-month gala sampling of these foods and customs from other lands, historical periods or areas.

In commercial food service, creation of a special atmosphere provides the escape for patrons that is known to be one of the strongest appeals going out to eat can have. A short time spent in a different life-style with a different pattern of surroundings, food and entertainment makes eating-out an occasion to be repeated and shared.

SPECIAL ATMOSPHERE THEMES FOR FOODSERVICE

In noncommercial settings, a special night of new, though temporary, decor themes and a menu of not-usually-encountered dishes is a morale booster for patrons and staff alike.

Foods and recipes in this book suggested for special theme menus have been toned down to American tastes, yet ways to make these dishes totally authentic are also included.

If you've settled on one of the themes in this book, you'll find an easy blueprint of the steps to be taken in building your foodservice around it. If you're just starting out in search of a special theme, study all four and select the one that seems most apt to intrigue your clientele.

Collected here are decor, menu planning, food presentation, promotion and merchandising ideas and recipes—all tested before publication in operations with successful performance records in special atmosphere food service.

OLE!

Adaptable is the word for the Ole theme. Whether its basis is Mexican, Spanish, Latin or South American, the theme is equally effective in drive-in operations and luxury dining rooms. If a spirited and colorful attraction is what you want to create, the formula is assembled on the following pages.

OLE!
Institutions Portfolio of Latin Food and Interiors

Olé—the spirited latin mix of food, decor and merchandising—
continues to work its magic on American food service. Kids everywhere
like the taste and texture of tacos; families relish the varied latin fare
(and like its low price too); and the dinner-at-eight crowd enjoys a
"trip" to Old Mexico or sunny Spain on an evening out.
The Olé package provides the kind of "total experience" experts
see as the future of dining out. Patrons at El Sombrero, in
San Francisco's Cannery, revel in the complete setting where they
can smell, hear, taste and watch Mexican. A colorful Mexican kitchen
is the main stage. There Act I may be preparation of guacamole;
Act II, frothing of chocolate with the beautifully carved molonillo
and Act III, mixing of "aguas frescas," drinks seldom encountered in the U. S.
Equally provocative ideas assembled in this section cover interior design,
food and merchandising efforts that are making latin (food) lovers
out of a growing number of Norte Americanos.

SEATTLE SAYS SI TO MEXICAN OPERATIONS

Right: Plaza 5 was a tasteful, attractive restaurant in the lower plaza of a downtown Seattle office building. It did well at noon, but like many urban operations it suffered from lack of patrons at night.

Above: Now very noticeable from the street above, La Plaza flags patrons with bold carved signs, rugged dark wood panelling, planter boxes with tile inserts, warm yellow tile flooring and bright striped awnings. Clarke's Restaurant Enterprises reports sales in the festive Mexican restaurant continue to increase. The hot color, spicy food, gay merchandising package has caught on quickly in the Northwest community where it rains more than it shines.

Left: At Los Arcos, one of Clark's suburban restaurants, the authenticity of the setting is established in the imposing entrance area.

Below: The interior structural detailing of Los Arcos includes Spanish Colonial beams of dark wood, recessed niches protected by spool-turned railings and detailed wood screens. Marshall Perrow, Seattle architect, who designed the restaurant, and Eugene Clark, of CRE, shopped in Mexico City antique shops for authentic pieces.

Left: La Plaza's interior was quickly converted to a Mexican restaurant through colorful ceiling treatment, positioning of big bright paper flowers in planter boxes behind every banquette and changing upholstery to a floral vinyl.

BORROW FROM TRADITION FOR SPANISH WARMTH

Spanish tradition in the San Diego area was researched by Fred Schmid and Assoc. for a design theme that would attract patrons to airport facilities. Borrowing from this tradition, food service areas are warm and informal, pleasantly punctuated with arches, red moresque shaped floor tiles, dark wood turnings, tropical foliage. In the airport's main dining area, the carpet design is reminiscent of decorative ceramic floor tile. Design results? An impressive increase in airport food service sales.

This gazebo, formed of wood turnings, is used for parties of six only. It provides some privacy yet gives a spacious feeling. The table setting shown is standard for lunch at the San Diego International Airport dining room. Fresh flowers are added for dinner in this Host International operation.

Left: Old army carbines form the handles on the doors at "The Widow and Pancho Villa", a dim, Mexican pseudo "dive" where Wallace Beery's lusty leer greets patrons. Designed by a creative and budget conscious architect, Monte Bell of San Francisco, this place doesn't take itself seriously but does amuse patrons. The 58-seat room with dramatic black and white movie stills on the walls is built entirely of old wood—aged telegraph poles, railroad ties, weathered wood from ranches and old tent poles. Booths resemble jail cells—a truly cloistered setting for patrons who like privacy.

Opposite page: The tall, vacant building, site of the "Widow", has an interesting window treatment at the front. Printed Finnish fabric was made into banners that hang on wooden poles. One banner that stretches across the ceiling turns at a 90° angle reads, "I am present my General", a famous quote from Villa's gravestone. Contrasted with the darker section of the restaurant, this is a bright pocket where businesslike lunchers can "see" to talk and eat.

OLE! A MERCHANDISING SUCCESS

The star of El Sombrero is Maria who when she's not doing exhibition cooking, walks about the restaurant serenely balancing great bowls full of food on her head.

An expert at Mexican settings, Architect Bruce Heiser uses authentic Mexican objects and natural materials to provide a believable backdrop for Maria's balancing act.

On the tables at Clark's La Plaza in Seattle, ideas abound. Paper napkin rings (see below) add color and suggest how to start a meal ala Mexico. Fresh sauce and tortilla chips are standard table top items, as are bright ceramic mugs.

Paper napkins rings have increased Margarita sales by 50%! Bulk-shipped flat, they are easily fastened around napkins via a slot into which the end tab fits.

A small exhibition kitchen was built into a corner of the first small El Sombrero designed by Donald Clever. Putting in a Mexican display kitchen takes up little room but is provides patrons with entertainment as they watch tortillas or guacamole being prepared. Also, it takes some of the action out of the main kitchen, leaving more room for the employees to work.

MERCHANDISING IDEAS AT LA PLAZA AND LOS ARCOS

To provide a fitting fiesta sound for the restaurants, Gene Clark, CRE, and architect Marshall Perrow taped authentic Mexican music from 50 long-playing records.

Telephones are answered in Spanish: "Buenos Dias!" and "Buenos Tardes!"

On Mexican Independence Day and Cinco Mayo, Mariachi Bands play while one flambouyant waiter becomes Pancho Villa and stages a stick-up.

Tostados in cellophane bags are given away to customers. (Mexican Fresh Sauce is sold for take-out.)

Clark's Mexican menus are easily understood by "gringoes" since every foreign term is translated to help patrons with their ordering. The luncheon menu is divided exactly in half diagonally, Mexican foods in one diagonal, American in the other.

CHAINS AND FRANCHISING GO ESPAÑA

Above: Taco Bell stands are set up for eating outside so diners can enjoy a South-of-the-Border scene. Surveys among housewives reveal high acceptance for the early California style of the structures. Informality, fast finger food, easy parking, low cost—these are the pluses in favor of the Olé drive-in. It's a carefree setting for young family dining.

Right: Trini's fiesta style buffet is featured each noon on this attractive counter. The interiors of the 139-seat operations are an appealing blend of contemporary and Mexican, with such colorful elements as ceramic tile facing on the counter, and stained glass windows. Tasteful landscaping around the self-contained building and ample parking attract patrons. At night there is full table service from waitresses in Spanish style costumes.

MAKE A FIESTA OF FOOD

The slap slap slap of tortillas being made by hand is a rare sound these days when most tortillas are factory products. In El Sombrero, Maria makes her own dough from corn flour (a prepared mixture), then forms the pancake-shaped tortillas and fries them on a griddle. The San Francisco restaurant also uses factory-made tortillas, as demand exceeds production.

COLORFUL FOODS FROM SPAIN

This is a luxury version of Paella, a favorite latin blend of foods and flavors. The saffron-flavored rice holds shrimp, clams, mussels, pork cubes, lobster, chicken breasts and Spanish sausage slices. The traditional tomatoes, pimientos, red onions and peas are colorful additions.

Sangria *offers a cooling contrast for fiery foods. Sangria mixtures vary; here frozen limeade concentrate and melon balls add contemporary convenience in prepared-ahead combination with dry red wine. At serving time, mixture is poured into ice-filled pitchers, then diluted with club soda.*

This Spanish finale with the flourishes of flamenco can be staged either from a cart or as a dessert display. Spanish Caramel Flan with Fruit, at center stage, contrasts chilled caramel-topped custard with tart fruits, whipped topping and chocolate curls.

OLE! FROM APPETIZERS TO ENTREE

Lemon yellow and pimiento red give a fiesta flair to Artichokes Spanish Style. Artichokes gain from flavor blending with bits of smoked ham, onions and lemon as they are cooked to tenderness. Capers and pimiento bits add savor during final heat-up.

Tamale Pies in 3-way tie as menu favorites: Top, Au Gratin Tamale Pie blends cream style corn, tomatoes, onions, garlic and chili powder with cornmeal, tomato juice and chunks of ripe olive. Cheese triangles top each serving. Center: Al Fresco Tamale Pie adds cut green beans to the layer of tomatoes, corn, ripe olives and onion with latin seasonings that is covered with a fluffy batter of cornmeal and baked to golden crunchiness. Bottom: Tuna is the twist in Seaside Tamale Pie. The traditional tamale ingredients are poured into a pastry shell for final baking of the colorful mixture.

Above: *A latin approach to seasonings puts peanut butter in the ole camp. As celery stuffing, castillian character comes from sour cream and horse radish; as a dip from deviled ham, celery salt and liquid hot pepper sauce.*

Right: *In Alaska King Crab a la Espanola, a sauce of onions, celery, green peppers, sauteed in olive oil, then simmered with canned tomato soup, stock and ole seasonings of garlic, crushed chili peppers and bay leaves is poured over Alaska King Crab meat and canned sliced mushrooms for oven heat-through. Steve B. King, right and Charles S. Hawley, students of the Hospitality and Food Service Industries Division, Seattle Community College prepared the dish recently for fellow students and instructors. It's a popular feature both on cafeteria lines and in the department's dining room.*

SOUP, ICED OR HOT WITH FIESTA ACCOMPANIMENTS

Above left: Sopa de Aguacate con Ajo (*Avocado Soup with Garlic*) is a chilled blend of pureed avocado, chicken broth, lime juice and seasonings thinned with cream. Add lemon slices or dollops of garlic-flavored whipped cream as garnish. An Olé add-to for frozen heat-and-serve cocktail beef tacos is this gala topping of red pepper relish and chopped green peppers. The pimiento-stuffed olive mound repeats the colors.

Above right: Guacamole is quick and easy when avocado meat is mashed in a blender and mixed with mayonnaise, onion seasonings and lemon juice. In Tacos con Aguacate (avocado to gringos) frozen heat-and-serve beef tacos get a build-up from avocado slices and shredded lettuce, heaped on after tacos are ready to serve.

Opposite page: A convenience standby, condensed tomato soup, instant diced onion, chili powder and instant garlic powder make a latin opener out of Chili Tomato Soup. Diced avocado completes the transformation. The Chili Cheese Ball in the center is a meld of grated sharp cheddar cheese and instant garlic powder. Ball is rolled in chili powder. Chili Chicken Con Carne joins a tomato-onion sauce sparked with chili powder and oregano with red kidney beans and chicken to provide a hearty entree.

The doorman at the Del Monte Hyatt House, Monterey, Calif., is a very convincing conquistador who welcomes guests into a rich "old" Spanish atmosphere. The entire inn, though only completed in 1969, has the rustic elegance of Old Mexico and this doorman's Cortez costume sets the stage immediately.

Right: A special party kit consisting of pinatas, garlands of paper flowers, fans and sombreros was used to decorate the tables at Texas A & M for the College's Mexican Fiesta Night (opposite page). Place cards and invitations can also be ordered with the kits.

The table tops at Del Monte Hyatt House accentuate the Spanish theme. Wrought-iron candles, pewter crested plates, gold foil napkin rings, amber footed goblets, heavy ornate flatware, and carved wood menus merchandise the motif handsomely. At breakfast and lunch white table cloths are replaced by colorful mats.

SELL A FIESTA SETTING

The serving crews wore sombreros that came with the manufacturers decorating kit, and there was Mexican music playing in the background. It was a colorful and welcome change from the customary Thursday evening dinner.

Mexican decor played a one-night stand at Texas A & M College recently when it was installed for a special Mexican dinner. The temporary fiesta setting was put in place for Col. Fred Dollar, director of food service, by a food broker and distributor who drew on a special kit of merchandising materials (shown at left). In return Col. Dollar served the distributor's complete line of frozen Mexican foods at the dinner. Using frozen prepared Mexican foods also simplified production for the outsize gathering. The especially good turnout for the Mexican meal was credited in large part by Col. Dollar to the "glamour of the paraphernalia." Decorating the enormous dining hall at Texas A & M was like trying to dress up a football field, but with flags, posters, bunting and streamers, the transformation was finally complete and the Mexican Fiesta for 5,000 college students could begin!

The meal of Mexican specialties (all convenience foods) consisted of enchiladas, tacos, re-fried beans and rice. Students enjoyed the foods saying that's what they'd buy if they were off campus for dinner.

'GRINGO-CATCHING' MERCHANDISING IDEAS

Above: Rhonda Olivera, 4, takes a bite of a taco as she sits on a Taco Mini-Bike she won in a contest sponsored by Taco Bell, Torrance, Calif. Watching her are three other winners all astride their Mini-Bikes. The contest, sponsored by the Mexican food take-out restaurant chain, featured two winners weekly for the first seven weeks and will have a winner a day for the eighth and final week.

Right: The "Revolutionary Times" is a collector's item. No. 1, Vol. 1, Last One, put out by the owners of The Widow and Pancho Villa Restaurant. It explains all the humorous approaches used in this mock "den of iniquity."

PANCHO LOVED WELL, NOT ALWAYS WISELY, BUT CERTAINLY OFTEN...

The Widow And Pancho Villa, San Francisco's newest and most intimate restaurant and cocktail lounge, is now open at 470 Pacific Avenue at Montgomery in the heart of the fabled Barbary Coast.

Fine Mexican cuisine and potables will be served.

Designed by world-famed architect, Monte Bell, the restaurant recreates a romantic and heroic era in Mexico's revolutionary history — pairing a young and lovely woman whose identity has been lost in the passing of time — and the towering figure of General Francisco "Pancho" Villa.

It justly celebrates the General who helped the Mexican people in their struggle to become masters of their own destinies.

Some say Villa was a bandit. He was most certainly a

THE NAME IS 'WIDOW AND PANCHO VILLA', SENOR, AND WHEN YOU SAY IT, SMILE!...

Why the name? General Francisco "Pancho" Villa personifies the Mexico of revolutionary excitement, of romantic legend and daring deeds. The days of tasty native dishes eaten hungrily around camp fires in the moonlight. On the isolated reaches of the broad deserts of our southern neighbor. Days of violence. Nights of plotting tomorrow's strategy and maneuvers in the sand with simple sticks.

The women who followed Villa's **Division of the North** prepared and served the food. They were called **soldaderas**, these wives and girl friends. Many who served their men in the evening became widows before dawn. And quite a few — depending upon which story you like — became widows of Pancho Villa.

We are recreating the romantic nights under the stars that live in the memory of these valiant women.

Our first inclination was to honor one of those widows as the inspiration for the superb Mexican cuisine created in our kitchen. But, when, having journeyed south for the purpose of making the acquaintance of one of these widows, in order to glean her culinary secrets, we were perplexed to come upon several disputing that distinction.

Rather than become embroiled in a very personal family matter, we found what we believe to be a most intriguing substitute in a widow with whom the great Villa surprisingly had no romantic attachment.

Stanton Delaplane, the Pulitzer prize winning columnist of the San Francisco Chronicle — himself a noted Villaphile —

Above: *This poster is the entire back of the colorful menu sold at Ferdinand's, a coffee shop with Spanish accents located in an unlikely spot, the Coral Reef Hotel, Honolulu. In bright oranges, purples and reds, the poster is a sell-out among the younger taco "afficionados."*

Left: *In an outdoor corral adjacent to La Plaza, two baby burros were rented for a display in honor of Mexican Independence Day—September 16, which Clark's used as an excuse for a great Fiesta.*

Below: *Bright buttons reading "Stamp Out Gringo Food . . . Clark's Plaza" are give-aways at the cash register.*

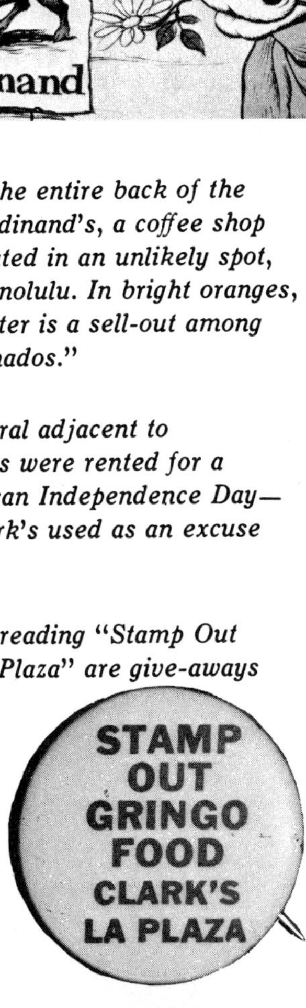

SPICES GIVE CHARACTER TO LATIN FOOD

SPICE	DESCRIPTION	USES
Red Pepper (Chilies)	Mexican cooks in particular use a variety of dried hot peppers (capsicums) which are generally known as chilies. Some of the hottest are tiny ones called variously "pequins", "tepines", "chiltepines" etc. The most readily available spice products of this type in the U.S. are "Red Pepper" (or "Cayenne") and "Crushed Red Pepper." Any of these will produce an adequate heat level for good Olé-type dishes.	Primarily to create the sharpness in Mexican and other Olé dishes (other spices produce the flavor and aroma). Likely to be used to varying degrees in all main dishes and sauces.
Chili Powder	A ground blend of chili peppers, oregano, cumin seed, garlic, salt and sometimes such spices as cloves, coriander seed and allspice.	A quick, convenient means of giving many dishes the Olé flavor (particularly Mexican). Traditional chili dishes, of course, but also basic stews, casseroles, sauces, soups, salad dressings, dips, cheese can all be given a touch of the Olé with a dash of chili powder.
Cumin Seed	Often called "Cominos" in Latin recipes. A small, oblong seed resembling caraway in shape. Strong, aromatic, somewhat bitter undertone. Very important to the character of chili powder and southwesterners often add it in addition to chili powder.	Latin American recipes of every kind are apt to list "cominos" seeds—meat stews, vegetables (i.e. corn butter), rice, sausages, salads, even cakes. It is a "something special" flavor they use universally.
Coriander Seed	Latin recipes frequently call for "cilantro" meaning leaves of the coriander plant. The seed is the most readily available source of coriander flavor. A distinctively fragrant, lemon-like odor and taste.	Like cumin seed, widely used throughout Latin cookery, and particularly in sauces (tomato avocado, etc.), rice, chicken, fish, eggs.
Anise Seed	The licorice flavor of these seeds is used in many Latin sweet goods.	Latin bakers often sprinkle anise seeds on cookies, use them in sweet rolls, coffee cakes and in conserves.
Cinnamon	Various barks of the *cinnamomom* family are marketed as cinnamon, but Latin cooks tend to prefer the milder lighter colored Ceylon-type cinnamon.	In Mexico, cinnamon is used in hot chocolate; in other Latin countries it is used as typically in the U.S.—sweet baked goods of all types, fruits and puddings.
Onion & Garlic	Both of these vegetable seasonings are extremely important throughout Olé cookery, but almost always in sliced, diced, chopped or minced forms. The dehydrated onion and garlic products of the spice shelf are therefore perfectly suited. In the onion, bear in mind that much larger particle sizes are now available.	Essential to all kinds of main dishes, soups, sauces, vegetables in all Latin countries. The Spaniards also make a garlic soup.
Paprika	Spanish cooks are particularly fond of this brilliant red powder with its mild-sweet flavor. A member of the capsicum family, it can have a nip of heat (i.e. Hungarian-type), depending on variety and processing of the peppers. But, the mild product is most common.	Primarily for its appetizing color and as a garnish in sauces, soups, main dishes, cheese, fish.
Parsley Flakes	All Latin cuisines utilize parsley, but the Spanish are possibly most avid. The dehydrated product makes the using vary convenient.	Spanish cooks are lavish with parsley, (as one cookbook author put it, "fistfuls") for flavor and garnish; especially in chicken and fish dishes, soups, eggs, seafood, rice.
Sesame Seeds	Mexican and Latin American cooks are sesame users in particular—as a flavor, for garnish and also as a thickening agent. The little light-colored seeds have a nut-like flavor, delicate crunch and a high oil content.	Latin American cooks use these seeds in chicken and fish dishes, as well as various sauces.
Oregano	A type of oregano grows in Mexico, accounting for the fact that this herb is so identified with that country's cookery. Actually, European oregano is more heavily used in the U.S. Strong, pleasant, somewhat camphoraceous odor and taste . . . often called the "pizza herb" for its close association with that dish.	A wide variety of main dishes, particularly in Mexico, but also in Spain; essential to chili-type dishes.
Saffron	The dried stigmas of a crocus plant, known as the world's costliest spice and probably associated more with Spanish cooking than any other. Actually, the little reddish strands are extremely potent and very little is required to flavor (and color) a dish. Flavor is strong, somewhat bitter and its coloring effect is yellow.	All Latin cookery, but especially Spain, where it is all-important in such famous dishes as paella, and arroz con pollo, as well as other meat or seafood combinations.

OTHER SPICES: Latin cooks regularly use many other spices also, as do good cooks everywhere. Typical are black pepper, bay leaves, cloves, allspice, nutmeg, mint, thyme and marjoram.

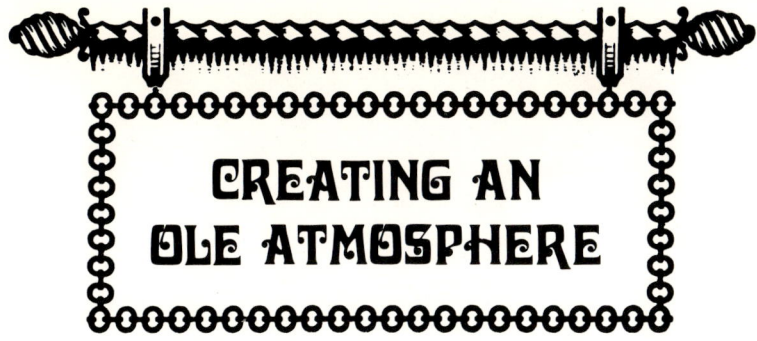

CREATING AN OLE ATMOSPHERE

The warmth and gaiety of colorful Olé interiors is contagious. The common component of the heritage that can be traced from Spain to the South of the Border countries in the New World is the predominance of vivid colors—made more vivid by the ever present dark woods, black iron and whitewashed walls that are inseparable elements of Olé decor.

Just stepping into interiors that draw on these decor traditions puts patrons in a fiesta mood. The long association in Norte Americano minds of Spanish settings and gaiety makes a transition to a holiday mood almost automatic.

In this country there is also a strong association between the words Spanish and Mexican. So closely aligned are the two that they have almost become one. The explanation for this fact goes back to the early Spanish settlements on this continent.

The manufacture of virtually the same Mexican and Spanish furniture and accessories that are being purchased today began in the early sixteenth century. Under the tutelage of the church and the Spanish nobility, the Indians of Mexico were taught to execute "European" designs. However, the Indians, already expert artisans, injected their own personalities into the work and a new style was born.

The native Mexican character continues to lend itself to a bold, vibrant interpretation of Indian-Spanish culture. In many instances, direct descendants of the original craftsmen are executing the same designs today.

The elements selected to establish Olé decor may be few or many, inexpensive or costly, but with careful planning they can be equally effective for the market they are designed to appeal to. Here are some of the ways food service operators throughout the country have developed the Olé theme.

ADD A MEASURE OF WARMTH AND CHARM

The tile-framed open kitchen is a favorite focal point. In addition to an instant stage setting, the open kitchen assures entertainment for guests waiting to be served; they can watch the deft preparation of menu specialties or examine the authentic and unfamiliar cooking utensils that can be displayed on its walls when not in use.

These display kitchens can be effective whether sizable or small. They offer the added advantage of taking some of the action out of the preparation kitchen.

Wrought iron fixtures too may range in elaborateness from simple candlesticks to room dividing gates. Wrought iron gates also make

SPECIAL ATMOSPHERE THEMES FOR FOODSERVICE

FOUR APPROACHES TO OLE DECOR

Wood turnings and arches keep El Sombrero's cocktail lounge interesting and intimate. Some walls in the San Francisco restaurant are stark white plaster, others are of patterned tiles in typical Spanish colors. Amber lights add soft warmth that flatters patrons.

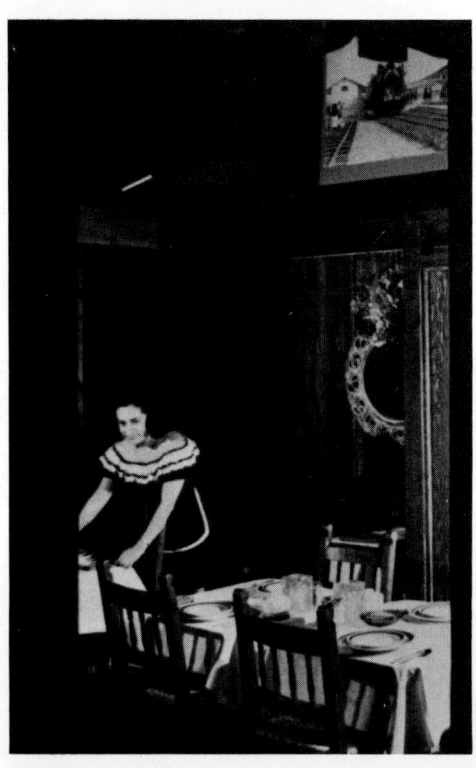

Rough wood poles create private dining room intimacy for seating areas of The Widow and Pancho Villa. Waitress uniforms keep focus on era of revolutionary excitement in Mexican history on which restaurant theme is based.

In the original El Sombrero, designed by Donald Clever, certain tables are dramatized with this special ceiling treatment. In Mexican fashion, wood turnings hang down against a panel of ceramic tile that stripes the wall. Plaster ornaments are placed on the wall to add decor impact in these areas.

The powerful presence of the Mexican hero whose legend sets the theme is introduced at the entrance of The Widow and Pancho Villa. Open wrought iron gate adds authenticity. Inside unusual decor elements are railroad ties, old beams and tent poles and bold posters depicting dramatic episodes in Villa's life.

COSTUMES ADD COLORFUL DESIGN ELEMENT

attractive guards for wine cellars or liquor storage areas. Wood carved with Spanish motifs has been successfully substituted for wrought iron in creating dividers for interior spaces.

The traditionally red floors may either be of tile or carpet. Sometimes a red area rug can be effectively centered on an expanse of tile to add texture interest or a warmer note.

Spanish furniture—the heavy, sometimes elaborately carved, wooden chairs; dramatic cupboards from earlier centuries that can be used for dining area storage needs; long wooden tables that lend dignity to private dining rooms—all should be considered when planning the furnishings for Olé interiors.

With Mexico an easy flight away from most U. S. foodservice, trips there to collect accessories are frequently part of the decorating activity. From one such excursion, the operator secured such attention-getting accessories as antique statues of saints, and old Spanish swords; wicked-looking maces; huge glass vases with gold applied inside; bas-relief plaques of Spanish Colonial motifs; and a group of oil paintings on tin done by Mexican Indians long ago under the direction of Spanish padres (they copied Renaissance paintings but added their own peasant interpretations).

Small bronze cathedral bells of Spanish origin can be hung from bronze chains for an effective arrangement on a white-washed wall. It's not necessary to leave the country to assemble effective design elements, however, as American companies have long manufactured the characteristic items needed.

Serapes in a multitude of bright colors are quickly converted into wall hangings or can be used to create a splash of color when artfully arranged on a table or chest with pottery from the same region. Stained glass is another way to introduce color and theme-setting design elements. The glass insets can be used to filter outdoor light or artificial lighting can be installed behind them.

Table linens and native costumes in the vibrant colors of the Olé culture add to interior interest. Because Olé draws its inspiration from so many countries, costumes for hostesses can be varied frequently to sustain patron interest. Promotion pieces to accompany such costume changes could tell a bit about the country where the dress is worn and at the same time perhaps sell a special dish developed to tie in.

The hostess in costume and a small display of native items would be enough to capture customer interest for a weekly or monthly Olé menu in a noncommercial food service. Displaying the accessory items against a vibrant wall hanging would increase their impact considerably.

Inspiring a fiesta mood should be the goal of every Olé interior design. People in a care-free mood spend more; when they've had a good time and good food they'll want to come again, and soon.

FOODS TO FEATURE ON OLÉ MENUS

Dishes that support the Olé theme can come from several geographic areas: Latin America, South America or Spain and Portugal. While many of these dishes were brought to the New World by Spanish and Portugese explorers and colonists, the recipes were often changed as foods found in the New World were added to the original ingredient list. These newly discovered ingredients were also used to create new dishes in the same Spanish food tradition that the colonists had enjoyed at home.

Gold and jewels in the anticipated mind-boggling quantities seldom materialized in the New World but many foods were encountered that never had been seen before. Tomatoes, beans, maize, potatoes, yams, pumpkins, squashes, gourds, chiles, vanilla, chocolate, peanuts, melons, avocados and pineapple were unknown in Europe before the return of the Conquistadors.

Even if they couldn't find gold, the early explorers could take seeds of the new fruits, vegetables and nuts back to Spain where the new foods were soon blended into ancient recipes. So creativity occurred on both sides of the sea and Olé cuisine is the more varied because of it.

Most familiar to the majority of American diners are the Mexican specialties—chili, tacos, enchiladas, tostados, refried beans, burritos.

The tortilla was undoubtedly inspired by the principal crop of Mexico—corn, in early times called maize by the English, masa by Spanish speaking people. Maize was pounded from the dry corn kernels into meal by the Indian women who made the meal into thin cakes that were cooked over open fires. Tortillas made from corn meal are said to have originated in the State of Sonora in Mexico.

Today, the flat, thin tortilla corn cakes are used either in a soft state to roll around a filling of meat or chicken or are deep fried to serve as a rigid holder for any one of several popular fillings. Tortillas are less often made on premise today since they are now factory prepared to meet quality standards.

Traditionally spicy, Olé foods can be successfully toned down to an acceptable level, bland enough to suit less adventurous American diners. Hot, hot dishes can be promoted as conversation-making challenges but the flavor focus should be set to meet majority tastes. A blander dish can always be spiced up if shakers of chili powder, garlic powder, or cayenne pepper are at hand.

As colorful as jewels, the Olé dishes often frame the reds and greens of spicy sauces against saffron-hued rice. However, no extravagance is involved in introducing these dishes on today's menus as the

**TELL PATRONS
WHAT'S IN
UNFAMILIAR
SPECIALTIES**

ingredients that go into them are low cost, with many of the items available pre-prepared and ready to combine and serve.

Mexican food is only one facet of the varied items composing the cuisine that has its roots in Castile. Paella from Spain probably has the widest menu following of the Spanish foods. The subtle flavors of shrimp and chicken get a Spanish spicing from bits of sausage, a golden hue from the saffron rice. The classic Flan that provides a mildly sweet wind-up to spicy fare also traces its origin to the land of the flamenco. These dishes are characteristic of the cookery that was fused long ago on the sunny Iberian peninsula. Flavors were further heightened as the influence of French, Italian and Moorish migrants was reflected in the original Spanish cuisine.

From South America come as many intriguing cuisine variations as there are countries. The basic elements of Spanish and Indian cookery have also gained accents from the variations introduced by German, Italian, French and English migrants in Argentina, Chile and other South American countries.

The availability of fish and shrimp in Brazil is reflected in uniquely flavored preparations like Casadinho de Camarao. Seafood styles are also set in Peru where Red Snapper, Caraqueno Style was first presented.

There's no problem of inspiration for planners of Olé menus. The difficulty is rather in determining which dishes to introduce first. By the same token there's no excuse for monotony. Since the same basic ingredients appear in many different guises, new dishes can easily be featured so often that there's no drop-off in patron interest in the menu.

What are some of the mainstays of Olé menus and how are they made—this basic information is essential to patrons making menu selections and it is just as important that the preparation of dishes should be understood by serving personnel as well.

Many more dishes could be added to the list that follows and certainly whenever a new specialty is introduced, a description should be provided. Since diners will not necessarily be familiar with these foods, the service staff should be ready with information on contents and cooking methods used in each dish. Posted descriptions similar to those on the facing page help the service staff in explaining menu specialties to diners:

Ole

Burrito—This is a tortilla made with flour rather than with the traditional Mexican corn. The flour tortilla may be rolled around a variety of fillings, either for an entree or for dessert service.

Chalupas—This is a fried tortilla spread with re-fried beans and topped with lettuce, tomato and a taco sauce.

Chili Con Carne—Authentically this chili dish does not have beans; it is a spicy meat sauce used as a topping for tamales, enchiladas, burritos, etc. As served on American menus, however, the dish does include beans so the difference needs to be made clear.

Empanado—A turnover filled with stuffing for out of hand eating as an entree or appetizer.

Enchilada—A corn tortilla rolled around a filling of onion and cheese or beef, covered with sauce and cheese, then baked.

Flan—Caramel coated rich custard, served chilled with fruit. Sometimes flavored with brandy.

Frijoles Refritos—Refried beans, pinto or red kidney beans are mashed, then simmered in hot lard or bacon drippings until fat is absorbed and mixture becomes a thick paste. Extra flavor comes with addition of tomato sauce, onions or cheese.

Guacamole—Used either as appetizer, salad or sauce: mashed avocado gets flavor from spices, tomatoes, onions, oil, lemon juice or limes.

Hot Sauce—This spicy sauce can be used on any dish for those who like a more seasoned food.

Margarita—A cocktail made with tequila, served in a salt-rimmed glass.

Paella—A saffron rice base made with tomatoes, garlic, and pimiento, holds pieces of chicken, clams, salami chunks.

Sangria—A robust red wine punch served in a clear glass pitcher.

Tacos—The Mexican style sandwich can be made either crisp or soft. Seasoned meat is placed in center of corn tortilla. Tortilla is then folded over and deep fried. Crisp fried tacos get more filling: shredded lettuce, grated cheese, spicy sauce, chopped onion, tomato, avocado.

Tamale—Seasoned dough made of cooked ground corn is spread on corn husks, topped with meat and sauce, then rolled up and steamed in the husks.

Tortilla—A thin pancake shaped cake, can be made in two ways: for soft service from flour; for crisp service from cornmeal and fried til crisp.

Tostada—A corn tortilla fried flat til crisp, then topped with heated re-fried beans, shredded lettuce and grated cheese. Sauce topping may be sour cream. Meat, chopped chicken or cheese may be added to re-fried bean filling.

SERVING OLÉ FOODS

Whatever the setting, the service of Olé foods can be easily adapted to fit in. At the luxury end of the service spectrum, diners should be reminded that dining in Spain is done at a leisurely pace. To make their Olé experience a refreshing escape, American diners should adopt for one evening a "Manana" time-sense. Getting into this relaxed frame of mind is made easier at San Francisco's Tia Maria with the suggestion that a guacamole appetizer be ordered to accompany cocktails.

Heel-tapping or dreamy in turn, the music of Spain and Latin America provides a good background mix for menus combining fiery food with cool drinks. A maraichi band on call can be a great assist in making special occasion banquet sales.

Olé food specialties are naturals for the speedy service drive-in or take-out set-up since many of them are finger foods. Descriptions of each item speed ordering. Another service speeder—as well as preventer of "too hot" complaints—is service of hot sauce on the side to be added in the amounts each individual prefers.

A modified buffet set-up simplifies service for the Mexican Adventure in Dining suggested by the Standards Dept. of ARA Services, Inc. for their contract operations.

Taking its pattern from the Mexican fiesta where celebrators sample foods from the booths (cantinas) of many vendors, this U. S. fiesta presents food from tables and hot carts decorated to look like Mexican cantinas.

HOW TO MAKE CANTINA FOR SELF SERVICE OF OLÉ SPECIALTIES

As the ARA instructions make clear, it's not difficult to create a cantina:

Tie 6- or 8-ft. lengths of moulding strips to table legs. Wrap table in wood-grained paper (can be purchased from display or art supply house). Around the top of the poles, stretch black crepe paper cut 18-in. wide. Over the crepe paper, drape strips of crepe paper in hot shades of blue, green, orange red and yellow. Cut these strips in varying widths of from 1 to 3 in. and 36 in. long. Fringe one end by clipping with scissors. The result will be strikingly like a Mexican serape with its brilliant color mix.

For eye-catching decorations at each cantina, the colorful raw ingredients used in Olé foods can be featured in pottery and straw containers or mounded alongside. The raw and dried peppers, gourds, squashes, yams, egg plants, pineapples and avocados with jars of vari-colored dried beans can have real impact. Also helpful as table decorations are miniature flags from the countries whose cuisine is being featured in the cantinas.

Costumes are suggested for service people and advance build-up for the events with travel posters, displays of native crafts is recommended. Their suggested menu—a useful promotion piece in itself, appears on the following page.

Waiters and waitresses should wear uniforms that further the Olé theme. If they do not speak Spanish fluently, they should master a few phrases to help set the mood. Most important of all, they should be able to describe the dishes and the ingredients that go into them.

Whatever the type of service, the personnel should be able to pronounce the names of the dishes properly. Construct a pronunciation list for your employees listing your own specialties. Lists can be posted at eye level at service windows or waitress stations out of patron sight yet easy for employees to re-check until pronunciation becomes familiar.

Group practice in pronunciation will help break the ice. Offer an emblem or a prize of Olé foods to take home to those who master the list.

How You Say It in Spanish is a good heading for such a list. The list that follows is based on pronunciation guides used in several food service operations.

HOW TO SAY IT IN SPANISH

Albondiquitas	Al-BON-dee-KEY-tahs
Anejo Rum	A-NAY-ho rum
Aperitivos	A-peqr-ee-TEE-vos
Arroz	Au-roz
Bebidas	Bay-BEE-das
Bistec Ranchero	BEE-steak ron-SHAIR-oe
Burrito	Bur-REE-toe
Cerveza	Sir vasa
El Bandido	El Bon-DEE-doe
El Toro Bravo	el-TOE-roe BRA-voe
Empanado	Em-pa-NA-doe
Enchilada	en-chi-LA-da
Ensalada	En-sa-LA-da
Frijoles Refritos	Free-HOLE-ays Ray-free-tohs
Guacamole	Gwah-kah-MO-lee
Margarita	Mar-gar-REE-ta
Pimientoes Rellenos	Pim-e-YEN-tohs Ray-YAH-nos
Quesdillas	Kay-sa-DEE-yas
Relleno	Ray-YAY-noe
Sangria	Son-GREE-a
Sopas	SOAP-as
Tacos	Tah-kos
Tamales	Tah-MAH-lace
Tortilla	Tor-TEE-yah
Tostados	Tohs-TAH-dohs

OLÉ MENU
(Standards Dept., ARA Services, Inc.)

"MAS VALE LLEGAR A TIEMPO QUE SER INVITADO"
(It is better to drop in at the right time than to be invited)

Empanaditas
(Small Chicken Turnovers)

Sole en Escabache
(Pickled Fish)

Huevos Endiablados
(Deviled Eggs)

Guacamole-Tostaditas
(Avocado Dip–Fritos)

Albondiquitas
(Tiny Chili Meat Balls)

Arroz Con Pollo
(Spanish Chicken with Rice)

Tostados

Roast Beef el Toreador

Pimientos Rellenos
(Stuffed Peppers)

Habichuelas con Hongos
(French Cut Green Beans and Mushrooms)

Peritas Pequeno
(New Potatoes, Parsley Butter)

Frijoles Refritos
(Refried Beans)

Ensalada Verde
(Tossed Salad)

Ensalada de Fruita Fresca
(Fresh Fruit Salad)

Ensalada de Repollo
(Calico Cole Slaw)

Fiesta Biscuits   Corn Bread Squares   Caramel Nut Rolls

Pumpkin Chiffon Tarts,
Whipped Cream

Chocolate Parfait,
Mocha Sauce

Spanish Cream

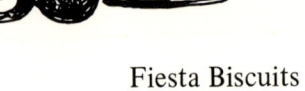

Ole

The wave of Mexican food enthusiasm began to roll on the West Coast though it's long since swept Eastward. Preparing school lunch items to please students of Mexican-American background helped to popularize tacos, enchiladas and burritos with the young.

In the Riverside City, Calif. school lunch operation, dessert burritos are a favorite. They are made by filling flour tortillas with fruit pie filling, rolling them up, brushing with melted butter and baking at 425°F. until hot and crisp. Another Olé special on Riverside menus is the Tortilla Wink—a frankfurter rolled in a tortilla, sometimes with a topping of beans as well, brushed with garlic butter, sprinkled with cheese (when available) and baked. Their Tacoburgers are burger patties in a taco. Elsewhere the Tacoburger may mean a burger bun filled with a taco meat mixture. Riverside is even considering a Mexican version of the perennial peanut butter and jelly sandwich—that's right they'll be putting the peanut butter and jelly in a tortilla.

When Olé menu specialties are purchased frozen-prepared, the battle is only half won. Thorough indoctrination in proper reconstitution methods and careful supervision is needed to insure that the items are as good on the plate as when they went into the pan.

In one operation with an impressive success record on sales of Mexican foods, the directions to be followed in the preparation of each specialty have been put on paper for employees and supervisors. These detailed instructions are presented both to handlers and servers to insure that all foods are at their finest when put in front of the guest.

OLE SPECIALS FOR SCHOOL LUNCH MENUS

INSTRUCTIONS REGARDING CONVENIENCE PREPARATION AND RECONSTITUTION
To All Servers and Handlers of Mexican Food

ENCHILADAS: Beef, Chicken or Cheese. Always keep covered with damp cloth when under refrigeration or after setting them out. Never expose product to air whether in freezer, refrigerator or out. This will prevent enchiladas from getting tough.

If prepared in microwave oven, always make sure product is completely covered with sauce and cover with plate. Add more sauce as you serve. Allow 2 minutes from frozen state and 1 minute when thawed.

TAMALES: Tamales should be _steamed_. Do not warm in oven or grill. If prepared in microwave oven, dip tamale with the husk in water and cover as you place in microwave. When you serve, cut off excess husk and place on plate with husk open. Smother with Red Enchilada Sauce. Sprinkle with shredded cheddar cheese. Allow 2 minutes in microwave from frozen state and 1 minute when thawed out.

DIRECTIONS FOR OLE CONVENIENCE FOODS

SAUCES: Sauces should be brought to a boil and wire-whipped before placing in steam table. Never serve a sauce that is off color, runny or extra heavy. Always taste and make sure of proper consistency before serving. With Taco Sauce and Hot Sauce, just stir and serve. Hot Sauce should be placed on all tables ordering Mexican food.

TACOS: Do not try to prepare Tacos on grill when in frozen state unless they go in the microwave oven first. Allow 1 minute. Be sure that grill is well oiled and cook on both sides until light golden color. Wipe off oil with absorbent towel before placing on plate. Serve Tacos with Taco Sauce only.

RE-FRIED BEANS: Beans should be kept at proper consistency when serving. They should not be runny or heavy and dried up. Add a little cooking oil with hot water and stir when heavy and dry. Place small thin slice of Jack cheese over beans on plate and a few tortilla chips around the beans.

SPANISH RICE: Rice should be placed in steam table in double insert with water in the one underneath to prevent drying out. When serving, it should be in a fluffy state. Do not let it get soggy or extra dry. When rice gets dry and hard, pull it out of the service line. You cannot reconstitute dried up hard rice.

RELLENOS: Can be reconstituted very well in steam table with a cover. Replace as they are used so they can remain fresh and tender. If microwave oven is used, smother rellenos in sauce on top and cover. Allow 1 minute in frozen state, 30 seconds when thawed. Add more sauce when placed on plate. If allowed to overheat, cheese will run out and pepper will be scorched and dry.

HOT PLATES: Mexican food must be served on very hot plates, about 400°F. Customers should be warned so they won't be burned. The food should be properly arranged and garnished so it will appear attractive and appetizing.

Pitfalls to be avoided and corrective steps to be taken in Olé food service are posted for employees in the same operation:

Beans, very dry—Add a little hot water and fresh frying oil and stir occasionally.

Cheese, not enough on beans—Cheese slice should be about 1 in. wide by 3 in. long.

Ole

Cheese and Sauce, not enough—Cover product entirely with sauce and cheese.

Rice, too dry—Place one insert pan into another holding water and keep rice pan covered when not serving from it.

Sauces, not properly whipped—Whip sauces and bring to a boil before serving; stir occasionally.

Product, not properly heated—Be sure product is sizzling hot in the center when it comes out of microwave oven or other heating unit before you place it on the table.

Tacos, too greasy—Tacos should be thoroughly thawed before browning on grill, then all grease should be absorbed with dry towel before adding relish and serving.

Product, not rotated—Product should be rotated after every new order; every item is dated.

Tamales—Tamales should be dipped in water before being put into microwave oven or else kept steamed until served.

These are just some of the many service gestures that make Olé eating out an experience so pleasant that patrons want to try it again. soon. Operations consistently report that their repeat business justifies their extra effort.

OLE FOOD PREPARATION

Enchiladas are a favorite menu item among the English-Spanish speaking students in the school lunch programs of the Rowland Unified School District. Preparing the necessary 2600-enchilada batches has been simplified through the use of the procedures pictured on these pages. Enchilada recipe appears on page 73.

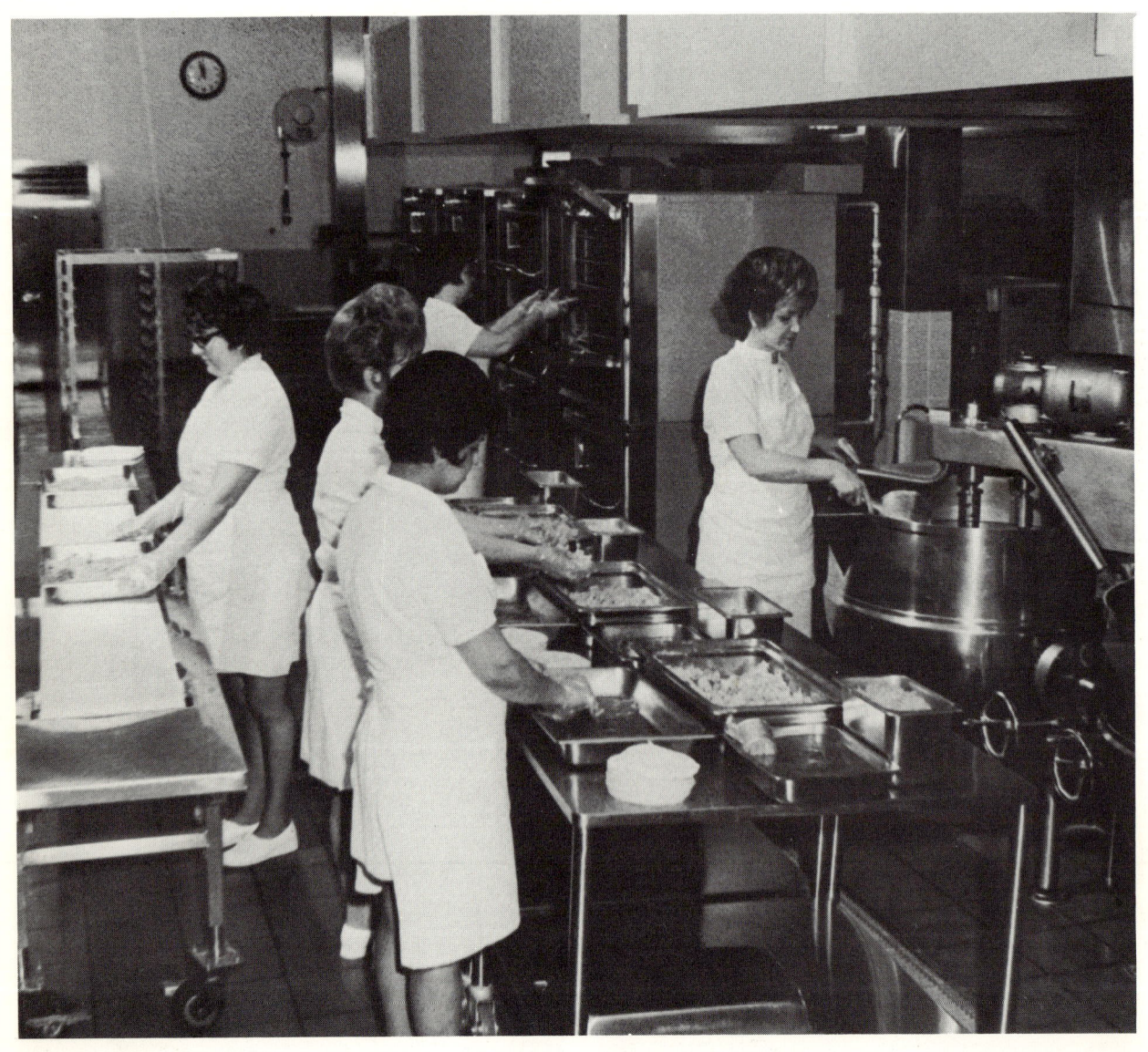

At Rowland Unified School District's new food center (Rowland Heights, Calif.), the set-up for enchilada making is compact and efficient. Mobile tables are lined up to make a long table just in front of the 80-gal. tilting cooker/mixer kettles. Tables are same height and width as stationary counters so they can be joined to counter to make it longer or to make it into a "T-" or "L-" shape. Here is a line-up for 3 workers, each with her own work station, to assemble pans of enchiladas.

Olé

In this close-up of a worker's station, note that pan to receive enchiladas is directly in front of worker, where she does her most efficient hand work, with a stack of tortillas on either side of the pan. Just above the tortillas are pans of sauce, above them pans of cheese and directly above the receiving pan is a pan of filling.

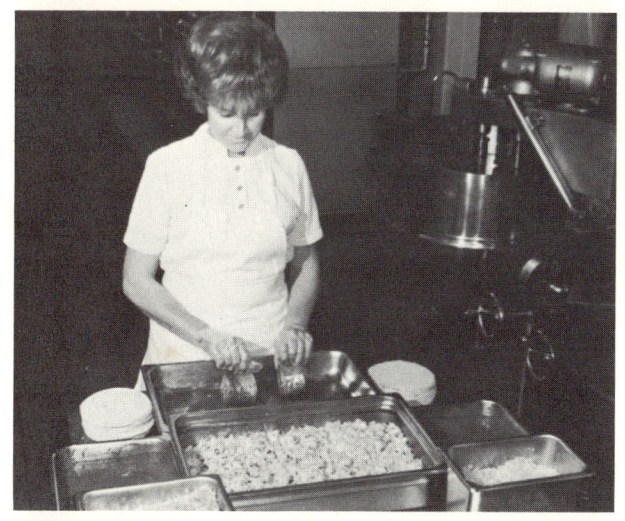

She dips tortillas in sauce.

Worker puts sauce in bottom of pan, dipping with both hands.

She layers sauced tortillas in pan, making 2 rows of 4 tortillas each.

Next she picks up 2 tortillas in each hand, keeping a finger between each. Worker wears plastic gloves.

She pours more sauce over tortillas.

Then she picks up the filling...

Cheese is spread over entire top. When spreading is completed, worker makes a turn and places pan on conveyor belt directly behind her. (see picture, p. 40.)

...and she sprinkles filling evenly over the surface. She repeats this for 3 layers.

Pans are taken off end of conveyor belt by the oven loader.

She picks up the cheese using both hands throughout completion of this step.

Ovens are filled in no time with this set-up as 6000-7000 enchiladas can be made in a very short time. Enchiladas are cut lengthwise down the middle of the pan and then cut crosswise of the pan into 12 servings. The serving is the same size and shape as a rolled enchilada, yet it takes much less labor to produce.

MENU PRESENTATION OF OLE FOODS

When menu items may be unfamiliar to patrons, detailed descriptions of each dish make selection speedier and more satisfactory as well. Sampling the cuisine of another culture can be an enjoyable adventure, if background is provided to heighten appreciation and to help the diner approach his meal feeling at ease.

Knowing whether it should be fingers or forks helps diners relax. This is made clear at Tia Maria in San Francisco where information about the tortilla gives patrons both the story of its development and tells how to handle it. This is their Introduccion a las Tortillas:

The tortilla is one of the earliest Mexican foods. It has passed through the centuries unchanged. Long before the Spanish conquistadors embarked for the American continent, the Aztecs were not only using the tortilla (Spanish for "little cake") as the staple food of their diet, they were also using it as an eating implement!

Tia Maria proudly continues this long Mexican tradition. We think you will enjoy watching the tortillas being pounded from the unleavened cornmeal in the manner that has been the age-old custom.

Today many people are at first confused about handling a tortilla. We suggest you attack it in the traditional Mexican fashion. Hold it flat in one hand, butter it, add the red sauce—sparingly at first—roll and eat! Your basket of hot tortillas will be delivered as soon as your order has been taken. We particularly recommend that you enjoy them with an imported Mexican beer.

Getting newcomers to try a strange cuisine suggests the use of a variety of sampling techniques. At Tortola's in San Francisco, a Tortolette cocktail tamale served with all drinks is an easy introduction to a spicy tidbit. Because it is just as good eaten at home, Tortola's cocktail menu notes that the Tortolette is available for take-home purchase.

Trini's Sampler is highlighted on the colorful menu of this Dallas operation. The Sampler is listed as an "introduction for the Mexican food novice or a treat for the AFICIONADO; our most complete taste selection in a single meal." The foods offered are: Guacamole tostada (tostadita), chili con queso tostada (tostadita), beef taco, cheese enchilada, tamale, chili con carne, refried beans and Spanish rice.

The menus reproduced on the following pages demonstrate successful ways to present Ole food items.

SPECIAL ATMOSPHERE THEMES FOR FOODSERVICE

the widow and pancho villa

470 pacific avenue
san francisco

Brown and orange on vivid yellow provide a colorful presentation for the menu specialties of The Widow and Pancho Villa. An information section on the menu explains items, translates Spanish words used. A Child's Plate offers a choice of Taco, small Enchilada or a ground Beef Patty with Rice or Beans.

For Your Information:
ENCHILADA is a corn tortilla in chile sauce, topped with cheese and your choice of filling. TORTILLA is made of corn meal or flour, fresh daily, used in place of bread. TAMALE is fresh corn spread on corn husk, wrapped around your choice of filling then steam cooked. TACO is a corn tortilla wrapped around filling and fried to a crisp. Served folded with lettuce and cheese added. CHILE RELLENO is green chile pepper filled with cheese, dipped in egg batter and fried. BURRITO is a rolled flour tortilla filled with pork. Served with chile verde sauce.

Carne — Beef
Gallina — Chicken
Queso — Cheese
Arroz — Rice
Refritos — Refried Beans
Postre — Dessert
Asada — Broiled
Frijoles — Beans
Carne Seca — Jerky Meat
Tostada — Toasted
Sopa — Soup
Maiz — Corn
Harina — Flour
Bebidas — Beverages

SIDE DISHES
Rice .... $.40
Beans .... .40
Salad .... .50
Tortillas (per basket) .... .25

CEVICHE $.95 STEAK PICADO $4.25

ENSALADAS
CHEF'S SALAD $2.25
WIDOWS SPECIAL (Avocado & Turkey) .. 2.10

APPETIZERS
GUACAMOLE, LARGE $1.95
GUACAMOLE, SMALL 1.50
TORTILLA PIZZA .... .95
 Mexico's Pizza — Open crisp flour tortilla with cheese, and strips of mild green chiles.

SOPA
(Soup of the Day) $.60

PANCHO RECOMMENDS:
ARROZ CON POLLO (½ Chicken & Rice) $2.70
SHRIMP RANCHEROS (Shrimp Sauteed in Spanish Sauce) 2.95
MOLE (Chicken & Spice Sauteed in Chocolate Sauce) .. 2.80
CHILE CON QUESO (Green Chile, Cheese, Rice & Beans) 2.25
CHILE CON CARNE (Chile with Beef, Rice & Beans) 2.35
HUEVOS RANCHEROS (Mexican Sausage,
 Eggs with Rice & Beans) 2.15
Salad served with above orders

CHILD'S PLATE:
Choice of Taco, small Enchilada
or Ground Beef Patty with Rice or Beans $1.50

THE WIDOW BRINGS TO YOUR ATTENTION:
Create your own combinations:
 Any two of the following combinations $3.50
 Any three of the following combinations 4.25
ENCHILADA (Beef, Chicken or Cheese) 2.35
GREEN CHILE ENCHILADA (Beef or Chicken or Cheese) 2.50
ENCHILADA SUIZA (Chicken Enchilada in Sour Cream) 2.50
BURRITO (Chicken, Beans or Beef) 2.20
TAMALE (Beef or Chicken) 2.35
TACO (Beef or Chicken) 2.10
TACO (Chicken or Beef in Sour Cream) 2.35
CHILE RELLENO 2.45
TOSTADA (Beef, Chicken, Cheese, Guacamole or
 Chile Con Carne with Beans, Lettuce & Sour Cream) 2.45
Beans, Rice and Salad served with above orders

BEBIDAS
Coffee .... $.25
Tea .... .25
Milk .... .25
Iced Tea .... .30
Sanka .... .25
Mexican Chocolate . .75
Soft Drinks .... .40
Mexican Beer ...... .75
Premium Beer ...... .75
Coors .... .60

POSTRES
Ice Cream .... $.35
Sherbet .... .30
Flan Custard ...... .50
Cheese Cake .... .65
Pecan Pie .... .65

THESE ORDERS DO NOT INCLUDE SALES TAX

SALUD!

For A Classic Flavor Experience Try A "South of The Border" Cocktail Made with Tequila.... *distilled juice of the cactus!*

MARGARITA 1.00
A classic, served in a chilled glass frosted with salt.

SANGRITA ..... .95
A peppery thriller, from Guadalajara. Sip one, then the other. DO NOT MIX.

TEQUILA SOUR ..... .95
A pleasant change of pace.

RAYO DE SOL ..... .95
Orangy as the sun. South of the Border version of a Screwdriver.

TROPICO ..... .85
A pleasing refresher made with the juice of fresh Toranja.

STRAIGHT ..... .75
With a wedge of fresh lime, and a pinch of salt.

A FINE SELECTION OF SPIRITS AVAILABLE FROM OUR BAR

CERVEZA DE MEXICO

BOHEMIA ALE	.60
CARTA BLANCA	.60
DOS EQUIS	.60

Wine List

	Bottle	½ Bottle
21 BEAULIEU BEAUROSE	2.75	1.50
22 ALMADEN GRENACHE (Rosé)	2.75	1.50
27 BEAULIEU CABERNET SAUVIGNON (Red)	3.25	1.85
26 BEAULIEU BURGUNDY (Red)	2.85	1.60
28 DIGARDI BURGUNDY (Red)	2.75	1.50
29 LOUIS MARTINI MT. BURGUNDY (Red)	2.75	1.50
36 DIGARDI CHABLIS (White)	2.75	1.50
37 DIGARDI SAUTERNE (White)	2.75	1.50
38 WENTE BROS. DRY SEMILLON (White)	2.75	1.50
39 WENTE BROS. GREY RIESLING (White)	3.00	1.75

SWEET WINES: A Fine Assortment of Domestic and Imported Sherries and Ports Available.

WINE BY THE GLASS: Red or White Dinner Wine (glass) .... .45

A SELECTION OF IMPORTED AND LOCAL BEERS AVAILABLE FOR YOUR PLEASURE

DOMESTIC BRANDY, IMPORTED FRENCH COGNACS AND SPANISH BRANDY FOR YOUR AFTER DINNER ENJOYMENT

If you have enjoyed your Tortolette cocktail tamale served with your cocktail, they are available to take home conveniently packed for your freezer

Tortola 1237 POLK STREET · SAN FRANCISCO 94109

Tamales

CORTEZ, High Life Tamale 2.65
Beans, Rice, Chili con Carne, Lettuce, Onions

TORTOLA SPECIAL TAMALE 1.95
All White Meat, in husks

SCARPULLA Special Beef CUP TAMALE 1.85
Not in husk, Chili con Carne. Melted Cheese

HIGH LIFE, not in husk 1.75
Sliced White Meat, Egg Garnish

SPECIAL CUP, not in husk 1.75
Beans and Rice

TAMALE, not in husk 1.65
Melted Cheese, Onions, Lettuce Garnish

TORTOLETTES, Cocktail Size Tamales, 4 for .60

Chili

CHILI CON CARNE 1.80
Spicy Stewed Beef in Pure Chili Sauce, No Beans

CHILI CON FRIJOLES 1.50
A Succulent Mixture of Spicy Beef and Little Red Beans in Pure Chili Sauce

CHILI CON ARROZ 1.50
Spicy Stewed Beef in Pure Chili Sauce, Served with Spanish Style Rice

FRIJOLES 1.30
Small Mexican Red Beans, Simmered Slowly with Spices, Onions, and Pure Chili Sauce

ARROZ 1.30
Spanish Style Rice, Long Grain, Fried, then Steamed with Green Peppers, Onions, Tomatoes, and Spices, Topped with Spanish Sauce

Enchiladas

PLATO TOMAS, Enchilada, Cheese, Olives, Sliced White Meat, Onions, Egg, Lettuce	2.85
PANCHO VILLA, Enchilada, Cheese, Beans Rice, Chili, Onions and Lettuce	2.75
DE LUXE, Enchilada, Spanish Beans, Queso Aji	2.75
SCARPULLA SPECIAL, Enchilada, Melted Cheese, Chili con Carne	1.90
SPECIAL, Enchilada, Spanish Beans, Shredded White Meat and Egg Garnish	1.70
DON JOSE, Enchilada, Melted Cheese, Onions, Ripe Olives, and Shredded Lettuce Garnish	1.70
GAUCHO, Enchilada, Spanish Rice and Spanish Beans	1.65
ENCHILADA CON QUESO, Enchilada with Melted Cheese	1.50
ENCHILADA CON FRIJOLES, Enchilada with Beans	1.50
ENCHILADA CON ARROZ, Enchilada with Rice	1.50

The separate Wine and Cocktail List (top of page) provided for customers at Tortola in San Francisco suggests, as a "Classic Flavor Experience," a South of the Border Cocktail made with Tequila and describes six variations. Also promoted on the Wine and Cocktail List are take-home packs of the Tortolette, the cocktail tamale served with each drink. The large food menu used at Tortola calls attention to their specialties by centering them against a colored background. Individual items are described in detail to help speed menu selection.

PRINCIPIAR — TO START

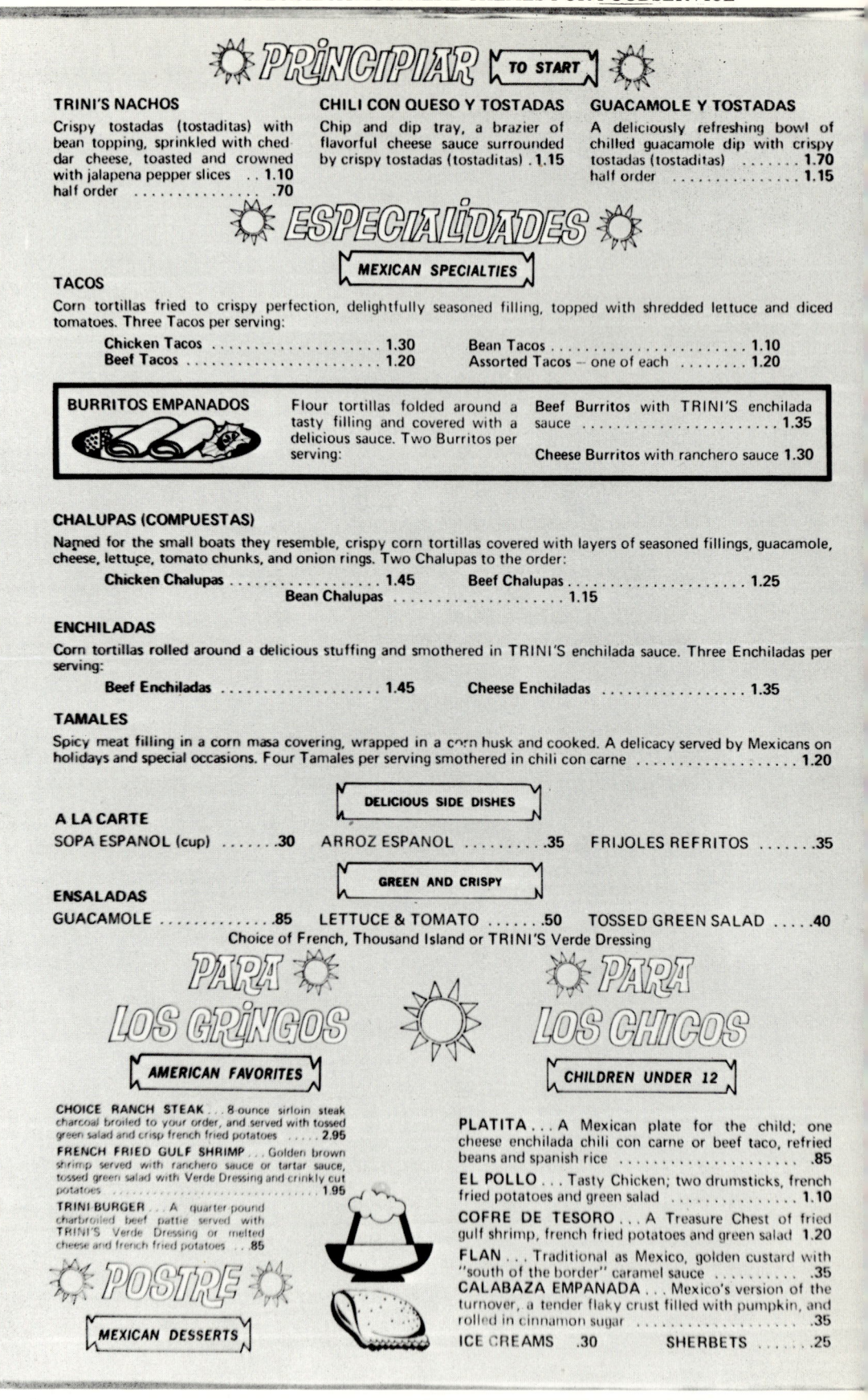

TRINI'S NACHOS
Crispy tostadas (tostaditas) with bean topping, sprinkled with cheddar cheese, toasted and crowned with jalapena pepper slices .. **1.10**
half order .... **.70**

CHILI CON QUESO Y TOSTADAS
Chip and dip tray, a brazier of flavorful cheese sauce surrounded by crispy tostadas (tostaditas) . **1.15**

GUACAMOLE Y TOSTADAS
A deliciously refreshing bowl of chilled guacamole dip with crispy tostadas (tostaditas) **1.70**
half order **1.15**

ESPECIALIDADES — MEXICAN SPECIALTIES

TACOS
Corn tortillas fried to crispy perfection, delightfully seasoned filling, topped with shredded lettuce and diced tomatoes. Three Tacos per serving:

Chicken Tacos .... 1.30   Bean Tacos 1.10
Beef Tacos .... 1.20   Assorted Tacos — one of each 1.20

BURRITOS EMPANADOS
Flour tortillas folded around a tasty filling and covered with a delicious sauce. Two Burritos per serving:
Beef Burritos with TRINI'S enchilada sauce 1.35
Cheese Burritos with ranchero sauce 1.30

CHALUPAS (COMPUESTAS)
Named for the small boats they resemble, crispy corn tortillas covered with layers of seasoned fillings, guacamole, cheese, lettuce, tomato chunks, and onion rings. Two Chalupas to the order:

Chicken Chalupas .... 1.45   Beef Chalupas 1.25
                      Bean Chalupas 1.15

ENCHILADAS
Corn tortillas rolled around a delicious stuffing and smothered in TRINI'S enchilada sauce. Three Enchiladas per serving:

Beef Enchiladas .... 1.45   Cheese Enchiladas 1.35

TAMALES
Spicy meat filling in a corn masa covering, wrapped in a corn husk and cooked. A delicacy served by Mexicans on holidays and special occasions. Four Tamales per serving smothered in chili con carne **1.20**

DELICIOUS SIDE DISHES

A LA CARTE
SOPA ESPANOL (cup) ...... .30   ARROZ ESPANOL .... .35   FRIJOLES REFRITOS ...... .35

GREEN AND CRISPY

ENSALADAS
GUACAMOLE .... .85   LETTUCE & TOMATO ...... .50   TOSSED GREEN SALAD ..... .40
Choice of French, Thousand Island or TRINI'S Verde Dressing

PARA LOS GRINGOS — AMERICAN FAVORITES

CHOICE RANCH STEAK ... 8-ounce sirloin steak charcoal broiled to your order, and served with tossed green salad and crisp french fried potatoes **2.95**

FRENCH FRIED GULF SHRIMP ... Golden brown shrimp served with ranchero sauce or tartar sauce, tossed green salad with Verde Dressing and crinkly cut potatoes **1.95**

TRINI-BURGER ... A quarter-pound charbroiled beef pattie served with TRINI'S Verde Dressing or melted cheese and french fried potatoes .. **.85**

PARA LOS CHICOS — CHILDREN UNDER 12

PLATITA ... A Mexican plate for the child; one cheese enchilada chili con carne or beef taco, refried beans and spanish rice .... **.85**

EL POLLO ... Tasty Chicken; two drumsticks, french fried potatoes and green salad **1.10**

COFRE DE TESORO ... A Treasure Chest of fried gulf shrimp, french fried potatoes and green salad **1.20**

FLAN ... Traditional as Mexico, golden custard with "south of the border" caramel sauce .... **.35**

CALABAZA EMPANADA ... Mexico's version of the turnover, a tender flaky crust filled with pumpkin, and rolled in cinnamon sugar .... **.35**

ICE CREAMS .30   SHERBETS ...... .25

POSTRE — MEXICAN DESSERTS

Avocado, grape shades and a splash of orange with white headings give Trini's menus a festive look. Headings in Spanish have English translations boxed below. For the unreconstructed American food lover, Trini offers three favorites: Steak, French Fried Shrimp; the Trini-Burger. Children under 12 may taste Mexican foods on the Platta:

COMBINACIONES
COMBINATION DINNERS

1. EL TORO
An ALL BEEF selection with hearty, robust flavor:
Guacamole salad, beef taco, beef enchilada, tamale, chili con carne, refried beans and spanish rice. 2.10

2. TRINI'S SAMPLER
TRINI'S introduction for the Mexican food novice or a treat for the AFICIONADO; our most complete taste selection in a single meal:
Guacamole tostada (tostadita), chili con queso tostada (tostadita), beef taco, cheese enchilada, tamale, chili con carne, refried beans and spanish rice. 1.95

3. RELLENO SABROSA
A TASTEFUL, STUFFED Mexican favorite:
Tossed salad with TRINI'S Verde Dressing, two chili rellenos, refried beans and spanish rice. 2.30

4. COMIDA GRANDE
A truly GRAND MEAL, traditional and delicious:
Beef taco, beef enchilada, cheese burrito, chili con carne and spanish rice. 1.80

5. ACAPULCO FESTIVO
FESTIVE ACAPULCO; as gay, colorful, and exciting as Acapulco itself:
Three guacamole enchiladas with sour cream dressing, spanish rice and refried beans. 1.75

6. COCINA REAL
A ROYAL KITCHEN meal prepared for you:
Tossed salad with TRINI'S Verde Dressing, beef burrito, tamale, chili con carne, refried beans and spanish rice. 1.75

7. FIESTA PEQUENA
A real LITTLE FEAST, well worth celebrating:
Tossed salad with TRINI'S Verde Dressing, beef taco, bean taco, chili con queso tostada and spanish rice. 1.35

8. CARNE TAMPIQUENA
TAMPICO STYLE STEAK charbroiled to perfection:
Tossed salad with TRINI'S Verde Dressing, 8-oz. sirloin steak, refried beans and spanish rice. 3.35

BEBIDAS

Coffee...15   Tea, Iced or Hot...15   Milk...20   Dr Pepper..15   Coca Cola...15   Fresca..15

SANGRIA
Traditional Spanish wine punch prepared by TRINI'S from vineyard selected wines and sun ripened tropical fruits.
Pitcher 1.50
Glass .... .55

VINOS	Bottle	½ Bottle
Burgundy, Taylor	2.50	1.50
Lake Country White, Taylor	2.75	1.75
Rosé, Taylor	2.50	1.50

CERVEZA
Imported Beer – Carta Blanca .... .55
Bohemia .... .55
Domestic Beers .... .45
DRAFT BEER   Glass.... .35   Pitcher... 1.50

T-A

one cheese enchilada chili con carne or beef taco, refried beans and Spanish rice, or they can enjoy those familiar child-choices: chicken drumsticks or fried shrimp with french fries. Desserts for adventurous or conservative choices: Flan and Cababoza Empanada (a pumpkin-filled turnover rolled in cinnamon sugar) or ice creams and sherbets.

SPECIAL ATMOSPHERE THEMES FOR FOODSERVICE

Grillwork designs frame the four columns of Clark's Plaza 5 menu. Columns are headed Aperitivos, Bebidas, Especialidadas, A La Carta with Postres below. The Seattle-based restaurant includes a Vocabulario Para Las Gringos which describes the contents and preparation of their Olé specialties in English.

1.25

GUACAMOLE DIP
Ripe avocado with onion, tomato, lemon juice and seasoning. Served with tortilla chips.
1.00

SOPAS
Soup of the Day   cup .35   bowl .50
Chili Con Carne   .95

Ensaladas

LA PLAZA
Avocado slices, grapefruit sections and crab legs on a bed of crisp romaine, vinaigrette dressing.
3.50

TOSTADA SOFISTICADA
Tortilla topped with refried beans, diced chicken, shredded lettuce, cheese and tomato.
2.75

CLARK'S TOSSED SALAD
Crisp romaine, torino salami, romano cheese and cheddar bits.
2.25

CRAB or SHRIMP LOUIS
Choice Dungeness crab or Alaska shrimp on a bed of shredded lettuce, egg and tomato garnish, Thousand Island dressing.
3.75

Bebidas

MARGARITA ESPUMOSA
Tequila, fresh lime, triple sec.
1.25

LAS BRISAS
Anejo Rum on the Rocks with Fresh Lime.
1.25

MEXICAN BEER
Carta Blanca Light.
.85

SANGRIA
Wine punch with fresh fruit juices.
glass **1.25**
pitcher **5.00**

EL TORO BRAVO
Tequila and Kahlua on the rocks
1.25

MEXICAN COFFEE
Mug of hot coffee spirited with Tequila and Kahlua.
1.25

Ole

Especialidades

Your entree selection includes
Fresh Sauce, Tortilla Chips
and Tossed Green Salad

LA FIESTA   3.55

Your choice of any two Mexican specialties, served with refried beans and Spanish rice.

CHICKEN ENCHILADA
CHEESE ENCHILADA
BEEF ENCHILADA
CHILI RELLENO
BEEF TAMALE
BEEF TACO

MUY GRANDE   4.25

Chili Relleno, Cheese Enchilada, Tamale, Spanish Rice Refried Beans.

EL BANDIDO   3.25

Two enchiladas filled with cheese and onions, topped with chili con carne served with Spanish rice.

BISTEC RANCHERO   3.95

Choice small steak, especially marinated and broiled to perfection. Served with Spanish rice and refried beans.

VOCABULARIO PARA LOS GRINGOS

Tortilla — Mexican bread molded into pancakes and quick heated on a grill.

Enchilada — Corn tortilla wrapped around a filling of cheese, beef or chicken, served with a spicy chili tomato sauce.

Taco — Crisp corn tortilla folded over a richly seasoned lean beef filling, shredded lettuce, tomato and cheese.

Chile Relleno — Green chile pepper stuffed with Monterey Jack cheese and souffled in a whipped egg batter, topped with a rich tomato sauce.

A La Carta

Your entree selection includes
Fresh Sauce, Tortilla Chips
and Tossed Green Salad

NEW YORK CUT STEAK   6.95
Choice, aged beef, 12-ounce cut

PRIME RIB EYE STEAK   5.95
Tender, full-flavored 8-ounce cut

FILET OF SALMON   4.95
Pride of the Pacific Northwest broiled in a wine-butter sauce

JUMBO GULF PRAWNS   4.95
Batter fried to a crisp golden brown

CHOPPED SIRLOIN STEAK   4.50
Our own choice ground beef with mushroom sauce and onion rings

All above entrees served with cheese enchilada and Spanish rice or French Fried Potatoes

Baked Potato with dressing   .50

Postres

FLAN FLAMBE'   .60
Flaming custard.

GHIRARDELLI SQUARE ICE CREAM   .60
A rich chocolate ice cream with a taste of what made San Francisco's Ghirardelli Square famous.

APPLE PIE   .50

GOURMET ICE CREAM   .50

CHEESE CAKE   .60

MEXICAN COFFEE
Mug of hot coffee spirited with Tequila and Kahlua.
1.25

Tia Maria Special

GREEN CHILE ENCHILADA WITH SOUR CREAM, CRISPY TACO, CHILE RELLENO, BEANS, RICE AND SALAD.

4.25

TOSTADA
This house favorite features chicken slices and Ripe Avocado complementing the crispy flavor of a Corn Tortilla. Generous helpings of Beans, Beef, shredded Lettuce and our Tangy Sauce are added.

2.40

VERACRUZ
Enchilada, Tamale (in husk), Beans, Rice, Salad.

3.30

DURANGO
Enchilada, Chile Relleno, Beans, Rice, Salad.

3.40

SONORA
Chile Relleno, Taco, Beans, Rice and Salad.

3.40

MONTEREY
Enchilada, Taco, Beans, Rice and Salad.

3.15

LAREDO
Two Rolled Tacos, crowned with Guacamole and Grated Cheese, Beans, Rice and Salad.

3.25

ACAPULCO
Two Enchiladas (Beef, Chicken or Cheese), Beans, Rice and Salad.

3.25

STEAK RANCHERO
Every country has its own steak and this is Mexico's. Sauteed Select Fresh Tomatoes, Tiny Onions and Choice California Peppers smother the Top Sirloin. Beans, Rice and salad accompany this unusual steak.

4.95

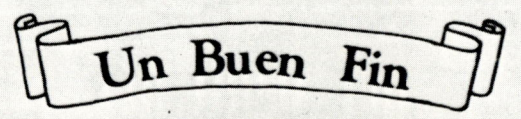

Un Buen Fin

MEXICAN COFFEE
An exotic blend of the Finest Liqueurs, Special Coffee and Spices, filled with tastes that are Mexico. A treat any time of day.

1.25

Luncheon

Especialidades Mexicanas

TOSTADA
This house favorite features Chicken Slices and Ripe Avocado complimenting the crispy flavor of a Corn Tortilla. Generous helpings of Beans, Beef, Shredded Lettuce and our tangy Sauce are added.
2.25

NUMBER 1
Taco, Beans, Rice and Salad.
1.85

NUMBER 4
Chile Relleno, Beans, Rice and Salad.
2.25

NUMBER 2
Enchilada, Beans, Rice and Salad.
1.85

NUMBER 5
Two Enchiladas, Beans, Rice and Salad.
2.60

NUMBER 3
Tamale (in the husk), Beans, Rice and Salad.
2.25

NUMBER 6
Enchilada, Taco, Beans, Rice and Salad.
2.60

Early California Fare

OLE!
You'll shout "Ole!" when you first taste this treasure of Early California. Tender chunks of Choice Lamb, Tiny Onions, fresh Californa Peppers, red Garden Tomatoes and broiled Mountain Mushrooms — all skewered on a sword. Charbroiled to your taste, served over Rice Pilaf with a Crisp Green Salad.
2.75

EL PESCADOR
Large succulent Gulf Shrimp deep fried to a Golden Brown served with our special Sauce. French Fries and a Crisp Green Salad.
1.95

EL TORITO
Chopped Tenderloin of Beef. Served with French Fries and a Crisp Green Salad.
1.95

EL POLLO
A tempting sandwich filled with sliced Breast of Chicken, served with a Fresh Salad containing Avocado, Tomato and Lettuce.
1.35

Tia Maria's regular luncheon menu (facing page) promotes a Special in the top frame, then lists 8 combinations appropriately named below. To complete any of these, they offer Mexican coffee—a brew that blends liqueur, a special coffee and spices.

The menu (above) of luncheon specials can be inserted easily and features combinations by number plus four selections of early California fare, that are Mexican in name only.

EL SOMBRERO

SOPA del DIA . . .65
[Soup of the day]

Salads

OUR SPECIAL SALAD [Chicken and Avocado]	2.35
HEARTS OF LETTUCE	1.30
LETTUCE AND TOMATO	1.45

Enchiladas

Beef Enchilada with Beans and Rice	2.35
Beef Enchilada with Chile Con Carne	2.25
Enchilada a Caballo [two fried eggs]	2.15
Chicken Enchilada with Beans and Rice	2.50
Cheese Enchilada with Beans and Rice	2.45
Green Chile Enchilada with Beans and Rice [Picante]	2.60
Enchilada Ranchera with Refried Beans and Rice	2.50

Salad served with above orders

Tamales
[in husks]

Chicken Tamale with Beans and Rice	2.50
Beef Tamale with Beans and Rice	2.50

Salad served with above orders

Chile con Carne [Pure]	2.25
Chile con Queso [Picante]	1.75
Chile con Carne with Beans and Rice	2.75
Chile con Carne with Refried Beans	2.45

Tortillas [hand made] [per basket]	.25
Chicken Sandwich with Salad	1.50
Child's Plate	1.35

Beverages

Coffee	.25	Mexican Chocolate	.90
Milk	.25	Soft Drinks	.40
Tea	.30	Local Beer	.60
Ice Tea	.40	Eastern Beer	.65
Sanka	.30	Mexican Beer	.75

Desserts

Pineapple Sherbet	.40	Ice Cream	.40
		Mexican Pastry	.30

Sales Tax will be added to the retail price on All Taxable items

---

A REAL TREAT!
Try Our Popular Combination Plate
Includes:
Enchilada, Taco, Chile Relleno, Beans
Rice and Salad
$4.25

El Sombrero Specialties

Chalupas [2], Beans and Rice	3.25
Tostadas Compuestas [2]	2.35
Tostada de Luxe [Chicken - Avocado]	2.50
Taco [Chicken or Beef] with Beans and Rice	2.10
Rolled Tacos [2] with Beans and Rice	3.00
Refritos [refried beans with cheese]	1.50
Guacamole [large order]	2.10
Guacamole [small order]	1.75

El Sombrero Suggestions

ARROZ con POLLO [half Chicken with Rice]	3.50
JOSE'S SPECIAL [Chicken with Sauce]	3.25
GALLINA en MOLE [Chicken with Mole Sauce]	3.75
GALLINA en PIPIAN [Pumpkin Seed Sauce]	3.75

Salad served with above orders

Chile Rellenos [2 Mexican Stuffed Peppers] with Beans and Rice	3.25
Half order	2.15
Chorizo con Huevo con Refritos	2.10
[Mexican Sausage with Eggs and Refried Beans]	
Spanish Omelette with Beans and Rice	2.10
Huevos Rancheros with Beans and Rice	2.25

Salad served with above orders

Sirloin Steak Picado [Mexican Style]
with Refried Beans and Salad . . 4.75

Wrought iron as a motif plus a scroll-presentation of El Sombrero specialties (printed on a beige menu board with headings in red) are the elements attractively combined in this Olé menu. Promotion of a Popular Combination Plate leads off on the page of Specialties and Suggestions.

Ole

Menu — GREAT MEXICAN FOOD

"ANY TIME IS TACO TIME"

CRAIG

TACO TIME

★ STORES NOW OPEN ★	★ STORES TO OPEN SOON ★
IDAHO - Boise (2) Nampa (1) Pocatello (1) MONTANA - Missoula (1) UTAH - Logan (1) Ogden (3) Roy (1) Salt Lake (2) WASHINGTON - Spokane (1)	IDAHO - Idaho Falls and Twin Falls MONTANA - Billings and Helena NEVADA - Reno and Las Vegas UTAH - Brigham, Clearfield, Salt Lake and Provo WYOMING - Cheyenne COLORADO - Colorado Springs and Denver ARIZONA - Phoenix NEW MEXICO - Albuquerque

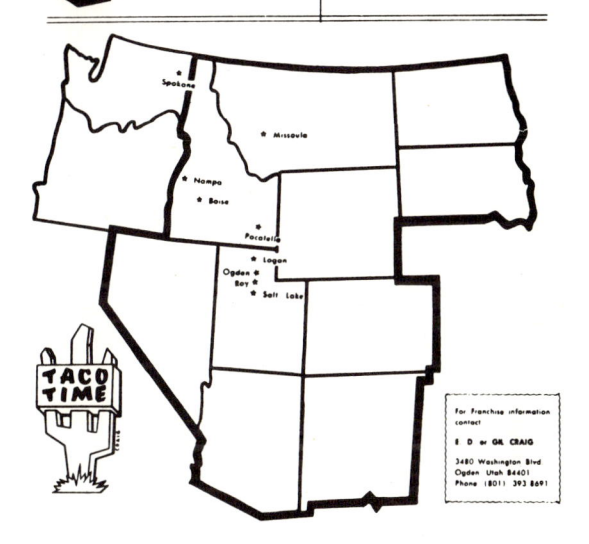

For Franchise information contact
E. D. or GR. CRAIG
3480 Washington Blvd
Ogden Utah 84401
Phone (801) 393-8691

Menu — GREAT MEXICAN FOOD

TACO	Crisp Corn tortilla with our lean ground beef, six month cheddar cheese, crisp lettuce and fancy tomato	.40
TOSTADO	An open face taco with lean ground beef, refried pinto beans, grated aged cheese, crisp lettuce and fancy tomato	.65
BURRITO	Flour tortilla with cheddar cheese, fried pinto beans, Ground beef, — rolled and deep fried	.40
MEAT BURRITO	Flour tortilla filled with lean ground beef and cheddar cheese, rolled and deep fried (all meat and cheese)	.60
TACO BURGER	Our delicious seasoned lean ground beef on a hamburger bun with cheddar cheese, crisp lettuce, fancy tomato and catsup	.65
BANDIDO	A real Texas corn tamale with taco meat and cheese, lettuce and tomato. A complete meal in itself	1.15
OUTLAW	A real Texas corn tamale with taco meat, cheese, lettuce, tomato and topped with chili. A complete meal in itself.	1.40
TAMALE	These delicious Texas tamales are made with choice beef and topped with our cheddar cheese	.70
REFRITOS	"Refried" pinto beans, topped with grated cheese, seasoned to please American taste	.30
CHILI	Our own Taco Time meaty chili seasoned to American taste	.40
MEXI-FRIES	Spicy french fried potatoes	.25
CRUSTOS	Deep fried crisp flour tortillas with sugar and cinnamon	.35
EMPANADAS	Sweet flour Tortilla filled with Taco Times own appetizing filling	.35

OUR SPECIALTY
delicious
TACO TIME
Hot Sauce
served individually
with each order
you are the Chef,
season food to
suit your taste

Hot Sauce 6 oz 30c
15 oz 55c
Corn Tortillas 2 doz.
.... 75c
Flour Tortillas 1 dz. 75c
Fried Taco Shells
.... 6 for 39c
Chili, quart $1.00

"ANY TIME IS TACO TIME"

This quick service, take-out menu is a vivid combination of bright orange and green. When closed (top left) cover is cut out to reveal promotion slogans on page 3 (above left). All Taco Time locations are printed on last page (top right). Mexican items are listed on the inside with helpful descriptions. A box promotes take-out quantity offers.

PROMOTING OLÉ FOODSERVICE

Many ways have been discovered that get prospective Olé patrons to stop, look and enter. Tia Maria in San Francisco uses a huge billboard on Highway 101—about 2 blocks from their door. Some of their successful billboard stoppers have been:

ST. PATRICK'S DAY SPECIAL: GUACAMOLÉ
TORTILLAS ARE CORNY
IT'S THE TACO THE TOWN
OUR CHEF HAS HOT PANS
TEQUILA OUR FOREIGN ADE PROGRAM

Letters of invitation enclosing a postcard (reproduced below) with a color picture of the restaurant's interior on one side and a certificate for 1 free combination dinner, when two or more are purchased, have also been successful in building business for Tia Maria.

POSTCARD OFFERS FREE DINNER

TIA MARIA
MEXICAN RESTAURANT
4470 EL CAMINO REAL - LOS ALTOS

Present this certificate to the cashier along with your dinner check. You will receive one FREE Mexican combination dinner with the purchase of at least one other Mexican combination dinner.

VALID SUNDAY THRU THURSDAY NIGHTS
OFFER EXPIRES Thursday, May 6, 1971

Their cleverly worded letter of invitation reads:

> 4470 El Camino Real
> Los Altos, California
>
> Amigo Mio:
>
> It's been a long time since I've written and I've lots to tell you, but it will have to wait until we meet again.
>
> Amigo, you remember Juan don't you? When he was in town last week he tried to look you up but he couldn't remember your address. He wanted you to be his guest at this great new Mexican restaurant he discovered in Los Altos, the Tia Maria at 4470 El Camino Real. The food is really authentic and is it good!—it's even better than it is here at the Chuahua Palace in Mexico City.
>
> Well, Juan was so disappointed in not seeing you and taking you to the Tia Maria, he says he told the manager you were a friend of his and the manager said, "Any friend of yours, Juan, is a friend of mine." So Juan arranged for a dinner for two for you at half price.
>
> Just present the enclosed card any day Sunday through Thursday for your half-price dinners. Juan says you will be so delighted you will be his best friend for life. Viva Tia Maria! Viva Mexico! Viva Juan!
>
> Your friend,
>
> *george Martinez*
>
> TIA MARIA Restaurant

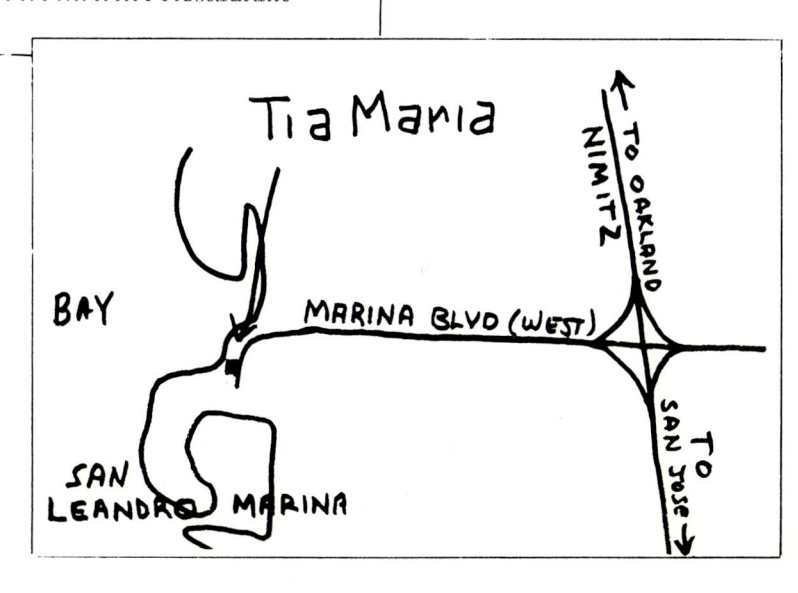

SPECIAL ATMOSPHERE THEMES FOR FOODSERVICE

This is the attractive format worked out for Tia Maria's courtesy dinner pass given for use by local groups or clubs requesting door prizes for charitable and other events.

Available as a souvenir to all who dine at Tia Maria's is the reproduction of their 4-page menu reduced to approximately 4 by 7 in. in size. Descriptions of menu items are easy to read on the bright gold paper and the mini menus have been used to persuade many customers to give Tia Maria's a try.

Ole
57

You don't have to go to Mexico for great Mexican food.

Los Arcos
CLARK'S NEW RESTAURANT AT SOUTHCENTER
CH 6-7360
11:30 AM – 11:30 PM
CLOSED SUNDAYS

Both radio and newspaper advertising has been effective for Clark's La Plaza and Los Arcos in Seattle. They have used humorous 10-second radio commercials narrated in a heavy Spanish accent and each one ends with "Viva La Plaza." High impact, one-column newspaper advertisements like the one at left get their message across as demonstrated by the fact that 50% of Los Arcos patrons select Mexican menu items.

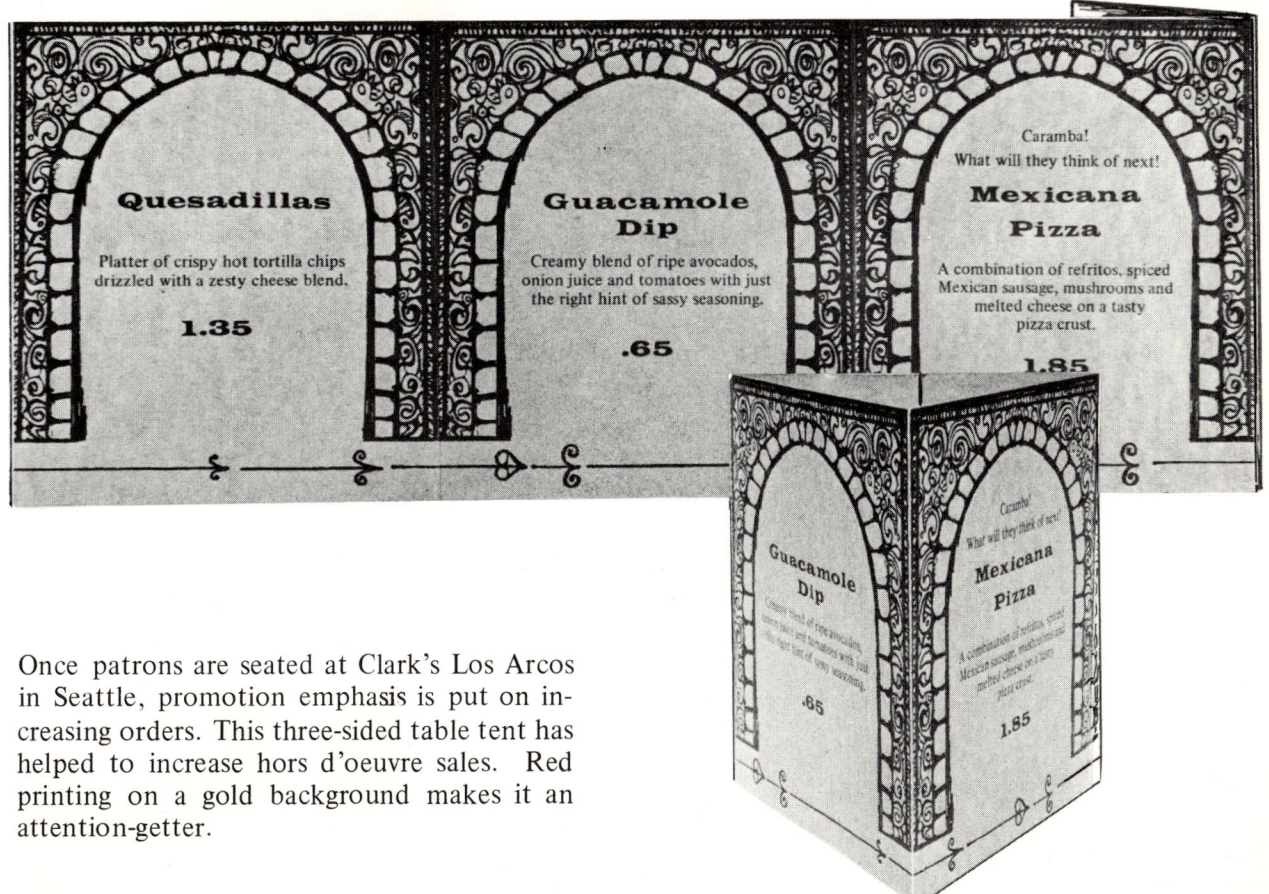

Quesadillas
Platter of crispy hot tortilla chips drizzled with a zesty cheese blend.
1.35

Guacamole Dip
Creamy blend of ripe avocados, onion juice and tomatoes with just the right hint of sassy seasoning.
.65

Caramba! What will they think of next!
Mexicana Pizza
A combination of refritos, spiced Mexican sausage, mushrooms and melted cheese on a tasty pizza crust.
1.85

Once patrons are seated at Clark's Los Arcos in Seattle, promotion emphasis is put on increasing orders. This three-sided table tent has helped to increase hors d'oeuvre sales. Red printing on a gold background makes it an attention-getter.

SPECIAL ATMOSPHERE THEMES FOR FOODSERVICE

This colorful menu-mailer, with room for a personal message on the back, helps get the word about Senor Pico's cocktails and appetizer-snacks to potential customers. Items are presented with the light touch characteristic of the expansive Senor pictured on the cover.

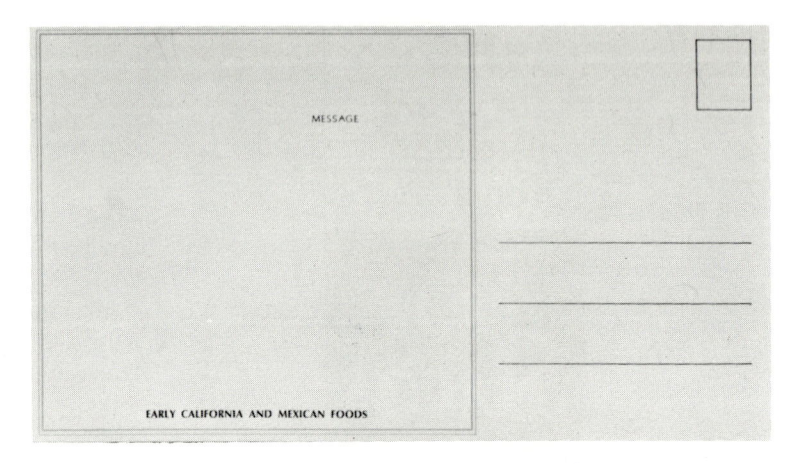

COCKTAILS

SONORA DAIQUIRI .85
FROM THE CACTUS COMES THE TASTE
FROM THE TEQUILA COMES THE BITE

MARGARITA .85
THE FAVORITE OF MEXICO—
SEÑOR PICO'S VERSION

AZTECA .90
A GOLDEN COCKTAIL, FROSTY AND SMOOTH

POTTED PARROT 1.50
WATCH THIS BIRD: WHEN HE STARTS
TALKING YOU STOP WALKING—HE'S
YOURS TO TAKE HOME

PONCHE 1.45
A BARREL OF FUN

DURANGO 1.35
AS RUGGED AS THE SIERRA MADRE
MOUNTAINS THAT RIM THIS TOWN
A GREAT NEW TEQUILA DRINK

SANGRITA .85
NO SISSY DRINK THIS—TEQUILA, LIME AND SALT,
WITH THE DEVIL'S OWN CHASER

KAFÉ-LA-TÉ .85
A FINE AFTER-DINNER DRINK OF STRONG COFFEE
AND RICH CHOCOLATE COMBINED WITH BRANDY.

FROM THE WINE BURRO

SANGRIA 1.85
A GLASS PITCHER FULL OF ROBUST
RED WINE AND SPARKLING JUICES

COPA DE VINO 1.85
A LIGHT, SPARKLING MIXTURE OF
WHITE WINE AND JUICES—SERVED
IN A BIG PITCHER

RED OR WHITE WINE:
BY THE GLASS .55   BY THE CARAFE 1.65

PINKY GONZALEZ 1.10
TOO MUCH OF THIS AND THEN TOO MUCH OF
THAT! THE CONTAINER TELLS THE STORY

APPETIZERS

BARBECUED "BONES" 1.35
BEEF "BONES" (RIBS) IN SEÑOR PICO'S
OWN MARINADE AND BARBECUED IN THE
BEEHIVE OVEN

GUACAMOLE 1.10
FRESH AVOCADO DIP MADE WITH SPICES,
TOMATOES; SERVED WITH CRISP TOSTADAS

NACHOS 1.10
TINY CRISP TOSTADAS—TOPPED WITH CHEDDAR
CHEESE AND PIECES OF CHILE

TAQUITOS 1.10
BITE SIZE TINY TACOS—PICADILLO FILLING

TAMALITOS 1.10
COCKTAIL SIZE TAMALES, SPICY AND FRESH

EMPANADAS 1.10
"LITTLE TURNOVERS" FILLED WITH SEAFOOD,
SPICES AND HERBS

CHILE CHEESE BALLS 1.10
CREAM CHEESE AND CHILES, ALL ROLLED INTO
ONE—FRIED TO A GOLDEN BROWN

QUESADILLAS 1.10
FAVORITE OF THE JAMAICA MARKET.
GOOD FOR EARLY OR LATE SNACK.

CHILI CON QUESO 1.10
A MIXTURE OF DIFFERENT SPICES, CHEESE
& CHILI SERVED PIPING HOT
WITH TOSTADA CHIPS

TURN ME OVER AND SEND ME!

FIVE PERCENT (5%) SALES TAX WILL BE ADDED TO THE ABOVE PRICES OF
ALL FOOD AND BEVERAGE ITEMS SERVED AT THE TABLES IN THIS ROOM
Copyright 1964 Señor Pico 6M 2-68 D.P.H.

APPETIZERS

ANTIPASTO

Make lettuce and endive beds on plates. Mound Lentil and White Bean Salad, (see recipe p. 75), in center. Surround with assortment of sliced salami, cheeses, hard-cooked egg, tomato wedges, tuna fish chunks, olives, pickled peppers. Garnish with pimiento strips, rolled anchovies stuffed with capers, and lemon wedges.

GUACAMOLE CON TOMATE
(Avocado Dip with Tomatoes)
YIELD: 12 servings
INGREDIENTS

Ripe California Avocados	4
Mayonnaise	½ cup
Chopped Onion	¼ cup
Salt	1 tbsp.
Chili Powder	2 tsp.
Garlic Powder	1 tsp.
Liquid Hot Pepper	½ tsp.
Tomatoes, peeled and chopped	2 medium

METHOD
Halve avocados lengthwise, twisting gently to separate halves. Plunge sharp knife directly into seeds and twist to lift out. Peel avocado halves. Mash avocado or blend a few seconds in electric blender. Mix with mayonnaise, onion, seasonings and lemon juice. Chill thoroughly. Garnish with tomato.

CHILI-CHEESE BALL
YIELD: 48 servings
INGREDIENTS

Sharp Cheddar Cheese, grated	3½ lb.
Instant Garlic Powder	4 tsp.
Chili Powder	

METHOD
In large bowl combine cheese with garlic powder; mix lightly. Shape into 8 balls, pressing firmly. Roll each ball in chili powder until well coated. Serve as an hors d'oeuvre with corn chips or crackers.

DEVILED DIP
For each 1 lb. peanut butter, blend in 2 (4½-oz.) cans deviled ham, 2 tsp. celery salt, ¼ tsp. liquid hot pepper.

STUFFED CELERY
For each 1 lb. peanut butter, add ½ pt. sour cream and 4 oz. prepared horseradish; mix well.

PEANUT BUTTER VEGETABLE DRESSING
INGREDIENTS

Peanut Butter	12 oz.
Garlic, crushed	2 cloves
Crushed Red Pepper	1 tsp.
Lemon Juice	1 oz.
Sugar	2 tsp.
Salt	1 tsp.
Bay Leaf	1 large
Water	1 pt.
Milk	1 cup

METHOD
Saute peanut butter with garlic and red pepper over low heat for about 3 min. stirring constantly. Add lemon juice, sugar, salt and bay leaf. Blend in water to make a smooth mixture. Add milk and bring just to a boil. Remove bay leaf. Serve hot over cooked green beans.

GAMBAS A LA CASTELLANA
(Shrimp Cocktail Castilian Style)
YIELD: 24 servings
INGREDIENTS

Cooked Shrimp, deveined	3 lb.
Red Apples, chopped	1 lb.
Peaches, chopped	1 lb.
Red Sour Cherries, drained	1 15-oz. can
Heavy Cream	1 cup
Ketchup	¾ cup
Prepared Horseradish	1 oz.
Salt	
Liquid Hot Pepper	¼ tsp.
Lettuce Leaves	24
Sociables Crackers	

METHOD
Dice shrimp. Combine with apples, peaches and cherries. Chill. Whip cream; fold in ketchup, horseradish, salt and liquid hot pepper to make sauce. Chill. Portion ½ cup of shrimp mixture onto lettuce leaves. Top with a dollop of sauce. Serve with crackers.

GUACAMOLE WITH BACON
YIELD: 3 cups
INGREDIENTS

Avocados, pureed	4
Salt	1 tbsp.
Lemon Juice	¼ cup
Tabasco	¾ tsp.
Garlic Cloves, crushed	3
Bacon, cooked crisp and crumbled	½ lb.
Walnut, chopped (optional)	¼ cup

METHOD
Blend avocado puree with salt, lemon juice, Tabasco and garlic. Cover and chill. Add bacon and walnuts.

GUACAMOLE WITH GREEN CHILI PEPPERS
YIELD: 3 cups
INGREDIENTS

Avocados, pureed	4
Canned Green Chili Peppers, finely chopped	½ cup
Onion, minced	¼ cup
Salt	1 tbsp.
Lemon Juice	¼ cup

METHOD
Blend all ingredients with avocado puree. Cover and chill.

MEXICAN SHRIMP BOATS
YIELD: 12 appetizers
INGREDIENTS

Raw Shrimp	1 lb.
Salad Oil	2/3 cup
Red Wine Vinegar	1/3 cup
Salt	1 tsp.
Paprika	½ tsp.
Ginger	½ tsp.
Pepper	¼ tsp.
Garlic Clove, minced	1
Avocados	3
Lemon Juice	
Salt	
Lemon Wedges	6

METHOD
Shell and devein shrimp. Combine oil, vinegar, salt, paprika, ginger, pepper and garlic in bowl; beat well. Add shrimp; cover and chill several hours. Drain shrimp, reserving 1/3 cup marinade.

Heat 2 tbsp. marinade in skillet. Add shrimp; cook quickly until just pink.

Cut avocados lengthwise into halves; remove seeds and skin. Brush avocados with lemon juice. Sprinkle with salt. Mound shrimp in avocados.

Heat remaining marinade; spoon over shrimp. Serve with lemon wedges.

ALASKA KING CRAB APERITIVOS A LA MEXICANA
INGREDIENTS

Alaska King Crab, fancy frozen	5 lb. pack

METHOD
Defrost and remove legs from pack, (approx. 2 lb.). Cut legs into bite size chunks. Arrange attractively on a platter impaled on cocktail picks. Serve accompanied with conventional cocktail sauce for dunking.

ALASKA KING CRAB SPREAD
YIELD: 2½ qt.
INGREDIENTS

Alaska King Crab Meat	3 lb.
Cream Cheese, softened	1½ lb.
Avocados, medium, 3 cups mashed	6
Lime Juice	¼ cup
Salsa Jalapena	2 tbsp.
Salt	to taste

METHOD
Place all ingredients in blender; whip until smooth. Adjust seasoning; chill thoroughly. Serve crab mixture in a bowl surrounded with tortilla chips for dipping.

CAMARONES EN FRIO
(Pickled Party Shrimp)
YIELD: Approx. 2 qt.
INGREDIENTS

Salad Oil	2 tbsp.
Shrimp, raw, peeled, deveined	2 lb.
Marinade	
Onion Flakes	½ cup
Instant Minced Garlic	1 tsp.
Water	1/3 cup
Salad Oil	½ cup
White Vinegar	1/3 cup
Chili Powder	1 tbsp.
Sugar	1 tsp.
Salt	1 tsp.
Ground Red Pepper	1/8-1/4 tsp.

METHOD
Marinade: Combine onion flakes, garlic and water and let stand to rehydrate for 10 min. Add remainder of marinade ingredients.

Saute shrimp in 2 tbsp. heated salad oil until pink. Drain and place in small bowl. Pour marinade over shrimp. Chill for 4 hrs. or longer.

To serve as appetizer, garnish with sliced avocado, tomato wedges and lemon slices.

GUACAMOLE
YIELD: 25 servings
INGREDIENTS

Avocados, large, peeled	4
Tomatoes, medium, peeled, diced	2
Onion, minced	4 tbsp.
Wine Vinegar or Lemon Juice	4 tbsp.
Salt	1 tsp.
Chili Powder	1 tsp.

METHOD
Mash avocado slightly. Add remaining ingredients and mix well.
CAUTION: To preserve color, make as near serving time as possible. Cover tightly with plastic wrap.

SOUPS

ALBONDIGAS
(California Beef Ball Soup)
YIELD: 24 servings
INGREDIENTS

Lean Ground California Beef	4 lb.
Soft Bread Crumbs	3 cup
Water	
Eggs	4
Salt	6 tsp.
Pepper	½ tsp.
Onion, thinly sliced	1 qt.
Butter	2 oz.
Canned Beef Broth	5 qt.
Canned Tomato Sauce	1 qt.
Chili Powder	¼ cup

METHOD
Mix together beef, crumbs, 1 cup water, eggs, 4 tsp. of the salt and pepper. Add beef broth, 3 qt. water, tomato sauce, chili powder and remaining 2 tsp. salt. Heat to boiling. Drop in beef balls. Simmer until beef balls are done, about 10 min.

SOPA DE AGUACATE CON AJO
(Avocado Soup with Garlic)
YIELD: about 1½ quarts
INGREDIENTS

Ripe California Avocados	4
Chicken Broth	1 pt.
Lime Juice	2 tsp.
Salt	½ tsp.
Garlic Powder	1/8 tsp.
Heavy Cream	1 pt.

METHOD
Halve avocados lengthwise, twisting gently to separate halves. Plunge sharp knife directly into seeds and twist to lift out. Peel avocado halves. In electric blender puree avocados with broth, lime juice, salt and garlic powder. Stir in cream. Chill thoroughly. Garnish with lemon slices or with dollops of whipped cream, flavored with garlic powder.

CHILI TOMATO SOUP
YIELD: 48 servings
INGREDIENTS

Condensed Tomato Soup	2 50-oz. cans
Water	3 qt.
Instant Minced Onion	8 oz.
Chili Powder	½ cup
Instant Garlic Powder	1 tsp.
Avocados, peeled and diced	8 small

METHOD
In large pot combine soup with water, onion, chili and garlic powders. Bring to boiling. Reduce heat and simmer, uncovered, for 15 min. Serve with diced avocado.

GAZPACHO ON HALF SHELL
YIELD: 24 servings
INGREDIENTS

Large Ripe Tomatoes	16
Cucumber	4
Green Pepper, chopped	1 cup
Red Onion, chopped	1 cup
Small Hot Red Pepper, finely chopped	2 to 3
Olive Oil	¾ cup
Red Wine Vinegar	3 tbsp.
Salt	1 tbsp.
Black Pepper, freshly ground	1/8 tsp.
Garlic Cloves	1 to 2
California Avocados	12
Fresh Lime or Lemon Juice	as needed
Salad Greens	as needed

METHOD
Remove skins from tomatoes. Chop tomatoes fine.

Peel and chop cucumbers.

Mix tomatoes and cucumbers with green pepper, onion, hot red pepper, olive oil, vinegar and seasonings. Crush garlic and mix in.

Chill until ice cold.

Cut avocados lengthwise into halves. Remove seeds and skin. Sprinkle avocados with fresh lime or lemon juice.

To serve, fill avocado halves with "Gazpacho" mixture. Serve on salad greens with spoons for eating.

ENTREES

CHICKEN ENCHILADAS
YIELD: 1
INGREDIENTS

Enchilada Sauce	1 oz.
Corn Tortilla	1
Chicken, chopped (cooked)	1 oz.
Onion, chopped	½ oz.
Sour Cream	1 oz.
Jalapene Chilies, finely minced	1/8 oz.
Sharp Cheese, grated	¾ oz.
Sharp Cheese, grated	1 oz.
Pimiento (¼ oz.)	3 strips
Ripe Olive Slices (3 whole olives for 2 enchiladas)	4 circles

METHOD
Dip tortilla into sauce, covering generously. If slightly warm, held at room temperature, tortillas will not crack as they are rolled.

Remove Jalapene chili seeds, wash, mince.

Place a row of chicken and onions across the tortilla. Add the sour cream on top. Scatter chili seeds as they are HOT. Top with grated cheese.

Roll tortilla around these ingredients; place on tray without crowding them. Brush more sauce on ends of tortillas to keep from drying out and cracking.

Sprinkle cheese over the top of each.

Place pimiento diagonally on top with ripe olives arranged in between.

Cook 45 seconds in microwave oven.

ALCACHOFAS A LA ESPANOLA
(Artichokes Spanish Style)
YIELD: 24 (4-oz.) servings
INGREDIENTS

Frozen Artichoke Hearts, thawed	3 lb. 6 oz.
Salt	1 tbsp.
Olive Oil	1 cup
Cooked Smoked Ham, chopped	7½ oz.
Onion, minced	12 oz.
Lemon, sliced	6 oz.
Capers, drained	3 oz.
Dromedary Pimiento Pieces	12 oz.
Wheat Thins Crackers	

METHOD
Cook artichoke hearts with salt, olive oil, ham, onion and lemon until tender. Add capers and pimientos. Serve hot with crackers.

TRINI'S CHILI CON QUESO
YIELD: 1 pt.
INGREDIENTS

Tomatoes and Green Chili	½ cup
Fresh Tomatoes, diced	2 tbsp.
Grated Onion	1 tbsp.
Process American Cheese, grated	1 lb.
Liquid Hot Pepper	¼ tbsp.

METHOD
Heat tomatoes and onion in double boiler. Add grated cheese and liquid hot pepper. Heat to melt cheese. Serve in warmer surrounded by crisp fried tostados.

CHICKEN CHILI CON CARNE
YIELD: 48 portions
INGREDIENTS

Instant Diced Onion	6½ oz.
Instant Minced Garlic	1 tsp.
Water	1½ cup
Oil	½ cup
Tomatoes, broken up—No. 10 cans	2 cans
Chili Powder	½ cup
Oregano Leaves	4 tsp.
Salt	4 tsp.
Sugar	2 tsp.
Ground Black Pepper	½ tsp.
Red Kidney Beans, undrained No. 10 cans	1½ cans
Cooked Chicken, diced	1 gal.
Cooked Rice	2 gal.

METHOD
Rehydrate onion and garlic in water for 10 min. In large saucepot heat oil; add rehydrated onion and garlic. Saute 5 min. Stir in tomatoes, chili powder, oregano, salt, sugar and black pepper. Simmer uncovered 15 min., stirring occasionally. Add kidney beans and chicken, Heat. Serve over hot rice.

TACOS CON AGUACATE
(Tacos with Avocado)
YIELD: 24 servings
INGREDIENTS

Large Beef Tacos	2 doz.
Ripe California Avocados	4
Lettuce, shredded	1 pt.

METHOD
Prepare beef tacos according to package directions for crisp tacos. Place peeled avocado halves cavity-side down and cut into thick slices.
TO SERVE: Open hot beef tacos gently and fill with avocado slices and shredded lettuce.

Ole

TOSTADOS CON CHORIZOS
YIELD: 24 tostados
INGREDIENTS

Western Iceberg Lettuce	3 lb.
	(about 3 heads)
Sausage, Chorizo or Italian	4½ lb.
	(about 24)
Boiling Water	
Corn Tortillas, 6 in.	24
Oil	
Pinto or Kidney Beans	1 No. 10 can
Onion Salt	½ oz.
Pepper	¼ tsp.
Barbecue Sauce	5 cup
Grated Parmesan Cheese	6 oz.

METHOD
Shred lettuce fine. Simmer sausages 5 min.; drain. Then brown sausages in skillet or broiler and cut diagonally into thin slices. Fry tortillas in hot oil until crisp, about 3 seconds. Drain beans and mash. Add onion salt and pepper. Heat with ½ cup of oil. With No. 12 scoop, portion mashed beans onto tortillas. Top each with 1 oz. lettuce, then 2 oz. sausage; ladle on 1½ oz. sauce and sprinkle with ¼ oz. Parmesan cheese. Broil just until cheese is lightly browned. Serve at once.

MINUTE STEAK ROLLS MEXICANO
YIELD: 24 servings
INGREDIENTS

California Beef Cube Steaks	24
Salt and Pepper	
Oil	2 oz.
Processed American Cheese, grated	1 lb.
Canned Corn	1 qt.
Canned California Green Chilies (seeds and pith removed), chopped, 7-oz. can	1 can
Canned Tomato Sauce	1 qt.
Chili Powder	1 tbsp.

METHOD
Season steaks with salt and pepper. Brown both sides quickly in hot oil. Combine half of cheese with corn and chilies. Spoon about 1/3 cup corn mixture on center of each steak. Roll up to enclose filling; secure with wooden pick. Place seam side down in shallow baking pan. Mix tomato sauce, remaining cheese and chili powder. Pour over steak rolls. Bake at 350°F. for 15-20 min. until steaks are tender.

OLIVE-EGG ENCHILADAS
YIELD: 24 enchiladas
INGREDIENTS
Filling

Chorizo Sausage	1 lb.
Hard-Cooked Eggs, chopped	2 doz.
California Ripe Olives, chopped	11 oz.
Red Sauce	1 cup
Salt	1 tsp.

Enchiladas

Corn Tortillas	24
Red Sauce (heated)	2½ cup
Oil (for frying)	

Garnish

Shredded Lettuce	
Onions, thinly sliced	4 oz.
Red Sauce	4½ cup
Dry Monterey Cheese, grated	2¾ oz.
Pitted California Ripe Olives	

METHOD
Filling: Remove sausage from casing. Crumble and cook until browned; drain. Combine sausage, eggs, chopped olives, 1 cup Red Sauce and salt.
Enchiladas: Dip tortillas lightly in sauce, and fry in a small amount of oil. Drain well. Roll about 2½ oz. filling in each tortilla; place seam side down in baking pan. Cover. Bake at 350°F. for 15 min., until heated through.
TO SERVE:
Place heated enchiladas on serving platter. Garnish with lettuce and onion. Spoon 1½ oz. Red Sauce over each. Sprinkle with cheese and top with pitted olives.

SPICY BEEF STEAK STRIPS
YIELD: Test recipe, 6 servings
INGREDIENTS

Beef Round Steak, ¼ in. thick	1½ lb.
Butter	2 tbsp.
Instant Minced Onion	1 tbsp.
Salt	1½ tsp.
Chili Powder	¼ tsp.
Cayenne Pepper	dash
Clove Garlic, finely chopped	1
Cinnamon	¼ tsp.
Celery Seed	¼ tsp.
Prepared Mustard	2 tbsp.
Water	1 cup

METHOD
Cut steak into ½- by 2-in. strips; brown in butter. Add all remaining ingredients; stir to mix. Cover and simmer 25 to 30 min., until fork tender. Serve over rice.

ARROZ CON POLLO

YIELD: 6 portions
INGREDIENTS

Instant Minced Onion	½ cup
Sweet Pepper Flakes	¼ cup
Olive Oil	1/3 cup
Ready-to-cook Chicken, cut into serving size pieces (½ to 3 lb.)	1
Salt	2½ tsp.
Oregano Leaves	1 tsp.
Paprika	½ tsp.
Ground Black Pepper	½ tsp.
Instant Garlic Powder	½ tsp.
Tomatoes, chopped, (1 lb. 12 oz.)	1 can
Smoked Ham, chopped	½ cup
Green Olives, sliced	¼ cup
Raw Regular Cooking Rice	1 cup
Frozen Peas	12-oz. pkg.

METHOD

Combine minced onion and pepper flakes with 2/3 cup water; let stand 10 min. to re-hydrate. Meanwhile, in a large saucepot heat oil. Add chicken and brown on all sides. Add re-hydrated onion and pepper flakes, saute about 5 min. Add seasonings, tomatoes, ham and olives. Cover and simmer 10 min.

Add 3 cups boiling water. rice and saffron; stir gently. Cover and continue simmering until chicken is tender, 25 to 30 min. longer.

Cook peas according to package directions, drain. Add peas to chicken. Place in serving casserole. Serve hot, with pimento strips if desired.

MONTEREY CHILI BEEF

YIELD: 24 servings
INGREDIENTS

California Beef Round Steak, cut in ¾-in. cubes	8 lb.
Oil	3 oz.
Onions, diced	3 qt.
Garlic, minced	6 cloves
Water	2 qt.
Canned Red Chili Sauce, (enchilada sauce)	1½ pt.
Salt	2 tbsp.
Pitted Ripe Olives	1 pt.

METHOD

Brown beef cubes in oil. Remove beef from pan. Add onions and garlic to pan, brown lightly. Return beef to pan with onions; add water, chili sauce and salt. Cover; simmer 1 to 1½ hrs. until beef is tender, adding water if needed. A few minutes before serving stir in olives. Serve with kidney beans or rice.

CHILI CON CARNE
(with Beef and Ham)

YIELD: Test recipe, 6 to 8 portions
INGREDIENTS

Onion Flakes	½ cup
Instant Minced Garlic	½ tsp.
Oil	3 tbsp.
Beef Round Steak	1½ lb.
Ham Steak	1 lb.
Tomatoes, cut up	1 1-lb. can
Chili Powder	1½-3 tbsp.
Salt	1 tsp.
Kidney Beans	1 1 lb. 4 oz. can
Water, Beef Broth or Red Wine (if needed)	¼ cup

METHOD

Mix onion flakes and minced garlic with 1/3 cup water; let stand 10 min. to soften.

Heat oil in a large skillet. Add softened onion and garlic; saute until golden. Dice steaks into ½-in. cubes. Add to skillet and cook until brown.

Add tomatoes, chili powder and salt. Bring to boiling point; reduce heat and simmer, uncovered, stirring occasionally, for 1 hr.

Stir in kidney beans and simmer ½ hr. longer. If necessary, thin mixture with water.

Top with a large dollop of sour cream, if desired.

MEXICAN MEAT LOAF

YIELD: Test recipe, 8 portions
INGREDIENTS

Eggs, lightly beaten	2
Tomato Sauce	8 oz.
Instant Minced Onion	½ cup
Sweet Pepper Flakes	¼ cup
Chili Powder	2 tbsp.
Salt	2 tsp.
Ground Red Pepper	1/8 tsp.
Instant Minced Garlic	¼ tsp.
Ground Meat Loaf Mixture	2½ lb.
Butter or Margarine, melted	1 tbsp.
Dry Bread Crumbs	3 tbsp.

METHOD

Combine eggs, tomato sauce, minced onion, pepper flakes, chili powder, salt, red pepper and minced garlic. Add meat; mix thoroughly but do not overmix. Press into lightly buttered 9- by 5- by 3-in. loaf pan. Drizzle top with melted butter. Sprinkle with bread crumbs.

Bake in a preheated hot oven (400°F.) 1 hr. or until done. Let rest in pan 10 min. before slicing.

Ole

SPANISH RICE

YIELD: 50 (5-oz.) servings
INGREDIENTS

Bacon	1 lb.
Onions, chopped	2½ lb.
Celery, chopped	1½ lb.
Green Peppers, chopped	1 lb.
Chili Powder	2 tbsp.
Italian Seasoning	2 tbsp.
Monosodium Glutamate	2 tbsp.
Oregano	2 tbsp.
Salt	2 tbsp.
Seasoned Salt	2 tbsp.
Celery Salt	1 tbsp.
Garlic Powder	1 tbsp.
Pepper	1 tsp.
Worcestershire Sauce	2 oz.
Stewed Tomatoes—No. 10 can	1 can
Tomato Sauce—No. 2½ cans	2 cans
Cooked Rice	12 lb.

METHOD
Cook bacon in 4-in. deep pan for 10 min. at 400°F. (convection oven) until crisp. Remove bacon; set aside. Saute onions, celery and green peppers in pan with drippings at 400°F. (convection oven) for 10 min. Stir occasionally. Dice or crumble bacon. Combine bacon, all seasonings, tomatoes and sauce. Add rice; stir to mix. Bake at 400°F. (convection oven) for 20 min.
NOTE: 1 lb. raw rice yields 4 to 4½ lb. or 2 qt. cooked rice; 3 lb. raw rice yields 12 to 13½ lb. cooked rice.

SOLE EN ESCABECHE—(Pickled Fish)
(Standards Dept. ARA Services, Inc.)

YIELD: 300 cocktail servings
INGREDIENTS

Butter	1 lb.
Olive Oil	2 qt.
Fillet of Sole cut in 1-oz. portions	20 lb.
Flour	
Salt and Pepper	
Onion, very thinly sliced, separated into rings	3 lb.
Green Peppers, sliced in rings	10
Garlic Cloves	10
Orange Juice	5 cups (or more)
Lime Juice	2 cups
Tabasco	2½ tsp.
Orange Slices	
Lime Slices	

METHOD
Heat butter and three-fourths (1½ qt.) of oil.
Flour fish lightly and saute until delicately brown on both sides. Season with salt and pepper.
Arrange fillets in steam table pan. Top with onion rings, pepper rings and garlic.
Combine remaining oil, juices and Tabasco. Pour over fish while still warm.
Let stand in refrigerator 12-24 hrs.
Serve garnished with orange slices, lime slices, grated orange rind and ripe olive rings.

TAMALE PIE

YIELD: Approx. 50 6- to 7-oz. servings
INGREDIENTS

Water, boiling	3½ gal.
Salt	6 tbsp.
Yellow Cornmeal	5 lb.

Filling

Onions, chopped	7 lb.
Ground Beef	25 lb.
Parsley, minced (1 bunch)	3 cup
Seasoned Tomato Sauce	1 No. 10 can
Mexicorn, 4-lb. 11-oz. cans	2 cans
Ripe Olives, chopped	4 lb.
Garlic, minced fine	10-14 cloves
Salt	6 tbsp.
Chili Powder	1-1/3 cup
Black Pepper	2 tbsp.
Worcestershire Sauce	½ cup
Tabasco	2 tbsp.
Sharp Cheese, grated	
Whole Ripe Olives	

METHOD
Remove water from heat to avoid splattering while adding salt and cornmeal.
Add salt and cornmeal slowly, stirring with wire whisk to prevent lumping. Boil until thickened. Line individual baking dishes with 2 oz. of mixture.

Filling
Saute onions and ground beef. Mix parsley, tomato sauce, mexicorn, chopped ripe olives, seasonings, Worcestershire sauce and tabasco with meat. Simmer 30-45 min. until done and thick.
Spread 4 oz. or 2 dips No. 12 scoop per bowl or use 1 extra large scoop. Cover center with 1½ to 2 oz. of cheese. Place ripe olive in center of dish.
With pastry bag place rosettes around edge of dish. Brush lightly with melted butter.
Cook 1½ min. in microwave oven.

EL SOMBRERO TOSTADO
YIELD: 24 portions
INGREDIENTS

Corn Tortillas	24
Oil for frying	as needed
Refried Beans	1 gal.
Sauteed Beef	6 lb.
Tomato Slices	72
Finely Shredded Lettuce	6½ gal.
Ripe Olives, coarsely chopped	1½ qt.
Sliced Turkey or Chicken	3 lb.
Avocados, sliced	8 small
Tomato Dressing	3 qt.
Grated Parmesan Cheese	1½ cup
Chopped Parsley	½ cup
Ripe Olives for garnish	96
Radishes for garnish	48

METHOD

For each Tostado, fry 1 tortilla until crisp. Drain; place on individual serving platter.

Cover with 2/3 cup hot refried beans, then 2/3 cup sauteed beef.

Place two tomato slices next to tortilla, one at each end of platter.

Toss lettuce with chopped olives. Mound 3 cups over tortilla and tomato slices for each serving.

Arrange 2 oz. sliced turkey or chicken around slices of lettuce mound, with avocado slices between.

Drizzle ½ cup Tomato Dressing over Tostado.

Top each with a tomato slice, a radish slice and a whole ripe olive; skewer.

Sprinkle with 1 tbsp. cheese and 1 tsp. parsley. Garnish with olive and radish roses.

DURANGO SPICED PORK AND EGGS
YIELD: Test recipe, 6 portions
INGREDIENTS

Olive or Salad Oil	2 tbsp.
Ground Lean Pork	1 lb.
Salt	¾ tsp.
Oregano Leaves, crumbled	½ tsp.
Instant Garlic Powder	¼ tsp.
Ground Red Pepper	¼ tsp.
Tomato, small, diced	1
Eggs, beaten	6

METHOD

Heat oil in skillet. Add pork and cook, stirring constantly, until brown. Stir in seasonings and tomato. Cook uncovered, over low heat 15 min. stirring occasionally. Pour eggs over mixture and cook, stirring constantly until eggs are set.

ALASKA KING CRAB A LA ESPANOLA
YIELD: 48 servings
INGREDIENTS

Celery, chopped	½ lb.
Green Peppers, chopped	½ lb.
Onions, chopped	½ lb.
Garlic, chopped	2 cloves
Olive Oil	4 oz.
Canned Tomatoes, drained	1 lb.
Tomato Soup, 50-oz. can	2 cans
Stock	1 pt.
Sugar	3 oz.
Chili Peppers, crushed	2
Bay Leaves	2
Salt and Pepper	
Alaska King Crab Meat	5 lb.
Canned Sliced Mushrooms, drained	1 lb.
Cooked Buttered Rice	1½ gal

METHOD

Saute celery, green peppers, onions, and garlic in olive oil until tender. Add tomatoes, tomato soup, stock, sugar, chili peppers and bay leaves. Add salt and pepper to taste. Bring to a boil, then simmer 15 min. Adjust consistency and seasonings. Place Alaska king crab meat and mushrooms in steam table pan; add sauce. Heat at 350°F. in oven; hold for service. Serve over hot buttered rice.

AU GRATIN TAMALE PIE
YIELD: 6-8 servings
INGREDIENTS

Instant Minced Onion	2 tbsp.
Garlic Powder	1/8 tsp.
Oil	¼ cup
Cream Style Corn, 1-lb. can	1 can
Tomatoes, 1-lb. 12-oz. can	1 can
Chili Powder	1 tbsp.
Seasoned Salt	1 tbsp.
Yellow Cornmeal	1 lb.
Tomato Juice, 13½-oz. can	1 can
Pitted California Ripe Olives, diced	8 oz.
Process American Cheese	2 slices

METHOD

Heat oil in pan. Add tomatoes, corn, onion, chili powder, salt and garlic. Bring to a boil; then simmer 20 min. Stir in cornmeal, tomato juice and ripe olives. Turn mixture into greased 2 qt. baking dish. Bake at 350°F. for 20 min. Cut each cheese slice into quarters and place on top of casserole mixture. Bake 5 to 10 min. longer.

AL FRESCO TAMALE PIE

YIELD: 6 servings

INGREDIENTS

Oil	3 tbsp.
Onion, chopped	3 oz.
Stewed Tomatoes, 1-lb. can	1 can
Corn, 12-oz. can	1 can
Cut Green Beans, drained, 1-lb. can	1 can
Chili Powder	1 tbsp.
Salt	1½ tsp.
Yellow Cornmeal	6 oz.
Pitted California Ripe Olives, diced	8 oz.
Flour	½ cup
Baking Powder	1¼ tsp.
Milk	½ cup
Egg	1 can
Melted Butter	3 tbsp.

METHOD

Saute onion in oil until soft. Stir in tomatoes, corn with juice, green beans, chili powder, 1 tsp. salt and ¼ cup cornmeal. Simmer 10 min. Add olives. Turn into 9-in. deep-dish pie pan. Combine flour, remaining ½ cup cornmeal, baking powder and salt. Beat egg; add milk and melted butter. Stir egg mixture into flour mixture to make a smooth batter. Spoon over ripe olive mixture. Bake at 425°F. for 25-30 min., until crust is lightly browned.

CHICKEN TORTILLA ROLLS
(City School Cafeterias, Riverside, Calif.)

YIELD: 36 portions

INGREDIENTS

Chicken Stock	4½ qt.
Evaporated Milk (14½-oz. cans)	3 cans
Butter, melted	1¼ lb.
Flour	8 oz.
Chicken Base	1½ tbsp.
Monosodium Glutamate	1½ tsp.
Salt	2 tbsp.
Pepper	1½ tsp.
Cooked Chicken, diced	5½ lb.
Corn Tortillas	3 doz.
Paprika	1 tsp.
Parsley, chopped	¼ cup
Cheese, grated	3 cup

METHOD

Heat chicken stock and undiluted evaporated milk.

Blend melted butter and flour. Add the milk mixture slowly, stirring constantly.

Add seasonings and bring to a boil. Turn off flame.

Moisten diced chicken with approx. ¼ of sauce.

Dip tortilla in warm sauce. Place No. 12 scoop of chicken mixture in center of tortilla. Roll and place in greased pan. Pour remaining sauce over tortilla rolls.

Sprinkle with paprika and chopped parsley. Bake at 350°F. for 20 min. (Convection oven—325°F. for 15 min.) Sprinkle with grated cheese and return to the oven for 5-10 min.

ENCHILADA BAKED PIE
(City School Cafeterias, Riverside, Calif.)

YIELD: 48 servings (3 gal. sauce)

INGREDIENTS

Ground Meat	3 lb.
Grated Cheese	3 lb.
Ground Onions	1 lb.
Salt	to taste
Oil	½ gal.
Tortillas	4 doz.

Sauce

Tomato Paste	1 No. 10 can
Water	3 No. 10 cans
Ground Onions	½ lb.
Chili Powder	½ cup
Cornstarch	to thicken

METHOD

Pre-cook meat. Mix 3 lb. of meat, 2½ lb. cheese, onions.

To make sauce, combine tomato paste, water, ground onions and chili powder. Bring to boil. Thicken with cornstarch.

Line bottom of a baking pan with tortillas. Spread with ½ of cheese, meat and onion mixture; cover with sauce.

Add another layer of tortillas and remaining filling mixture. Cover with sauce. Sprinkle with cheese.

Bake 30 min. at 350°F. Cut in squares and serve.

MEXICAN DOGS

YIELD: 48 servings, 1 chili enchilada each

INGREDIENTS

Frankfurters	48
Tortillas	48
Kraft Chili Con Carne	1 No. 10 can
Kraft Tomato Juice	1¼ qt.
Old English Pasteurized Process Cheddar Cheese, shredded	1½ qt. (1 lb. 8 oz.)

METHOD

Place a frank on each tortilla. Roll tortillas around franks. Portion each 24 servings, seam side down, into a 12- by 20- by 2-in. steam table pan.

Combine ingredients; pour over tortillas. Bake at 350°F. for 25 minutes.

Top with cheese. Continue baking 5 min.

SEASIDE TAMALE PIE

YIELD: 6 servings

INGREDIENTS

Unbaked Pastry Shell, 9-in.	1
Oil	2 tbsp.
Scallions, chopped	1/3 cup
Garlic Salt	1 tsp.
Chili Powder	2 tsp.
Corn, 12-oz. can	1 can
Tomatoes, 1-lb. can	1 can
Tomato Juice, 13½-oz. can	1 can
Yellow Cornmeal	12 oz.
Pitted California Ripe Olives	8 oz.
Tuna, drained, 7-oz. can	1 can

METHOD

Saute scallions in hot oil until soft. Add tomatoes and tomato juice, corn, chili powder and garlic salt. Bring to a boil, then simmer 15 min. Slowly stir in cornmeal. Cook, stirring constantly, until mixture is thick, about 10 min. Add olives and tuna. Turn into unbaked pastry shell. Bake at 450°F. for 25 min., until brown.

TOSTADOS CON POLLO
(Tostados with Chicken)

YIELD: Test recipe, 6 servings

INGREDIENTS

Western Iceberg Lettuce	1 med. head
Tortillas, fresh, frozen or canned	12
Corn Oil	½ cup
Kidney Beans, drained	2 lb.
Garlic Powder	¼ tsp.
Salt and Pepper	
Tabasco	
Boned Chicken	12 oz.
California Avocados, small, peeled and sliced	2
Parmesan Cheese	1 cup
Tomato, medium, thinly sliced	1
Salsa Pica*	

METHOD

Core, rinse and drain lettuce thoroughly. Shred lettuce. Fry each tortilla in hot oil about 3 seconds; drain on paper towels.

Drain off all but 2 tbsp. oil; add beans and garlic powder. Cook and mash beans until thick paste is formed. Add salt and pepper to taste. Spread bean mixture on tortillas, sprinkle with Tabasco. Top with chicken, avocado, Parmesan, remaining tortillas, tomato lettuce and Salsa Pica*.

*SALSA PICA: Combine 1 or 2 seeded canned green chiles, 1 medium tomato, quartered, and 1 small onion in blender; blend until smooth (or chop ingredients fine.)

PAELLA

YIELD: 24 servings

INGREDIENTS

Shrimp, large	2 doz.
Clams (optional)	4 doz.
Mussels	4 doz.
Pork, cut in ½ in. cubes	2 lb.
Lobsters, 1¼ lb. each	8
Olive Oil	1 pt.
Dry White Wine	1 qt.
Chicken Breasts, boned, 5 oz. each	24
Red Onions, diced	2 lb.
Pimientos or Red, Sweet Peppers diced	12
Tomatoes, coarsely chopped	5 lb.
Uncle Ben's Converted Rice	1 qt.
Saffron	1 tsp.
Paprika	1 tsp.
Chicken Stock or Bouillon	9 cup
Salt	1 tsp.
Pepper	½ tsp.
Spanish Sausage (chorizos), sliced ¼ in. thick	20
Cooked Peas, drained	1 lb.

METHOD

Devein shrimp; set aside. In a deep kettle, boil clams and mussels in lightly salted water JUST until shells open. Clean, cut out muscle; set aside.

Roast pork cubes at 375°F. for 20 min.; stir occasionally to prevent sticking. Set aside.

Remove tails and claws from lobsters. Cut tails into 4 pieces each and claws into 3 pieces. Saute in olive oil over medium heat for 3 min. Salt and pepper to taste. Remove from pan; add ½ cup wine and set aside.

Brown chicken breasts in olive oil until golden. Remove from pan; set aside. Add onion, red peppers and tomatoes to pan; cook over medium heat until onions are crisp-tender, not brown. Add remaining olive oil. Add rice and cook until golden brown. Stir in saffron, paprika, stock, remaining wine, salt and pepper. Bring to a boil.

Arrange lobster pieces and shrimp around edge of pan and chicken breasts in the center. Roast at 375°F. for 15 min. Add clams, mussels, pork and chorizos. Cook for 10 min. longer, until liquid is absorbed and rice is tender. Heat peas and sprinkle over all.

ENCHILADAS CON POLLO
(Tortilla Chicken Casserole)

YIELD: Test recipe, 6 servings

INGREDIENTS

Western Iceberg Lettuce	1 large head
Tortillas, fresh, canned or frozen	12
Softened Cream Cheese	8 oz.
Chicken, cut in strips	24 oz.
Butter	
Grated Parmesan Cheese	1 cup
Heavy Cream	2 cup
Salsa Verde (see below)	
Guacamole (see below)	

METHOD

Core, rinse and thoroughly drain lettuce. Chill.

Spread tortillas generously with cream cheese and lay strips of chicken down center; fold each tortilla once. Place tortillas in buttered 3 qt. shallow baking dish. Sprinkle with grated cheese and pour cream over top.

Bake in 350°F. (moderate) oven 30 min. Serve with Salsa Verde and Guacamole.

Salsa Verde

To prepare Salsa Verde: Combine 1 lb. canned tomato sauce; two canned green chilies, seeded and finely chopped; 1 clove garlic, crushed; 1 medium onion, finely chopped, and ¼ tsp. salt in saucepan. Simmer 30 min., stirring occasionally.

Guacamole

To prepare Guacamole: Remove 5 or 6 outer leaves from lettuce; place on salad plate to form "bowl."

Mash 1 ripe avocado with 2 tbsp. lemon juice, 1 tsp. grated onion, ½ tsp. salt and 1/8 tsp. Tabasco.

Fill lettuce "bowl" with mixture.

Shred remainder of lettuce and serve over enchiladas on removal from oven.

BAKED STUFFED POTATOES COLOMBIAN STYLE
(With Cumin Seed)

YIELD: Test recipe, 6 servings

INGREDIENTS

Baking Potatoes, medium-large	6
Sour Cream	½ cup
Salt	1¾ tsp.
Ground Cumin Seed	½ tsp.
Ground Black Pepper	1/8 tsp.
Garlic Powder	1/8 tsp.
Hard-Cooked Eggs, chopped	2
Milk	1/3 cup
Butter or Margarine	6 pats

METHOD

Wash potatoes and wipe dry. Puncture ends with a fork or pointed knife. Bake 1 hr. 15 min. or until done in a preheated very hot oven (450°F.) (If oven is in use at lower temperature, bake potatoes at the same time, but increase the cooking time which will depend upon oven temperature.) Cut a slice from top of each potato. Scoop out the inside and place it in a bowl being sure the potato shells are intact. Combine sour cream, seasonings, hard-cooked eggs and milk. Add to potatoes and mix until fluffy. Spoon lightly into potato shells. Serve hot at once with a pat of butter or margarine, if desired.

MEXICALI PIE
(City School Cafeterias, Riverside, Calif.)

YIELD: 100 portions, 3½- by 2¼- by 2-in.

INGREDIENTS

Ground Meat	15 lb.
Celery	2 qt.
Onions	1 qt.
Green Pepper	1 qt.
Tomatoes, 1-1/3. No. 10 cans	1 gal.
Tomato Puree, 2/3 No. 10 cans	2 qt.
W. K. Corn, 1-1/3 No. 10 cans	1 gal.
Salt	¼ cup
Chili Powder	¼ cup
Flour, sifted	2½ qt.
Cornmeal	1¼ qt.
Sugar	½ cup
Salt	2 tbsp.
Baking Powder	2/3 cup
Dried Eggs	1 pt.
Dried Milk	1 cup
Cheese, shredded	2 lb.
Water	3 qt.
Shortening, melted	1 cup

METHOD

Cook meat; add celery, onions and green pepper. Cook until tender. Drain off excess fat.

Heat together tomatoes, tomato puree and corn; add meat mixture and seasoning and simmer for 15 min. Place mixture in baking pans to depth of about 1½-in. (Four No. 200 pans.)

Sift together the sifted flour, corn meal, sugar, salt, baking powder, dried eggs and dried milk. Add cheese to dry ingredients. (Part of the cheese may be reserved and sprinkled over casserole upon removing from oven.) Then add water and melted shortening. Pour thin batter over the hot meat mixture (about ¼ in. thick). Bake at 400°F. for 30 min.

CHILI PIE
(City School Cafeterias, Riverside, Calif.)
YIELD: 100 portions
INGREDIENTS

Ground Beef	12½ lb.
Onions, chopped	1½ qt.
Shortening	1½ cup
Tomatoes, cooked	1¼ gal.
Kidney Beans, cooked	1¼ gal.
Salt	1-1/3 tbsp.
Pepper	1 tsp.
Chili Powder	1-1/3 tbsp.

Cornbread Topper

Flour	1¼ qt.
Cornmeal	1 qt.
Sugar	2 tbsp.
Salt	2 tbsp.
Baking Powder	3 tbsp.
Eggs	3
Dry Milk	1 cup
Water	1 qt.
Shortening, melted	¼ cup

METHOD
Brown onions in shortening. Add meat. Cook until browned. Add remaining ingredients and continue cooking for about 20 min.

Pour into a pan and cover with Cornbread Topper batter. Bake in hot oven 425°F. for 20 min.

Mix dry ingredients together.

Blend eggs with milk. Add to dry ingredients and mix slowly until blended. (DO NOT OVERMIX). Treat as for muffins.

Fold in melted shortening last.

Spread topping over hot meat mixture as thinly as possible, pouring very gently.

BURRITOS
YIELD: About 20 lb. (50 3-oz. servings)
INGREDIENTS

Pork, cubed	22 lb.
Onions, chopped	6 lb.
Green Peppers, chopped	2-3 lb.
Chili Sauce	1 No. 10 can
Chili Powder	½ cup
Prepared Mustard	½ cup
Worcestershire Sauce	¼ cup
Wine Vinegar	½ cup
Seasoned Salt	¼ cup

Per Serving Portion:

Meat Mixture	1½ oz.
Ortega Green Chile Salsa	1 oz.
Sharp Cheese, grated	1 oz.
Salsa	½ oz.

METHOD
Saute pork, onions and green pepper. Add chili sauce, chili powder, mustard, Worcestershire, vinegar and salt. Cook until done—about 45 min.
TO SERVE
Put meat mixture, Salsa, cheese across flour tortilla, then roll together. Cook 45 seconds in microwave oven. Top with more Salsa after tortilla is cooked.

ALASKA KING CRAB TOSTADOS CON JOCOQUI
YIELD: 12 servings
INGREDIENTS

Alaska King Crab Legs, sliced diagonally	1 qt.
Sour Cream	1 pt.
Green Chile Relish	¼ cup
Oregano	¼ tsp.
Salt	to taste
Corn Tortillas, crisp hot	12
Refried Beans, prepared, hot	2 cup
Onions, chopped	¾ cup
Jack Cheese, grated	1 cup
Lettuce, shredded	1 qt.
Ripe Olives, pitted	24
Red Chiles	12

METHOD
Prepare all ingredients prior to serving time; assemble the tostados quickly, serve warm and crisp.

Combine sour cream, green chile relish, oregano and salt. Set aside.

Place a layer of beans on each tortilla; add chopped onions, grated cheese and shredded lettuce. Top with Alaska King Crab leg slices. Pour over sour cream dressing.

Garnish with a slice of crab leg, two olives and a red chile.

FRIJOLES RE-FRITOS (Refried Beans)
(Standards Dept., ARA Services, Inc.)
YIELD: 25 servings
INGREDIENTS

Red Kidney Beans	1 No. 10 can
Salt	to taste
Lard or Bacon Drippings	2-2½ cup

METHOD
Mash beans slightly and season. Add 1 cup melted fat and stir to combine. In skillet, cook very slowly, stirring frequently to prevent sticking.

Refrigerate overnight.

Heat additional fat in skillet. Add beans and stir until beans are completely dry.

CHILES RELLENOS
YIELD: 4 servings
INGREDIENTS

Peeled Green Chiles	8 oz.
Monterey Jack Cheese	8 oz.
Flour	
Eggs, separated	3
Cold Water	1½ tsp.
Peanut Oil	

METHOD
Cut chiles lengthwise, removing seeds. Wrap around a rectangular piece of cheese so that cheese is completely covered. Roll in flour; set aside.

Beat egg whites and water until stiff; add egg yolks and continue beating until well blended.

Dip floured cheese-stuffed chiles into beaten egg and deep fat fry in peanut oil preheated to 350°F. Spoon hot fat over top and cook until golden brown. Drain on paper towels. Continue until all chiles are browned.

Place in hot Tomato Sauce and simmer for a few minutes until heated through. Serve hot with sauce.

Tomato Sauce

Whole Canned Tomatoes	2 cup
Onion, finely chopped	1 large
Peanut Oil	1/3 cup
Oregano, crushed	1 tsp.
Salt	to taste

METHOD
Put tomatoes into blender bowl and blend a few seconds until smooth. In large skillet, saute onion in peanut oil until limp. Add tomatoes, oregano and salt to taste. Simmer, covered, for 10 min. Add Chiles Rellenos as above.

TOSTADOS
(Standards Dept., ARA Service, Inc.)
YIELD: 100 servings
INGREDIENTS

Tortillas	100

Beef Filling

Ground Beef	14 lb.
Tomato Paste	2½ cup
Water	1¼ qt.
Tomato Soup	1 No. 5 can
Worcestershire Sauce	1 tbsp.
Ground Cumin Seed	1 tbsp.
Chili Powder	1 tbsp.
Garlic Powder	½ tsp.
Salt	to taste
Onions, chopped	1 lb. 8 oz.

METHOD
Brown meat. Add all other ingredients. Simmer 2 hrs.

Fry tortillas in deep fat until crisp. This may be done the day before. If they need freshening, they can be heated in oven before serving.

Have separate containers of refried beans and grated cheddar cheese close to tortillas and filling.

Assemble tostados with tortillas on bottom, beef filling next, then re-fried beans, then grated cheese, lettuce. Tiny pickled beets and diced avocado can also be added. Have bottled taco sauce available since some like it <u>hot</u>.

CHICKEN CORTEZ
YIELD: Test recipe, 6 portions
INGREDIENTS

Chicken Breasts	4
Butter or Margarine	¼ cup
Hot Water	2 cup
Instant Minced Onion	1 tbsp.
Salt	2 tsp.
Pepper	1/8 tsp.
Cornstarch	¼ cup
Cold Water	2 tbsp.
Ripe Olive Wedges	½ cup
Green Pepper, diced	½ cup
Chopped Pimiento	1 tbsp.
Lemon Juice	1 tbsp.
Crushed Rosemary	½ tsp.
Avocados	2
Dry Sherry	4 tbsp.
Unsweetened Chocolate, grated	½ sq.

METHOD
Brown chicken in melted butter; add hot water, onion, salt, and pepper. Cover; cook over medium heat 35 min. or until chicken is tender. Reserve broth, adding enough water to make 2 cups. Cut chicken into bite-size pieces.

Combine cornstarch and cold water; add to chicken broth. Cook over low heat, stirring constantly until mixture is thickened. Add chicken, ripe olives, green pepper, pimiento, lemon juice and rosemary. Cook over low heat about 6 min. or until pepper is just tender.

Cut avocados lengthwise into halves; remove seeds and skin. Cut fruit into balls with melon ball cutter or ½ tsp. measure. Stir into hot chicken mixture with sherry and chocolate. Place over low heat, stirring gently until chocolate melts.

BEEF TACOS
(El Monte Elementary School District)
YIELD: 100 servings (1½ gal.)
INGREDIENTS

Ground Beef	10 lb.
Taco Seasoning Mix	9-oz. pkg.
Water	1½ qt.
Cheese, shredded	2½ lb.

METHOD
Brown meat until crumbly. Drain off all excess fat.
    Add taco seasoning mix and water. Stir thoroughly, blending all ingredients well.
    Bring to boil. Reduce heat and simmer, uncovered, 20 to 30 min. or until meat is of suitable moistness. Stir occasionally to prevent sticking.
    If meat becomes dry, more water may be added as needed.
    Cool meat.
    Add shredded cheese.
    Fill each taco shell with No. 30 scoop meat mixture.
    Heat in 400°F. oven for 15 min. Serve immediately.

MEXICAN FIESTA
YIELD: Test recipe, 4 portions
INGREDIENTS

Chef-mate Chili with Beans	1 lb. 10 oz. can
Contadina Tomato Sauce	2 oz.
Corn Chips, crushed	2 cup
Ripe Olives, pitted	¼ cup
Chef-mate Cheese Sauce	½ cup

METHOD
Mix Chili with Beans and tomato sauce.
    Layer Chili with Beans, corn chips, olives and Cheese Sauce in 7- by 7- by 2-in. pan ending with corn chips.
    Bake in 350°F. oven 50-60 min.

TACO MEAT MIXTURE
YIELD: 28-30 servings
INGREDIENTS

Ground Beef	10 lb.
Lawry's Taco Seasoning Mix	9 oz.
Water	1½ qt.

METHOD
Brown beef until crumbly; drain off excess fat. Add seasoning mix and water. Simmer, uncovered, 20 to 30 min. Stir occasionally to prevent sticking. (Mixture may be refrigerated overnight or frozen.)

TO SERVE: Place 28 to 30 taco shells in a No. 200 steam table pan, so open edges stand up. Spoon meat mixture into each taco shell. (This may be done 3 to 4 hrs. in advance of the meal period. Hold for heating as required.) Heat at 400°F. for 5 to 10 min. until hot throughout. Garnish each Taco with grated cheese and shredded lettuce placed directly on top of the hot mixture.

TAMALE STEAK ROLLS
YIELD: Test recipe, 6 servings
INGREDIENTS

Tomato Sauce	8 oz.
Tomato Paste	1/3 cup
Chopped California Ripe Olives	4½ oz.
Onion, chopped	¼ cup
Pimientos, chopped	2
Chili Sauce	1 tbsp.
Worcestershire Sauce	1 tbsp.
Marjoram	1/8 tsp.
Salt	½ tsp.
Pepper	¼ tsp.
Beef Cube Steaks	6
Grated Parmesan Cheese	1/3 cup

METHOD
Combine all ingredients except steaks and cheese. Spread steaks with two-thirds of ripe olive mixture. Roll to enclose filling and secure with wooden picks. Place in greased baking dish. Cover with remaining ripe olive mixture; sprinkle with cheese. Bake at 375°F. (moderately hot) 25 to 30 min.

TACOS DE COCTEL Y ACIENTUNAS RELLANAS
(Cocktail Tacos with Stuffed Olives)
YIELD: 24 servings
INGREDIENTS

Cocktail Beef Tacos	2 doz.
Red Pepper Relish	2 lb.
Green Pepper, chopped	2
Pimiento-Stuffed Olives	

METHOD
Prepare beef tacos according to package directions for crisp tacos.
TO SERVE: Open hot tacos gently and fill with relish and chopped pepper. Arrange on platter and garnish with olives.

ENCHILADAS
(Rowland Unified School District)

"This recipe for 96 enchiladas, each of which meets Type A Lunch protein requirement of 2 oz. cooked meat or cheese, 1 egg or 1/3 cup cooked dry beans and peas or 3 tbsp. peanut butter, can be varied. Sometimes we use only cheese and egg to meet the protein requirement. At other times we add ground beef and reduce the quantity of both egg and cheese. The original recipe using no beef is one of our most popular meatless dishes.

"We, of course, do batch cooking and expand the recipe to fit our 80-gal. tilting cooker/mixer kettles. From our 80-gal. kettle of sauce we can make approx. 2600 enchiladas. Anyone planning to increase this recipe needs to keep in mind that the quantities of spices should not be multiplied at the same rate as the other ingredients are or the finished product will be far too spicy. The rate of quantity increase on the spices should be lowered as the multiplication factor of the entire recipe increases. As we enlarge the recipe, we also decrease the quantity of fat (butter) which we use. *(Preparation sequence for efficient enchilada production is pictured on pp. 40-42.)*

Ruth D. Richard
Director of Food Services

YIELD: 96 portions
INGREDIENTS
Sauce

Celery, chopped	3 cup	
Onion, chopped	2 cup	
Green Pepper, chopped	1½ cup	
Garlic Powder	1 tbsp.	
Fat	1¼ cup	
Tomato Paste	½ No. 10 can	
Water	5 qt.	
Salt	¼ cup	
Chili Powder	1/3 cup	
Pepper	1¼ tsp.	
Paprika	¾ tsp.	
Cinnamon	¾ tsp.	
Nutmeg	¼ tsp.	
Cloves	¼ tsp.	

Enchiladas: | | | Alternate
Onions, chopped	3 lb.	Same
Fat	1¼ cup	Same
Cheese, shredded	8 lb.	4 lb.
Ripe Olives, chopped	3 cup	Same
Hard-cooked Eggs, chopped	3 doz.	2 doz.
		Ground Beef, 8 lb.
Tortillas	8 doz.	Same

METHOD
Sauce

Saute chopped vegetables in fat until golden brown in color. Do not over-brown.

Add vegetables to tomato paste and water. Mix.

Mix seasonings together and add to tomato mixture. Cook slowly 6 hrs. Stir occasionally.

Enchiladas:

Dip 8 tortillas in hot sauce. Place in bottom of 200 pan.

Cover with 1 qt. of filling.

Repeat steps 1 and 2.

Top with third layer of tortillas (24 per pan).

Cover with 1 qt. sauce, then a layer of cheese.

Bake at 375°, 15-20 min.

Cut down center of pan lengthwise, then make 12 cuts crosswise of pans. Makes 24 servings the same size and shape of rolled enchiladas.

BEEF STEW A LA BOGOTANA
(with Cumin Seed)

YIELD: Test recipe, 6 portions
INGREDIENTS

Beef Stew Meat, lean	2 lb.
Flour	¼ cup
Salt	3¾ tsp.
Shortening	2 tbsp.
Water	2 cup
Potatoes, medium	3
Carrots, medium-large	6
Snap Beans	1 cup
Green Peas	1 cup
Ground Cumin Seed	¾ tsp.
Ground Black Pepper	¼ tsp.
Ground Coriander, optional	2 tsp.

METHOD

Trim off excess fat and cut meat into 1½-in. cubes. Roll in flour mixed with salt. Brown in hot shortening. Add water, cover and cook slowly 1½ hrs. or until meat is almost tender. Peel potatoes and carrots and cut each into 4 pieces. Add to meat. Cover and cook 15 more min. or until vegetables are tender.

SALADS

FIESTA SALAD
YIELD: 50 (½ cup) servings
INGREDIENTS

Unflavored Gelatin	3 oz.
Cold Water	1 qt.
Boiling Water	3 cup
Heinz Restaurant Pack Undiluted Tomato Soup, 51-oz. can	1
Heinz Distilled White Vinegar	1 cup
Cream Cheese, softened	1½ lb.
Heinz Salad Dressing	1½ lb.
Celery, chopped	1½ lb.
Green Peppers, finely chopped	1 lb.
*Pimientos, chopped	½ lb.
*Pitted Black Olives, chopped	¼ lb.

METHOD
Soften gelatin in cold water for 10 min. Dissolve in boiling water. Add soup and vinegar; blend well. Chill until partially set. Combine cheese and salad dressing; whip until smooth. Combine soup mixture with cheese mixture; whip until smooth. Fold in celery and remaining ingredients. Pour ½ cup mixture into each individual mold. Chill until firm. Turn into lettuce cup and serve.

*¾ lb. stuffed green olives, chopped may be substituted for pimientos and black olives.

COLOMBIAN TOSSED VEGETABLE SALAD
(with Cumin Seed)
YIELD: Test recipe, 6 portions
INGREDIENTS

Lettuce	½ head
Cabbage, shredded	1
Carrots, thinly sliced	½ cup
Onion, sliced	½ cup
Celery, sliced	½ cup
Salad or Olive Oil	¼ cup
Fresh Lemon Juice	1 tbsp.
Cider Vinegar	1 tbsp.
Salt	1 tsp.
Sugar	½ tsp.
Ground Black Pepper	1/8 tsp.
Garlic Powder	1/8 tsp.
Ground Cumin Seed	½ tsp.
Tomatoes, medium, sliced	2
Beets, cooked, cut into julienne strips	½ cup
Hard-Cooked Eggs	2

METHOD
Tear lettuce into bite-size pieces. Place in a salad bowl. Add cabbage, carrots, onion and celery. Combine oil, lemon juice, vinegar and seasonings. Pour over salad. Toss lightly. Top with sliced tomatoes and beets as desired. Garnish with sliced hard-cooked eggs.

CRAB-GRAPEFRUIT SALAD ESPANOL
YIELD: Test recipe, 4 servings
INGREDIENTS

California Grapefruit, large	4
Avocados, large ripe	2
Mayonnaise	¼ cup
Fresh Lemon Juice	2 tbsp.
Salt	1½ tsp.
Hot Sauce	2 dashes
Crab Meat, cooked	1¼ lb.
Salad Greens	
Tortilla Chips	

METHOD
Peel grapefruit; slice into 3/8-in. cartwheels, removing any seeds. Chill.

To prepare guacamole dressing, peel and seed avocados. With electric mixer or fork, mash avocados. Add mayonnaise, lemon juice, salt and hot sauce, blending thoroughly. Shred ½ cup of crab meat and add to guacamole dressing.

When ready to serve, arrange grapefruit cartwheels and remaining crab meat on bed of crisp salad greens. Garnish with fresh lemon cartwheels or wedges. Serve with guacamole dressing and tortilla chips.

ENSALADA DE PERA A LA VINAGRETA
YIELD: 100 servings
INGREDIENTS

Canned Pear Halves	100
Anchovies, chopped	¾ cup
Capers	¼ cup
Pimientos, julienne cut	¼ cup
Chives, chopped	1/3 cup
Parsley, chopped	1/3 cup
Lemons, sliced paper thin	½ cup
Lemon Juice	1 cup
Orange Juice	1 cup
Tabasco Sauce	1 tsp.
Salt	to taste
Wine Vinegar	¾ cup
Olive Oil	2¼ cup

METHOD
Place pear halves in container. Combine all other ingredients and pour mixture over the pears. Chill thoroughly before serving.

ENSALADA DE ALASKA KING CRAB CON SALSA DE AGUACATE

YIELD: 12 servings, 1 qt. sauce
INGREDIENTS

Alaska King Crab, meat and legs (3-oz. portion)	2 lb. 4 oz.
Lettuce Beds, crisp in chilled bowls	12
Tomatoes, sliced	6
Asparagus Tips	48
Eggs, hard-cooked, quartered	9
Pimientos, cut in strips	4 oz.
Ripe Olives, pitted	24
Lemon Wedges	12
Salsa de Aguacate (recipe below)	3 cup

METHOD
On chilled lettuce bed arrange one-half tomato and 4 asparagus tips. Top with 3 oz. of Alaska King Crab meat; ladle over 2 oz. of Salsa De Aguacate.

Garnish with a crab leg, pimiento strips, 3 egg quarters, 2 olives and a lemon wedge.

Salsa de Aguacate

Avocado, pureed	2 cup
Tomatoes, peeled, seeded	½ cup
Onions, chopped	½ cup
Green Chiles, canned peeled	¼ cup
Sugar	2 tbsp.
Salt	to taste
Lemon Juice	¼ cup
Mayonnaise	1 cup

METHOD
Combine all ingredients; blend together until smooth. Adjust seasonings. Cover and store under refrigeration.

LENTEJAS CON FRUITA

YIELD: 48 servings
INGREDIENTS

Lentils	4 lb.
Butter	8 oz.
Onions, thinly sliced	8 oz.
Celery, thinly sliced	8 oz.
Cumin, ground	½ tsp.
Pepper	to taste
Salt	to taste
Stock	1 gal.
Bananas, sliced	1½ qt.

METHOD
Saute vegetables lightly in butter. Add lentils, seasonings and stock. Bring to a boil, cover and cook slowly, approx. one hr., until the lentils are tender and the liquid is absorbed. Serve garnished with sliced bananas.

VARIATION
Sliced pears, cubed pineapple; light, sweet cherries.

AVOCADO HALF-SHELLS WITH SALSA VERDE

YIELD: 8 filled halves
INGREDIENTS

Green Pepper, finely chopped	¼ cup
Chopped Parsley	¼ cup
Celery, finely chopped	2 tbsp.
Scallion, finely chopped	1 tbsp.
Pimiento, finely chopped	1 tbsp.
Capers, drained, finely chopped	1 tbsp.
Anchovy Filets, finely chopped	1 tsp.
Salt	½ tsp.
Pepper	1/8 tsp.
Basil	1/8 tsp.
Spanish Olive Oil	½ cup
Lemon Juice	2 tbsp.
California Avocados, fully ripe	4
Lemon Juice	

METHOD
Combine all ingredients, except avocados, for salsa and chill thoroughly.

When ready to serve, halve avocados lengthwise, twisting gently to separate halves. Whack a sharp knife directly into seeds and twist to lift out. Brush half-shells with lemon juice; fill with salsa and serve.

LENTIL AND WHITE BEAN SALAD

Yield: 48 servings
Ingredients:

Lentils	2 lb.
White Beans	2 lb.
Sugar	½ cup
Salt	1 tbsp.
Dry Mustard	2 tsp.
Pepper	½ tsp.
Garlic, crushed	2 cloves
Oil	1½ cup
Vinegar	½ cup
Green Onions, finely sliced	1 pt.
Pimientos, chopped	8 oz.
Lettuce Leaves	
Hard-cooked Eggs, sieved	1 cup
Parsley Sprigs	

METHOD
Cook lentils and beans separately in salted boiling water. Drain and cool. Combine next 7 ingredients; blend well and set aside. Add onions and pimientos to lentil-bean mixture. Pour dressing over lentil mixture and toss lightly. Marinate, covered, in refrigerator at least 4 hours, or until flavors are well blended. Serve on lettuce leaves. Garnish with sieved egg and parsley.

SAUCES

SALSA BUENO
YIELD: about 2 pt.
INGREDIENTS

Fresh Tomatoes, diced	1 lb.
Avocados, peeled and diced	½ lb.
Cucumbers with Peel, diced	½ lb.
Canned Green Chili Peppers, drained and chopped	1-2 oz.
Sunkist Lemons (grated rind and juice)	2

METHOD
Combine all ingredients. Cover and refrigerate for several hours. Serve with hamburgers, chops or steaks.

RED SAUCE FOR ENCHILADAS
YIELD: 2 qt.
INGREDIENTS

Oil	2 oz.
Flour	1½ oz.
Garlic, crushed	3 cloves
Beef Stock	3 cup
Tomato Puree	1½ qt.
Chili Powder	1 oz.
Cumin	¼ tsp.
Salt	½ oz.

METHOD
Blend oil with flour and garlic in large kettle. Add remaining ingredients and cook, stirring frequently, until mixture boils. Turn heat low, and simmer about 15 min.

AVOCADO SALSA NO. 1— FOR GRILLED MEATS AND FOWL
YIELD: Approx. 5 cups
INGREDIENTS

California Avocados, fully ripe	2
Tomatoes, large, peeled and chopped	2
Red Onion, medium, coarsely chopped	1
Green Pepper, medium, coarsely chopped	1
Green Chili, minced	1
Salt	1 tsp.
Dash Pepper	
Lemon Juice	2 tbsp.

METHOD
Halve avocados lengthwise, twisting gently to separate halves. Whack a sharp knife directly into seeds and twist to lift out.

Peel avocados; then dice, placing cavity-side down to prevent breaking.

Toss diced avocado with remaining ingredients; chill.

CHILI VERDE (HOT SAUCE)
YIELD: 1 qt.
INGREDIENTS

Fresh Hot Green Jalapena Peppers	20
Fresh Tomatoes	1¼ lb.
Garlic	1 clove
Salt	

METHOD
Cook peppers until tender. Cook tomatoes until soft. Drain, remove stems from peppers and tomatoes. Blend peppers and garlic at low speed of electric blender until as smooth as preferred. Add tomatoes and peppers and blend until slightly coarse or smooth. Add salt to taste.
NOTE: Hot Sauce will keep fresh for up to 10 days in refrigerator.

TRINI'S RANCHERO SAUCE
YIELD: Approx. 1 pt.
INGREDIENTS

Ro-Tel Tomatoes, (tomatoes and green chili), ½-in. dice	1 cup
Onion, medium, ½-in. dice	1
Green Pepper, ½-in. dice	3 tbsp.
Tomato Puree	4 tbsp.
Pepper	¼ tsp.
Salt	½ tsp.
Water	½ cup
Cornstarch	4 tsp.

METHOD
Bring tomatoes, onion, green peppers, tomato puree, salt and pepper to a boil. Combine cornstarch and water to smooth consistency. Add to boiling tomatoes. Stir and simmer until onions and peppers are tender but still crisp.
TO SERVE: Provides a colorful accompaniment over omelets, steak, pork chops or fish.

AVOCADO SALSA NO. 2— FOR COLD, COOKED SEAFOOD OR GRILLED FISH
YIELD: Approx. 5 cups
INGREDIENTS

California Avocados, fully ripe	2
Frozen Chives, chopped	¼ cup
Parsley, chopped	¼ cup
Watercress, chopped	¼ cup
Salt	1 tbsp.
Lemon Juice	1 cup
Dairy Sour Cream	1 cup
Mayonnaise	¼ cup
Anchovy Paste	4 tsp.
Tabasco	2 dashes

METHOD
Prepare diced avocados as directed in recipe above; then whirl in electric blender with remaining ingredients until well blended; chill.

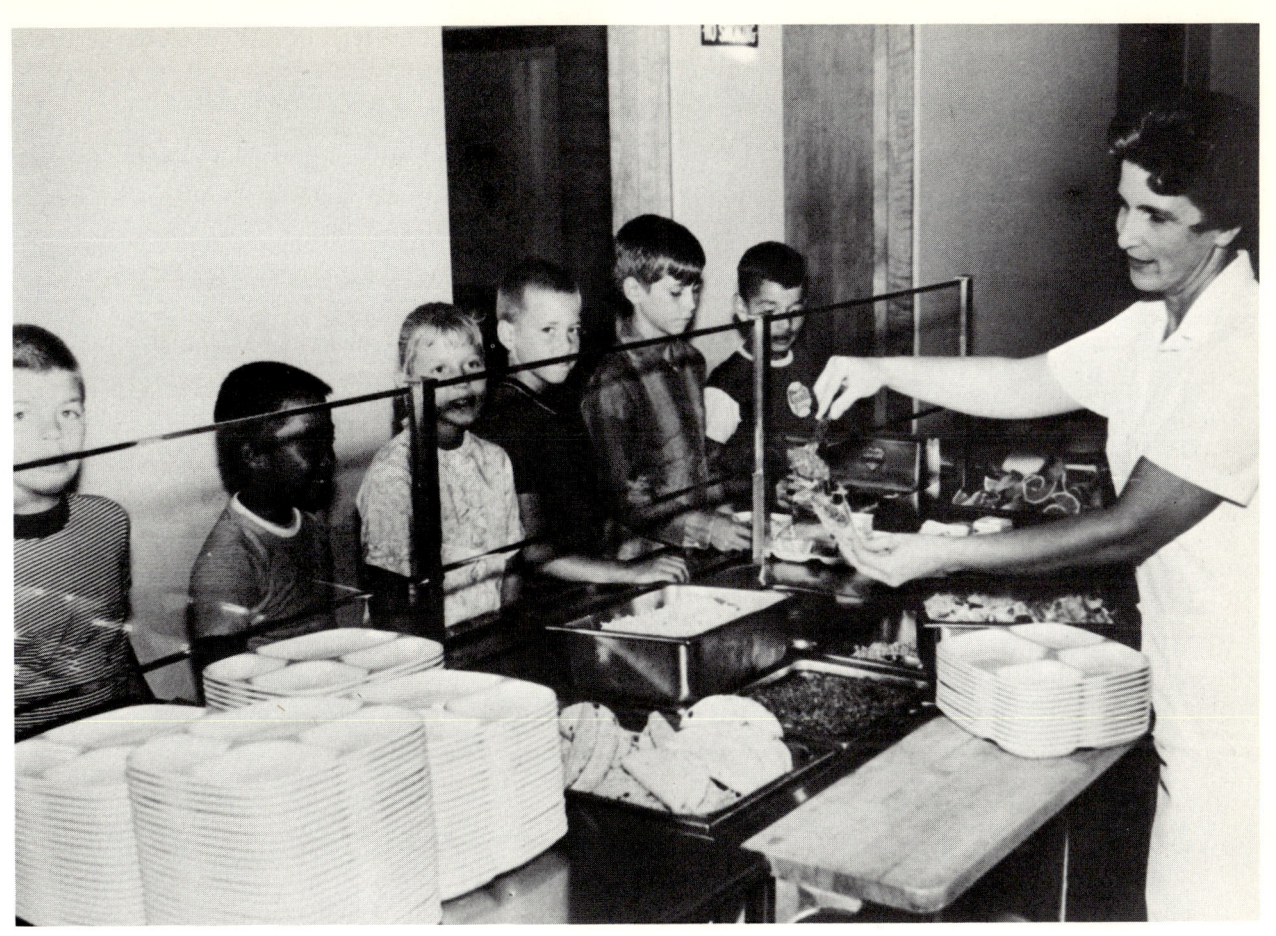

Tacos rate ahead of hamburgers in some school lunch popularity polls and are welcomed by children even when served as often as every other week.

DESSERTS

CREMA CATALONIA

YIELD: Test recipe, 5-6 servings
INGREDIENTS

Eggs, slightly beaten	3
Sugar	¼ cup
Salt	¼ tsp.
Light Cream, scalded and cooled	2 cup
Vanilla	½ tsp.
Sugar	½ cup
Cinnamon	½ tsp.
Bananas, peeled and sliced	3

METHOD
Combine eggs, ¼ cup sugar and salt. Slowly stir in slightly cooled cream and vanilla. Fill 5 or 6 custard cups; set in shallow pan on oven rack. Pour hot water into pan, 1-in. deep. Bake at 325°F. 40 to 45 min.

Remove from oven and cool slightly (or refrigerate several hr.)

TO SERVE
Just before serving, sprinkle tops with mixture of ½ cup sugar and ½ tsp. cinnamon. Broil about 5 or 6-in. from heat until bubbly crust forms. Arrange banana slices over top of sugar crust; serve immediately.

PERA CON DUDIN Y KAHLUA

YIELD: 24 servings
INGREDIENTS

Prepared Vanilla Pudding	1½ qt.
Whipped Cream (sweetened), or prepared whipped topping	1½ pt.
Kahlua Coffee-Flavored Liqueur	½ cup
Pacific Coast Canned Pear Halves, drained	48
Pomegranate Seeds	

METHOD
Gently fold pudding into whipped cream to blend; add Kahlua and blend well. Chill thoroughly. Use 2 pear halves per serving. Fill hollows of each pear with Kahlua pudding. Garnish with pomegranate seeds. An optional garnish of Kahlua may be poured over top.

BUDIN DE CHOCOLATE
(Mexican Chocolate Pudding)
METHOD

For each 4 portions of Instant Chocolate Pudding Mix, mix in 1 tsp. ground cinnamon, 1 tsp. grated orange peel and ½ tsp. pure vanilla extract. Mexican Chocolate Pudding may be topped with whipped cream garnished with shaved chocolate.

MANZANAS FRITAS
(Spanish Fried Apples)
YIELD: Test recipe, 6 portions
INGREDIENTS

Apples, large	3
Cream Sherry	¼ cup
Sugar	¼ cup
Flour	3 tbsp.
Ground Cinnamon	1½ tsp.
Butter or Margarine	6 tbsp.

METHOD

Peel, core and slice apples into ½-in. wedges. Dip wedges first into sherry, then into mixture of sugar, flour and cinnamon. Fry apples in butter or margarine until nicely browned and crisp, turning once.

Can be served as a dessert or as an accompaniment for pork, chicken or veal.

CHERRIES DULCE BORRACHA
(Sweet Cherry Kabobs)
METHOD

Marinate cherries in mixture of 1 cup bar syrup and ¼ cup rum. String two light and dark cherries on skewers. Center with pineapple cube.

SPANISH CARAMEL FLAN WITH FRUIT
YIELD: 24 servings
INGREDIENTS

Sugar	2¼ lb.
Eggs	3½ cup
Salt	2 tsp.
Milk	3 qt.
Vanilla	1 tbsp.
Frozen Whole Strawberries, thawed and drained	48 oz.
Frozen Sliced Peaches, thawed and drained	30 oz.
Frozen Raspberries, thawed and drained	30 oz.
Frozen Whipped Topping, thawed	
Chocolate Curls	

METHOD

Heat 3 cups of the sugar in a large skillet until it melts and is a caramel-colored syrup. Divide syrup into bottoms of three 6-cup ring molds. Cool. Beat together remaining sugar, eggs, and salt. Gradually beat in milk and vanilla. Pour egg mixture carefully over caramel in ring molds. Set molds into pans with 1-in. water. Bake at 350°F. for 1 hr., or until knife inserted in center comes out clean. Cool, then chill.

TO SERVE:

Loosen edges of custard; invert onto platter. Surround each ring with drained fruits. Fill centers with whipped topping; garnish with chocolate curls. Serve chilled.

BEVERAGES

LIME SANGRIA
YIELD: 24 (4-oz.) servings (3 quarts)
INGREDIENTS

Frozen Limeade Concentrate, partially thawed	12 oz.
Frozen Melon Balls, partially thawed	12 oz.
Burgundy or other Dry Red Wine	2 12-oz. bottles
Club Soda, chilled	
Mint Leaves, Lemon Peel	

METHOD

Stir limeade and melon balls in 1 gal. container. Add wine and mix well.

TO SERVE

Fill 1 qt. pitchers half full of ice cubes, pour in 1 pt. Sangria mixture; add about 4 oz. club soda, mix well. Garnish with mint and lemon peel.

SANGRIA, ORANGE
YIELD: 30 servings, 4 oz. size
INGREDIENTS

California Burgundy or other Red Dinner Wine	1 gal.
Unsweetened Orange Juice	1 46-oz. can
Lemons, sliced	3
Oranges, sliced	3
Sugar	to taste
Variety of fresh fruit, if desired (such as sliced fresh peaches, sliced plums and fresh berries)	
Sparkling Water (optional)	

METHOD

Mix wine, orange juice and sliced fruit. Let stand, covered, in refrigerator for several hours or overnight. Add sugar and sparkling water, if desired. Pour Sangria into wine glasses, half-filled with ice cubes.

DRY SANGRIA
(Los Gallos Restaurant, San Francisco)
METHOD

Mix a base of four parts California Burgundy to one part orange juice. Fill the glasses with crushed ice and pour half glass with the base and top up with California Champagne. Squeeze lime juice and twist on top.

Ole

SUPPLIERS OF MEXICAN FOODS

Armour & Co., Special Products Div., Phoenix, Ariz. 85001
Frozen: chili con carne in Volume Fare line is packed 3/12 per case.

Banquet Foods, Corp., St. Louis 63101
Frozen: chili sauce with beans, meat and tomato is available in individual servings designed for school lunch programs.

Calavo Growers, Los Angeles 90058
Frozen: avocado pulp is available in 1 lb. cans; guacamole is packed in 1 lb. & 7¾ oz. cans and avocado halves are packed 30 per case.

Campbell Soup Co., Food Service Product Div., Camden, N. J. 07018
Canned: chili con carne is available in both 12/50 oz. case pack and 48/8¾ oz; chili mac is packed 48/8½ oz.
Frozen: beef tamales in chili sauce with meat contain 72 tamales per case; beef enchiladas in chili sauce with meat are packed 64 per case.
Distribution: frozen products are presently available in the Omaha District and in Western and Southwestern divisions only.

Carnation Co., Los Angeles 90036
Canned: chili without beans and chili with beans are packed 12/50 per case.

Chef Boy-Ar-Dee, Food Service Div. of American Home Foods, New York City 10017
Canned: chili con carne with beans, choice chili con carne with beans and chili con carne (plain) are all packed 6/No. 10 cans per case; chili hot dog sauce with meat is available packed 12/30 oz. or 6/No. 10; beef taco filling is packed 6/No. 10.

Claridge Frozen Foods, Inc., Great Neck, N. Y. 11021
Frozen: chili meat sauce and chili with beans are available in 8/5 tubs per case.

Colonial Foods Intl., Philadelphia 19148
Frozen: el ranchero macaroni shells with Mexican chili and beans is designed for school lunch.

The DOB Corp., Los Angeles 90016
Frozen: beef tamales, chili & bean tamales and refried bean with cheese sauce tamales are packed in both 24/5 oz. and 24/7 oz. individual servings; bean & beef burritos, fried bean and beef (with or without foil bags) burritos, apple pie burrito and fried apple pie burrito are all packed 36/4 oz.; bean & beef burritos, plain or "red hot," beef & potato burritos, plain or "red hot," red chili and bean and cheese burritos are all packed 24/5 oz.; fried bean & beef and fried apple pie burritos are packed 24/4 oz.; chili & beans and refried beans are available in 3/7 lb. pans per case; beef, cheese and chicken enchiladas are packed 6/4 doz.; taquitos and fried taquitos are packed 6/7 doz.; fried taquitos are also available 24/3½ oz.; enchilada, taco and avocado sauces are all packed in ½ gal. containers.

Don's Prize, Miami, Fla. 33150
Frozen: chili with beans is packed in 6/5 tubs per case.

Durkee Food Service Group, Cleveland 44115
Frozen: chili con carne with beans is available in 4/60 oz. trays per case.

El Chico Corp., Dallas 75234
Canned: (6/#10) Delgado chili, no beans; parchment wrapped tamales; chili hot dog sauce, fried beans; taco meat and jalapeno peppers; (24/#300) Delgado chili without beans, chili with beans, parchment wrapped tamales, chili hot dog sauce; beef taco filler.
Frozen: rice Mexican style, 6/3 lb.; tamales, 2/11 lb.; tortillas, 3/36 ct.; cheese enchiladas with gravy, 8/18 ct. and beef enchiladas with gravy.
Distribution: Southeastern United States.

Fearn Intl., Inc., Le Gout Foods Div., Franklin Park, Ill. 60131
Canned: chili con carne with beans and chili con carne no beans are both packed 6/#5.

Foster Frosty Foods, Denver 80220
Frozen: taco patties are fully cooked and preportioned for 8, 6, 5 and 4 patties to a lb.—packed 10 lbs. to a carton.

Fred's Frozen Foods, Noblesville, Ind. 46060
Frozen: chili con carne with beans packed either 6/6 lb. or 8/3¼ lb. and chili without beans packed 8/3¼ lbs.

Gold Metal Products Co., Cincinnati 34214
Dry: "taco-pop" spiced popcorn is available in 1 pt. plastic coated cartons packed 12 per case or in bulk 45# drums.

Green Giant Co., Le Seur, Minn.
Canned: Mexican brand whole kernel corn with sweet peppers is available in institutional and retail pack.

S. Gumpert Co., Inc., Jersey City, N. J. 07302
Canned: tamales with chili gravy, chili con carne with beans and chili con carne without beans are all packed in 6/#10 tins; chili con carne designed for camping is packed 24/15 oz. tins.

H. J. Heinz, Pittsburgh 15230
Canned: chili con carne with beans is packed in 3 lb. 3 oz. cans and 8¾ oz. for individual servings; chili macaroni is available in 8¼ oz. cans.

Henderson's Portion Pak, a division of Borden Foods, Coral Gables, Fla. 33134
Frozen: chili patties.

Horn & Hardart Co., Institutional Products Div., New York City 10019
Frozen: chili con carne with beans is packed 4½ steam table pans per carton.

Kadison Foods, Div. of Kadison Labs, Inc., Flavor Sq., Chicago 60609
Dry: chili con carne is packed in 8 oz. pouches; only the addition of water is needed.

Kitchen Ready Foods Corp., Food Service Div., Great Neck, Long Island, N. Y. 11021
Frozen: chili-mac is packed 4/5 lb.

Kraft Foods, Chicago 60611
Canned: chili con carne with or without beans in 50 oz. cans.

Lawry's, Los Angeles 90047
Dry: ready-to-use taco shells come 200/case; seasoning mixture for meat filling is packed 6/9 oz. packages per case.

Manning's Famous Foods, Inc., Eugene, Oregon 97401
Frozen: beef tamales packed 32/6 oz.; chili con carne and tamale pie are also available and chicken tamales can be obtained by special order.
Distribution: west coast and midwest at present; national expected soon.

Mar-Kes Foods, Compton, Calif. 90224
Frozen: all beef chili, tacos, taquitos and burritos are available.

Nalley's Fine Foods, Div. of W. R. Grace & Co., Tacoma, Wash. 98411
Frozen: 5 oz. beef tamales, cheese enchiladas, and beef enchiladas; 8 lb. chili brick; taco shells and corn tortillas and 5 lb. taco meat filler are available.
Distribution: primarily Southern California but some in Arizona and No. California also.

Nuggett Distributors, Inc. Stockton, Calif. 95204
Canned: refried beans, enchilada sauce, green chiles, jalapena, taco sauce, tamales and tortillas are all available.

Oh Boy Corp., San Fernando, Calif. 91340
Frozen: beef and cheese enchiladas (dry), 6/24/2 oz., beef or cheese enchiladas with sauce, 12/1 doz. trays; beef and bean burritos, 6/4 lb.; refried beans, 6/5 lb.; enchilada sauce, 6/5 lb.; beef tacos, 6/18's; beef and bean tacos, 36/6's, chili brick, 8/4 lb.
Distribution: limited institutional dist., products are handled by retail wholesalers in many cities.

Pronto Food Corp., Chicago 60618
Frozen: chili meat sauce packed in 6/5 lb. tubs; chili with beans in 6/5 lb. tubs and 9/8 lb. bricks; hot dog chili sauce is available in both hot and mild varieties.

R. J. Reynolds Foods, Inc., New York City 10017
Frozen: Patio tamales shuck wrapped or in chili gravy; both are packed 4/20 count trays as are large beef-filled tacos; enchiladas in chili gravy are packed 4/15 count trays; refried beans in 4/4½ lb. trays; Mexican style rice in 4/3 lb. trays; beef, and bean and bacon cocktail burritos are packed 200 ct. per case; beef cocktail tacos are available 4/60 count trays per master.

Rosarita Mexican Foods, Mesa, Ariz. 85201
Frozen: cheese and onion enchiladas with grated cheese and sauce, beef enchiladas with grated cheese and sauce, refried beans with cheese, cocktail tacos, red chili burritos, green chili burritos, bean and cheese burritos, taco stix, tamales, cheese enchiladas and beef enchiladas are all available in institutional sizes.
Canned: refried beans in 6/10, 48/8 oz., or 12/40 oz.; enchilada sauce packed 6/10; hot tomato sauce packed 12/40 oz.; taco sauce, 12/7 oz. and hot sauce packed 12/7 oz.

Sara Lee, Food Services Div., Deerfield, Ill. 60015
Frozen Chili Bouquet, dumplings, U. S. choice beef in chili sauce, 2 12-lb. trays per pack.

John Sexton & Co., Chicago 60632
Canned: chili con carne with or without beans in No. 10 and No. 5 cans, tamales packed #4.

Frank G. Shattuck Co., New York City 10010
Frozen: chili con carne is available packed 4/80 oz.

Swift & Co., HRI Dept., Chicago 60604
Canned: chili with or without beans packed in No. 10 cans.

Vienna Sausage Co., Chicago 60607
Frozen: Mexican flavored hot dogs are wrapped in tortillas.

Nautical

Drawing on the sea and lakes to create settings for fish and seafood service permits endless variations on the nautical theme. With the availability of fish and seafood today, the difficult task is determining which of the many menu items to feature. Presented in this section—in sea-chart detail, are profitable patterns for operations at all levels.

The Nautical Way

SPECIAL ATMOSPHERE / FOOD I

"Out to sea"—that's where a growing number of diners want to eat. To capture these patrons, nautical interiors and seafood specialties are creating a seagoing sensation in landlocked areas as well as on the waterfront. For your sea chest, operation-tested decorating, food and equipment ideas from nautical America's Award-Winning installations.

Gentle curving staircase sweeps up to detailed crow's nest landing at Castagnola's Lobster House, Santa Barbara, Calif.
Designed by: Vern H. Estes, Fred W. Griswold Co.; Thomas H. Headley, Richard S. Headley, Castagnola's Lobster House.

Starting the Voyage

Sailing away from it all is a believable destination for patrons approaching the Windjammer, even though it is in Cincinnati, Ohio. Constructed to scale and locked on a reef, the Windjammer is surrounded by wharves which also provide the entrance to the 230-seat restaurant. The encrusted 22-ft. anchor, recovered from a Spanish Galleon believed to have sunk in 1630 in the Florida Keys, is another mood-building artifact. The Windjammer's exterior design serves as its own sign and is easily identifiable from the adjacent interstate highway.

Designed by: Homer A. Shrewsbury, Jr. Inc.

At Nantucket Cove, another inland seafood house, interiors were plotted to give Chicago patrons "a trip Down East." The trout pond at the entrance has a water wheel turned by a constant stream of water that creates a current like those trout enjoy in their natural habitat. Trout in constant motion retain continuing interest of waiting patrons. Other aquatic activity goes on in the lobster pond at the end of the Oyster Bar where water cascades down a rock wall into ponds kept filled with lively crustaceans.

Designed by: A. S. R. Designs, Ltd.

Castagnola's (right) doesn't settle for salt air alone to get patrons in a sea-going mood. The lighthouse lantern and rusted anchor at the entrance to the parking lot heighten the nautical first impression. The mood is set as the guest enters "below deck" through antiqued paneled mahogany doors and feels "the roll of the ship" as he steps upon the slightly pitched, planked floor. Slanted head walls, massive beams and hand-hewn ship's knees (originally made from tree roots, where they branch out from massive trunks, to brace the hulls of great wooden sailing ships) add further realism to the scene.

Designed by: Vern H. Estes, Fred W. Griswold Co.;
Thomas H. Headley, Richard S. Headley, Castagnola's Lobster House.

Pilings formerly used to tie up riverboats in the Grand River alongside Holly's Landing have moved inside. At one entrance a line of rope-circled weathered piles adds atmosphere and aids in traffic control. Used effectively at the entrance to the Grand Rapids, Mich. dining room as reminders of nautical America's travel-by-river era, pilings stand alongside teak-decked gangways. Holly's Landing was planned to give all rooms continuous orientation to the river.

Designed by: Fred Schmid Associates;
Holly Grills, Inc.

THE NAUTICAL WAY

Sea-Styled Interiors

The sea takes over with air travelers at San Diego's International Airport food service. Again, simulated lantern light between rugged ship's beams soon has patrons feeling they're on board a sturdy ship. Tall pilings, roped top and bottom, form a divider at the rear; three more pilings roped together at the entrance are an eye-catching introduction to the room. Ship's lanterns suspended from the ceiling, a ship's wheel against the wall, rope ladders and the curved prow-like solid divider help create a snug ship.

Designed by: Fred Schmid Assoc.; Interstate Hosts, Inc.

Sounds of splashing water provide background at Chicago's Nantucket Cove for the Oyster Bar built of weathered timbers. Captain's chair bar stools, ships fittings, nets and floats from lobster boats are sea-accented design notes. Small blackboard at right has Oyster Bar menu specials chalked on it.

Designed by: A. S. R. Designs, Ltd.

An authentic, fully rigged ship's mast with crow's nest dominates the main dining room at Castagnola's Lobster House. The mast supports the high beamed, peaked ceiling with its wide areas of light, drift tone acoustical tile. The turn column rail outlining the widow's walk around the perimeter of the room adds an extra dimension of nautical interest. Reflected sunlight, often creating uncomfortable glare in waterfront dining rooms, is here controlled by wide overhanging eaves and woven basswood blinds that can be raised or lowered as patrons prefer in this Santa Barbara, Calif. dining room.

Castagnola's coffee shop welcomes guests of all ages into a relaxed nautical atmosphere. An arched, planked, dark-tone ceiling and golden brown, veined beams contribute to a spacious feeling. Booth enclosures are canted and faced with pegged, V-grooved planks in a gray-tone driftwood finish. Authentic "dead-eye" blocks and shroud lines are conversation-provoking dividers. Sunshine-yellow china and tangerine toned coverings for seats and booths lend warmth to the room.

Designed by: Vern H. Estes, Fred W. Griswold Co.; Thomas H. Headley, Richard S. Headley, Castagnola's Lobster House.

THE NAUTICAL WAY

Detailed to Welcome Aboard

Seafaring settings are kept stimulating with interest-arousing details. Authentic objects or replicas, when carefully chosen and placed, are equally interesting. At Castagnola's, a replica of a ship chandler's desk, like those used in the sailing ships of the 17th century, surrounds the maitre d's station. Above it a hanging ship's lantern shines down on a diving helmet. In this setting the modern notes of the communication system and cigarette machine are properly subdued.

Between courses Castagnola's guests study one of the eight cannon, above left, raised from the depths of the Atlantic ocean, off the coast of Florida. Gun carriage, rope rigging and racked cannon balls follow plans common to gunboats of the 1600's from which these cannon were fired.

Design by: Vern H. Estes, Fred W. Griswold Co.; Thomas H. Headley, Richard S. Headley, Castagnola's Lobster House.

A snug corner at San Diego International Airport draws on maritime history for ship's fittings like the rope screen and lantern.

Designed by: Fred Schmid Assoc.; Interstate Hosts, Inc.

Seafood in the Spotlight

Shrimp Louis Salad catches the eye of the dieting contingent. This salad is an adaptation of the well-known Crab Louis created in Seattle at the turn of the century. It's a well designed combination of shrimp, wedges of hard cooked egg and tomato centered with fresh parsley and framed with lettuce.

Another California inspiration, Halibut Tokay, below, combines fish with grapes, the tokays grown in the Napa Valley. Fresh or defrosted halibut is placed on a layer of finely chopped onion, seasoned with salt and pepper and dotted with butter. Lemon juice and wine are added; then fish is covered with foil for baking. Juices are drained from baked fish and combined with thin white sauce to which grapes are added. Sauce is cooked just long enough to heat grapes. Baked fish is portioned, covered with sauce and broiled til lightly brown. Halibut Tokay can also be placed in individual casseroles and sauced ahead of time, then given final browning to order.

A "Captain's Club Sandwich," above, follows the two-decker club sandwich idea—and is at home in a wide range of seafood menus. A golden-crusted hot fish portion makes one of the layers. Chutney, the extra layer, is a change from the more frequently served ketchup or tartar sauce. Pickle relish, sweet or hot, could also serve as the contrast to the firm, moist flesh of the breaded fish portion. Suggested as garnishes are potato chips and a tomato-olive-pickle combination.

Rich and creamy Lobster Stew, right, is hearty enough to provide a tasty meal by itself and yet versatile enough to invite a cool, crisp salad or sandwich in addition. Instant nonfat dry milk and non-dairy creamer are responsible for the smooth, rich blend of this stew extraordinaire. Generous bits of lobster accented with clam broth, basil and onion combine flavorfully in this delectable stew which rates special attention on a seafood menu.

THE NAUTICAL WAY

Seafood in the Spotlight

When seafood's in the spotlight, it needs the build-up that comes with vivid color styling, the flair of table-side flaming or a uniquely-flavored sauce to set off its presentation. At the Ambassador in Chicago, Polynesian Pike gets order-building attention when cognac is added to the accompanying chafing dish of fruit sauce for flaming at table side. The sauce itself is a combination of such uncommon ingredients as soy sauce, white wine, sliced bananas and cubed pineapple. Sauced fish is served with a portion of fluffy rice garnished with toasted coconut.

See table of contents for seafood recipes referred to in this section.

Atun a la Marina is a baked fish dish color-styled to stand out on the steamtable. Onions, tomatoes and tuna are layered, then sprinkled with coating of chopped pimiento-stuffed spanish green olives, parsley, granulated garlic and seasonings. Cinnamon adds a tantalizing flavor to each portion.

Rock Lobster Stew, right, is a rich amalgamation of vegetable-laden fish broth sharpened with lemon juice. Red-circled slices of rock lobster float on each serving of the essence that results from the slow simmering of shellfish, tomatoes, parsley, onion and garlic.

Baked Haddock Fillets gain a fiesta air when blanketed with a rich red spanish sauce. Sauce is easy-to-combine blend of onion, green pepper, bay leaves, whole cloves, peppercorns, canned tomatoes, garlic and slices of pimiento-stuffed spanish green olives.

Paprika-sparked scallops, below left, eye-catchingly arranged in an attractive casserole, get follow-up dash from vermouth poured over the broiled pieces of scallop just before service. This is a dish that qualifies for the gourmet section of the seafood menu though speedy preparation keeps costs low.

At Hogate's famous seafood restaurant in Washington, D. C., directions for seafood presentation are all colorfully plotted. At left, in Swordfish Creole pale swordfish squares and centered serving of rice are set off in a vivid red frame. Another menu headliner, broiled Fishkabobs Swordfish also have built-in color coordination. Three scallops, one piece of swordfish, one piece of salmon, four pieces of green pepper and four white onions are threaded alternately on skewer, marinated, then broiled.

Seafood in the Spotlight

Something different for special luncheon or dinner menus, Alaska King Crab Mantua. Large crab chunks in a tomato flavored sauce are an elegant menu item served in shells or portioned from a casserole.

Crisp-coated trout, center, on a plank with vivid vegetables and a piped border of mashed potatoes is an easily promoted menu specialty.

South African Souffle Sandwiches, bottom, are puffy open face specials. Rock lobster chunks, blended with mayonnaise, parmesan cheese and egg yolks, have stiffly beaten egg whites folded in, go under broiler for last minute browning.

QUICK TRICKS WITH TROUT

Boiled Trout Mimosa—Coat poached trout with sauce made of roux, fish broth, seasonings, lemon juice, butter and chopped hard cooked eggs.

Fried Trout and Tomato Orly—Deep fried trout is drained, salted and served with a tomato sauce flavored with lemon juice and liquid hot pepper sauce.

Trout Castellane—Dip seasoned trout in milk, then flour. Saute in sweet butter with oil until crisp and golden. Serve hot with parsley butter.

Trout Hors D'Oeuvres—Fillet trout; cut into small strips. Roll in corn meal; fry in vegetable or peanut oil. When trout strips are golden brown, serve hot with cocktail sauce.

THE NAUTICAL WAY

An easy-to-merchandise fish favorite of the young: breaded fish sticks. The clown on this Circus Supper Plate is easily assembled: Place 1 No. 10 scoop mashed potatoes on warm plate. Cut 1 cooked fish stick in half diagonally and press into potato to form pointed hat. Cross 2 fish sticks at base of potato for collar. Cut stuffed olives in half, push into potatoes for eyes; add curved gherkin for mouth. Arrange 3 carrot curls for ears and topknot on hat. Mound child-sized serving of green beans under crossed fish sticks.

Backyard Barbecue Fish and Chips, below left, is a popular teen plate. A zippy barbecue sauce spices up deep fried or oven finished fish portions and frozen shoestring potatoes. Add a flaky biscuit and Cheese-Apple Crisp for dessert.

How well do you know your fish? That's the question posed on a guessing game place mat, section below, to keep children occupied while waiting for dinner. The approach for each of a dozen fish is like the one pictured here; place mat is excellent merchandising for Fish Fry for Small Fry.

A hardfighting fish that splashes through clear, rocky-bottomed streams and lakes. His name sounds like a singer, he rhymes with class, and he tastes elegant.

Equipped to Serve Seafood

At Dale's Secret Harbor, Los Angeles, preparation of seafood items is made time-and-motion speedy with well placed equipment and proper working heights. At left, a table height, 6-drawer unit is insulated, has removable ice pans in each drawer for fish storage and work space extends in counter branching off at right angles. More seafood is stored in the refrigerated 12-drawer fish file which has a stainless steel ice pan in each drawer.

Designed by: A. K. Grimshaw, Rehco Corp.; Louis L. Armet, Armet & Davis, A. I. A.

Fish and rough vegetable preparation are combined at Castagnola's, Santa Barbara, Calif., in one station, efficiently located facing walk-in refrigerators and the freezer. Unit has fully enclosed self-closing drawers with removable pans. Hose reel provides spray rinse for food products. Work counter has a special lip below the saw table to prevent drippage. Raised curb forms undershelf. Stainless steel shelf around prep station serves adjacent vegetable and salad areas.

The salad pantry was designed to turn out a large volume of fresh produce and frozen and fresh shellfish salads. At end of line, large dual-temperature refrigerator assures adequate backup storage of bulk items. Small range alongside it is flanked by two large pull-out ice bins for storing fresh shellfish. Large refrigerated bases in work counter, with pan recesses, serve for a la carte salad preparation. Plate dispensers in refrigerated areas chill salad plates. Scrap chute alongside sink makes discard of unusual items easy.

Seafood preparation dictated many equipment choices in Castagnola's main cooking battery: infra red broiler was chosen for short preheat time and speedy cooking; warming oven above it can hold prepared food; volcanic under-fired broiler has intense heat and high production; grill top range, oven and built-in fryers complete battery. Refrigerated drawers between range and broiler are sized for modular pans.

THE NAUTICAL WAY

Equipped to Serve Seafood

CASTAGNOLA'S LOBSTER HOUSE MENU

APPETIZERS	
Shrimp	1.50
Seafood	1.75
Crab	1.50
Marinated Herring	1.25
Lobster	2.25
Baked Oysters Rockefeller	2.95
Oysters on Half Shell	2.50
Cracked Crab in Season	2.45
Steamed Clams	2.25

SOUPS	Bowl	Cup
Clam Chowder	.75	.50
Soup du Jour	.75	.50
Bouillabaisse Marseillaise		3.95
(Served with French Garlic Bread)		

SALADS
Caesar Salad per person	1.50
Mixed at table (for two or more)	
Louie Salad crab or shrimp	3.50
Lobster Louie	4.25

GOLDEN FRIED DINNERS
All dinners include: Soup or Salad, Rice Pilaf or choice of Potato

Guaymas Shrimp Platter	3.75
Eastern Scallops Platter	3.50
Combination Seafood Platter	3.95
Shrimp, Scallops, Filet of Sole	
Filet of Sole saute meuniere	3.25
Chesapeake Bay Oysters saute meuniere	3.75
Barbecued Shrimp	3.95
Stuffed Shrimp wrapped in bacon	3.95

SEAFOOD DINNERS
All dinners include: Soup or Salad, Rice Pilaf or choice of Potato

Broiled Catalina Swordfish	3.75
Poached Filet of Sole marguery	3.95
Poached Salmon	3.95
Abalone Steak saute almondine	4.50
Seafood Brochette on rice pilaf	4.25
Steak and Lobster	6.50

Abalone Gourmet saute with creamed Lobster, Crab, Shrimp and Scallop supreme	4.95
Lobster Supreme Lobster, Crab, Shrimp, Scallops in cream sauce with mushrooms served in Lobster shell	4.95
Broiled California Lobster served in shell with dressing and drawn butter	5.95
Toasted Garlic Bread	.50
Local Stone Crab Legs a rare seasonal treat, on crisp lettuce, piquant sauce— enough for two persons	1.75

Braised Mahi Mahi: Wedding Style Selected filets of this queen of the sea, braised in papaya, and light rum, with toasted coconuts, and slivered almonds, garni supreme

Soup du Jour or Tossed Garden Green Salad
(New England Clam Chowder 35c additional)

Au Gratin Potatoes
Fresh Vegetables du Jour
(Idaho Baked Potato: Sour Cream and Chives .35c extra)
Frozen Dessert   Beverage   3.95

served only til 7 P.M.
EARLY-DINER "SPECIAL"
Soup du Jour or Tossed Garden Greens
Fresh Filet of Red Snapper a la Bretonne, white wine sauce, imported capers, bay shrimp, and fine herbs garni
Au Gratin Potatoes
Vegetable du Jour
Dessert   Beverage   2.95

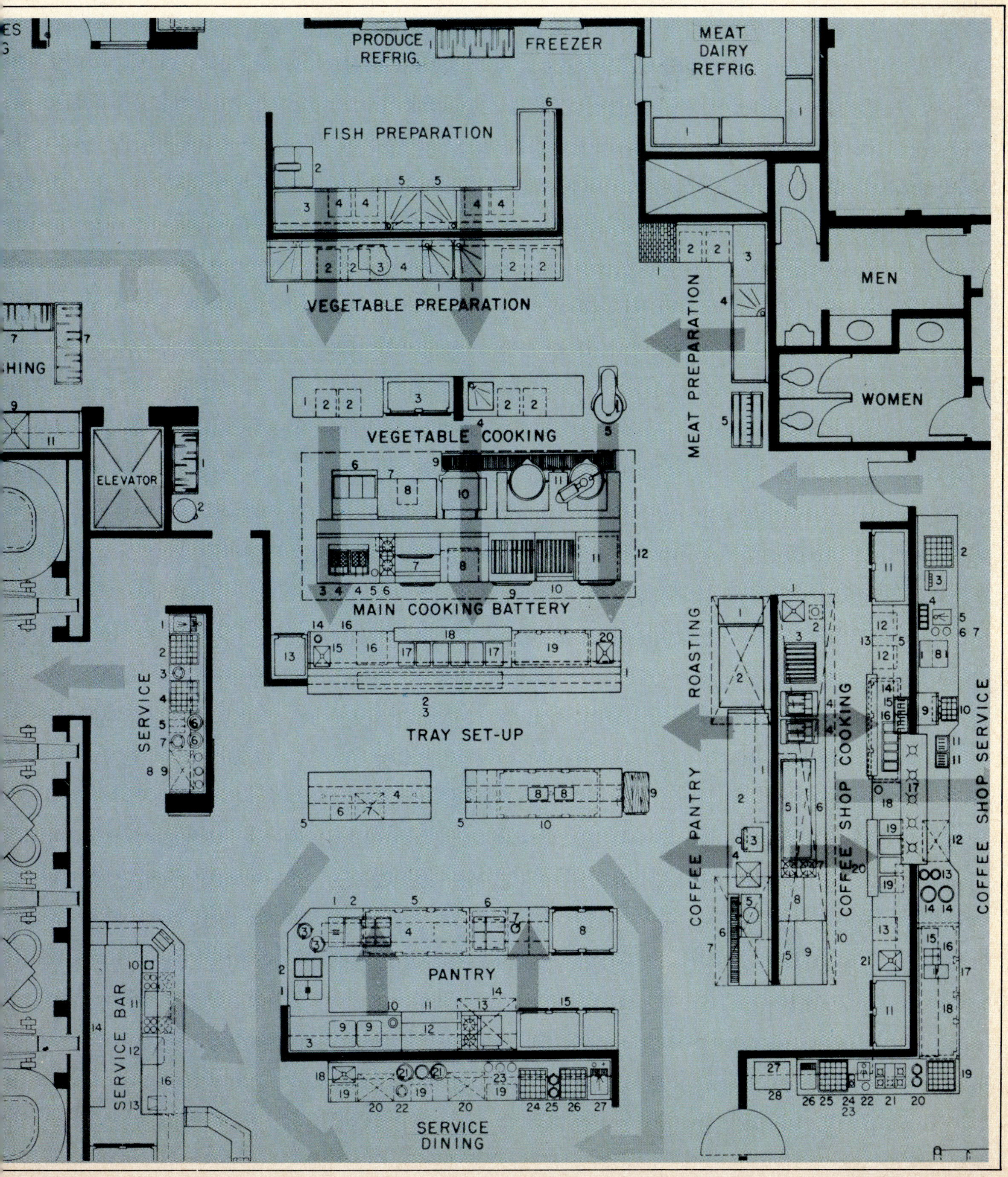

PRODUCE REFRIG.
FREEZER
MEAT DAIRY REFRIG.
FISH PREPARATION
VEGETABLE PREPARATION
MEAT PREPARATION
MEN
WOMEN
VEGETABLE COOKING
ELEVATOR
MAIN COOKING BATTERY
SERVICE
ROASTING
TRAY SET-UP
COFFEE PANTRY
COFFEE SHOP COOKING
COFFEE SHOP SERVICE
PANTRY
SERVICE BAR
SERVICE DINING

Equipped to Serve Seafood

The back counter, waitress serving area and milk dispenser at Castagnola's coffee shop are faced with a durable wood grain plastic laminate. Nautical interest is added with the brass boat cleats used as door and drawer pulls. Pastry cases above counter at left are framed in a burnished coppertone hardwood, have self-closing clear glass doors, easily removed for cleaning. Antique copper hood at right conceals heat lamps, gets a nautical note from the bands of studded brass that decorate it.

CASTAGNOLA'S EQUIPMENT

Employee Facilities
1. locker
2. clothes pole

Dry Stores
1. shelving
2. files
3. desk

Receiving
1. scale
2. cantilevered receiving table
3. elevated shelf
4. drawer

Walk-in Refrigerator & Freezer
1. refrigerator shelving

Dishwashing & Pot Washing
1. cup and glass rack dolly
2. dish cart
3. silver sorting table
4. burnisher
5. burnishing table
6. dishwashing machine
7. pot racks
8. cantilevered pot washing assembly
9. pot sink
10. overflow compartment
11. elevated shelf

Fish Preparation
1. mobile rack
2. saw
3. cantilevered preparation table
4. drawer
5. preparation sink
6. elevated shelf

Meat Preparation
1. meat block
2. drawer
3. cantilevered preparation table
4. preparation sink
5. mixer attachment rack

Vegetable Preparation
1. preparation sink
2. drawer
3. vegetable cutter
4. cantilevered preparation table

Vegetable Cooking
1. pedestal supported work table
2. drawer
3. reach-in refrigerator
4. preparation sink
5. floor mixer—80 qt.
6. hot top range w/oven
7. cantilevered work table
8. drawer
9. drain trough
10. cantilevered 3-compartment steamer
11. dual 40-gallon kettles and mixer

Main Cooking Battery
1. mobile rack
2. fat filter
3. fryer stand
4. fryer
5. scrap well
6. open burners
7. griddle top range w/salamander
8. refrigerated drawers
9. over and under fired broiler
10. under fired broiler
11. over fired broiler w/warming oven
12. hood
13. reach-in refrigerator
14. scrap hole
15. cook's sink
16. refrigerated drawers
17. hot food section
18. removable cutting board
19. undercounter refrigerator
20. cook's sink

Tray Setup
1. elevated shelf
2. suspended warmer
3. dish storage shelving
4. elevated shelf
5. tray setup table
6. drawer
7. warming drawers
8. refrigerated insert pans
9. mobile serving cart
10. undercounter refrigerator

Pantry
1. top refrigerator access
2. cold inserts
3. self-leveling plate dispenser
4. elevated shelf
5. pass-thru undercounter refrigerator
6. ice cream cabinet
7. disher well
8. pass-thru refrigerator
9. sink
10. disher well
11. refrigerated drawers
12. work table w/removable cutting board
13. range—open and hot top burners
14. hood
15. reach-in refrigerator and freezer

Service Stands & Service Bar
1. water station
2. self-leveling glass dispenser
3. self-leveling saucer dispenser
4. self-leveling cup dispenser
5. silver dispenser
6. soup warmer
7. self-leveling soup liner dispenser
8. roll warmer
9. coffee warmer
10. blender
11. mix station
12. glass washer
13. bar sink
14. back bar
15. refrigerator
16. counter
17. cash register
18. silver sink
19. silver dispenser
20. roll warmer
21. soup warmer
22. self-leveling soup liner dispenser
23. coffee warmers
24. self-leveling cup dispenser
25. self-leveling saucer dispenser
26. self-leveling glass rack dispenser
27. water station

Roasting
1. mobile rack
2. two-deck roast oven

Coffee Pantry
1. elevated shelf
2. work table
3. milk dispenser
4. sink
5. coffee urn
6. urn stand
7. hood

Coffee Shop Cooking
1. sink
2. scrap well
3. broiler
4. fryer
5. elevated shelf
6. griddle
7. open burners
8. salamander
9. hot top range
10. hood
11. reach-in refrigerator
12. drawer
13. work counter
14. undercounter refrigerator
15. toasters
16. garnish wells
17. service counter w/warming bulbs above
18. scrap well
19. hot food section
20. removable cutting board
21. sink

Coffee Shop
1. cash register
2. self-leveling glass dispenser
3. drink dispenser
4. syrup pumps
5. sink
6. disher well
7. scrap well
8. ice cream cabinet
9. milk dispenser
10. self-leveling glass dispenser
11. toaster
12. warming drawers
13. self-leveling soup liner dispenser
14. soup warmer
15. elevated pastry display case
16. garnish wells
17. salad crisper
18. undercounter refrigerator
19. self-leveling cup dispenser
20. self-leveling saucer dispenser
21. coffee maker
22. sink
23. scrap well
24. tea maker
25. self-leveling glass dispenser
26. water station
27. elevated shelving
28. mobile buss cart
29. self-leveling cup dispenser
30. silver dispenser
31. service stand
32. water station
33. coffee warmer
34. ice bin
35. sink
36. counter

Dining Room Service Stand
1. coffee warmer
2. self-leveling coffee dispenser
3. silver dispenser
4. self-leveling cup dispenser
5. water station
6. self-leveling glass dispenser

Bar
1. blender
2. mix station
3. scrap well
4. sink
5. glasswasher
6. ice bin
7. undercounter refrigerator
8. cash register
9. undercounter refrigerator
10. liquor display shelving

All pictures in this section from winning installations in the 1968 Interiors Award and Food Service Award programs.

INSTITUTIONS AWARD

THE NAUTICAL WAY

Elements of a Sea Going Setting

The sea has always represented adventure to a sizable share of the American public. It was the lure of the sea that brought the first discoverers to the New World's shores. That lure is just as strong for America's sons today, as the growing number of marinas and boat owners bears out.

Going to sea is an experience that can be produced in a land-locked area just as readily as on water. Perhaps the sea-going vessel is a fresh water side wheeler. That's all right with the average patron. To him a ship is a ship is a ship.

TAKE PATRONS TO SEA FOR ESCAPE

The excitement for the knowledgeable patron comes from authentic artifacts used to establish a nautical atmosphere. When explained on signs or menus, these same items are of special interest to patrons seeing them for the first time.

The place at the top of the list when Americans go out to eat is the one designed to take them far from their everyday environment. Surveys in all categories verify that the happiest eating-out experience offers the extra attraction of an escape dimension.

Building a ship's exterior into the exterior of the operation, or anchoring a replica alongside quickly points up that patrons are getting outside their daily setting, starting on a sea-styled adventure.

Sunset over Cincinnati's Windjammer provides an excellent silhouette of mast, spars and rope rigging. Standing high against the sun they are a combination that appeared originally on the American square rigger or a Spanish treasure galleon.

At Anthony's Grotto in San Diego, the change in environment is first experienced as patrons cross over bridges between streams of rushing water on their approach to the four sea-surrounded dining rooms.

When the marine theme cannot be introduced on the exterior, effective arrangement of objects of maritime interest at the entrance will establish the new environment. At the Windjammer (although it does have a ship as part of the exterior) heightened emphasis for the theme is contrived at the entrance with a ship's wheel, binnacle and diver's helmet (dating from the 90's), coral, seafans and ballast rock; a sign constructed with weathered rope on a hatch cover, a harpoon.

Entrance to the Windjammer is gained by climbing four solid wooden steps to a simulated wharf. From here, a slightly curved wooden gangplank takes the visitor through massive, decorative wooden doors to the artifact-laden lobby of the Windjammer.

AUTHENTIC ARTIFACTS SET STAGE

In the main dining room and lounge, through an ingenious blend of breath-taking blues and greens, distressed wood, coral and artifacts

—plus the judicious use of lighting, the interior designer has evoked a truly unique effect.

The undersea effect is enhanced by murals which capture the brilliance and splendor of highly imaginative underwater scenes. The fantasies inspired by King Neptune and his court are similar to hallucinations described by many early divers. In murals, they present another-world aura to Windjammer diners. Many of the marine artifacts used at the Windjammer were recovered from the Spanish galleon by Martin Meylach, a Florida treasure diver.

The seagoing mood, induced as patrons approach, is extended to each room of Castagnola's Lobster House, Santa Barbara, Calif. with unique lamps, accessories and antique adaptations.

As viewed from the foyer, the Dinghy Room is softly lighted by converted oil-burning ship lanterns that give a warm closeness to this intimate area. Dark rich tones of mahogany doors are enhanced by driftwood finish inset panels. Large brass cleats on doors repeat the nautical theme.

Emphasis on authenticity determined the design of the Cannon Room. The aft section with curved braces, sloping bulkhead and tapered windows, duplicates in its details those that were built into the stern quarters of the Spanish galleons.

CAPTURING THE MOTION OF THE SEA

A mural of the storm-swept sea outside the windows seems to roll the "great ship" in optical motion as guests enjoy the warmth of the cabin. The banquet-sized tables, draped in white linen and contrasting sharply with the vivid red booths seem warm and natural additions to the nautical interiors.

Dramatically poised on the "gun deck" in one dining room is one of eight cannons that were raised from a ship—probably from the Spanish Gold Fleet—sunk in the Atlantic Ocean off the coast of Florida in 1733.

As they view the centuries-old cannon, there is exciting interest for diners of all ages in sharing for a brief period a page in world naval history. Markings on the cannons indicate they are the type originally used on Spanish and English gunboats of the 1600's. Gun carriages to hold them were built from drawings obtained from the U. S. Navy Dept. Originally the carriages were used in the restoration of the U.S.S. Constitution. Spanish ships often used English weapons because of superior workmanship.

The massive ropes that anchored the cannon and the block and tackle, mounted on both sides to absorb the recoil, are in place. Cannon balls are racked above the cannon in position for possible use.

Seagoing interiors at Castagnola's extend to the coffee shop where vinyl covered, padded counter stools are backed by sections of authentic "water casks" and are bound in studded brass.

Nautical

WHEN INLAND WATERS PROVIDE THEME

At Holly's Landing, the site of the Inn-restaurant complex, on the bank of the Grand River near downtown Grand Rapids, provided a natural setting for a 19th century nautical atmosphere. The name Holly's Landing itself identifies the corporate name with the actual pleasure boat landing for guests.

All fixtures are custom designed to fill specific requirements of operation and have been treated to resemble artifacts associated with a nautical atmosphere. Dining chair is a classic American captain's chair which has been produced for over 100 years and is both rugged and economical.

The entrance to the cocktail lounge is flanked by piling, bulkhead and steamboat lanterns. Clerestoried ceiling and ship's mast revive feeling of shipboard dining from the captain's buffet.

TELL TALES ABOUT ARTIFACTS ON MENUS, TABLE TENTS

Menus and table tents are the best way to explain the history and use of marine artifacts that have been selected as specific elements of nautical decor. Nantucket Cove's Treasure Map and Menu describes and locates for patrons such unique maritime objects as a Pelorus liquid compass in gimbals, one of the finest navigating instruments used in early whaling boats. A floor plan outlining areas of Nantucket Cove makes it easy to find the items. The map-menu, which offers detailed background on the artifacts that are pictured, also serves as a mailing piece.

The nautical approach permits a wide range of treatment. From total and expensive reproductions of a ship's interior in fine dining rooms to a few well chosen nautical pictures and artifacts in a coffee shop, the interior designer can set his sights at several levels in capitalizing on the universal lure of the sea.

Purchasing Fish, Seafood

Fish is one of the most delicate and perishable of foods. Under favorable conditions, it is an excellent media for the growth of bacteria. Bargains in fish, therefore, should never be considered unless top quality is assured. Only the best at all times—but not necessarily the most expensive fish—should be purchased. Nothing less will give customer satisfaction. Once purchased, the fish must be kept refrigerated until preparation time.

Market Forms—The manner in which the fish is to be cooked will influence the form in which it is purchased. The market forms are known to all food operators—whole or round fish; drawn fish; dressed or pan-dressed; steaks; single fillets; butterfly fillets, and fish sticks.

CHOOSING FRESH FISH
Look for—
- fresh, mild odor
- bright, clear, convex eyes
- red gills
- firm, springy flesh
- scales, bright and tight

Of the two forms of fillets, the single fillet is the one most commonly used. It is cut from one side of the fish. Butterfly fillets are the two sides of the fish and are similar to two single fillets held together by uncut flesh and skin. Fish steaks are usually cut ¾ to 1 in. thick. Fish sticks are cut lengthwise or crosswise from fillets or steaks into portions of uniform length, width and weight. An average size is 3- by 5/8- by 5/8-in., each weighing an ounce.

Fresh Fish—When fish is purchased whole or round, the eyes should be bright, full and never sunken; the gills, a reddish pink free from slime and odor; the scales, bright, shiny and adhering tightly to the skin; the flesh, moist, firm, elastic, and not separating from the bone.

Frozen Fish—Frozen fish should be kept in the sharp-freezer until it is to be used. Fillets, steaks and dressed fish may be cooked without defrosting but will take a longer cooking time. When fish is to be defrosted, it should be thawed in the refrigerator at 40°-45°F. and only long enough to permit ease in preparation.

Fish should not be thawed at room temperature as the thin parts will defrost before the thicker ones, and become a good breeding place for undesirable bacteria. Whole or drawn fish may be thawed by immersing them in cold running water.

Fish once defrosted should never be refrozen, because the flavor may become changed.

Average Per Portion Amounts of Fresh or Frozen Fish to Buy

Steaks	5-8 oz.
Fillets	4-5 oz.
Sticks	4 oz.
Dressed Fish	8 oz.
Whole or Round Fish	12 oz.

Recommended Uses for Different Trout Sizes

All trout sizes listed below are dressed sizes:

Breakfast or Light Meals— 1 quarter-pound trout per serving
1 third-pound trout per serving

Lunch— 1 third-pound trout per serving
1 5- to 2-pound trout per serving
1 half-pound trout per serving
2 quarter-pound trout per serving

Dinner— 1 5- to 2-pound trout per serving
2 quarter-pound trout per serving
1 half-pound trout per serving
1 10-ounce trout per serving
2 third-pound trout per serving
1 12-ounce trout per serving
1 16-ounce per extra large serving

SHRIMP

Raw, or "green" shrimp as it is called in the trade, varies from a greenish-grey to a reddish-brown depending on its production area. The common varieties are: white or common, brown or grooved; pink or coral. When cooked, all are similar in appearance and flavor.

Unless otherwise specified, the term "shrimp" refers to the fresh, frozen or cooked tail section of the shrimp. They are graded according to size, and the count is frequently designated by such terms as jumbo, large, medium, small. They are classified according to the following sizes per pound: 15 and under; 16 to 20; 21 to 25; 26 to 30; 31 to 42; 42 and over.

Among the shrimp imported by the United States is a king-sized variety known as scampi. It is shipped frozen from Italy, Panama and parts of South America, and is served largely in exclusive Italian restaurants.

Midget shrimps, averaging 150-300 per pound are also received frozen from Iceland and Holland.

LOBSTERS

Lobsters may be purchased for shipment live to all parts of the country. They may also be obtained in three other forms: cooked in the shell, lobster meat, and canned lobster meat. Except in the producing areas, lobsters cooked in the shell and lobster meat are not found on the markets in large quantities. No lobster is canned in the United States, but comes from Canada, the world's largest producer.

Live lobsters may be purchased in weights varying from ¾ lb. to 3 lb. or heavier. The meat comes from the claws, and must not be confused with crayfish or spiny lobster, of which only the tail is marketed.

ROCK LOBSTER TAILS

Only the tail of the crayfish is marketed. This comes to the United States in a frozen state largely from South Africa. They usually run from 6 oz. to 1 lb., but can be much heavier.

CHOOSING FRESH SHELLFISH
Look for—
- Lively lobsters
- In-shell oysters, clams and mussels with tightly closed shells.
- Plump shucked mollusks in clear liquid
- Scallops that are creamy pink
- Crabs that move and smell sea-fresh
- Firm, meaty shrimp with mild odor

STORING FRESH SEAFOODS
- Place dry, dressed fish in dish and loosely wrap with foil or saran.
- Keep fresh shellfish in cracked ice in the refrigerator
- Store fish in upper section of refrigerator or in meat keeper.
- Cook within one day.

STORING FROZEN SEAFOODS
- Keep frozen seafoods frozen solid in original wrapper
- Best storage temperature 0°F.
- Use immediately after defrosting
- Do not defrost and refreeze

CRABS

Crabs may be purchased in four forms: live, cooked in the shell, crab meat, and canned meat. Near the production areas, crabs are generally sold alive by the dozen for the institutional trade. Like lobsters, they must be kept alive until the time of cooking.

Hard-shell crabs are frequently cooked by steaming or boiling almost as soon as taken from the water. As the meat is very perishable, the crabs must be refrigerated or packed in ice till time of use. The meat is picked from cooked crabs and shipped in iced containers. (Alaska crab is discussed under a separate heading).

Cooked crab meat is available in the following forms:

Blue Crab of East and Gulf coasts:
1. Lump meat—comes from the large muscles. It is known as "special" or back-fin. The meat is white.
2. Flake meat—also white in color as it is the remaining portion of the body meat.
3. Flake and lump meat—in some sections both kinds of white meat are packed together.
4. Claw meat—as the name implies, it comes from the claws. The outer color of the meat is brownish in color. There is only one grade.
5. Pacific Coast or Dungeness Crab—meat from body and claws packed together. Is reddish in color.

Canned crab meat is available in all parts of the country and can be used interchangeably in recipes calling for cooked crab meat.

ALASKA KING CRAB

The Alaska king crab is butchered, washed, cooked, cooled, the meat shaken from the shell, then weighed, packed in molds and frozen—all within two hours after the catch is landed.

Crab legs are frequently frozen in the shell without precooking. Other fish are now processed on board ship in a similar way.

SCALLOPS

The highly-prized scallop of New England can be either a bay scallop or a sea scallop. Bay scallops, taken from inshore waters, are small, and are considered the greater delicacy as the flesh is more tender, and inclined to be sweeter. But the supply is very limited. The large sea scallop, an inhabitant of offshore banks and deep waters, is the one used extensively in quantity food operations. Both species have sweet, firm, white meat.

CLAMS

The marketed varieties on the Atlantic coast are the hard clam, the soft clam, and the surf clam. The hard-shelled clams are found from Cape Cod to Texas. In New England, they are commonly called quahaugs (or quahogs).

Littlenecks or cherry stones are trade names for the smaller-sized hard clams. They are usually served on the half-shell. Soft-shell clams, found from Cape Cod to the Arctic, are said by many New Englanders to be the only "true" clam.

Among the many varieties on the Pacific Coast, the most common species are the butter, littleneck, razor and pismo. Clams are bought in three forms: live in the shell, shucked fresh or frozen, or canned.

Shell clams, like oysters, should be alive when purchased. Gaping shells that will not close when handled mean that the hard-shell clam is dead, and no longer usable. With other varieties, there will be some constriction of the siphon or neck when the clam is touched. Shell clams will remain alive for several days if refrigerated at about 40°F.

Shucked clams should be plump, with clear liquor, and free from any pieces of shell. They should be kept refrigerated or packed in ice. When properly handled, they will remain fresh and in good condition for a week or 10 days.

Frozen shucked clams should not be thawed until ready to use and once thawed, never refrozen.

Hard, soft, razor, surf and pismo clams are canned whole, minced, or as clam chowder and are widely used in many quantity food establishments. For institutional use, the following containers are available in addition to the domestic sizes: No. 5 cans, 51 oz., for canned clams; Nos. 5 and 10 cans for clam chowder; Nos. 5 and 10 cans or glass jars for clam broth or juice.

OYSTERS

Oysters vary in size, texture and flavor according to their production area. They inhabit the Atlantic, the Pacific and the Gulf. Those taken from the waters of the Atlantic, from the Maritime Provinces of Canada to Texas, are known as Eastern. The Olympia, a small delicately flavored oyster, is found in Puget Sound. The giant Japanese oyster is taken from the Pacific.

Oysters may be purchased in three forms: live in the shell, fresh and frozen shucked, and canned.

Shell oysters are sold by the dozen, peck, bushel or crate. They should be alive when purchased, as indicated by a tightly closed shell. Oysters with gaping shells that do not close when handled are dead, and unfit for consumption. Shell oysters refrigerated at 40°F. or lower will keep for a considerable time.

Shucked oysters should be plump, and have a natural creamy color, with clear liquor, free from shell particles. Fresh shucked oysters are packed in metal containers or waxed cartons and should be kept refrigerated. They are sold by the gallon. When properly refrigerated, they will remain fresh for a week or ten days. Frozen shucked oysters should not be thawed until ready to use. Once thawed, they should not be refrozen.

THAWING FROZEN SEAFOODS
- Defrosting at room temperature causes sogginess and flavor loss.
- Partially thaw fillets and steaks in the refrigerator or under cold water. (Be sure you leave them in the watertight wrapping.)
- Defrost only until the portions separate easily.

Eastern oysters are usually packed in the following commercial grades:

Grade	Oysters per Gallon
Counts or Extra Large	Not more than 160
Extra Selects or Large	Not more than 161-210
Selects or Medium	Not more than 211-300
Standards or Small	Not more than 301-500
Standards or Very Small	Over 500

Canned oysters are available in No. 5 and 10 cans and in several forms for quantity menus.

SEAFOOD CALORIE COUNTDOWN

	Calories
Haddock, fried-3 oz.	135
Fishsticks- 5 sticks-4 oz.	200
Crabmeat-3 oz.	90
Mackerel-3 oz.	200
Salmon-3 oz.	120
Oysters-1 cup	160
Shrimp, cooked-3 oz.	110

Preparing Fish, Seafood

As ocean fish travel refrigerated in planes to all parts of the country, so fresh water fish are carried in tank trucks with freshly pumped water and delivered alive daily to operators everywhere.... lobster from New England, pompano from Florida, king crab from Alaska, dolphin from the islands of Hawaii, shrimp from the gulf ports and Mexico, oysters from New Jersey and salmon from the Pacific Northwest.

With the advances in processing, quick frozen blocks of seafood seriously challenge the flavor of the fresh catch and seafood preparation time is reaching a highly profitable minimum. Today, the processor's goal is a prefabricated cut or portion of fish to meet every menu need, a seafood pack that fits most profitably into production schedules.

Fish in quantity food operations is more frequently deep fried than cooked in any other way. When properly fried, it is appetizing and inviting for it has an attractive brown color, a crisp crust, a thoroughly cooked interior without being overcooked, a dry, non-greasy exterior, and the characteristic flavor of the specific fish.

Frying Fats—The quality of the frying fat is of utmost importance as it influences the flavor of the cooked fish. If fat develops off-flavors while in use, these will be transferred to the fish. For this reason, the fat must be frequently checked.

The following fats are the ones commonly used for deep frying: hydrogenated shortening; salad oils of good quality produced from cottonseed, peanut or corn oil; and modern lards that have an antioxidant added.

The frying-kettle should never be over-loaded. The ratio to use is 1 : 8, that is 1 lb. fish to 8 lb. fat.

Frying Temperatures—The temperature of the frying fat also affects the quality of the fish. Fish fried at too low a temperature absorbs a great deal of fat, while that cooked at the correct temperature has a low absorption. It is agreed that the temperature should not be lower than 325°F.-350°F., nor higher than 385°F. Fish cooked in the frozen state is generally cooked at the lower temperature. 375°F. is a good average temperature for all other fish.

Fish should never be overcooked. Leaving it one minute longer than necessary in the hot fat destroys its fine flavor. It is advisable to cook it for the shortest time possible.

Dredging the Fish—For deep frying as well as for some other methods of cooking, the fish must be properly dredged or coated with seasoned flour, crumbs or dipped in batter. If batter is used, it should be thin, as a thick batter absorbs fat.

DEFROSTING
- Do not defrost breaded fish portions, sticks or shellfish. They go directly from the freezer to oven, broiler or fry-pan.
- If you do your own breading, defrost your seafoods before deep frying.

FRYING TIMES—PRESSURE FRYING
Fish Fillets
   4 oz.   3½ min.
Whole Fish
   1-1½ lb.   5 min.
Shrimp, jumbo   4 min.
Oysters   1½ min.
Crab   3 min.

Broiling—Frozen fish is usually thawed before broiling. Fresh or thawed fillets and steaks are placed in a preheated broiler 2 in. from the broiling unit; the distance from the source of heat for split fish and whole fish varies from 2 to 6 in. Frozen fish or fish of a very delicate texture are placed about 4 in. from the direct heat.

The fish is brushed several times with oil, melted butter or margarine. Some chefs prefer to first dust the fish lightly with seasoned flour when preparing it for broiling.

Steaks are turned once; fillets are never turned.

When fish is charcoal grilled, the grill should be sufficiently hot to mark the fish.

Pan Frying or Sauteing—This method is usually employed for small whole fish. Many cooks are of the opinion that this is the preferred method for smelts and small game fish if they are first dipped in milk and then in seasoned cornmeal. Fillets and fish steaks are frequently pan-fried.

Steaming—This is a favorite method of cooking cod, haddock, salmon, bass, halibut and similar fish as it seals in flavor and juices. A savory sauce adds additional succulence to an already flavorful fish.

Baking—Unlike meat, fish even in the raw state is already tender. It is, therefore, the consensus that it is more flavorful and moist when baked at a moderately high temperature (400-425°F.) for the shortest period of time.

Poaching—The fish is immersed in a liquid to barely cover it. White wine is frequently used as part of the liquid to add a flavor dividend. Some fish that readily lend themselves to this method of cooking are: flounder, ocean perch, haddock, halibut, cod, sea bass, English sole, salmon, pompano, etc.

Fish, like vegetables, are ruined when overcooked. Yet this happens all too often. Overcooking robs the fish of its moisture and leaves it dry. Cooking time should be accurately watched as the flesh of the fish even in the raw state is already tender. Cooking brings out the natural flavors, improves the appearance, and makes it more appetizing.

Boiled Fish—Fish, with the exception of shellfish such as lobster, crab, etc., should never be boiled. Rather it should be simmered or poached with the bubbles breaking gently beneath the surface of the liquid.

To supply acidity and help keep the flesh firm, vinegar or lemon juice in the proportion of ¼ cup for every 2 gal. water is frequently added.

Salt and pepper are the only seasonings needed to step up the natural flavors of some fish, while herbs, fish stock, court bouillon, or wine may be required to complement fish of a milder flavor.

FRYING TIMES-HIGH INPUT FRYERS
(All 350°F.)

Frozen Breaded Shrimp	4 min.
Fresh Breaded Shrimp	3 min.
Frozen Fish Fillets	4 min.
Fresh Fish Fillets	3 min.
Fresh Breaded Scallops	4 min.
Breaded Fried Clams	1 min.
Breaded Oysters	5 min.
Frozen Fish Sticks	4 min.

Rosemary, thyme, tarragon, marjoram, oregano, bay leaves, parsley, or other herbs may be added to the liquid in which the fish is being cooked, but care must be taken to use them sparingly as the delicate flavor of the fish is easily overwhelmed.

SEASON SPARINGLY— DON'T OVERWHELM DELICATE FLAVOR OF FISH

Monosodium glutamate in the proportion of ½ tsp. to each pound of fish, rubbed into the flesh or added to the liquid, will step up the natural fish flavor.

Wines have an affinity for almost all fish, but the wine flavor must never predominate. It is added to the liquid while the fish is cooking to mingle with the fish flavor and impart a delicious, mellow and characteristic taste.

Fish Stock—This is prepared by simmering the head, bones, skin and tail of the fish. It can be used as: the liquid in court bouillon; to baste fish; or it can be reserved for sauces, chowders, or molded seafood salads.

Court Bouillon—The strength of the court bouillon will vary with the kind of fish being cooked. The liquid may boil before the fish is put into it, but never afterwards. Slow cooking allows the fish to absorb the flavor of the bouillon.

The court bouillon, like the fish stock, may be used in sauces.

Boiling Green Shrimp—Shrimp may be peeled, deveined and boiled, or boiled, peeled and deveined. Some famous chefs believe that shrimp cooked in the shell are more flavorful.

The amount of salt used varies according to the method. For every 15 lb. of shrimp, allow 3 gal. of water and 1½ cups of salt for the unpeeled; ¾ cup of salt for the peeled. Cover and boil 5 to 10 minutes. Remove from water and chill.

If the recipe calls for further cooking in a sauce or casserole, reduce the initial cooking time.

Some cooks prefer to cook shrimp in a court bouillon claiming it more fully develops the shrimp flavor. A simple vegetable bouillon is made with chopped onions, lemon slices, bay leaves, peppercorns, salt and water.

Breaded Frozen Shrimp—One of the greatest boons to the quantity food operator has been the development of frozen, breaded, uncooked shrimp. No kitchen preparation is necessary; no thawing is needed. The shrimp are cooked from their hard-frozen state in 2 to 3 minutes in 350°F. deep fat. Cooked to order, there is no delay even in the busiest rush periods; no waste, no standing on the steamtable for undue periods of time.

While large-size shrimp will cook from the hard-frozen state in approximately 2 to 3 min. in 350°F. deep fat, jumbo shrimp require 3 to 4 min.

Boiling Live Lobsters—There are two schools of thought on the meth-

**BEST WAY
TO RELAX
A LOBSTER**

od of boiling lobsters. One is to drop live lobster into the boiling water. The other is to kill the lobster just before placing it in the boiling water. This is done by inserting the point of a sharp knife between the body shell and the tail segment, and cutting down to break the spinal cord.

Advocates of this latter method claim that putting the live lobster into the boiling water causes the muscles to become rigid, and this rigidity is seen in the less-tender flesh of the cooked lobster.

The lobster is boiled in a covered kettle for about 20 min. Overcooking makes the meat tough and stringy. Once cooked, the lobster should be immediately immersed in cold water and left to cool. The meat can then be easily removed from the claws and tail. The tomalley or green liver—a delicious morsel—is taken from the body. The roe of female lobsters—a pink-reddish deposit—is also a choice part of the lobster, and is frequently used in sauce if not eaten with the lobster.

Broiled Lobster—Allow one whole 1 lb. lobster per serving. Place lobster on back; kill by inserting point of sharp knife between the eyes. Split lobster from head to tail. Remove stomach, sac at the back of the head, and the intestines and black vein which runs the length of the tail. Crack claws.

Brush flesh with melted butter or margarine. Place lobster, with shell side up, on greased broiler rack 4 to 5 in. from source of heat. Broil 5 to 8 min. Turn. Brush generously with melted butter or margarine. Broil 10 min. longer or until flesh shrinks from shell. Serve with melted butter and lemon wedges.

Rock Lobster Tails—For casseroles and some other dishes, the lobster tails are cooked in boiling salted water, usually without pre-thawing. The cooking time varies from 9 to 20 min. according to the size of the lobster. (They usually run from 6 oz. to 1 lb. but can be much heavier).

After cooking, thorough chilling makes it easy to remove the meat from the shell. By cutting through the under shell with scissors, the meat can be pulled away from the shell with the fingers and removed.

Crab Cooked in the Shell—Hard-shell crabs are frequently cooked by steaming or boiling almost as soon as taken from the water. As the meat is very perishable, the crabs must be kept refrigerated or packed in ice until time of use.

Alaska King Crab—With its habitat the Bering Sea and surrounding waters, the Alaska king crab is entirely different from the blue crab of the Atlantic and Gulf Coasts or the dungeness of the Pacific. It weighs up to 15 lb., and may measure 5 ft. stretched.

Only the legs and claws of large male Alaska king crabs are used. When cooked, the meat is white attractively marked with red.

Prior to the last decade, this crab was marketed solely as canned meat, with the entire supply being put up by the Japanese and other Orientals. When an American discovered that the Alaska king crab remained fresh when frozen, it was soon being shipped frozen or flown fresh to the coastal and inland markets of the U. S.

Its use in these forms has steadily increased until Alaska king crab is found today on menus of famous eating places in almost every section of the United States. It has a delicate flavor, and lends itself to a variety of delicious dishes.

Secrets of Seafood Success

MARINADES ADD SPECIAL FLAVOR

Step up the flavor of some fish by using a marinade, made by sauteing minced onions and chopped green peppers in garlic butter, then adding water, lemon juice, vinegar, sugar, salt and pepper, marjoram or ginger and boiling the mixture 10 min. The liquid is poured over the fish in the bakepan, and the fish baked in a 450°F. to 500°F. oven, or the marinade may be used to poach fish in.

* * *

To give an added touch of color to the serving of light-colored fish, sprinkle paprika over the fish during its preparation.

* * *

Use attractive garnishes to add additional zest to fish dishes. Some of these are: marinated fluted cucumber slices; lemon or lime rings; lemon or lime wedges lightly dipped in paprika or minced parsley; mushroom caps; celery curls; radish roses or slices; tomato slices or wedges; parsley; watercress; beet and horseradish relish; watermelon pickle; tomato relish; sweet, sour or dill pickles, etc.

* * *

For that added touch, put a small amount of sherry wine, white wine, tarragon or herb vinegar in the egg mixture for dipping fish before baking.

* * *

Shape codfish cake mixture into tiny balls. Place in frying basket and fry in deep fat until a golden brown. Serve as appetizers on toothpicks.

* * *

Complement the mild flavor of fish with a tart relish, such as pickled or harvard beets, cole slaw, green pepper and celery relish, marinated cucumbers, onion relish, etc.

* * *

To make pigs in blankets, wrap each oyster in a thin half-slice of bacon. Fasten with toothpick. Bake at 425°F. about 20 min. or until bacon is crisp. Remove toothpick and serve each oyster in its blanket on a small piece of toast, allowing 4 to 6 per entree. For hors d'oeuvre, do not remove toothpick; omit toast.

* * *

When broiling fish, brush often with melted butter, margarine, or salad oil. If desired, sauteed minced onions or grated parmesan cheese may be added to the butter or other shortening.

* * *

A table piece giving instructions on how to bone a fish or eat a lobster encourages the timid gourmet.

* * *

Make quick service quicker by preportioning salmon or tuna loaves. Individual loaves topped with a slice of hard-cooked egg make for convenient service.

* * *

FISH PIZZA

Deep fat fry breaded 4 oz. frozen fish portions or sticks at 375°F. for 3 min., shaking basket occasionally. Remove and let drain. Spread one side with tomato sauce and top with slice of mozzarella cheese. Sprinkle with oregano and place under broiler until cheese melts. Serve immediately on toasted bun with potato chips and cole slaw. Merchandise as Fish Pizza.

Sauces for Seafood

Sauces play an important role in the serving of fish. Certain sauces have an affinity not only for the fish but also for the method of cooking it. For instance, tartar sauce is a natural to team with fried fish, while egg sauce adds to steamed fish.

The sauces that follow have been placed in the category of their most general use.

STEAMED, POACHED, BOILED FISH

Bechamel: a rich, white sauce seasoned with nutmeg and bay leaf.

Bordelaise: a rich, brown sauce with red wine, chopped shallots, tarragon and parsley.

Drawn Butter

Hollandaise

Mock Hollandaise: a Bechamel Sauce with egg yolks added.

Maitre D'Hotel: see description in section on broiled fish which follows.

Mornay: a rich, white sauce with cheese and egg yolks added.

Newburg: a rich cream sauce with egg yolks, cream and sherry or brandy.

Ravigote: a white sauce with fine herbs, white wine, vinegar, fish essence, butter and cream.

Tomato

Rarebit: prepared mustard, eggs, and grated cheese added to white sauce.

White Sauce Variations: with cheese, hard-cooked eggs; green and red peppers, pimientos, parsley, peas, shrimp, etc.

Creole Sauce

SAUCE FISH
TO FIT
COOKING
METHOD

FOR BROILED FISH

Specialty Butters: amandine butter, anchovy butter, caper butter, lemon butter, parsley butter, paprika butter, scallion butter, watercress butter, shrimp butter.

Black Butter: (Beurre Noir): Butter heated until brown, and vinegar, capers or chopped parsley and seasonings added.

Maitre D'Hotel Butter: butter, lemon juice, finely chopped parsley, salt and pepper.

Colbert Butter: similar to Maitre d'Hotel Sauce with finely chopped herbs added.

Bearnaise: Hollandaise Sauce with minced onions, fresh tarragon, parsley and vinegar.

Horseradish Cream: Bread crumbs, horseradish, light cream, seasonings, whipped cream.

Mariniere: White Wine Sauce with fish essence, finely chopped shallots and herbs.

Meuniere: butter, lemon juice and parsley.

Mustard Sauce

SPECIAL ATMOSPHERE THEMES FOR FOODSERVICE

FOR FRIED FISH
    Caper Hollandaise
    Cucumber Dressing: heavy cream, vinegar, finely chopped cucumber, seasonings.
    Hollandaise
    Lobster, Shrimp or Crab Meat Mayonnaise Piquante: minced onions, capers, vinegar, seasonings, chili sauce or mixed pickles and sugar.
    Tartar
    Remoulade: similar to mayonnaise with chopped fennel, parsley, shallot and tarragon leaves added.

FLAVOR LIFTS FOR SEAFOOD

    Lemon Barbecue Sauce: To give a flavor lift to broiled fish fillets, defrost fillets in lemon juice and water. Make a smooth mixture of ½ cup fresh lemon juice, ¼ cup salad oil, 2 tbsp. grated onion, 1 tsp. dry mustard, ½ tsp. salt and 2 tbsp. brown sugar. Pour over fillets just before broiling.

    Butter 'n Nutmeg Sauce: Suggested as a savory accompaniment to fresh fish is this blend of 1/3 cup butter softened in fresh lemon juice plus 1 tsp. nutmeg. Add mixture to fish as it browns in butter.

    Cocktail Sauce: To glamorize shrimp or scallops, serve this quick sauce. Into ½ cup of tomato catsup blend 6 tbsp. fresh lemon juice, 3 drops hot pepper sauce and 1 tbsp. horseradish sauce.

    Lemon Supreme Sauce: Bake this simple flavor mixture right into a salmon steak. Place fish on foil-lined baking dish and pour over it this mixture: equal parts of fresh lemon juice and butter, chopped green onions (tops and all), salt and pepper.

    Salmon steaks can become gourmet treats when they are baked or broiled with a special sauce. Three ideas are Caper Sauce, which comes straight from the bottle, Italian Sauce, which can be purchased bottled and Horseradish Sauce, a blend of mayonnaise base and bottled horseradish. Dill, of course, can be added to most any mayonnaise base fish sauce.

    Remember in seasoning fish that you are enhancing natural flavor, not trying to hide it. Some fish requires only salt and pepper for great taste appeal while some is elegant with special sauces.

    Fish that is delicate in flavor usually needs a piquant sauce; bland fish served cold lends itself to hot sauce; fried fish is best with tart sauces based on mayonnaise. Many shellfish are delicious served in their own broth or with melted butter. Sizzling steaks or fillets are ideal when spread with cold butter before serving.

SHRIMP AND SAUCES

    Shrimp in the shell are marketed by size or number to the pound.

Uncooked, Fresh or Frozen	No. Per Serving
15 and under	4
16-20	5
21-25	6
26-30	8

Use about 2½ oz. of cooked shrimp per cocktail.

If you buy uncooked shrimp in the shell, whether fresh or frozen,

Nautical

prepare them this way: Clean and devein before or after cooking. Boil shrimp three to five minutes in salted water to which pickling spices have been added. Allow 1 tsp. spices per lb.

REMOULADE SAUCE FOR SHRIMP COCKTAIL
YIELD: 100 portions
INGREDIENTS

Mayonnaise	1 gal.
Anchovies, chopped	4 oz.
Capers	2 oz.
Lemon Juice	4 oz.
Instant Onion	½ oz.
Instant Garlic	1 tbsp.
Pickle Relish	1 cup

METHOD
Combine all ingredients. Serve over chilled shrimp. Allow 1 oz. per serving.

LEMON MUSTARD SAUCE
YIELD: 100 1-oz. portions, 3¼ qt.
INGREDIENTS

Butter or Margarine	¾ cup
Flour, all-purpose, sifted	¾ cup
Salt	1 tbsp.
Milk, hot	3 qt.
Lemon Juice	1 cup
Prepared Mustard	1 cup
Parsley, chopped	1 cup

METHOD
Melt fat, blend in flour and salt. Stir into the milk. Cook until thickened, stirring constantly. Remove from heat. Gradually stir in lemon juice and mustard. Add parsley. Heat. Serve over fish.

CUCUMBER SAUCE
YIELD: 100 1-oz. servings
INGREDIENTS

Cucumbers, diced	2 qt.
Mayonnaise	2½ qt.
Salt	1½ tbsp.
Pepper	½ tbsp.
Paprika	1 tbsp.
Lemon Juice	½ cup

METHOD
Peel, drain cucumbers, put through food mill. Combine with other ingredients, mix, chill.

TARTAR SAUCE
YIELD: 100 1½-oz. servings
INGREDIENTS

Olives, finely chopped	1 pt.
Pickles, finely chopped	1 qt.
Parsley, finely chopped	1 cup
Onions, finely chopped	1 cup
Mayonnaise	1 gal.

METHOD
Combine all ingredients and chill.

THAWING FROZEN SHRIMP
- Frozen shrimp may be dropped directly into boiling water. Frozen lobster tail, crab legs and chunks, may be cooked without defrosting.
- Other frozen shellfish because they cook quickly, should be defrosted before cooking.

GREEN GODDESS DRESSING
FOR SEAFOOD COCKTAIL

YIELD: 2¼ cups
INGREDIENTS

Ingredient	Amount
Garlic Clove	1
Salt	¼ tsp.
Anchovy Paste	3 tbsp.
Commercial Sour Cream	½ cup
Mayonnaise	1-1/3 cup
Tarragon White Vinegar	¼ cup
Scallions or Chives, finely cut up	¼ cup
Parsley, finely cut up	½ cup

METHOD

Crush garlic clove with salt. Combine with anchovy paste, sour cream, mayonnaise and vinegar; stir in scallions and parsley.

Serve over pieces of rock lobster and whole cooked sea scallops.

AVOCADO DIP

YIELD: Approx. 1½ cups
INGREDIENTS

Ingredient	Amount
Ripe Avocado	2
Mayonnaise or Salad Dressing	2 tbsp.
Lemon Juice	2 tbsp.
Onion, grated	1 tbsp.
Worcestershire Sauce	1 tsp.
Liquid Hot Pepper Sauce	¼ tsp.
Salt	¼ tsp.

METHOD

Cut avocados in half lengthwise and remove seeds. Peel and mash avocados until smooth. Add remaining ingredients and mix thoroughly. Cover and chill 1 hour. Makes approximately 1½ cups dip.

Merchandising Seafood

To whet visitor's appetites and sell an extra bit of local seafood, restaurants along Fisherman's Wharf in San Francisco have counters on the street where they sell cold crab and shrimp cocktails in paper cups with sauce and oyster crackers.

On one street all cocktails are 70¢ each. On a less populated street they sell for 60¢ each. Restaurateurs stick together on these prices, but compete fiercely via their barkers' colorful personalities and strong sales pitches to passersby.

CARRY-OUT SEAFOOD COCKTAILS

Some of the stands sell 4 oz. miniature wine samples to accompany the shellfish snacks.

Tourists are interested in watching the attendants remove the steaming crabs from huge cauldrons, brush them clean, crack them with traditional tools, and prepare them for later sale when chilled.

Very few sophisticated props are used for the sale of the cocktails—some trays full of them are covered with sheets of polyethylene and some have plastic domes. Business is good at every stand and profit ratio is high on these quick-sale items served in disposable containers.

America's children have learned to enjoy fish as a school lunch special. To capitalize on the established appeal, the National Fisheries Institute recommends these menu items for the young:

Buccaneer Sea Burger—A thick, deep fried fish portion or fillet on a grilled bun. . .topped with a hearty helping of Treasure Island Sauce . . .served with a mound of frozen french fries and Gold Doubloon Corn.

FISH FRY FOR THE SMALL FRY

Moby Dick Dinner—A whale of a meal for small fry. . .finger-size fillets. . .frozen crinkle-cut french fried potatoes. . .served with a mildly-seasoned Clipper Dippin' Sauce. . .Sea Green Beans.

Robinson Crusoe Special—An eating adventure for young explorers . . .a tender fish fillet covered with a tomato-based Seaman's Sauce. . served with crunchy frozen potato rounds. . .cole slaw.

Long John Silver Sandwich—Try this tasty feast. . .a generous fish portion on a bun. . . topped with a tomato slice, crisp lettuce and creamy cheese and olive Pirate's Sauce. Served with french fried potatoes. . .cole slaw.

Fun "take home" items will bring the young ones to your operation—and because the kids want to come, the parents will be there too. Try these ways to increase your young following:

Tiny Toy Boats—"floating" on a seafood plate. They are ideal reminders of your fish and seafood specialties.

Small Buried Treasure Maps—rolled up and tied with string, perfect accompaniments for the Buccaneer Burger, Robinson Crusoe Special or Long John Silver Sandwich.

Gold Coins—(chocolate pressed into a coin shape and covered with gold foil) make very special "clean plate awards." Have the waitresses serve them from a Treasure Chest or Pirate's Booty Bag.

Merchandise seafood specials for your dieting patrons. They'll be a welcome change from the ever-present ground beef item so often offered on low calorie menus. Try rotating these low calorie dishes under a Sea-Slimmer heading on your menu:

LOW CALORIE SEAFOOD SPECIALS

Slimline Shellfish Salad—King Crab chunks, cucumber slices, hard-cooked egg and tomato wedges in a dressing of low calorie mayonnaise, lemon juice, prepared mustard and liquid hot pepper sauce.

Slender Spicy Fillets—Fillets of haddock, halibut, flounder, ocean perch or red snapper broiled with a topping of minced onion, grated cucumber, chopped pimiento, salt and pepper.

Low-Cal Curried Fillets—Cod or other fillets baked in a curry-seasoned sauce of sliced celery, onion, skim milk.

Fish Fillet Gourmet—Brush fillets with mixture of lemon juice, salt, white pepper, chopped fresh mint, oregano and broil. Serve with garnish of ripe olives and lemon wedges.

Dieter's Sea-Green Delight—Fillets of cod, flounder, whitefish, red snapper, haddock, simmered in lemon-lime beverage and served with a low calorie mayonnaise sauce blended with minced watercress, parsley and scallions.

SEA-STYLED MENU

The sea can tie the menu together even when it's not all seafood. At Stouffer's Pier W in Cleveland, the sea is reflected in five of the six major menu headings, while line drawings of a pirate and lantern plus the Pier W logo further emphasize the seafarin' food. The Pirate's Grill and a Captain's Bounty are headings covering meat and chicken entrees. Lighthouse Specialties are lobster and steak. Neptune's Treasures are all seafood items and Yo-Ho-Ho and a Rum Dessert is the heading for the finale of the meal.

Nautical

CLAMBAKES

Staging a clambake is now possible in any American establishment since the ingredients are available in most locations. As the clambake travels inland, it may have to be changed slightly. A study of the traditional method may suggest changes that will make this unusual seafood gala a feasible promotion.

At one Clambake reported in INSTITUTIONS Magazine the feast starts with Clam Bouillon (broth), then an exquisite clam chowder, made from a treasured recipe. It seems to be a cross between the creamy New England chowder and the tomato-laden Manhattan style—a smooth, savory formula which is carefully guarded by the management.

With the chowder, pilot crackers and homemade brown bread are served. Then a salad appears. Both the broth and chowder are prepared in the kitchen, but the management insists that these items are as much a part of the clambake meal as the foods cooked over the rocks outside.

Next come heaping bowls of steamed clams that waitresses rush to the table straight from the bake stones. These are served with drawn butter, kept in a warmer at the table. Before long, the diner finds a plate containing sausage (a type similar to bratwurst), sweet potatoes (both from the bake) and clam fritters (from the kitchen),

At this point, it's time for a break. The guests sit back, relax and enjoy a dish of "Squantum Punch." This is similar to frozen eggnog—stiffly laced with brandy—having the consistency of milk sherbet. It should be mentioned that patrons are welcome to partake of as much of any dish as desired. However, considering the menu, this is a rarely exercised privilege.

The second part of the dinner begins with a fish course—a generous portion of fresh fish of the season (from the bake). The usual service calls for a whole fish per table (large, round tables seating 10 to 14) which the senior member at each table carves. Accompanying this are corn-on-the-cob (also from the bake) and white potatoes (saratoga-style).

Next comes the kingly lobster, which has been given a special succulence and flavor by the intermingling aromas from other foods in the bake. The lobster benefits not only from the other seafoods cooked with it, but the steam cooking produces especially tender, moist meat.

At this Clambake the portion is half a 1-lb. lobster (with the other half ready and waiting if you're up to it). Hot, drawn butter is the Yankee idea of the perfect accompaniment for lobster.

Then, another traditional dish—baked Indian Pudding. Finally, dessert—fresh melon of the season.

Preparations for a bake start in the morning. The fire is made entirely above ground. Other authorities believe it should be placed in a pit, but the pit method can be troublesome. Since the fire in the

CLAMBAKES COME INLAND WITH VARIATIONS

BAKE STARTS EARLY

pit tends to create a vacuum, if the soil is slightly sandy, the fire will suck in the sides of the hole and cover the food with dirt.

Today, it is common to use pieces of iron (known as bake irons) as the heat source in the bake.

However, stones are traditional and provided they are well seasoned, the stones are just as effective. The stones should be about the size of a football and should have been above ground for a long time. When rocks are taken out of the ground and immediately subjected to the intense heat of a bake fire they often split apart. Then, there is real danger from flying fragments. Rocks that are newly dug up should be left out to "season" (dry out) for at least a summer before they are used.

The food in a bake takes at least 45 min. to cook. It may be left under the canvas up to an hour and a half if need be, but any longer will probably overcook it. All the foods take about the same time to cook.

While a particular sequence is followed in laying the food on the bake, it is merely to make it convenient to remove one course at a time while keeping the others hot. The lobsters and corn go on the bottom; next the steamer clams, then the sausages and sweet potatoes—and on top, the fish.

PUTTING ON A CLAMBAKE

The fire is laid on concrete platform under a tin roof. While the clams are soaking, the oysters are cleaned by scrubbing thoroughly with a stiff-bristled brush. Clams are soaked in several saltwater "baths."

Clams are picked over to cull out dead ones or those with badly broken shells. Clams are dead when their necks are outside of the shells—the surest sign.

Clams are replaced in clean salted water. Next, a hearth of fire bricks about 8 ft. sq. is laid with wood, then crumpled paper; kindling goes on last.

A solid layer of heavier wood is added. Following this will be three more layers of similar pieces, placed at right angles to each other.

The pyre is now about 3 ft. high, and when bake stones are placed on top, the fire is ready for lighting.

Fire is lit about 1½ to 2 hr. before food is added. As wood burns, stones gradually settle to hearth. After wood has burned, stones are shoved aside, ashes cleared and rearranged in single layer. Stones should be white hot.

Next, large pieces of wood are laid around bed to frame in rockweed. Finally, the rockweed is spread over stones. This Clambake took about 5 bu. of rockweed. Rockweed which has large pods filled with salt water, is excellent seaweed for steaming.

Nautical

Food, wrapped in cheesecloth, is placed in shallow wire baskets. Foods are placed on fire in reverse order of way they'll be removed when done.

Fast action is required to cover bake with 3 layers of heavy, soaked canvas. Next, soaked burlap bags are put around canvas to seal in heat.

FAST ACTION WHEN BAKE IS READY

When the steamer clam course is ready, one end of the canvas is lifted so that fish, sausages and lobster will remain hot. Waitresses rush to dining room with clams.

While bake is being "laid up" in the afternoon, kitchen staff is busy preparing other dishes. Clam broth is made with one part quahogs (larger clams) and three parts steamer clams. They are thoroughly cleaned. Clams are cooked on top of the range in a pan to which slightly salted water is added to cover.

MENU FOR CLAMBAKE

Clam Broth
Clam Chowder
Pilot Crackers
Brown Bread
Steamer Clams
Sausage
Sweet Potato
Clam Fritters
(kitchen prepared)
Fresh Fish Portion
Corn on the Cob
Saratoga Potatoes
Lobster
Baked Indian Pudding
Melon

Seafood Recipes

FILENE'S NEW ENGLAND CLAM CHOWDER
YIELD: 250 - 5 oz. portions
INGREDIENTS

Clams, shucked, in liquor	1 gal.
Water	2 gal.
Quahaugs, in shell	2 peck
Potato, ½ in. cube	30 lb.
Pork, ½ in. cube	1½ lb.
Onion, thinly sliced	3 lb.
Flour	2 lb.
Milk	1 gal.
Butter	1 lb.
Cream, 20%	2 gal.
Salt and Pepper	to season

METHOD
Cook clams in their own liquor with 2 gal. water. Save liquid.

Wash quahaugs thoroughly, and cook in 9 gal. water. Save liquid.

Combine clam and quahaug liquid and strain through cheesecloth.

Shuck quahaugs. Remove black necks from clams and quahaugs. Chop remaining soft part very fine.

Cook cubed potatoes in clam liquid, or steam them separately. Saute cubed pork. Add onions and cook until tender. Remove pork and onions from pan.

Add flour to pan, and blend well with fat to make a roux. Cook thoroughly. Add clam liquid, stirring well with wire whip.

Then add onions, pork, potatoes, and milk. Add cream and butter. Cook until well blended. Serve hot.

NOTE: The necks of the clams and quahaugs may be finely chopped, cooked with potatoes or in clam water and added to chowder. Clam chowder develops flavor upon standing. Best made 1 hr. before serving.

COURT BOUILLON
INGREDIENTS

Carrots, diced	2 cup
Celery, diced	2 cup
Green Peppers, chopped	1 cup
Onions, minced	1 cup
Butter or Margarine	½ cup
Peppercorns	9
Whole Cloves	7
Bay Leaves	3
Salt	3 tbsp.
Lemon Slices	6
Mild Vinegar or Lemon Juice	¾ cup
Parsley, chopped	¼ cup
Water, cold	2½-3 gal.

METHOD
Saute carrots, celery, green peppers and onions in melted shortening.

Combine all ingredients. Boil 30 min. Strain.

ALASKA KING CRAB CASSEROLE MANTUA
YIELD: 24 portions
INGREDIENTS

Alaska King Crab, cut in large chunks	4½ lb.
Butter	12 oz.
Flour	4 oz.
Half & Half	2 qt.
Tomato Puree	3 oz.
Salt	to taste
Pepper	to taste
Tomatoes, peeled, seeded and diced	6
Truffles, chopped	4

METHOD
Saute crab in butter. Remove crab and hold.

Add flour to butter and stir 3 min. Add half & half and tomato puree, simmer until thickened.

Season, add Alaska King Crab and tomatoes. Place in buttered casserole. Srpinkle truffles over top.

Bake in moderate oven 30 min.

ATUN A LA MARINA
(Tuna a la Marina)
YIELD: 35 servings
INGREDIENTS

Onions, sliced	3 lb.
Tomatoes, fresh or canned, drained	9 lb.
Tuna, drained and flaked	7 lb.
Pimiento-Stuffed Spanish Green Olives, chopped	1½ qt.
Prepared Parsley, minced	1 cup
Instant Granulated Garlic	1½ tsp.
Salt	2 tbsp.
Pepper	1½ tsp.
Cinnamon	1½ tsp.

METHOD
Layer one-half the onions, one-half the tomatoes and one-half the tuna in steam table or baking pan. Repeat layers, ending with tuna.

Sprinkle with all remaining ingredients. Cover and bake at 350°F. for about 45 min.

Serve with rice or boiled potatoes.

Crab

CRAB MEAT AU GRATIN
(Hackney's Restaurant, Inc.)
YIELD: 25 portions
INGREDIENTS

Crab Meat, fresh	6 lb.
Butter	1 cup
Flour	2 cup
Milk, scalded	5 qt.
Salt	2 tbsp.
Hot Pepper Sauce	4 dashes
Egg Yolk	8
Sherry Wine	½ cup
Nippy Cheese, grated	1½ cup
Green Pepper, cut in rings	5
Mushrooms, sliced, sauteed	15

METHOD
Melt butter. Stir in the flour and salt. Add scalded milk and hot pepper sauce. Stir until thickened.

Add a little of the hot sauce to the beaten egg yolks. Blend well.

Combine egg mixture with the remaining sauce. Stir in the sherry wine. Add crab meat. Adjust seasonings, if necessary.

Fill individual greased casserole dishes with the crab meat mixture. Top with grated cheese, and green pepper ring filled with sauteed mushrooms.

Bake in 350°F. oven until cheese is melted and sauce is bubbly.

Serve with french fried potatoes and tomato salad.

CRAB CASSEROLE DELUXE
YIELD: 6 servings
INGREDIENTS

Eggs, beaten	2
Bouillon or Light Cream	½ cup
Butter, melted	2 tbsp.
Hot Pepper Sauce	1 tsp.
Onion, minced	1 tbsp.
Mustard, prepared	1 tsp.
Salt	½ tsp.
Pepper	¼ tsp.
Crabmeat, cooked, chopped	2 cup
Crumbs, bread or cracker	1 cup

METHOD
Combine eggs, bouillon, butter, and seasonings, and mix well. Stir in crabmeat and half the crumbs and mix well. Pour into greased 1½ qt. casserole or fill crab shells with this mixture, top with remaining crumbs and dot with butter.

Bake in moderate oven until crumbs are lightly browned.

ALMOND DEVILED CRAB
YIELD: 24 servings, about ½ cup each
INGREDIENTS

Eggs, hard cooked	12
Medium White Sauce	1½ qt.
Crab Meat, shelled and picked	2 lb.
Celery, chopped	2 cup
Green Pepper, chopped	2 cup
Onion, chopped	½ cup
Worcestershire Sauce	1 tbsp.
Soft Bread Crumbs	1 cup
Process Swiss Cheese, grated	2 cup
Blanched Slivered Almonds	2 cup

METHOD
Chop eggs coarsely.

Combine white sauce, crab meat, celery, pepper and onion. Heat through thoroughly. Remove from heat; stir in eggs and worcestershire. Divide into well-greased scallop shells or individual bakers, allowing a generous ½ cup crab meat mixture per portion.

Combine bread crumbs, cheese and almonds; sprinkle over portions.

Bake at 400°F. 20 min.,* or until crumbs are browned and almonds lightly toasted.

*If crab meat mixture is allowed to cool to room temperature prior to baking, allow 30 min. baking time.

TRITON'S TRIUMPH
(Washington, D. C. Mayflower Hotel)
YIELD: 50 servings, approx. 2/3 cup each
INGREDIENTS

Mayonnaise	2 qt.
Worcestershire Sauce	3 tbsp.
Mustard, prepared	¼ cup
Capers (optional)	1/3 cup
Sherry, dry (optional)	1½ cup
Cayenne Pepper	¼ tsp.
Salt	as needed
Curry Powder	2½ tsp.
Parsley Flakes	¾ cup
Onions, chopped fine	3 cup
Celery, chopped fine	3 cup
Bread, soft, shredded	3 qt.
Water	1¼ qt.
Crab Meat, flaked (13 oz. cans)	5 cans
Shrimp, drained (2 lb. 6 oz. cans)	2 cans

METHOD
Combine mayonnaise, worcestershire sauce, mustard, capers and sherry.

Combine all other ingredients and add to the mayonnaise mixture. Place in individual baking shells or greased casseroles.

Bake in moderate oven (350°F.) about 20 to 30 min., until heated through.

MANHATTAN FISH CHOWDER

YIELD: 50 servings of approx. 9 oz. or 1 cup each

INGREDIENTS

Bacon or Salt Pork, diced	1 lb.
Onions, chopped	1 qt.
Celery, chopped	1 qt.
Potatoes, chopped	2 qt.
Water	2 qt.
Salt	2 tbsp.
White Fish Cubes (cod, halibut, haddock, etc.)	6 qt.
Tomatoes, strained	1 No. 10 can
Pepper	1 tsp.
Butter	¼ lb.
Parsley, chopped	as needed

METHOD

Fry bacon until crisp and brown. Add onions and celery and fry until tender.

Cook potatoes in water with salt for 10 min.

Add bacon, onions, celery, fish, tomatoes and pepper to potatoes. Simmer for 30 min.

Just before serving, add butter and simmer for 5 min. longer.

Sprinkle with finely chopped parsley.

CRAB CAKES

YIELD: 80 cakes (40 portions)

INGREDIENTS

Backfin Crab Meat	10 lb.
Bread Crumbs, fresh, soft	1¾ qt.
Salt	1½ tbsp.
Cayenne Pepper	½ tsp.
Dry Mustard	2½ tbsp.
Parsley, fresh, chopped	¾ cup
Cream Sauce, medium	1 qt.

METHOD

Look over crab meat and remove shell. Combine first 6 ingredients and toss lightly together. Add cream sauce and blend carefully. Using a No. 12 ice cream scoop, dip mixture in portions.

Pat out each portion into a cake 2½-in. in diameter and ¾ in. thick. Brush a bun pan with oil or melted shortening. Place cakes in pan. Brush top of cakes with melted shortening.

Broil 5 min. Turn cakes and broil another 5 min.

Serve with cole slaw.

NOTE: Crab cakes should have a loose appearance so that the lumps of crab meat show. Handle carefully. If preferred, the cakes may be breaded and fried in deep fat.

NEW ENGLAND CODFISH CAKES

YIELD: 83 portions, 6-oz. size

INGREDIENTS

Dried Salt Codfish	9 lb.
Potatoes, A. P.	30 lb.
Eggs	30
Fine Bread Crumbs	1 cup
Black Pepper	1 tsp.
Baking Powder	1 tsp.

METHOD

Soak codfish strips in hot water 30 min. Bring to simmering point; drain very thoroughly. Put codfish through grinder.

Peel, boil, and drain potatoes. Mash in power mixer. Add eggs, codfish, crumbs, pepper and baking powder. Beat in power mixer until light and thoroughly blended.

Cool mixture. Drop by spoonful (2 oz. each) into 375°F. fat. Fry until a golden brown. Drain on brown unglazed paper.

Serve 3 to the order, with or without sauce. Garnish with parsley or watercress.

ITALIAN DIAVOLO

YIELD: 25 servings

INGREDIENTS

Linguine	4 lb.
Rock Lobster Tails (4 oz. each)	12
Shrimp, medium	4 lb.
Crabmeat, flaked	4 lb.
Garlic, chopped	4 cloves
Olive Oil	1½ cup
Plum Tomatoes, canned	3 qt.
Red Pepper Seeds, crushed	1½ tsp.
Oregano, crumbled	1 tbsp.
Salt and Pepper	

METHOD

Cook linguine in boiling salted water until firm but tender.

Drop lobster tails into boiling salted water. When water reboils, cook 5 min. Drain and drench with cold water. Cut away underside membrane and remove meat. Dice.

Cook shrimp in boiling salted water until they turn pink. Drain, shell and devein.

Saute garlic in olive oil. Add tomatoes, red pepper and oregano. Simmer sauce for 20 min. Stir occasionally. Add lobsters, shrimp and crab meat. Season to taste with salt and pepper.

Put linguine into individual casseroles and top with seafood sauce. Sprinkle with grated Parmesan cheese.

Serve with bread sticks and a tossed salad.

Fish Portions

FISH FLORENTINE
YIELD: 25 servings
INGREDIENTS

Fish Portions, breaded	25
Spinach, cooked, chopped, drained	3 qt.
Stroganoff Sauce, made from mix	2 qt.
Parmesan Cheese, grated	1¾ cup

METHOD
Prepare fish portions according to package directions.

    Into each individual casserole put ½ cup hot spinach. Top with fish portions and 1/3 cup stroganoff sauce.

    Sprinkle top with 1 tbsp. cheese. Put under broiler and broil until top is golden brown.

    Serve casserole with tossed salad and chunks of crusty bread.

OLD ENGLISH FISH AND CHIPS BATTER
(White Spot)
YIELD: Approx. 5 gal.
INGREDIENTS
Fish Batter

All-Purpose Flour	20 lb.
Baking Powder	1¾ cup
Salt	6 tbsp.
Sugar	2-1/8 cup
Milk	3 gal.
Eggs	24

METHOD
Weigh 2 lb. of the flour with the baking powder, salt and sugar. Sift. Weigh the remaining 18 lb. flour into three 6-lb. lots.

    Pour milk into large power-mixer bowl. Start power mixer on speed No. 2. Add the first lot of flour with the baking powder, salt and sugar. Mix well. Separately add the three remaining lots of flour mixing well after each addition.

    Break eggs into a large measure, and gradually add to the flour and milk mixture.

    Increase speed to No. 3 when the mixture reaches the non-splash consistency. When smooth, pour into cans, and keep refrigerated until ready to use.

    Cut cod or halibut into pieces 2½ by 2½ in. Dip in batter. Drain. Place fillets in frying basket.

    Fry in deep fat at 375°F. until a golden brown. Drain on unglazed brown paper.

    Allow 4 oz.—3 or 4 fish sticks—per serving. Serve with potato chips.

BREADED FISH STEAKS—CHINESE STYLE
YIELD: 24 servings
INGREDIENTS

Frozen Breaded Fish Steak Portions	8 lb.
Salt	4 tsp.
Vinegar	2 cup
Sugar	4 cup
Water	5-1/3 cup
Chicken Bouillon Cubes	12
Green Peppers, large, cut into strips	4
Pineapple Chunks, canned, drained	4 cup
Cornstarch	¾ cup
Water	6 tbsp.
Soy Sauce	2 tbsp.

METHOD
Deep fry frozen fish portions at 375°F. for 3 to 5 min. Drain on absorbent paper.

    Combine vinegar, sugar, water, bouillon cubes, green pepper and pineapple. Simmer for 10 min.

    Combine cornstarch, water and soy sauce to make a thin paste. Add gradually to hot sauce and cook until thick, stirring constantly. Serve over fish.

FISH PORTIONS IN WINE SAUCE
YIELD: 32 servings
INGREDIENTS

Frozen Breaded Fish Portions	1 lb. pkg.
Fresh Mushrooms, sliced	4 cup
Butter	1 cup
Flour	4 cup
Basil	2 tsp.
Salt	2 tsp.
Pepper	dash
Milk	4 cup
White Wine	4 cup
Paprika	dash

METHOD
Saute mushrooms in butter 3 to 4 min. Blend in flour, basil, salt and pepper until smooth. Stir in milk and white wine and cook over medium heat until thickened.

    To broil frozen fish portions, preheat oven. Sprinkle portions with salt and pepper. Brush both sides with mixture of melted butter and lemon juice. Broil 5 min. on one side and 4 min. on other side. Take portions from broiler immediately.

    Arrange portions on serving platters. Pour sauce over fish and sprinkle top with paprika for color.

SUNSHINE FILLETS

YIELD: 25 portions
INGREDIENTS

Flounder Fillets or other thin Fish Fillets, fresh or frozen	7 lb. 8 oz.
Orange Juice Concentrate (frozen)	5 oz.
Butter or Margarine, melted	4 oz.
Salt	½ oz.
Nutmeg	1 tsp.

METHOD

Thaw fillets. Divide into portions, about 4½ oz. each. Place skin side down in a single layer on well-greased sheet pans.

Thaw orange juice. Combine orange juice, butter, and seasonings. Pour sauce over fish.

Bake at 350°F. (moderate oven) 20 to 30 min. or until fish flakes easily when tested with a fork.

BAKED HADDOCK FILLETS IN SPANISH SAUCE

YIELD: 50 servings (5 oz. fillets; 2 oz. sauce)
INGREDIENTS

Haddock Fillets (5 oz. each)	50
Prepared Chopped Onion	¾ cup (rounded)
Prepared Chopped Green Pepper	¼ cup (rounded)
Bay Leaves	2
Whole Cloves	2 tsp.
Peppercorns	2 tsp.
Tomatoes, canned, No. 10 can	1 can
Salt	3 tbsp.
Instant Granulated Garlic	½ tsp.
Butter or Margarine	12 oz.
Pimiento-Stuffed Spanish Green Olives, sliced	3 cup

METHOD

Rehydrate onion and green pepper. Drain and fluff.

Tie bay leaves, cloves and peppercorns in a cheesecloth bag. Add to tomatoes and heat to simmering. Stir in salt and instant granulated garlic.

Saute onions and green peppers in butter or margarine. Add to tomatoes. Simmer for 10 to 15 min. Stir in sliced olives.

Place haddock fillets on well-greased baking sheets. Remove cheesecloth bag of spices from sauce, and pour sauce over fish.

Bake at 400°F. for 15 to 20 min.

GOURMET FISH FILLETS

YIELD: 24 servings
INGREDIENTS

Fish Fillets (haddock, sea bass, white fish or halibut)	8 lb.
Lemon Juice	1 cup
Salt	1 tsp.
Cashew Nuts, coarsely chopped	4 cup
Cheddar Cheese, shredded	4 cup
Fine Dry Bread Crumbs	2 cup
Onion, finely minced	¾ cup
Cayenne Pepper	½ tsp.
Tomato Sauce	1 qt.
Melted Butter	½ cup
Sherry Wine or Dry White Wine	½ cup

METHOD

Marinate fish fillets in lemon juice and salt for 2 hrs. in refrigerator. Drain and place in well-greased baking pans.

Combine nuts, cheese, bread crumbs, onion and cayenne. Pour in tomato sauce mix. Cover fish with mixture.

Bake at 375°F. for 45 min., basting often. Garnish with whole cashews.

HOGATE'S BROILED FISHKABOBS
(Hogate's Seafood Restaurants, Washington, D. C.)

YIELD: 6 servings
INGREDIENTS

Scallops	36
Swordfish Chunks (approx. 1-in. each)	12
Fresh Salmon Chunks (approx. 1-in. each)	12
Green Pepper Pieces (1-in. pieces)	48
Small White Canned Onions	48
Thyme	2 tbsp.
Oregano	2 tbsp.
Salt	¼ cup
Black Pepper	2 tbsp.
Garlic Powder	2 tbsp.
Oil	

METHOD

Thread 3 scallops, 1 piece swordfish, 1 piece salmon, 4 pieces green pepper, and 4 white onions alternately on skewer.

Mix thyme, oregano, salt, black pepper, and garlic powder together and sprinkle on fishkabobs.

Arrange skewers in refrigerator dish; cover with oil. Refrigerate several hours. Drain.

Broil 4 in. from source of heat until fish flakes easily when tested with a fork and is attractively brown. Turn as needed.

Flounder

FILLET OF FLOUNDER WITH DILL STUFFING

YIELD: 50 servings
INGREDIENTS

Chopped Dehydrated Onions	1 cup
Water	1 cup
Dill Pickle Relish, drained (reserve liquid)	1¼ lb.
Soft Bread, cubed	2½ lb.
Green Pepper, diced	7 oz.
Salt	2½ tsp.
Pepper	½ tsp.
Butter or Margarine, melted	1¼ lb.
Eggs, beaten	3
Fillet of Flounder	16 lb.
Dill Pickle Relish Liquid	½ cup
Condensed Cream of Tomato Soup, undiluted, 51 oz. cans	2 cans

METHOD
Heat oven to 350°F.

Soak onions in water 20 min. Toss together onions, relish and next six ingredients.

Weigh out fillets at approx. 5 oz. each; sprinkle with salt. On each fillet, place a No. 16 dipper of stuffing; roll as jelly roll, secure with toothpicks. Place stuffed fillets in 2 baking pans (18- by 12- by 2-in.)

Add relish liquid to soup; pour over stuffed fillets.

Bake for 25 min. or until fish flakes easily with fork.

To serve, spoon sauce over each fillet; garnish with parsley.

FILLING FOR BAKED STUFFED FLOUNDER
(University of Miami, Coral Gables, Fla.)

INGREDIENTS

Bread Crumbs, fresh ground	1 qt.
Almonds, chopped toasted	¼ cup
Onions, chopped, sauteed until tender	5 oz.
Parsley, chopped	1 tsp.
Lime Juice	½ oz.
Eggs, whipped	3
Capers	1 level tsp.
Salt and Pepper	to taste

METHOD
Combine filling ingredients lightly. Roll 1 tbsp. filling in each 4 oz. fillet of flounder. Lay in buttered casserole and bake for 5 min.

Cover with 2 oz. mornay sauce and return to oven until brown.

Garnish with buttered parisienne potatoes and asparagus spears.

SEVEN SEAS STUFFED FLOUNDER
(Seven Seas Restaurant, Panama City, Fla.)

YIELD: 4 servings
INGREDIENTS

Flounder	4
Crab Meat, lump	1 lb.
Celery	1 stalk
Pepper	1 bell
Onion, medium	1

METHOD
Chop vegetables fine and mix with 1½ cups mayonnaise, 2 tbsp. prepared mustard and dash of cayenne pepper, garlic powder, worcestershire sauce, salt and pepper. Add 1 egg, slightly beaten and ½ lb. salted crackers, crumbled. Mix well, add crabmeat and toss.

Split the flounder down the thick side to the backbone and widen out. Put stuffing inside and garnish with 3 or 4 shrimps and paprika.

Place in well buttered pan and bake at about 450°F. 12 to 15 min. or until done. If not brown, place under broiler a couple of minutes.
NOTE: This same stuffing recipe may be made into fried crab patties.

FROGS' LEGS A L'AMERICAINE

INGREDIENTS

Frogs Legs, frozen	1 lb.
Flour	1½ cup
Salt	¼ tsp.
Pepper	as needed
Baking Powder	¼ tsp.
Egg	1
Water	¾-1 cup

METHOD
Thaw frogs' legs.

Sift dry ingredients into bowl. Break egg on top and gradually beat in water with a whisk.

Dip frogs' legs in batter and deep fry at 385°F.

Serve two per portion.

FROG LEGS MANIER

YIELD: 1 serving
INGREDIENTS

Frog Legs	2
Butter	2 tbsp.
Garlic	1 clove

METHOD
Saute 2 jumbo frog legs about 6 or 8 min. in 2 tbsp. butter to which has been added one clove of garlic, crushed.

Fry until golden brown.

FISH STICKS PARMIGIANA
YIELD: 6 servings
INGREDIENTS

Chili Sauce	½ cup
Olive Oil	1 tsp.
Onion Salt	¼ tsp.
Garlic Salt	1/8 tsp.
Tabasco	dash
Mozzarella Cheese	¼ lb.
Fish Sticks	
Oregano	to taste

METHOD
Combine chili sauce with olive oil, onion salt, garlic salt and Tabasco.

Cut cheese into thin slivers about 3 in. long and ¼ in. thick.

Following directions on package, bake or broil fish sticks up to point of turning. Remove from oven; turn fish sticks and arrange half of them on top of remaining sticks. Top each pair with some of chili sauce mixture, then with sliver of cheese. Sprinkle with oregano. Finish baking or broiling as label directs.

FISH STICKS WITH HOT TARTAR SAUCE
YIELD: 25 servings
INGREDIENTS

Fish Sticks	100
White Sauce, seasoned, made from mix	2 qt.
Pickle Relish, well drained	1¾ cup
Parsley, chopped	1¾ cup
Stuffed Olives, chopped	1¾ cup
Cooked Rice	1 gal. plus cup

METHOD
Prepare fish sticks according to package directions.

Heat white sauce and stir in remaining ingredients.

For each serving put 4 fish sticks on top of ¾ cup cooked rice. Spoon ½ cup of sauce over sticks. Garnish with parsley and green beans.

SEA-GOING DIP
(Ship's Haven, Lynnfield, Mass.)
YIELD: Approx. 1 lb.
INGREDIENTS

Shrimp, cut into tiny pieces	1 lb. can (or fresh)
Eggs, hard boiled, chopped very fine	4
Chili Sauce	2 tbsp.
Lemon Juice	¼ tsp.
Onion or Garlic Salt	to taste
Mayonnaise	enough to bind
Salt and White Pepper	to taste

METHOD
This should be a thick spread. Serve in a pretty bowl and surround on platter with party rye bread and chips. This can be made a few days ahead.

BAKED FILLET OF FRESH FLORIDA RED SNAPPER—A LA CREOLE
(Henrici's, Inc. Restaurant)
YIELD: 100 portions
INGREDIENTS
1. Creole Sauce

Butter	1½ cup
Celery, diced	1 gal.
Green Peppers, diced	2½ qt.
Green Olives, chopped	48
Fresh Mushrooms, sliced	2¾ qt.
Canned Whole Tomatoes, No. 10	2 can
Tomato Puree, No. 10	½ can
Consomme	1 qt.
Worcestershire Sauce	2 tbsp.
Hot Pepper Sauce	½ tsp.
Garlic Juice	¼ tsp.
Sugar	2 tbsp.
Salt	1½ tbsp.
Pepper	1 tsp.
Cornstarch	1½ cup
Cold Water	1½ cup

2. Fresh Florida Snapper

	100 lb.
Salt	to season
Salad Oil	
Paprika	

METHOD
Saute celery, green peppers, olives and mushrooms in the butter. Add the next 9 ingredients, and bring mixture to a boil. Mix cornstarch and water and combine with other ingredients. Boil 5 min. Reduce heat and simmer gently 30 min.

Wipe fish with damp cloth, and fillet into 8-oz. portions. Place red snapper fillets on greased baking sheet. Sprinkle with salt, salad oil and paprika.

Bake in a 375°F. oven 10 min. or until fillets are done.

Serve immediately.

Allow 2 oz. creole sauce for each individual serving. Garnish with parsleyed lemon wedges.

SHRIMP BEAN SALAD
For this distinctive Meal-in-a-Dish Salad, use cooked great northern beans instead of the potatoes in your favorite potato salad recipe and add shrimp.

Halibut

BAKED NORTH PACIFIC HALIBUT WITH ALASKA KING CRAB DRESSING, TOMATO SAUCE

YIELD: 50 portions
INGREDIENTS

North Pacific Halibut fletch, cut in 5 oz. portions	50
Alaska King Crab Dressing*	3 qt.
Melted Butter	8 oz.
Salt	to taste
Pepper	to taste
Tomato Sauce	1 gal.

METHOD
Cut a pocket in each fillet and fill cavity with 2 oz. of dressing. Place filet in baking pan and dribble with melted butter. Season with salt and pepper.

Bake at 350°F. oven for approx. 20 min. until fish flakes, but is moist.

Spoon tomato sauce on serving dish; place baked halibut in center.

*Alaska King Crab Dressing

Alaska King Crab Meat	1½ lb.
Onion, chopped	8 oz.
Celery, chopped	8 oz.
Butter, melted	1 lb.
Bread Crumbs	4 lb.
Lemon Juice	4 oz.
Salt	to taste
Pepper	to taste
Marjoram	1 oz.
Parsley	½ cup

METHOD
Saute onion and celery until golden. Combine all ingredients and mix well.

NORTH PACIFIC HALIBUT POLYNESIAN

YIELD: 3 qt.
INGREDIENTS

North Pacific Halibut Fillets	100
Soy Sauce, Japanese (Shoyu)	1 qt.
Pineapple Juice, Syrup from Canned Peaches, half and half	1 qt.
Water	1 qt.
Vinegar	1½ cup
Granulated Sugar	3 lb.
Ginger, ground	2 tsp.
Garlic, fresh	3 clove

METHOD
Mix all liquid ingredients thoroughly, then mash garlic, combine it with the ginger, and add to liquid ingredients. Simmer mixture for 20 min.; strain and store until needed.

Baste liberally with the sauce while pan-frying the halibut steaks on both sides. Sauce gives them a beautiful golden brown appearance when served.

HALIBUT, POACHED FILLET AU GRATIN
(Malahat Chalet)

YIELD: 25 portions
INGREDIENTS

Halibut, cut 4 oz. portions	25
Salt and Pepper	to season
Milk	1 qt.
Butter	4 tbsp.
Canadian Cheddar Cheese, cut in slices	25
Paprika	few dashes

METHOD
Fillet halibut in 4-oz. pieces. Season with salt and pepper. Place fillets in well-greased bake pan. Pour milk over fish.

Cut cheese in pieces the size of the halibut fillets. Top each fillet with a slice of cheese. Sprinkle lightly with paprika.

Bake in 375°F. oven 35 min. or until the fish flakes easily with a fork.

GRILLED HALIBUT ORIENTAL

YIELD: 25 servings
INGREDIENTS

Halibut Steaks, fresh or frozen, 6 oz. portions	25
Salt	1½ tsp.
Pepper	1½ tsp.
Garlic Powder	¼ tsp.
Ground Ginger	1 tbsp.
Peanut Oil or other vegetable oil	2¼ cup
Vinegar	1 cup
Soy Sauce	2 tbsp.

METHOD
If halibut is frozen, thaw it at room temperature until it is no longer icy.

Prepare basting sauce by measuring salt, pepper, garlic powder and ginger into bowl. Add 6 tbsp. oil and 6 tbsp. vinegar. Beat with a wire whisk. Add ¾ cup oil and 6 tbsp. vinegar and beat again. Add remaining oil, vinegar and soy sauce and beat until well mixed.

Arrange halibut steaks on greased grill. Brush liberally with sauce and grill about 5 min. on each side, brushing frequently with sauce.

Serve with french fries, tossed green salad, rolls and butter.

HALIBUT FLORENTINE IN CASSEROLE
(Tarantino's)
YIELD: 1 casserole (Use 10-in. Welsh Rarebit dish)
INGREDIENTS

Halibut Steak	6-8 oz.
or	
Halibut Fillet	5-6 oz.
Water, hot	½ cup
Spinach	2 oz.
Green Onion, chopped	1 tbsp.
Lemon Juice	4 tbsp.
White Wine	1 oz.
Cream Sauce, heavy, hot	¼ cup
Egg Yolk	1
Cheese, nippy, grated	1 oz.
Salt	to season
Pepper	to season

METHOD
Place halibut in shallow casserole or saucepan. Add water and lemon juice. Simmer gently 5 min. Add white wine. Simmer 2 min. longer or until flavors are blended. (The simmering should reduce the liquid to about two-thirds its volume.)

Remove halibut from heat. Drain off the stock. Combine stock with the heavy cream sauce; stir until thoroughly smooth. Add chopped spinach and onion. Season with salt and pepper.

Bring sauce to boiling point. Remove from heat. Pour some of the hot sauce over the beaten egg yolk. Combine with rest of sauce. (This is now Sauce Florentine.)

Pour Florentine Sauce over halibut. Sprinkle with grated cheese.

Bake in 375°F. oven until cheese is melted and sauce is bubbly. Serve hot in dish in which it has been cooked.

HALIBUT TOKAY
YIELD: 25 servings
INGREDIENTS

Halibut Steaks, fresh or frozen, 6 oz. portions	25
Chopped Onion	1 cup
Salt	4 tsp.
Pepper	½ tsp.
Butter or Margarine	¾ cup
Lemon Juice	½ cup
Rose Wine	1 pt.
Flour	½ cup
Light Cream	1 qt.
Tokay Grapes, seeded	1 qt.

METHOD
If halibut is frozen, let stand at room temperature about 30 min. to defrost.

Sprinkle onion in bottom of buttered baking dish. Place halibut steaks over onions in dish; sprinkle with salt and pepper and dot with half of the butter. Pour lemon juice and wine over fish. Cover dish with aluminum foil and bake in a preheated moderate oven (350°F.) 15 to 20 min. or until fish flakes easily when tested with a fork.

Meanwhile melt the remaining butter in a saucepan; stir in flour.

When fish is cooked, remove baking dish from oven and reset oven to broil. Drain juices from fish and reserve.

Gradually pour juices into butter-flour mixture in saucepan, stirring constantly. Stir in light cream and cook while stirring until slightly thickened. Add grapes and cook just long enough to heat grapes. Spoon sauce over portion of fish.

Put fish under broiler and broil until lightly browned. Serve garnished with finely chopped parsley. Complete entree with rice, glazed carrots and a heart of lettuce salad.

NOTE: Fish steak can be placed in an individual casserole and covered with sauce and then broiled as needed.

SEAFOOD AU GRATIN
(The Frances Virginia Tea Room)
YIELD: 24 portions
INGREDIENTS

Shrimp, cooked, cleaned	1 lb.
Crabmeat	1 lb.
Fish, cooked, flaked	1 lb.
Egg Noodles, medium, cooked	1½ qt.
Cream Sauce	1½ gal.
Nippy Cheese	12 oz.
Bread Crumbs	2½ cup
Butter	3 oz.

METHOD
Place a bed of cooked noodles in the bottom of each individual greased shallow casserole or scallop shell. Put equal portions of each fish on top of the noodles. Cover with medium cream sauce.

Sprinkle each casserole with ½ oz. of grated nippy cheese. Top with bread crumbs. Sprinkle with paprika. Pour melted butter over crumbs.

Bake in a 350 to 375°F. oven until seafood mixture bubbles and crumbs are browned—approx. 20 to 25 min.

Lobster

LOBSTER STEW
YIELD: 2¾ gal.
INGREDIENTS

Diced Lobster Meat	3 lb.
Butter	9 oz.
Liquid Non-Dairy Creamer*	1 gal.
Onion, chopped	12 oz.
Reconstituted Instant Non-Fat Dry Milk	1 gal.
Clam Broth	1 qt.
Chopped Parsley	1 cup
Basil	2 tbsp.
Salt	1 tbsp.

METHOD
Saute lobster in butter.

Heat liquid non-dairy creamer with onions until hot; add lobster. Add instant non-fat dry milk, clam broth, parsley, basil and salt. Heat thoroughly. Serve.

*Reliquefied according to package directions.

BAKED STUFFED LOBSTER SHELL
(LOBSTER, SHRIMP AND CRAB MEAT AU GRATIN)
(Miller Bros.)
YIELD: 10 portions - 1 lb. stuffed lobster shell
INGREDIENTS

Lobster Meat	2½ lb.
Scallops, cooked	2½ lb.
Shrimp, cooked	2½ lb.
Crab Meat	2½ lb.
Butter (1 cup)	½ lb.
Flour	3 cup
Milk, rich	2 qt.
Salt	to season
Pepper, white, freshly ground	to season
Nippy Cheese, grated	6 cup
Bread Crumbs	4 cup

METHOD
Make cream sauce using butter, flour, milk, pepper and salt. When thoroughly cooked, stir in 1 lb. of grated cheese. Combine seafood and add to cream sauce.

Fill lobster shells with mixture being careful to place an equal amount of each seafood in each shell. Sprinkle top with bread crumbs. Top with remainder of the cheese.

Place in a 425°F. oven and bake 10 to 15 min. or until cheese is melted and slightly browned.

CREAMED LOBSTER AND MACARONI WITH SHERRY WINE AND CHEESE
(Parker House, Boston)
YIELD: 30 8-oz. size casseroles
INGREDIENTS

Macaroni, uncooked	2 lb.
Lobster Meat	4 lb.
Butter	8 oz.
Paprika	4 oz.
Cream Sauce	3 qt.
Salt	to season
Pepper, white	to season
Sherry Wine	10 oz.
Parmesan Cheese	10 oz.
Butter, melted	8 oz.

METHOD
Cook macaroni in rapidly boiling water until tender. Drain, wash.

Cut lobster meat in ½ in. pieces. Saute in butter 5 min. Add paprika and cream sauce and blend well. Then add sherry wine. Fold in cooked macaroni. Season with salt and pepper. Remove from heat.

Place the lobster-macaroni mixture in individual greased casserole dishes, or in one large casserole. Sprinkle with parmesan cheese. Pour melted butter over top of cheese, allowing about 1½ tsp. for each individual casserole.

Bake in 350°F. oven until cheese is lightly browned.

SEAFOOD PANCAKES
(A specialty at The Village Nook, West Englewood, N. J., served with a spiced peach and a simple salad.)
YIELD: Filling for 20 pancakes
INGREDIENTS

Pancakes, from mix	20
Butter or Margarine	1 cup
Flour	1 cup
Monosodium Glutamate with Lemon Flavor	1 tbsp.
Prepared Mustard	1 tbsp.
Salt	1 tbsp.
Cayenne Pepper	½ tsp.
Milk	2 qt.
Lobster Meat, Shrimp, or Crabmeat, cooked	2 qt.

METHOD
Melt butter. Blend in flour, monosodium glutamate with lemon flavor, mustard, salt and cayenne. Gradually stir in milk. Cook, stirring constantly, until mixture thickens and comes to a boil.

Add seafood; heat through.

RIJSTAFEL-CURRY OF LOBSTER, SHRIMP, CRAB MEAT WITH SHERRY AND SAFFRON RICE PILAW
(Pump Room, Ambassador East)

YIELD: 25 portions

INGREDIENTS

Lobster Meat, cooked	2 lb.
Shrimp, whole, cooked	2 lb.
Lump Crab Meat	2 lb.
Curry Sauce	1½ gal.
Cream (18%)	1½ pt.
Sherry Wine	1 cup
Butter	8 oz.
Salt	to season

METHOD

Cut cooked lobster meat into ½-in. pieces.

Boil shrimp, shell and clean. Leave whole.

Heat crab meat separately, in oven so as not to break it too much.

Cook lobster and shrimp in butter for 5 min. Add cream, sherry wine and crabmeat. Mix gently. Keep at low heat for 2 min. Season to taste.

Serve with Saffron Rice Pilaw.

Rijstafel-Curry Sauce

Butter	1 lb.
Onion, chopped	2 cup
Celery, diced	½ cup
Apples, diced	1 cup
Garlic Clove, minced	1
Bay Leaves	2
Whole Black Peppercorns	6
Whole Cloves	4
Flour	¾ lb.
Curry Powder	4 tbsp.
Chicken Broth, hot	1½ gal.
Sugar	1 tsp.
Lemon Juice	4 tbsp.
Worcestershire Sauce	1 tbsp.
Salt	to season

METHOD

In the melted butter, cook the next seven ingredients 8 min.

Mix curry powder with the flour, and stir into the butter mixture. Cook slowly 5 min. Add chicken stock, stirring constantly. Cook 15 min. Add sugar, lemon juice, worcestershire sauce, and salt. Stir thoroughly.

Pour through a fine strainer (china cap).

Rijstafel-Saffron Rice Pilaw

Rice, long-grained	2 lb.
Chicken Stock	2 qt.
Onion, finely chopped	1 cup
Butter	4 oz.
Saffron	½ tsp.
Salt	to season

METHOD

Wash rice and dry in towel.

Melt butter, add onion and cook 2 min. Add rice; cook 5 min., stirring frequently. Add hot stock, saffron and salt. Bring to boiling point. Cover saucepan, and cook in 375°F. oven until rice is tender, with most of the broth absorbed.

Spread cooked rice in flat pan. Place in a 300°F. oven until any remaining liquid evaporates, and rice is light and fluffy.

PECKETT'S ON SUGAR HILL SEAFOOD CASSEROLE

YIELD: 25 servings

INGREDIENTS

Scallops	1½ lb.
Scallop Liquor	1 to 2 cup
Fresh Crab Meat	1½ lb.
Fresh Lobster Meat, diced	2 lb.
Butter	4 oz.
Flour	1 cup
Milk	3 qt.
Heavy Cream	2 cup
Sherry	1 cup
Salt	to season
Pepper	to season
Cheese, grated	2 cup
Bread Crumbs	2½ cup
Butter	4 oz.

METHOD

Put scallops in pan with barely enough cold water to cover. Bring to boiling point; reduce heat, simmer 2 min. Remove from heat. Drain scallops. Reserve liquor.

Remove any small pieces of shell from crab meat.

Boil lobster for the time prescribed according to weight. Remove flesh from shell and cut in large pieces.

Make cream sauce with the butter, flour, milk, and scallop liquor. When thoroughly cooked, add the heavy cream. (Important not to add the cream till now.) Add lobster, scallops and crabmeat to the sauce. Season with salt and pepper. Add sherry.

Place mixture in buttered baking dish or in individual casserole dishes. Sprinkle top with grated cheese. Top with bread crumbs. Dot over with butter. Sprinkle with paprika.

Bake in 350°F. oven until cheese is melted and crumbs are brown—about 30 min.

Oysters

HANGTOWN FRY
(Tarantino's, San Francisco)
YIELD: 1 portion
INGREDIENTS

Oysters (15 Olympias or 5 blue points)	1/3 cup
Fine Crumbs or Prepared Meal	1/3 cup
Enriched Flour	3 tbsp.
Eggs, slightly beaten	2 or 3
Cold Water	1 tbsp.
Bacon	2 strips
Salt and Pepper	to season

METHOD
Drain and strain oysters.

Combine crumbs or meal and enriched flour. Dip oysters in mixture. (If preferred, dip oysters in egg mixture and crumb again).

Fry oysters in butter until a golden brown, being careful not to get butter too hot. Pour off most of butter, or remove oysters to second heated frying pan.

Grill 2 strips bacon until crisp. Add to pan with oysters.

Add cold water to eggs and beat slightly. Pour over oysters and bacon in pan. Cook until eggs are set.

Fold like an omelet or serve in circular shape on heated plate with french fried potatoes; add parsley or watercress, lemon wedge.

BIENVILLE SAUCE FOR OYSTERS
(Commander's Palace, New Orleans)
YIELD: Sauce for 12 doz. oysters
INGREDIENTS

Bacon	¼ lb.
Mushrooms, sliced	8 oz.
Garlic, chopped	8 clove
Butter	¼ lb.
Shallots, chopped	½ bunch
Milk, hot	3 qt.
Oyster Juice	1 pt.
Sherry Wine	1 cup
Lemon Juice	1 cup
Parsley, chopped	½ cup
Flour	2 cup
Shrimp, boiled (cut)	1 lb.
Egg Color	½ tsp.

METHOD
Cut bacon into small pieces, fry until brown; add sliced mushrooms and cook until they are brown. Add garlic, cook until done but not brown; add butter, let butter melt and add flour, blend and cook slowly for 5 min.; add hot milk and stir until thick.

Add egg coloring, small cut shrimp, oyster juice, lemon juice, sherry wine and chopped parsley.

Cook slowly for 15 min.

OYSTER AND CORN CASSEROLE
YIELD: 65 4-oz. servings. Size pan: 12-in. by 20-in.
INGREDIENTS

Oysters, standard	1 qt.
Corn, cream-style, No. 10 can	1 can
Whole Kernel Corn, No. 10 can	2 qt.
Milk	1 qt.
Salt	1 tbsp.
Pepper	to season
Cracker Crumbs	1 qt.
Butter	5 oz.

METHOD
Heat milk and oyster liquor. Add oysters to scalded milk and cook until edges curl.

Butter cracker crumbs. Remove oysters from milk. Add corn and one-half the buttered crumbs to the milk. Season with salt and pepper.

Place one-half of the remaining buttered cracker crumbs on the bottom of a greased casserole dish or bake pan. Place alternate layers of other ingredients on top of crumbs, by first adding one-half of the corn-milk mixture, then a layer of oysters, followed by the remaining corn-milk mixture.

Top with the rest of the buttered crumbs.
Bake in 375°F. oven until crumbs are golden brown (approx. 35 min.).

BAKED OYSTERS WITH CRABMEAT AU GRATIN
YIELD: 2 servings
INGREDIENTS

Butter	2 oz.
Shallots, chopped	2
Oysters, freshly opened	12
Crabmeat Lumps	6 oz.
Dry White Wine	2 oz.
Medium Cream Sauce	1 cup
Parmesan Cneese, grated	1 oz.
Chives, chopped	2 tsp.
Hot Pepper Sauce	dash
Salt and Pepper	to taste

METHOD
Put the butter and shallots in a small pan with the oysters and simmer slowly, until the oysters are half done. Add the crabmeat and wine and cook until the wine is completely absorbed. Add the cream sauce and mix thoroughly. Add remaining ingredients.

Place in skillet and bake in 350°F. oven until top is browned.

FRIED OYSTERS

Pour breader into a large shallow breader pan. Dust oysters by tossing into a pan of dry batter mix. Shake off excess duster. (NOTE: Dusting is optional. If dusted, the oysters take on a heavier coating, are more attractive in color and stay crisp longer. If not dusted, there is a more distinctive oyster flavor.)

Blend together 1 lb. batter mix and 1 qt. water. Coat dusted or undusted oysters with batter. Drain excess batter.

Immediately toss batter-coated oysters into breader. Press breader into the oyster with palm of hand to flatten oyster. This results in a more attractive fried oyster.

Fry in deep fat at 350°F. to 375°F. 1½ to 2 min.

ISLAND HOTEL SEAFOOD BISQUE
(Island Hotel, Cedar Key, Fla.)

YIELD: 6 servings
INGREDIENTS

Crabmeat, fresh	½ lb.
Shrimps, fresh or frozen	½ lb.
Oysters, raw	½ pt.
Stock, chicken	1 pt.
Cream, heavy	½ pt.
Milk, whole	½ pt.
Butter or Margarine	2 tbsp.
Worcestershire Sauce	½ tsp.
Pepper, cayenne	dash
Nutmeg	dash
Sherry, dry	3 tbsp.

METHOD

Combine in a large saucepan the chicken stock, cream, milk, juice from oysters, butter, worcestershire sauce, and pepper. Bring to simmer but do not boil. Set aside.

Flake crabmeat with fork. Peel and coarsely chop shrimp. Very small oysters may be used whole, otherwise quarter or halve into bite size pieces. Add seafoods to liquid and return to stove.

Simmer for 15 min. Remove from fire, add sherry and dash of nutmeg. Serve hot.

Garnish tureen or individual soup bowls with sprinkle of paprika.

SOUTH AFRICAN SOUFFLE SANDWICHES

YIELD: 12 open-face sandwiches
INGREDIENTS

South African Rock Lobster Tails (3-4 oz. ea.)	6
Mayonnaise	½ cup
Parmesan Cheese, grated	¼ cup
Egg Yolks	2
Egg Whites, beaten till stiff	2
Round White Bread Slices	12

METHOD

Drop frozen South African rock lobster tails into boiling salted water. When water reboils, cook for 3-5 min. Drain immediately, drench with cold water and cut away underside membrane. Remove meat in one piece and cut into 1-in. crosswise slices.

Mix mayonnaise with parmesan cheese and egg yolks. Fold in beaten egg whites. On a cookie sheet in broiler, toast slices of bread on one side. Turn and arrange rock lobster pieces on untoasted side of the bread. Cover slices with mayonnaise mixture. Return to broiler, six inches away from the source of heat. Broil until golden brown.

Serve at once, garnished with parsley and radish roses.

GOURMET STUFFED ROCK LOBSTER

YIELD: 6 portions
INGREDIENTS

South African Rock Lobster Tails (4 oz. tails)	6
Butter	6 tbsp.
Dry Mustard	2 tbsp.
Worcestershire Sauce	2 tsp.
Lime Juice	3 tbsp.
Mango Chutney, chopped	6 tbsp.
Salted Peanuts, finely chopped	½ cup
Grated Parmesan Cheese	as needed

METHOD

Drop frozen lobster tails into kettle of boiling, salted water. After 1 min., remove tails from kettle, drench with cold water, cut away underside membrane and carefully remove meat from shell. Reserve shells. Cut up rock lobster meat, which will be translucent and only partly cooked, into small pieces.

In heavy skillet, melt butter, add mustard, worcestershire sauce and lime juice. Stir in chopped chutney. Add rock lobster pieces and peanuts. Saute very slowly until heated through.

Stuff shells with mixture, sprinkle lightly with grated parmesan cheese and quickly brown under broiler.

Salmon

BAKED FILLET OF SALMON, SAGE DRESSING
(Ivan's Acres of Clams Restaurant, Seattle)

YIELD: 8 portions

INGREDIENTS

Celery, diced	1½ cup
Onion, diced	1½ cup
Bread Crumbs, dried	
Bacon, minced	4 slices
Eggs	4
Chicken Stock	1 cup
Sherry Wine	¼ cup
Salt	1/8 tsp.
Pepper	1/8 tsp.
Monosodium Glutamate	¼ tsp.
Sage	½ tsp.
Salmon Fillets	8

METHOD

Fry bacon. Add celery, onions and sage and saute until golden brown. Pour mix over bread crumbs; add eggs and seasoning; mix thoroughly. Blend in chicken stock and wine.

Spoon mixture into large baking dish. Sprinkle fillets with monosodium glutamate. Baste with wine and butter and arrange on dressing.

Bake 30 min. in 350°F. oven.

Serve with cole slaw.

BAKED SALMON AND MACARONI

YIELD: 60 6-oz. servings or 90 4-oz. servings

INGREDIENTS

Monosodium Glutamate	1 tbsp.
Elbow Macaroni	4 lb.
Pink Salmon	1 4-lb. can
All Purpose Sauce Base	2 lb.
Hot Water	4½ qt.
Process American Cheese	2 lb.
Tomato Slices	as needed
Butter, melted	2 oz.
Cracker Meal	4 oz.
Parmesan Cheese, grated	2 oz.
Monosodium Glutamate	1 tsp.

METHOD

Add 1 tbsp. monosodium glutamate to boiling, salted water. Cook macaroni in water until just tender. Drain and blanch in cold water.

Drain salmon, reserving liquid. Break up meat and divide evenly into two 12½- by 20-in. pans along with cooked macaroni.

Stir all purpose sauce base into hot water. Bring to a boil and simmer for 5 min. When thickened and smooth, add some liquid drained from salmon. Dice or shred American cheese and add to hot sauce, stirring until melted.

Pour over mixture in pans and mix well. Place tomato slices on top of mix. Prepare crumbs using butter cracker meal, cheese and monosodium glutamate and sprinkle over tomatoes. Brown under broiler or in oven.

SALMON FIESTA

YIELD: 24 servings

INGREDIENTS

Canned Salmon	4 1-lb. can
Eggs	8
Onions, medium, finely chopped	4
Dry Mustard	4 tsp.
Worcestershire Sauce	4 tsp.
Packaged Seasoned Bread Dressing Mix	6 cup
Shortening	½ cup
Condensed Tomato Soup	46-oz. can
Dairy Sour Cream	1 qt.

METHOD

Drain salmon, reserving 1-1/3 cups of the liquid. Remove skin and bone from salmon and flake with a fork.

Beat eggs; add the 1-1/3 cups liquid, onion, mustard, worcestershire sauce and bread dressing mix. Mix in salmon; shape into balls. Brown salmon balls in hot shortening, turning frequently.

Blend soup and sour cream; pour over salmon balls in skillet. Cover and heat over low heat to serving temperature, but do not boil.

Serve with confetti rice.

Confetti Rice

Combine 3 qt. hot cooked rice, 1 cup melted butter, 1 cup each chopped parsley and pimiento.

DILL SAUCE FOR SALMON
(Bit of Sweden, Chicago)

YIELD: 1 pt. approx.

INGREDIENTS

Sour Cream	2 cup
Salad Dressing	¼ cup
Milk	½ cup
Dry Mustard	2 tsp.
Medium Onion	½
Brown Sugar	2 tsp.
Dill Seed	4 tsp.
White Vinegar	½ cup
Cucumber, chopped	1 cup
Allspice	½ tsp.
Salt	to taste

METHOD

Combine all ingredients in order listed. This sauce is served on the smorgasbord; also as accompaniment to poached salmon.

Scallops

SAVORY NEW BEDFORD SCALLOPS
YIELD: 48 servings, approx. 4-oz.
INGREDIENTS

Scallops	14 lb.
Flour	2 cup
Olive Oil	3 cup
Garlic Cloves, large	7-8
Parsley, minced	1 cup
Salt	to season
Coarse Ground Black Pepper	to season
Lemons	6

METHOD
If scallops are frozen, defrost. Rinse and dry well. Roll in flour.

Half the olive oil may be replaced by the same amount vegetable oil or melted shortening, if desired. At least half the oil should be olive oil for flavor. Heat oil.

Add scallops and cook quickly in the hot oil, tossing and turning to coat and cook on all sides. Add some garlic and parsley to each panful of scallops as they cook.

Remove scallops to warm baking pan and keep hot until ready to serve. Sprinkle generously with salt and pepper. Serve with a lemon wedge.

This recipe is best cooked 1/3 at a time (divide ingredients in 3—more or less—and cook in 3 pansful.) The bits of brown adhering to the pan are good scraped off with a spoon, drained and added to the scallops.

After cooking, only a small amount of oil should remain. Reduce still further by rapid heating; stir in flour and water to make a thin sauce; season with hot prepared mustard. Salt to taste. Serve with scallops as Garlic-Mustard Sauce.

Coarse Grind Black Pepper is suggested to give a gourmet touch that regular pepper lacks.

Serve these savory scallops with a side dish of tartar sauce and crisp toast crackers. Or serve with a small portion of hot Chinese mustard for dipping.

A simple green salad, or sliced tomatoes and cucumbers with a tart dressing, makes a good flavor combination with this dish. Suggest a very light dessert.

Relishes such as black olives, melon rind pickles, sweet-sour cucumber slices are good with these scallops.

SCALLOP THERMIDOR OR COQUILLES ST. JACQUES
(Mr. Donald Fleming, Fleming's Cafeteria, St. Louis, received the Gourmet Award Plaque from the Missouri Restaurant Assn. for this seafood dish.)
YIELD: 25 ½-cup portions
INGREDIENTS

Scallops, fresh or frozen	5 lb.
Boiling Water	3 qt.
Salt	2½ oz.
Butter or other Fat	6 oz.
All-Purpose Flour, sifted	4 oz.
Salt	1 tbsp.
Powdered Mustard	1½ tsp.
Cayenne Pepper	¼ tsp.
Hot Milk	1½ qt.
Mushroom Stems and Pieces, drained	1½ (8-oz.) can
Parsley, chopped	½ cup
Grated Parmesan Cheese	3 oz.

METHOD
Thaw frozen scallops. Remove any shell particles and wash. Place in boiling salted water. Cover and return to the boiling point. Simmer for 3 to 4 min. depending on size; drain.

Chop scallops coarsely. Melt butter; blend in flour, salt, mustard and cayenne pepper. Stir into hot milk. Cook until thick, stirring constantly. Add mushrooms, parsley and scallops.

Portion scallop mixture with a No. 8 scoop (½ cup) into well-greased individual shells. Place about 1½ tsp. cheese over each serving. Sprinkle with paprika.

Bake at 400°F. for 15 to 20 min. until cheese browns.

SCALLOPS ROADHOUSE
(The Ambassador Hotel, Chicago)
YIELD: 1 portion
INGREDIENTS

Scallops	12
Green Pepper	½
Red Pepper	½
Salt	to taste
White Wine	2 tbsp.

METHOD
Wash and clean scallops. Cut red and green peppers into ½-in. squares. Salt lightly and saute scallops and peppers together until tender. Season to taste. Sprinkle with white wine.

Serve on toast with longbranch potatoes.

Nautical

SCALLOPS AU GRATIN VIRGINIA
(Cape Cod Room, The Drake, Chicago)

YIELD: 4 portions

INGREDIENTS

Bay Scallops	1½ pt.
Butter	¼ cup
Virginia Ham, cooked, cubed	¼ cup
Salt and Pepper	to season
Cream Sauce	¾ cup
Cream (30%)	¼ cup
Parmesan Cheese	6 tbsp.

METHOD

Saute scallops in butter until tender. Add cubed ham. Season with salt and pepper. Slowly stir in the cream sauce mixed with the heavy cream. Heat to boiling point. Adjust seasonings, if necessary.

Place mixture in individual serving dishes. Top with parmesan cheese.

Pop under broiler for 3 to 5 min.—until cheese is melted and sauce is bubbly.

BROILED SCALLOPS WITH VERMOUTH

YIELD: 12 servings (6 oz. ea.)

INGREDIENTS

Scallops	4 lb.
Water	6 cup
Sweet Vermouth	12 oz.
Salt	sprinkling
Pepper	sprinkling
Paprika	sprinkling
Butter	6 oz.

METHOD

Cut 1-oz. sea scallops in half in width. Rinse. Arrange 12 pieces (6 oz.) in casserole dish. Add water to half cover scallops. Pour 1 tbsp. Vermouth over scallops. Sprinkle with salt, pepper and paprika. Dribble with 1 tbsp. melted butter.

Bake at 350°F. for 10 min.—until scallops begin to whiten. Finish under broiler to color.

Pour 1 to 2 tsp. vermouth over scallops upon serving. Serve with baked potato and tiny whole carrots.

SCALLOPS POLYNESIAN EN BROCHETTE FLAMED WITH COGNAC
(Kon-Tiki Ports Restaurant, Sheraton-Chicago Hotel)

YIELD: 2 servings

INGREDIENTS

Scallops	20
Bacon	6 slices
Kumquats, whole	8
Ginger-Flavored Pickles (green)	12 slices
Pineapple Chunks	12

METHOD

Cut slices of bacon in half. Wrap 12 scallops with ½ slice bacon. Stuff remaining 8 scallops into whole kumquats from which centers have been removed.

Place 3 bacon wrapped scallops, 2 stuffed kumquats, 3 ginger pickles, and 3 pineapple chunks on 4 10-in. skewers.

Grill brochettes on broiler until bacon is crisp, turning once.

To serve, place brochettes upright in a half coconut filled with a sweet-sour sauce. Flame brochettes with cognac when served.

May also be served on fried or steamed white rice. Pour sweet-sour sauce (recipe follows) on brochettes and rice.

Sweet and Sour Sauce

Sugar	6 tbsp.
Vinegar	4 tbsp.
Soy Sauce	3 tbsp.
Pineapple Juice	½ cup
Sherry	1 tbsp.
Cornstarch	1½ tbsp.
Water	1 cup

METHOD

Mix first 5 ingredients. Bring to a boil.

Mix cornstarch and water. Gradually add cornstarch to boiling pineapple juice mixture, stirring constantly until thickened. Remove from heat.

Serve sauce over brochettes.

SCALLOPS AND SHRIMP IMPERIAL

YIELD: 15 6-oz. servings

INGREDIENTS

Scallops	3 lb.
Shrimp, medium size	3 lb.
Onion, finely chopped	1 cup
Garlic, minced	1 clove
Butter or Margarine	2 tbsp.
Condensed Cream of Mushroom Soup	1 can (3 lb. 2 oz.)
Light Cream	1 cup
Sherry	½ cup
Soy Sauce	1 tsp.
Liquid Pepper Sauce	¼ tsp.

METHOD

Poach scallops in small amount of water for 6 to 8 min. or until tender.

Cook, shell and devein shrimp.

Cook onion and garlic in butter until tender but not brown. Add mushroom soup; stir until smooth. Blend in cream, sherry, soy, liquid pepper sauce. Fold in scallops and shrimp; heat slowly, just to boiling. Serve 6 oz. portion.

Shrimp

BAKED STUFFED SHRIMP
YIELD: 20 to 25 servings
INGREDIENTS

Shrimp, fresh or frozen	8 lb.
Crabmeat	8 lb.
Fresh Bread, crusts removed and cubed	8 slice
Mayonnaise	½ cup
Hot Pepper Sauce	2 tsp.
Worcestershire Sauce	4 tsp.
Prepared Mustard	4 tsp.
Salt	2 tsp.
Onion, large, minced	1
Green Pepper, finely chopped	2
Melted Butter or Margarine	2 cup

METHOD

Shell uncooked shrimp, leaving tail shells on. Split shrimp down the back and spread apart, butterfly fashion. Combine crabmeat, bread cubes, mayonnaise, hot pepper sauce, worcestershire sauce, mustard and salt.

Saute onion and green peppers in butter until soft; add to crabmeat mixture.

Firmly stuff shrimp with crabmeat mixture. Place shrimp, tail sides up, on a greased shallow baking dish; brush with remaining butter.

Bake in hot oven 400°F. about 15 min. or until browned.

SHRIMP A LA NEWBURG
(Rohr's Restaurant, Cleveland)
YIELD: 1 portion
INGREDIENTS

Shrimp, shelled and cleaned	1 cup
Butter	2 tbsp.
Flour	1 tsp.
Cream, sweet	2 cup
Egg Yolks, beaten	2
Sherry, dry	3 oz.
Lemon Juice, fresh	1 tsp.
Paprika	½ tsp.

METHOD

Cook the shrimp in 1 tbsp. butter, using care that the butter does not burn.

In another saucepan, melt the remaining 1 tbsp. butter and stir in the flour until well-blended. Add the cream, heat, and stir until it is smooth. When it starts to boil, remove from the heat. Add the beaten egg yolks and sherry and stir until mixture thickens. Add the shrimp, lemon juice and paprika, but do not heat again or the newburg will curdle.

Serve with toasted crackers or melba toast.

SHRIMP IN BEER O'DONNELL
(O'Donnell's Sea Grill)
YIELD: 25 portions
INGREDIENTS

Onions, large, chopped	3
Carrots, large, finely chopped	3
Paprika	4 tbsp.
Sweet Basil	4 tbsp.
Thyme	2 tsp.
Rosemary	2 tsp.
Shortening	3 oz.
Water, boiling	1 gal.
Beer	1 qt.
Flour	2½ cup
Shortening	2½ cup
Salt and Pepper	to season
Shrimp	10 lb.

METHOD

Combine the first 6 ingredients and saute 20 min. in the 3 oz. shortening. Add the water and beer, and simmer 20 min. Strain through china cup.

Heat stock to boiling point. Thicken with roux or use flour and shortening designated in recipe for sauce. Season with salt and pepper.

In greased individual casserole dishes, place 6 oz. cooked and cleaned shrimp. Cover with beer sauce. Top with Holland rusk.

Place casseroles in 375°F. oven or on top of range until sauce is bubbly, and shrimp is thoroughly hot.

FRIED SHRIMP
(Seven Seas Restaurant, Panama City, Fla.)
YIELD: 1 serving
INGREDIENTS

Shrimp, large	12
Egg	1
Salt and Pepper	to taste
Oregano	1 dash
Garlic	to taste
Olive Oil	½ cup
Lemon, juice of	½ lemon

METHOD

Prepare 12 large shrimp for cooking. Mix salt, pepper and egg with a dash of oregano and garlic powder. Dip each shrimp in egg and seasoning, roll individually in flour and cook in ½ cup olive oil in a frying pan over a slow fire. Stir occasionally and when shrimp is done, sprinkle juice of half a lemon over it.

Nautical

SHRIMP JAMBALAYA

YIELD: 24 servings
INGREDIENTS

Onion, chopped	1
Garlic, minced	1 tbsp.
Butter	¾ cup
Parsley, minced	½ cup
Bay Leaves	4
Thyme	½ tsp.
Flour	¼ cup
Chili Powder	1 tsp.
Canned Tomatoes, drained and chopped	1½ qt.
Chicken Broth	4½ qt.
Salt	as needed
Rice, uncooked	1 qt.
Shrimp, shelled, deveined	8 lb.

METHOD
Saute onion and garlic in butter until tender, about 10 min. Add parsley, bay leaves and thyme. Stir in flour and chili powder. Add tomatoes; simmer 10 min., stirring frequently. Add chicken broth and salt to taste. Bring to boil. Stir in rice, reduce heat.

Cover and simmer 25 min., stirring occasionally. Add shrimp to rice mixture and simmer, covered, for 15 min., or until shrimp is tender.

CHEF SPENCER'S FLAKED SHRIMP AND SEAFOOD AU GRATIN IN CASSEROLE
(Hilaire's Restaurants)

YIELD: 24 portions
INGREDIENTS

1. Cream Cheese Sauce	
Flour	2 cup
Butter or Shortening	1 cup
Salt	2 tbsp.
Pepper	2 tsp.
Milk	1 gal.
Nippy Cheddar Cheese	1 qt.
2. Salmon and Halibut, cooked Shrimp	
(Prawns or Alaska Shrimp)	3 lb.
Onion, large, chopped	2
Butter or Margarine	4 tbsp.
Sherry Wine	½ cup
Bread Crumbs	2½ cup
Butter or Margarine	½ cup
Paprika	3 tsp.

METHOD
1. Melt shortening; stir in the flour and blend well. Add salt and pepper. Cook over low heat 5 to 7 min. Stir while cooking. Add scalded milk, stirring constantly with wire whip. Cook until of the proper consistency.

Add nippy cheese, and stir until cheese is melted.

2. Chop shrimp and combine with the flaked salmon and halibut.

Saute onions in the 2 oz. butter. Add sauteed onions and sherry wine to the cheese sauce. Combine fish and cheese sauce.

Place in individual greased casseroles. Top with buttered crumbs. Sprinkle with paprika.

Bake in 350°F. oven 20 min. or until crumbs are delicately browned and ingredients bubbly.

Serve topped with thick tomato slice or garnished with parsley and lemon wedge.

NOTE: The fish au gratin may also be put in greased baking pan.

CURRIED SHRIMP SALAD

YIELD: 48 portions
INGREDIENTS

Shrimp, fresh or frozen, peeled and deveined	8 lb.
Minced Onion	¾ to 1 cup
Minced Celery	1 qt.
Mayonnaise	1 qt.
Curry Powder	1/3 to ½ cup
Soy Sauce	1/3 to ½ cup

METHOD
Cook shrimp in court bouillon 2 to 5 min. Drain and chill.

Combine onion and celery.

To prepare dressing combine mayonnaise, curry powder and soy sauce.

Toss ingredients lightly in dressing. Garnish with cherry tomatoes and whole ripe olives.

SHRIMP CREOLE

YIELD: 5 qt.
INGREDIENTS

Flour	½ cup
Liquid Shortening	1 cup
Onions, chopped	2 cup
Tomato Sauce (No. 10 can)	3 qt.
Thyme	1 tsp.
Bay Leaves	2
Parsley Flakes	¼ cup
Hot Pepper Sauce	¼ tsp.
Shrimp, cooked and peeled	6 lb.

METHOD
Brown flour. Add shortening and onions. Cook 15 min. Add tomato sauce and seasonings. Simmer for 20 to 30 min. Remove bay leaves. Add shrimp and heat for about 10 min.

Serve over cooked rice.

SHRIMP GUMBO
YIELD: 12 8-oz. portions
INGREDIENTS

Shrimp, fresh or frozen	3 lb.
Bay Leaves	2
Water	4 cup
Onion, chopped	1½ cup
Celery, diced	½ cup
Parsley, chopped fine	¼ cup
Fresh Tomatoes, peeled and quartered	2 cup
Salt	2 tsp.
Red Pepper	pinch
Okra, chopped in 1-in. pieces	2 cup
Cooked Rice	3 cup
Butter or Margarine	½ cup
Fish Stock	4 cup

METHOD
Cook shrimp with bay leaves in boiling water. Drain and reserve stock. Peel and devein shrimp. Replace shrimp shells only in stock. Simmer for 30 min., strain and set aside.

Saute onions and celery in butter or margarine. Add parsley, tomatoes, seasoning and okra. Cook until tender, about 20 min. Add hot fish stock and cooked rice. Simmer for 10 min. Add shrimp and serve immediately in hot bowl. Garnish with fresh parsley.

STUFFED PEPPERS, CREOLE STYLE
YIELD: 40 servings
INGREDIENTS

Green Peppers, whole	40
Rice, cooked	1 gal.
Fish, cooked and flaked	1½ qt.
Shrimp, cleaned, cooked and chopped	1 qt.
Onions, chopped	3 cup
Thyme	1 tsp.
Parsley Flakes	½ cup
Tomato Sauce (2 No. 10 cans)	6 qt.
Celery, chopped	3 cup
Bread Crumbs, buttered	1½ qt.

METHOD
Steam clean peppers for 5 to 10 min., depending on thickness.

Combine rice, fish, shrimp, onions, thyme, parsley flakes, 3 qt. (1 No. 10 can) tomato sauce and celery.

Stuff peppers, using about ¾ cup stuffing for each pepper. Sprinkle buttered bread crumbs on top of each. Pour tomato sauce to about 1/8-in. depth in bottom of baking pans.

Bake at 375°F. for 30 to 40 min.

Heat remainder of sauce and serve over baked peppers.

SHRIMP LOUIS
YIELD: 25 servings
INGREDIENTS

Shrimp, fresh or frozen	6 lb.
Heads of Lettuce, large	3
Eggs, hard-cooked and quartered	10
Tomatoes, cut in wedges	10
Parsley	as needed
Louis Dressing	

METHOD
Clean and cook shrimp by boiling 3 min. in 3 qt. of water to which 4 tsp. pickling spices have been added. Drain and chill shrimp. Arrange shrimp, egg and tomato wedges on salad. Garnish with parsley. Serve with Louis Dressing (recipe below).

Louis Dressing

Mayonnaise	2 cup
Chili Sauce	2/3 cup
Onion, large, grated	1
Parsley, chopped	2 tbsp.
Horseradish, grated	1 tsp.
Cayenne Pepper	dash
Tarragon Vinegar	2 tbsp.
Olives, chopped, stuffed	¼ cup
Worcestershire Sauce	1 tsp.

METHOD
Combine all ingredients. Chill.

FRESH SHRIMP AND MUSHROOMS EN CASSEROLE
(Toll House, Inc., Whitman, Mass.)
YIELD: 12 portions (½ cup each)
INGREDIENTS

Butter	3 tbsp.
Salt	1 tsp.
Pepper	½ tsp.
Worcestershire Sauce	½ tsp.
Paprika	few grains
Mushrooms, quartered	1½ lb.
Onion, minced	4 tsp.
Parsley, chopped	2 tsp.
Green Pepper, minced	4 tsp.
Flour, all-purpose	4 tbsp.
Milk	1½ cup
Shrimp, cooked, cleaned and whole	1 lb.
Grated Cheese	2 tbsp.

METHOD
Melt butter. Add seasonings, mushrooms, onions, green peppers, parsley. Simmer until mushrooms are tender. Blend in flour. Add milk; stir until smooth. Cook 5 min. Add shrimp and grated cheese.

Fill buttered ramekins with mixture. Cover with buttered bread crumbs or crumbled cornflakes. Brown in 450°F. oven. Serve piping hot.

SPANISH MARINATED SHRIMP
(Beasley's)
YIELD: 30 salads
INGREDIENTS

1. Shrimp in Shell	10 lb.	
White Onions, large	4	
2. Pure Olive Oil	1 qt.	
Cider Vinegar	1½ pt.	
Capers with Juice	1 pt.	
Garlic, crushed	2 tsp.	
Lemon Juice	¼ cup	
Salt	2 tsp.	
Sugar	2 tbsp.	
Hot Pepper Sauce	few drops	
Worcestershire Sauce	2 tbsp.	

METHOD
1. Cook shrimp. Peel and devein. Wash and drain well. Cut onions in thin rings on commercial cutter.
   In a deep, flat pan place alternate layers of shrimp and sliced onions until all ingredients are used.
2. Make a dressing of the other ingredients. Pour over shrimp and onions. Cover and let stand in refrigerator overnight.
   To serve, lift shrimp out of dressing. Place in crisp lettuce cups. Garnish with tomato wedges, sliced cucumber and watercress.

NOTE: Spanish marinated shrimp makes a delicious salad, cold plate, or hors d'oeuvre platter.

SHRIMP de JONGHE
(The Cape Cod Room, Drake Hotel, Chicago)
INGREDIENTS

Shrimp, fresh or frozen	8 to 10 per serving
de Jonghe Butter	3 oz.

METHOD
Place shrimp evenly in round silver dish and place sliced de Jonghe Butter on top. Place in 350°F. oven until the butter becomes brown.

De Jonghe Butter - 8 servings

Sweet Butter	1 lb.
Garlic Cloves	2
White Wine	2 oz.
Lemon Juice	¼ tsp.

EGG, SHRIMP AND ANCHOVY SALAD BOWL
(Greenfield-Mills Restaurant Co.)
YIELD: 1 serving
INGREDIENTS

Head Lettuce Cup	¼ head
Egg, hard-cooked, cut in sixths (3 sections)	½ egg
Stuffed Olive	2 (only)
Anchovy Fillets	2 (only)
Tomato, cut in 8 wedges	1 wedge
Shrimp	3 (only)
Special Salad Bowl Greens	5 oz.

Salad Greens for Egg, Shrimp and Anchovy Salad Bowl
YIELD: 38 servings
INGREDIENTS

Head Lettuce Hearts	1½ gal.
Watercress	1 qt.
Escarole	2 qt.
Romaine	2 qt.
Endive	3 qt.
Spinach	2 qt.
Radishes, sliced thin	1 pt.
Tomatoes, cut ¾-in. cubes	1½ qt.
Salt	2 tbsp.
Salad Bowl Dressing	3 cup

METHOD
Cut leafy vegetables into pieces approximately 1½-in. long. Wash carefully. Drain well. Chill thoroughly. Mix all ingredients together. Do not add salad dressing until ready to use.

Sole

DOVER SOLE, SAUTE AMANDINE
(The Bird and Bottle Inn, Garrison, N. Y.)

Clean and completely skin a 20-oz. English sole. Do not remove the bone. Saute in sweet butter over a hot open flame until the fish is brown on both sides. Shake pan and keep the fish moving so that it does not stick to the bottom of the pan. Do not let the butter burn.

Remove the fish from the pan and place it on an ovenproof platter. Sprinkle with a tbsp. of finely sliced blanched almonds and pour the butter from the pan over the fish. Place in a hot (450°F.) oven for about 7 min., to finish cooking and brown the almonds.

Serve on a preheated plate.

SOLE, CHEF BERTIL'S FILLET, A LA STOCKHOLM
(Evan's Coffee Shop, Arlington, Va.)

YIELD: 3 portions
INGREDIENTS

Fillet of Sole or Flounder	1 lb.
Butter	1 tbsp.
Chives, Green Onion Tops, or Onions, finely chopped	1 tbsp.
Carrots, finely chopped	1 tbsp.
Celery, finely chopped	1 tbsp.
Salt	¼ tsp.
Pepper	1/8 tsp.
Lemon Juice	4 tbsp.
Lobster, Alaska King Crab, Shrimp or Mushroom Sauce	½ cup
Egg White	3
Parmesan or Cheddar Cheese	1 tbsp.
Mayonnaise	2 tbsp.
Salt and Pepper	to season

METHOD

Melt butter in shallow saute pan. Add vegetables. Cook 5 min. Place fillets on top of vegetables. Sprinkle with salt and pepper. Add lemon juice.

Bake in 350°F. oven 10 min.

Cover fish with lobster, Alaska king crab, shrimp or mushroom sauce.

Beat egg whites until stiff. Fold in grated cheese and mayonnaise. Season with salt and pepper. Pile whites on top of fish. Bake in 350°F. oven until whites are a delicate brown.

Use lobster tail shells as a garnish with lobster sauce; crab meat pieces for Alaska king crab sauce; shrimp with shrimp sauce, and mushroom caps with mushroom sauce.

Pike

POLYNESIAN PIKE
(The Ambassador Hotel, Chicago)

YIELD: 1 portion
INGREDIENTS

Pike Fillet or other Fish Fillet	1 lb.
Butter	2 tbsp.
Banana, sliced	½
Chop Suey Sauce	2 tsp.
White Wine	1 oz.
Cubed Pineapple	2 tbsp.
Salt	to taste

METHOD

Thaw fillet, if frozen. Saute fillet in 1 tbsp. butter; when done set aside on warm platter. Return pan to stove, add rest of butter, pineapple, banana, chop suey sauce, wine and salt. Saute off, and pour pineapple mixture over fish.

Serve with fluffy rice garnished with toasted coconut. For flame at table side use chafing dish, and place fish on platter, finish sauce, add cognac to it and light, pour over fish.

Tuna

TUNA CHEESE ROLL
YIELD: 50 servings
INGREDIENTS

Chunk Style Tuna, drained	16 (6½-oz.) cans, or 8 (12½-oz.) cans
Processed American Cheese, grated	2 lb.
Bisquit Mix	4 qt.
Milk	1 qt.
Sauce	
Butter or Margarine	1 cup
Chopped Green Peppers	2 cup
Tomato Puree	2 qt.
Onion Salt	3 tbsp.
Celery Salt	1 tbsp.
Sugar	½ cup

METHOD
Break tuna into pieces. Combine tuna and cheese.

Combine bisquit mix and milk; mix lightly. Turn out on lightly floured surface; knead gently 10 times. Divide into 8 parts.

Roll out into 8- by 12-in. rectangles, about ¼-in. thick. Sprinkle with tuna mixture. Roll up jelly-roll fashion. Place on baking sheets. Prick tops.

Bake in hot oven (400°F.) 20 min., or until lightly browned.

Meanwhile, melt butter or margarine, add green peppers and saute until tender. Add remaining ingredients and heat to boiling point. Simmer 5 min.

Serve sauce with Tuna Cheese Roll.

DAYTON'S BAKED TUNA FISH SOUFFLE
(Dayton's, Minneapolis)
YIELD: 16 4-oz. portions
INGREDIENTS

White Tuna Fish, finely flaked	4 cup
Butter	1 cup
Green Peppers, diced ¼-in.	7/8 cup
Onions, chopped	2/3 cup
Celery, diced ¼-in.	1¼ qt.
Quick Tapioca	7 tbsp.
Whole Milk	1¾ cup
Egg Whites	8
Egg Yolks	8
Salt	2 tbsp.

METHOD
Melt butter. Add onions, green peppers, and celery. Saute until tender but not brown. Combine with finely flaked tuna fish.

Beat egg yolks. Add milk, salt, tapioca and add to tuna fish mixture. Fold in stiffly beaten egg whites. Turn into greased steamtable pan.

Bake in pan of hot water in 275°F. oven 1½ hr. or until firm.
NOTE: The souffle may also be baked in individual molds set in a pan of hot water.

TUNA SOUFFLE SANDWICH
YIELD: 45 sandwiches
INGREDIENTS

Enriched Bread, fresh or day-old	90 slices
Tuna, drained and flaked	1 No. 5 flat can
Celery, chopped	¾ lb.
Green Pepper, chopped	¾ lb.
Dry Mustard	2 tbsp.
Stuffed Olives, chopped or sliced	9¾ oz.
Process American Cheese, grated	2¼ lb.
Eggs, whole	4½ lb.
Milk	4½ qt.
Paprika	1½ tsp.

METHOD
Trim crusts from bread. Arrange 15 slices of bread in the bottom of three 12- by 20- by 2½-in. greased steam table pans, fitting them close together.

Combine tuna, celery, green pepper, mustard and olives in a 1½ gal. bowl. Spread 1½ qt. of tuna mixture over bread in each pan. Sprinkle cheese evenly over tuna mixture. Cover with second bread slice.

Beat eggs and milk together in a 2 gal. bowl. Pour 2½ qt. of egg and milk mixture over sandwiches in each pan. Sprinkle paprika over top of sandwiches.

Bake in 325°F. oven for 45 min., or until custard is set and sandwiches are light and golden brown.

Low Calorie Selections

FISH FILLET GOURMET
Calories per Serving: Approx. 165
YIELD: 24 servings
INGREDIENTS

Fish Fillets (haddock, cod, sole, whitefish or flounder)	8 lb.
Low-Calorie Soft-Type Margarine	as needed
Lemon Juice	¾ cup
Salt	1 tbsp.
White Pepper	½ tsp.
Fresh Mint, chopped	¼ cup
Oregano	1 tbsp.
Ripe Olives	as needed
Lemon Wedges	as needed

METHOD
Place fillets on cold, greased broiler grid. Brush with soft margarine. Combine lemon juice and seasonings. Spoon over fillets.

Broil 3 in. from heat 3 to 5 min., or until fish flakes easily when tested with a fork.

Garnish with ripe olives and lemon wedges to serve.

Suggested Menu: Tossed salad with low-calorie dressing and melba toast.

LOW-CAL CURRIED FISH FILLETS
Calories per Serving: Approx. 140
YIELD: 24 servings
INGREDIENTS

Cod Fillets (haddock or other fillets may be used, too) skinned	8 lb.
Celery, sliced	1 qt.
Onion, sliced	1 qt.
Vegetable Oil	¼ cup
Curry Powder	1 tbsp.
Pepper	¼ tsp.
Skim Milk	1 qt.
Paprika	as needed

METHOD
Place fillets in single layer in buttered baking pan.

Saute celery and onion in oil 5 min. Stir in seasonings and milk. Pour over fish.

Bake in 350°F. oven 25 to 30 min. Sprinkle with paprika and serve.

Suggested Menu: Broccoli spears seasoned with lemon juice, cottage cheese salad and crisp relishes.

SEA-GREEN DELIGHT FILLETS
Calories per Serving: Approx. 185
YIELD: 24 servings
INGREDIENTS

Watercress, minced	1-1/3 cup
Parsley, minced	1-1/3 cup
Scallions, minced	1 cup
Low-Calorie Mayonnaise	1 qt.
Whole Peppercorns, cracked	¼ tsp.
Low-Calorie Lemon-Lime carbonated beverage	4 qt.
Fish Fillets (cod, flounder, whitefish, red snapper, haddock	8 lb.

METHOD
Combine minced watercress, parsley and scallions. Mix 1 cup watercress mixture with mayonnaise. Chill.

Place remaining watercress mixture in skillets with peppercorns and lemon-lime beverage. Bring to boil. Add fillets, cover tightly. Reduce heat and simmer 10 min. or until fish flakes easily when tested with fork.

Lift fillets to serving dishes and serve with mayonnaise sauce.

Suggested Menu: Green vegetable seasoned with lemon juice and plain rye wafers.

SLENDER SPICY FILLETS
YIELD: 24 servings
INGREDIENTS

Oil or Low-Calorie Margarine	as needed
Fish Fillets (haddock, halibut, flounder, ocean perch, or red snapper)	8 lb.
Onion, minced	½ cup
Cucumber, grated	1 qt.
Pimiento, chopped	¼ cup
Salt	2 tsp.
Pepper	½ tsp.

METHOD
Brush fillets lightly with oil or margarine. Place on greased, cold broiler grid and broil 3 in. from source of heat for about 7 min.

Combine remaining ingredients. Spread over fish and broil 3 min. longer, or until fish flakes easily when tested with fork. Serve immediately.

ALTERNATE SUGGESTIONS: Brush choice of fish fillets lightly with worcestershire sauce and season to taste. Broil to desired doneness (about 10 min.)

Sprinkle oiled fish fillets with prepared herb mixture (or personal choice of herbs.) Broil to desired doneness (about 10 min.)

Nautical

SLIMLINE SHELLFISH SALAD
Calories per Serving: 160
YIELD: 24 servings
INGREDIENTS

Lettuce Leaves	as needed
Cucumbers, sliced	2
Torn Lettuce	as needed
Eggs, hard-cooked and halved	1 doz.
Tomato, cut in wedges	3
King Crab Meat Chunks	8 lb.

METHOD
Line salad bowls with lettuce leaves and mound torn lettuce in center of bowls to provide base.

Arrange cucumbers, 2 egg halves and 4 tomato wedges on torn lettuce. Mound crabmeat on top. Drizzle with dressing and serve.

DRESSING INGREDIENTS

Low-Calorie Mayonnaise Dressing	2 cup
Lemon Juice	¼ cup
Prepared Mustard	2 tsp.
Hot Pepper Sauce	as needed

METHOD
Combine all ingredients and chill. Serve over Slimline Shellfish Salad.

SEA FOOD SPECIES CHART National Fisheries Institute

SPECIES	OTHER NAMES	WHERE CAUGHT	FAT OR LEAN	MARKET FORMS*	FAVORITE WAYS TO SERVE
Catfish	Bullhead, Blue Channel	Great Lakes, other U.S. lakes, inland rivers, ponds, creeks.	Lean	Whole, dressed; fresh, frozen	Southern Catfish Stew
	Wolf fish	Iceland, Germany, England, Denmark, Norway	Lean	Fillets, frozen	Deep-fried Catfish with Hush Puppies
Cod	Codfish, Scrod (Baby)	New England, Middle Atlantic, Pacific Coast, Iceland, England, Norway, Germany, Denmark, Canada	Lean	Breaded and pre-cooked sticks and portions. Drawn, dressed, steaks, fillets; fresh, frozen, salted, smoked	Baked Cod with Cream, Sticks or portions Served with Zesty Mustard Sauce
Croaker	Hardhead	New Jersey, Atlantic Coast to Texas Gulf	Lean	Round or pan-dressed, fillets; fresh, frozen	Chowder
Flounder	Sole, Fluke	Northwest Coast, Gulf Coast, New England, Middle Atlantic, Canada Denmark, England, Iceland	Lean	Whole, pan-dressed, dressed, steaks, fillets; fresh, frozen, smoked	Grilled Steaks, Baked Fillets in Orange Sauce
Grouper	Red, Black, Yellowfin, Speckled Hind, Gag, Scamp	South Atlantic, Gulf	Lean	Whole, steaks, fillets; fresh, frozen	Fillet Rollup with Spanish Sauce
Haddock	Scrod (Baby)	New England, Canada, Iceland, Norway, England	Lean	Whole, drawn, fillets; fresh, frozen, salted, smoked. Breaded and pre-cooked sticks and portions	Fillets in Wine and Tarragon Sauce, Finnan Haddie, Baked au Gratin, Hearty Fish Sticks or Portions in Sandwiches
Hake	White, Red, Squirrel, Ling, "Deep-Sea Fillet"	Gulf of St. Lawrence south to North Carolina	Lean	Dressed, fillets; fresh, frozen, salted, corned	Baked, Chowder
Halibut		New England, Pacific Coast, Alaska	Lean	Drawn, dressed, steaks; fresh, frozen, smoked, canned	Halibut Steaks in Herb Sauce, Baked, Stuffed, Broiled
Lake Perch	Yellow Perch	Great Lakes, other U.S. lakes, inland rivers	Lean	Whole, pan-dressed, fillets; fresh, frozen	Deep-fried, Pan-fried
Lake Trout	Togue	Great Lakes, Lakes of British Columbia, Alaska, Northern U.S.	Lean	Whole, drawn; fresh, frozen	Trout Amandine, Baked Whole with Herb Stuffing
Mackerel	Blue, American	New England, Norway	Fat	Whole; fresh, frozen	Broiled or Baked, Seafood Casserole
Spanish		South Atlantic, Gulf	Fat	Whole, drawn; fresh, frozen	
King	Cero, Kingfish	South Atlantic, Gulf	Fat	Drawn, steaks; fresh, frozen	

SEA FOOD SPECIES CHART National Fisheries Institute (cont.)

SPECIES	OTHER NAMES	WHERE CAUGHT	FAT OR LEAN	MARKET FORMS*	FAVORITE WAYS TO SERVE
Mullet	Striped, White, Jumping, Silver	Atlantic (Florida to North Carolina), Gulf (Florida to Texas)	Fat	Round, fillets; fresh, frozen, smoked, salted	Baked Atop Herb-seasoned Stuffing
Ocean Perch	Rosefish, Redfish	New England, Northwest Coast, Iceland, Germany, England, Norway, Canada	Lean	Whole, fillets; fresh, frozen	Pan-fried, Baked in White Wine Sauce, Perch Amandine
Pollock	"Deep-Sea Fillet", Boston Bluefish	Cape Cod to Cape Breton	Lean	Drawn, dressed, steaks, fillets; fresh, frozen, salted, smoked	Baked, Broiled with Herb Sauce
Rainbow Trout	Brook, Speckled	Northwestern United States (commercial fish farms), Denmark, Norway	Lean	Dressed, boned; fresh, frozen	Trout Amandine, Charcoal Broiled with Lemon Butter, Saute Meuniere
Red Snapper		Gulf, Middle Atlantic, Formosa	Lean	Drawn, dressed, steaks, fillets; fresh, frozen	Poached Snapper, Snapper Fillet Amandine, Baked, Stuffed

Salmon
  Sockeye
  Chinook
  Silver
  Pink
  Chum
	
	Red
	Spring, King
	Silversides, Coho
	Humpback
	Fall
		Pacific Coast, Alaska, North Atlantic	Fat	Dressed, steaks, fillets; fresh, frozen, smoked, canned	Poached or Baked, Salmon Steaks Florentine, Planked, Charcoal Broiled

Scup	Porgy, Paugy	Southern New England to North Carolina	Lean	Whole, pan-dressed, fillets; fresh, frozen	Baked, Broiled with Lime and Butter
Sea Bass Black & White		Pacific Coast	Lean	Steaks, fillets; fresh, frozen	Sauteed Bass with Tartar Sauce, Baked Stuffed Bass
Common	Blackfish, Black Sea Bass	New England, Middle and South Atlantic	Lean	Whole, pan-dressed, fillets; fresh, frozen	
Sea Herring	Atlantic or Pacific Herring	New England, Middle Atlantic, Iceland, Denmark, Norway, Germany, England, Scotland, Holland, Sweden (virtually world-wide)	Fat	Whole, chunks; fresh, salted, pickled, smoked (sardines)	Herring in Sour Cream or Wine Sauce
Sea Trout Gray	Weakfish, Squeteagues	Middle and South Atlantic	Lean	Whole, drawn; fresh, frozen	Trout Amandine, Pan-fried Trout, Saute with Lemon Butter
Spotted	Speckled Trout	Middle and South Atlantic, Gulf	Lean	Whole, drawn, dressed; fresh, frozen	
White	White or Sand Trout	Gulf	Lean	Whole; fresh, frozen	
Shad	Buck, Roe or White Shad	Coastal rivers from Maine to Florida, Washington to California	Fat	Whole, drawn, fillets, boned; fresh, frozen, smoked, canned. Shad roe: fresh, frozen, canned	Broiled with Bacon, Baked with Toasted Sesame Topping
Smelts	Whitebait, Surf Smelt, Grunion, Eulachon or Columbia River Smelt, Silverside, Jacksmelt, Bay Smelt	North Atlantic, Pacific Coast, Columbia River, and bays from Mexico to Canada, Great Lakes	Fat to Lean (changes by type)	Whole, dressed; fresh, frozen	Pan-fried, Broiled
Sole	Rex, Petrale, Sand, Grey, Lemon Sole	Pacific Coast, Alaska Canada, Atlantic Coast, England, Holland, Belgium, Denmark	Lean	Whole, fillets; fresh, frozen	Sole Amandine, Baked Fillet of Sole with Seafood Stuffing, Charcoal Broiled with Lemon Butter
	Dover or English	England	Lean		
Spot	Goody, Lafayette	New Jersey to Florida	Lean	Whole, pan-dressed; fresh, frozen	Pan-fried, Broiled
Striped Bass	Rock, Rock Bass, Rock Fish	Atlantic Coast Pacific Coast	Lean	Whole, drawn, steaks, fillets; fresh, frozen	Baked with Herb Stuffing, Pan-Fried with Mushrooms
Tuna	Albacore Yellowfin Skipjack Blue Fin Little	Pacific Coast Pacific Coast Southern waters Atlantic and Pacific Coast Atlantic (all tuna world-wide)	Fat Fat Fat Fat Fat	Canned Canned Canned Canned Drawn	Tuna Salad, Scalloped Tuna Casserole Marinated and Grilled

Nautical

SPECIES	OTHER NAMES	WHERE CAUGHT	FAT OR LEAN	MARKET FORMS*	FAVORITE WAYS TO SERVE
Whitefish		Great Lakes, Minnesota, Canada	Fat	Whole, drawn, dressed, fillets; fresh, frozen, smoked	Baked, Broiled, Poached with Hollandaise
Whiting	Frostfish, Silver Hake	New England, England	Lean	Drawn	Breaded and Deep-fried

*Many species are marketed in forms other than those listed. This chart attempts to show the most popular market forms of the various species.

SHELLFISH SPECIES CHART
National Fisheries Institute

SPECIES*	OTHER NAMES	WHERE THEY ARE CAUGHT	MARKET FORMS	FAVORITE WAYS TO SERVE
Clams				
Butter		Pacific Coast, Alaska	Live in shell; shucked, fresh, frozen; frozen breaded raw or fried; canned, whole or minced	Scalloped Clams, New England Quahog Cakes, Clam Chowder, Fried, Paella, Clam Cocktail
Hard	Quahog, Hard Shell, Cherrystones	New England, Middle and South Atlantic		
Little Neck		Pacific Coast, Alaska		
Razor		Pacific Coast, Alaska		
Soft	Soft Shell	New England, Middle Atlantic		Steamed Clams
Surf	Skimmer	Middle Atlantic		
Crabs				
Blue		Middle and South Atlantic, Gulf	Live in shell; frozen cooked in shell; fresh, frozen, or canned meat	Deviled Crab Cakes, Crab Mornay, Crab Bisque, Crab Louis, Avocado Stuffed with Crab Salad
Dungeness		Pacific Coast, Alaska		
King		Alaska		
Stone		Florida		
Lobsters				
True		New England, Canada	Live in shell; frozen in shell; canned meat	Lobster Thermidor, Lobster Newburg, Lobster Stew, Broiled Lobster, Broiled Stuffed Lobster
Spiny	Sea Crawfish, Rock Lobster, Rock Lobster Tail	South Atlantic, Gulf, Pacific Coast, S. Africa, Australia, New Zealand, Brazil, Ecuador, British Honduras, Haiti		
Deep Sea Lobster Tail		Denmark, Iceland, Scotland		
Oysters				
Eastern		New England, Middle and South Atlantic, Gulf	Live in shell; shucked, fresh, frozen; frozen breaded raw or fried, canned	Oyster Stew, Oysters Rockefeller, Oysters on the Half Shell, Fried Oysters
Pacific	Japanese	Pacific Coast, Japan		
Olympia	Western	Pacific Coast		
Scallops				
Bay		Middle and South Atlantic, New England, Gulf	Shucked, fresh or frozen	Scallops Au Gratin, Fried, Scallop Stew, Broiled Scallops
Sea		New England, Middle Atlantic, Australia	Frozen, breaded, raw or cooked	
Shrimp				
White, Brown and Pink	Prawn	South Atlantic, Gulf	Fresh or frozen, frozen raw and peeled; fresh or frozen cooked, peeled and unpeeled; frozen breaded raw or fried; canned	Shrimp Creole, Paella, Shrimp de Jonghe, Shrimp Egg Foo Yoong, Shrimp Curry, Pickled Shrimp, Shrimp Cocktail, Shrimp Newburg, Breaded, Deep-fried, Tempura, Jambalaya
Alaska Pink		Alaska		
California Gay		Maine, Mexico, French Guinea, Dutch Guinea (imports virtually world-wide)		

*All Shellfish are lean.

SUPPLIERS OF SEAFOODS AND SEAFOOD ENTREES

Acadia Fisheries, Inc., Gloucester 01930
Frozen fillets; portions; shell fish.

Alaskan Seafoods, Inc., Homer, Alaska 99603
Canned and frozen Alaska King crab, shromp; frozen halibut and salmon.

Armour Food Service Co., Chicago 60611
Frozen prepared seafood entrees.

B & B Fisheries, Inc., Kodiak, Alaska 99615
Canned and frozen Alaska King crab, shrimp; frozen scallops.

Bayou Foods, Inc., Mobile, Ala. 36607
Frozen prepared seafoods; stuffed crab, shrimp, flounder; crab and shrimp burgers; crab rolls.

Blue Channel Corp., Port Royal, S. C. 29935
Frozen crab cakes; seafood entrees.

Blue Water Seafoods, Cleveland 44142
Frozen fish fillets; shellfish, clams; breaded frozen portions, shrimp, oysters and scallops; frozen raw oysters. Pre-cooked portions, croquettes, sticks, cakes, chips.

Booth Fisheries, Chicago 60606
Frozen portions; shellfish; prepared entrees, prepared portions, sticks.

Brilliant Seafood, Inc., Boston 02110
Shrimp products.

Campbell Soup Co., Camden, N. J. 08101
Frozen seafood entrees.

Carnation Seafoods, Oceans of the World, Inc., New York City 10014
Prepared frozen fish portions, sticks, steaks; rainbow trout; shellfish; breaded and precooked fish; shellfish entrees.

Coldwater Seafood Corp., Scarsdale, N. Y. 10583
Icelandic brand fish sticks, fillets, portions, steaks; shellfish, prepared breaded portions; pre-cooked portions; fish cakes.

Continental Coffee Co., Chicago 60614
Frozen prepared entrees.

Del Monte Corp., San Francisco 94105
Canned seafoods.

Dolphin Seafoods, Inc., Cleveland 44102
Frozen fillets; shellfish; prepared breaded portions, fillets, scallops, shrimp; pre-cooked fish portions.

Don's Prize Meats, Miami 33150
Frozen fish.

Duffy-Mott, Inc., New York City 10019
Tilghman brand fish cakes; breaded crab and oysters; fried clams; shellfish specialties.

Empress Fisheries Co., Inc., New York City 10007
Frozen fish fillets, steaks, Rainbow trout; shellfish; turtle meat; breaded oysters.

Forty Fathom Seafoods, Inc., Chestnut Hill, Mass. 02167
Frozen fish, shellfish.

Frionor Norwegian Frozen Fish, New Bedford, Mass. 02741
Frozen fillets; breaded sticks and portions; fish cakes; prawns, shrimp; roe

H. J. Heinz Co., Pittsburgh 15230
Canned seafoods.

The Gorton Corp., Gloucester 01930
Frozen fish fillets; steaks; shellfish; prepared breaded portions; pre-cooked breaded portions.

Icelandic Products, Inc., Harrisburg, Pa. 17101
Frozen fish sticks, steaks, portions.

Idaho Trout Processors Co., Boise 83705
Frozen fish; Rainbow trout; prepared, boned and breaded trout.

Howard Johnson Co., Brockton, Mass. 02689
Frozen fried clams; shrimp croquettes; prepared entrees.

Kraft Foods, Chicago 60611
Canned tuna; canned clam products.

Libby, McNeill & Libby, Chicago 60604
Prepared entrees (tuna & noodles, tuna pie)

Marriott Hot Shoppes, Inc., Bethesda, Md. 20036
Pre-cooked frozen seafood entrees.

Moore's Seafood Products, Inc., Fort Atkinson, Wis. 53538
Prepared seafoods; breaded fish portions, sticks, scallops; frozen fillets, steaks; breaded shrimp; pre-cooked portions, sticks; shrimp patties.

Morton Frozen Food Div., Continental Baking Co., Rye, N. Y. 10580
Prepared fried shrimp and scallops; fish portions.

New England Fish Co., Seattle 98114
Frozen shrimp, fillets, portions, steaks, breaded portions and shrimp; shellfish (San Juan brands)

NIFDA, Atlanta, Ga. 30325
Frozen seafood portions.

O'Brien, Spotorno, Mitchell, San Francisco 94133
Prepared frozen entrees, (poached salmon, sauced fish, gourmet entrees)

Ocean Products, Inc., Tampa 33601
Frozen entrees; shrimp; fish patties; (Treasure Isle brands)

Ocoma Foods Co., Omaha, Neb.
Seafood entrees.

Pacific Pearl Quality Seafoods, Seattle 98104
Canned and frozen Alaska King crab, Dungeness crab; canned oysters and shrimp.

Ralston Purina Co., St. Louis, Mo. 63188
Chicken of the Sea canned tuna and oyster stew; frozen shrimp products.

Robinson Canning, Inc., New Orleans, La.
Canned shrimp.

Rubenstein Foods, Inc., Dallas, Tex. 75276
Frozen fish fillets, portions; whole fish (trout); shellfish; prepared breaded portions and shrimp; stuffed fish entrees.

Sara Lee, Food Services Div., Deerfield, Ill. 60015
Frozen entrees in steamtable pans: Seafood Creole—bay scallops, Alaska King crab, shrimp in creole sauce; Scallops Florentine—bay scallops, shell macaroni, fine-chopped spinach in wine-accented cream sauce; Tuna and Noodles au Gratin, white albacore tuna with pimento, sliced mushrooms in cream sauce.

Seabrook Farms Co., Inc., Seabrook, N. J. 08302
Frozen prepared entrees.

Seapak Corp., St. Simons Island, Ga. 31522
Frozen fish; shellfish; clams.

Sea Pass Corp., St. Louis 63110
Shrimp products

Shoreline Seafoods, Ltd., Tampa, Fla. 33605
Frozen shellfish; breaded oysters, shrimp, scallops.

Snake River Trout Co., Buhl, Idaho 83316
Frozen Rainbow trout, boned and breaded trout.

Star-Kist Foods, Inc., Terminal Island, Calif. 90731
Frozen fish; shellfish; prepared entrees; canned seafood.

Stouffer Foods Corp., Cleveland 44115
Frozen prepared entrees (tuna and noodles, crab, shrimp and lobster Newburgs; shrimp curry).

Wakefield Seafood, Inc., Seattle 98199
Shellfish, Alaska King crab.

ASSOCIATIONS

Alaska King Crab Marketing and Quality Control Board, Subport Bldg., Juneau, Alaska 99801

American Seafood Distributors Assn., 821 15th St. N. W., Washington, D. C. 20005

Canned Salmon Institute, 618 Second Ave., Seattle, Wash. 98104

Fishery Council, 118 South St., New York City 10038

Gloucester Fisheries Assn., c/o Addison Gilbert Hospital, Gloucester, Mass. 01930

Halibut Assn. of North America, 911 Western, Seattle, Wash. 98104

International Shrimp Council, 1200 18th St., N. W., Washington, D. C. 20036

Maine Sardine Council, 15 Grove St., Augusta, Me. 04330

Massachusetts Seafood Council, Admin. Bldg., Fish Pier, Boston 02210

Middle Atlantic Fisheries Assn., 118 South St., New York City 10038

National Fisheries Institute, 1614 20th St., Washington, D. C. 20009

National Shrimp Breaders Assn., 2 N. Riverside Plaza, Chicago 60606

New Bedford Seafood Council, 18 Commercial St., New Bedford, Mass. 02740

Northwest Fisheries Assn., 66 Marion St., Seattle, Wash. 98104

Shrimp Assn. of the Americas, 910 E. Levee St., Brownsville, Tex. 78521

South African Rock Lobster Service Corp., 70 Wall St., New York City 10005

Southeastern Fisheries Assn., Inc., 330 S. Adams St., Tallahassee, Fla. 32301

U. S. Bureau of Commercial Fisheries, 100 E. Ohio St., Chicago 60611

U. S. Trout Farmers Assn., 67 W. 9000 South Sandy, Utah 84070

U. S. Dept. of Interior Fish and Wildlife Service, U. S. Government Printing Office, Washington, D. C.

National Assn. of Frozen Food Packers, 919 18th St. N. W., Washington, D. C. 20009

Country/Colonial

Both Farm Style and Early American food and decor win popularity polls in all areas of the country. The following section offers easy answers on assembling decor elements, setting a service style and developing menus for these basic American themes.

Special Atmosphere: The Charm of Country/Colonial

America's food heritage goes back to the early colonists...
taught to plant corn by the Indians... celebrating their first successful
crops with a feast. The first food service establishments were
country inns where the stages stopped for their passengers to dine
and rest. The keen desire, repeatedly expressed, for a return to earlier,
simpler ways gives the country–colonial food service experience
an appealing aura. Here are interiors, menus and dishes that
capitalize on happy memories of "Sunday dinner on the farm"...
foods that have been popular ever since the days of the Pilgrims.

The Charm of Country/Colonial

Stephenson's Apple Farm Restaurant uses appropriate names, appointments and seating arrangements for each of its various dining areas... the Backporch Room, Backyard Room, Cupboard Room, Parlor and Larder, shown below. Soft light dramatizes the Larder's weathered wood ceiling and highlights bags of produce placed on the rafters. Nine couples or an 18-member party sit family style at the long table in the center of the room. Railings separate these guests from twosomes at tables and in booths.

Above, the close-up of Groff Farm Specialties, Mt. Joy, Pa., illustrates the bounty of this country inn's tables.

In early America, fresh tomatoes were considered poisonous and Bibb lettuce was unheard of. But, farmers grew bountiful crops of crisp green cabbage. This practical vegetable was a basic "material" used in making the New England boiled dinner, and the frontier's colorful Calico Slaw, shown on the opposite page.

The cider press that dominates the Cider Mill Cocktail Lounge, Stephenson's Apple Farm, at left, is filled with real apples. Half-bushels, also holding real apples, mask lighting to provide indirect wall illumination. Guests enjoy helping themselves from the baskets.

> **GROFF'S FARM SPECIALTY**
>
> Family Style Dinner
> $4.85—Home Cured Ham
> with Chicken Stoltzfus or Chicken Pot Pie
> Children 10 years and under—$2.40
>
> This dinner includes:
> Fruit cup or juice
> Rolls and butter
>
> Potatoes—mashed with browned butter
>
> 2 vegetables: Peas, French green beans,
> corn, carrots, beets,
> cauliflower w/cheese sauce
> or green beans in ham broth
>
> Relishes: Cranberry apple sauce, chow chow,
> spiced Persian melon, pickles, etc.
>
> Pudding: Cracker, tapioca,
> caramel or vanilla pudding w/fruit
>
> Cake: Chocolate, white w/cocoanut glaze,
> spice or angel food
>
> Pie: Almost any kind
>
> Ice Cream: Vanilla
> Chocolate Sundaes may be substituted
> for pie and ice cream
>
> Coffee and tea
>
> These prices do not include the 6%
> sales tax or the gratuities.
>
> When choosing a menu for a group, please
> choose one that will be suitable
> for everyone, as we do not serve
> one beef, one chicken, etc.

Farm plenty is the immediate impression of diners at the Groff Farm in Mt. Joy, Pa. Their first sight is the table where all the famous Pennsylvania Dutch dishes are spread out in a lavish display. Menu specialties are listed in the announcement, above, sent to groups inquiring about reservations for meals served in Groff's Early American home. Garden crispness for their vegetables, same-day baked cakes, pies, puddings by Betty (Mrs. Abe) Groff, hams, cured on premises, and roasts carved by Abe Groff, are important factors in the growing fame of Groff Farm.

Extra emphasis for the bountiful larder implied in country decor comes from Stephenson's Fruit Cellar passageway, right. Patrons also enjoy a glimpse of the wine cellar.

Designed by: Dr. John W. Welch, University of Missouri; Lloyd J. Stephenson, Leslie W. Stephenson; Henry Schoenfeld, Greenwoods, Inc.; Roger T. Sermon, Mitchell Anderson, Sermon & Anderson.

The Charm of Country/Colonial

Apples... rural... farm... quaint early Missouri... these were key words for designers of Stephenson's Apple Farm Restaurant. Old farm tools that decorate the rustic lobby quickly establish this theme; a complimentary cup of cider from the keg placed at the center of the back wall of the lobby pleasantly confirms it. "Hay Storage" door at top of stairs is entrance to office. The Country Store just off the lobby, above, sells items in harmony with their rural theme, chosen to produce in the viewer a feeling of having stepped back in time. Stephenson's own apple butter, jams, jellies, preserves and relishes are also sold from the antique showcase with its glass top and front.

Left, windows facing the counter and shelves displaying merchandise in Country Store filters light through a collection of colored glass bottles, ornately painted canisters and antique bric-a-brac.

The Charm of Country/Colonial

Designed for use as a banquet room as well as for regular dining, Stephenson's Apple Farm Quilt Room, at left, has carpets woven to resemble an old-fashioned hooked rug. Carpet colors of red, blue, amber, green and black are used in other furnishings to provide color accents. Table cloths of blue and white are designed in a quilt pattern. Water goblets and tumblers used on the tables are blue, green, amber and ruby red. Quilts hanging in the room are antiques.

Saved from the Hessian mercenaries who in July 1779 destroyed all but three buildings in Pound Ridge, N. Y., Emily Shaw's Inn, bottom left, served varied purposes before it was opened as a restaurant in 1939. The character of the interior retains the original architectural elements of the 175-year old building: wide board floors, rough plaster, beamed ceilings. Pewter sconces and plates, windsor and captains chairs, portraits and Currier & Ives prints, colorful tablecloths underscore its historical importance. Lump Crabmeat Cocktail, Shaw's Famous Cheddar Cheese Soup are among starred items on an attractively handwritten menu. Wide boards, beamed ceilings, colonial stools, continue Early American theme to tap room.

Two hundred years of experience stand behind Williamsburg's reputation for fine food and drink. Visitors of the famed city find that a mug of beer and a hearty meal are still served in the finest Virginia tradition at Chowning's Tavern, opposite page. Chowning's is an alehouse reminiscent of the boisterous pre-revolutionary period. Last year, 305,750 people were served house specialties such as the Welch Rabbit pictured, Brunswick Stew and delicious breads. Jugs, bottles and pewter plates, once practical articles of tavern equipment, now act as part of the decor.

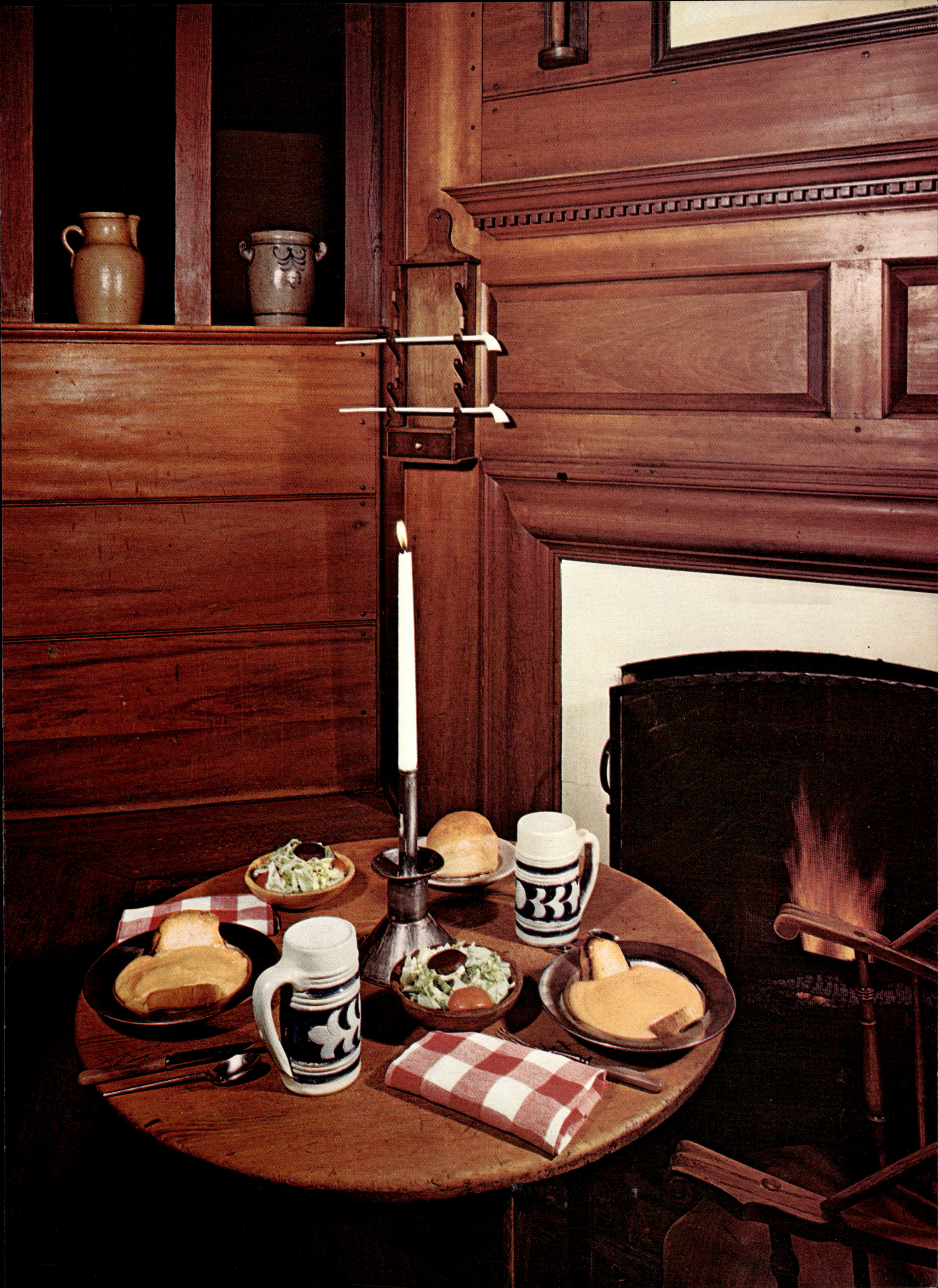

The Charm of Country/Colonial

Country/Colonial

CALICO COLESLAW
YIELD: 71 (½ cup) servings
INGREDIENTS:

Vacuum-pack golden whole kernel corn or corn with sweet peppers, drained	1 75 oz. (#10 can)
Cabbage, shredded	6 qt.
Onion, finely chopped	3 cups
Sharp cheddar cheese, cubed	12 oz.
Black olives, sliced	¾ cup

CREAMY MUSTARD DRESSING:

Mayonnaise	1½ qt.
Vinegar, apple cider	1 cup
Sugar	¾ cup
Prepared mustagrd	1 cup
Celery seed	2 tbsp.

METHOD:
Drain corn, toss with shredded cabbage, onion, cheese and olives. Combine mayonnaise, mustard and sugar. Add vinegar and celery seed, blend thoroughly. Toss cabbage mixture with dressing, chill.

OPTIONAL DRESSING
INGREDIENTS:

Tarragon vinegar	2¼ cups
Sugar	2¼ cups
Salad oil	1½ cups
Salt	¼ cup
Celery seed	1 tbsp.

METHOD:
Combine sugar, salt and vinegar in jar with tight-fitting cover; shake until sugar is dissolved. Add salad oil and celery seed to vinegar mixture; shake until well combined. Toss cabbage mixture with dressing; chill.

COUNTRY CAPTAIN
YIELD: 24 servings
INGREDIENTS:

Broiler-fryer chickens, cut in 8ths or use half breasts, thighs & drumsticks	6-3 lb.
Salt *	
Pepper *	
Butter or margarine *	

Country Captain Chicken made its first appearance in the South, where the recipe was brought back from India by our early American sea captains who knew a great dish when they tasted it. Today, Country Captain, opposite page, is eaten with zest from Maine to California, in city cafeteria or rural restaurant.

Onions, medium	4
Garlic cloves, crushed	3 to 4
Curry powder	⅓ cup
Leaf thyme	1 tbsp.
Stewed tomatoes or use regular pack*, seasoned	3 qt.
Currants or raisins	1½ cups
Hot cooked rice	
Toasted blanched almonds	
Chutney	

METHOD:
Sprinkle chicken pieces on both sides with salt and pepper.* Heat butter in large skillet; add chicken and brown on all sides. Remove chicken from skillet and add onion, green pepper, garlic, curry powder and thyme. Cook until onion is tender but not brown. Add tomatoes, currants and chicken. Cook, covered, 20 to 30 minutes, until chicken is tender. Serve over rice with almonds and chutney.
*Amount will depend on the strength of the curry and whether seasoned tomatoes are used.

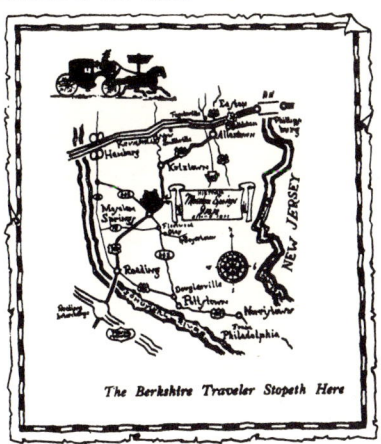

FRESH APPLE BREAD
Stephenson's Apple Farm

YIELD: 35 servings (2-in. sq.)
INGREDIENTS:

Shortening	1 qt.
Sugar	5 cups
Eggs, whole	10
Flour	1 gallon
Baking powder	2 tbsp.
Baking soda	4 tsp.
Salt	1 tbsp.
Orange rind	¼ cup
Raisins	3 cups
Nuts	1 cup
Apples, raw, peeled, and chopped	1 gallon
Apple cider	3 cups

METHOD:
Cream shortening, add sugar gradually. Beat eggs thoroughly and blend with shortening. Sift together flour, baking powder, baking soda and salt, add to shortening mixture. Mix together and add to the above mixture the orange rind, raisins, nuts, chopped apples and apple cider. Pour into well-greased 1½-in. by 14 by 10-in. cobbler baking pan, bake at 350°F. for 45 minutes.

COUNTRY HARVEST BUFFET

In the summertime Stephenson's Apple Farm Restaurant patrons may fill their plates from the Country Harvest Buffet and dine under the trees of an apple orchard. Buffet foods, below are easily carried the few steps to the orchards.

APPETIZER TABLE
Brisling Sardines
Fillet of Sardine
Smoked Oysters
Cheese Tray
Cold Cuts
Cold Baked Whitefish (Haddock)
Tiny Smoked Sausages

SALAD TABLE
Tiny Whole Spiced Beets
Marinated Green Beans
Corn Relish
Sweet Sour Cucumber & Onion Slices
Ripe Sliced Tomatoes
Stuffed Celery Sticks
Green Onion & Radish Tray
Deviled Eggs
Creamed Cottage Cheese
Potato Salad
Garden Salad
Marshmallow Salad
Jellied Cinnamon Apple Salad
Jellied Waldorf Salad

RELISHES
Stuffed Olives
Sweet Cherry Peppers
Snef Gerkins (Mustard Pickles)

VEGETABLE TABLE
Wax Beans & Ham
Creamed New Potatoes & Peas
Green Rice
Country Style Corn in Cream
Baked Cinnamon Apples

MEAT STEAM TABLE
Hickory Smoked Brisket of Beef
Hickory Smoked Sliced Ham
Hickory Smoked BarBQ Ribs
Hickory Smoked BarBQ Chicken
Hickory Smoked BarBQ Gizzards
Hickory Smoked Weiners with Creole Sauce

BREADS & MISCELLANEOUS
Hot Light Rolls
Muffins (variety of flavors, i.e. apple, banana, chocolate chip etc.)
Apple Butter

DESSERT TABLE
Fresh Fruit Bowl (center piece)
Old Fashioned Strawberry Shortcake
Fresh Apple or Cherry Cobbler
Tomato Cake
Caramel Pecan Pie
Butterscotch Whipped Cream Pie

The Charm of Country/Colonial

At Salem Tavern, Winston Salem, N. C., a waiter, dressed in authentic 19th century garb, places service on table. Flatware is stainless steel copied from 18th century pewter. Pistol handled knives and three tined forks complete the service. The butterfly sconces above the mantel are copies of a local Moravian design.

Table and chairs in the dining rooms are largely reproductions of pieces in the Old Salem collection, top right. The sawbuck tables are copies of an early Moravian table in the "Single Brothers House," another of the six exhibit buildings in the historic area. Records indicate that the chair boards around the room were introduced in 1816.

Hostesses in 19th century Moravian dress greet guests in hallway of Salem Tavern Dining Rooms, at right. Cupboard on left, sometimes called a welsh dresser or hutch, was made in early Salem.

SALEM : TAVERN

Wednesday Dinner

Pickl'd Herring
Clear Mushroom Broth

Rouladen ~ Oven Brown'd Potatos   4.00
Bak'd Chicken, Rosemary Dressing   3.85

Beets with Dill
Spic'd Cream'd Onions
Butter Beans

Cabbage Salad   Tavern Bread

Winklers Cream Puffs
Rice Pudding, Rasberry Sauce
Apple Dumpling ~ Orange Gustav

Coffee   Tea   Milk   Cider

Draft Beer
Wine: bottle
      half-bottle
      glass

ALWAYS AVAILABLE

Strip Sirloin Steak $6.25
Rib Eye Steak   6.00
Double Loin Lamb Chops   6.95
Chicken Pie   4.25
Chopped Sirloin Steak   3.25
Green Salad

Part of the restoration of a Moravian congregation in Winston-Salem, N.C., the six Salem Tavern Dining Rooms are furnished in early 19th century style. Lighting is almost exclusively by candlelight. Curtains are in yellow, red or blue checks. According to the custom of the period, no tablecloths or placemats are used. German specialties, always a feature of the menu, include such items as sauerbraten, rouladen, goulash, knackwurst with sauerkraut and filled German pancakes. Other menu choices are always available.
Designed by: John E. Markham; Laventhol, Krekstein; Horwath and Horwath, Architect, John C. Page, Lashmit, Brown & Pollock.

Above, a typical menu from Salem Tavern Dining Rooms lists Winklers cream puffs. The Winkler Bakery, a few doors from the Dining Rooms began operation in 1807. It is now open to demonstrate 18th century baking methods for visitors and purveys limited bakery products from a small retail shop.

The Charm of Country/Colonial

Top left, the Lenape Inn, West Chester, Pa. has panelling in main dining room as background for Currier & Ives prints. Shutters are used as dividers when privacy is needed for parties, yet when open add to spaciousness. Large fireplace provides focal point for second room.

Bottom left, the Moselem Inn's first diners came in Conestoga wagons a hundred years ago. Today's guests find interiors furnished with reminders of an earlier day. The Blue Willow Room, transformed from a combination sitting and waiting room to a light and airy dining room, was planned as a setting for the Blue Willow ware crockery used for the Inn's early guests. The Presidential Room, not pictured, is the formal dining room at Moselem Springs Inn. As one guest reported, "The big problem is to hold back on the homemake bread and tub butter to save room for everything else." Diners with hearty appetites have been eating in this room since the Inn opened some 100 years ago in Fleetwood, Pa. Presidential portraits, in gold frames, white tablecloths, red and blue menus, golden chandeliers with red electric candles, golden draperies and Pennsylvania windsor chairs are used to develop the Presidential motif.

The King's Arms Tavern, across the street from the famous Raleigh Tavern in Williamsburg, specializes in Virginia ham, peanut soup and Sally Lunn bread. Breast of chicken is served with the ham in an authentically simple and elegant atmosphere.
Beer is served in classic colonial glassware.

The Charm of Country/Colonial

BAKED LOBSTER PIE
Colonial Inn
YIELD: 4 servings
INGREDIENTS:

Lobster meat	1 lb.
Milk, hot	3 cups
Sherry	1 oz.
Paprika, good size pinch	1
Monosodium glutamate, good size pinch	1
Salt and pepper	to taste
Butter or margarine	1/8 lb.
Bread flour (heaping)	1 tbsp.

METHOD:
Saute lobster meat in butter or margarine, with the paprika until it crackles. Add flour and cook about 1 minute. Add sherry and milk, bring to a boil and simmer for a few minutes. Season with salt and pepper and monosodium glutamate.

Put in casserole and top with fresh bread crumbs and melted butter. Bake in 400°F. oven until crumbs brown.

TOPPING: Mix fresh bread crumbs with salt, pepper, monosodium glutamate, paprika, sherry, lemon juice and dash of Worcestershire sauce.

CHICKEN STOLTZFUS
Amish Wedding Chicken—
Groff's Farm
YIELD: 6 portions (At Groff's Farm, this dish is prepared 1 roasting hen at a time)
INGREDIENTS:

Roasting hen	1 5-lb.
Saffron	pinch
Salt and pepper	to taste
Whipping cream	1 cup
Celery, diced	1 cup
Parsley flakes	1 tsp.
Cornstarch	3 tbsp.

METHOD:
Put hen in enough water to cover. Add saffron, salt, pepper and simmer 1¼ hours or until tender. Cool, drain, reserving broth. Cut meat from bones and into chunks.

Mix cornstarch with ½ cup broth until smooth. Heat 2 cups broth with cream, celery and parsley flakes and when boiling stir in cornstarch mixture. When mixture has thickened, add chicken, taste for seasoning and spoon over pastry biscuits. Garnish servings with chopped parsley.

ESCALLOPED SWEET POTATOES & APPLES
Stephenson's Apple Farm Restaurant
YIELD: 50 servings
INGREDIENTS:

Sweet Potatoes (canned)	15 lb.
Apples (canned or frozen)	8 lb.
Oleo	2 lb.
Brown sugar	6 lb.
Water	1 qt.
Salt	2 oz.
Cinnamon	2 tsp.
Pineapple	1 #2-can
Maraschino cherries	1 cup

METHOD:
Slice sweet potatoes ¼-in. thick; alternate with sliced apples in 12 by 20-in. pan. Make syrup combining oleo, brown sugar, water, salt and cinnamon and pour over the sweet potatoes and apples. Sprinkle pineapple over apple and sweet potato layers. Sprinkle the cherries over the pineapple. Bake 1 hour at 325°F.

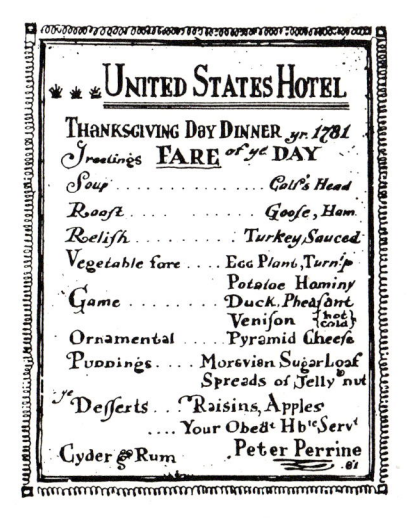

```
UNITED STATES HOTEL
THANKSGIVING DAY DINNER yr. 1781
Greetings    FARE of ye DAY
Soup.............Calf's Head
Roast............Goose, Ham
Relish..........Turkey Sauced
Vegetable fare..Egg Plant, Turnip
                Potatoe Hominy
Game............Duck, Pheasant
                Venison (hot cold)
Ornamental......Pyramid Cheese
Puddings.......Moravian Sugar Loaf
               Spreads of Jelly nut
Ye Desserts....Raisins, Apples
             ...Your Obedᵗ Hbˡᵉ Servᵗ
Cyder & Rum      Peter Perrine
                        '81
```

BREAST OF CAPON
Colonial Inn

Boil breast of capon in a rich chicken stock until almost done. Remove and split in two. Remove all bones. Brush breast with butter and brown under the broiler on both sides. Brown thin slices of ham, place on slice of toast, and place capon breast over ham and cover with a rich almond sauce. Garnish with a kumquat in a small bed of chicory and serve.

ALMOND SAUCE: Saute slivered almonds in butter, add a few drops of almond extract and sauterne wine and add rich supreme sauce. Simmer for 10 minutes and strain through a fine strainer.

BEERSHIRE CHEESE PIE
YIELD: 24 servings
INGREDIENTS:

Bacon, sliced	1 lb.
Swiss cheese, grated	2 lb.
Flour	¼ cup
9" unbaked pastry shells	4
Butter or margarine	¼ lb.
Onions, peeled and sliced	2 lb.
Eggs, slightly beaten	12
Beer	3 cups
Milk	1 cup
Tabasco	1 tsp.
Salt	2 tsp.
Dry mustard	½ tsp.

METHOD:
Cook bacon until crisp, drain on absorbent paper and crumble into small pieces. Beat together eggs, beer, milk, Tabasco and seasonings. Combine bacon and cheese; dredge with flour. Melt butter; add onion slices and cook until tender, not brown. Distribute cheese-bacon mixture evenly in 4 unbaked pastry shells. Place layer of cooked onion on each pie and fill shells with egg-beer mixture. Bake 350°F., 30 to 35 minutes.

STUFFED BAKED FLOUNDER
Colligan's Stockton Inn
YIELD: 30 servings
INGREDIENTS:

Titi shrimp	10 lb.
Flounder fillets (6 oz. ea.)	30 pcs.
Shallots	1½ cups
Mushrooms	2 lb.
Parsley, chopped	½ cup
Flour	2 lb.
Milk	1½ qt.
Dry white wine	1½ cups
Butter	1½ lb.
Lemons, juice of	2
Worcestershire sauce	2 tbsp.
Salt and white pepper	to taste

METHOD:
Melt butter, add shallots, parsley, mushrooms, flour blend roux blanc, milk, wine, lemon juice, Worcestershire sauce, salt and pepper. Stir until smooth. Remove from heat and add pre-blanched shrimp. Fill flounder with stuffing. Bake in moderate oven for 20 minutes.

The Charm of Country/Colonial

Above, the fine food and the atmosphere of yesteryear can be found at Christiana Campbell's Tavern in Williamsburg, Virginia. In the 1700's George Washington was a frequent visitor here. Tavern pot pie and beer in pewter mugs are served in the tap room.

Mushrooms grew wild near most early country inns and taverns, and undoubtedly found their way into many pots. Today, cultivated varieties bring their earthy goodness to country recipes like Chef Manuel Alicia's steak sauce, served at Lenape Inn, above left. Mushroomy biscuits, bottom left, a house specialty at Lenape Inn make country dining memorable.

Country/Colonial

LENAPE MUSHROOM STEAK SAUCE
YIELD: 1 gallon
INGREDIENTS:

Fresh mushrooms	2 lb.
or	
Canned sliced mushrooms	1 can (1 lb.)
Medium onions, chopped	1 lb. (4 cups)
Garlic cloves, minced	8 (2½ tbsp.)
Butter or margarine, divided	1½ cups
Beef bouillon, undiluted	2 cans (3 lb. 3 oz. ea.)
Tomato paste	¾ cup
Ground black pepper	1 tsp.
Cornstarch	⅓ cup
Marsala wine	1 cup

METHOD:
Rinse, pat dry and slice fresh mushrooms or drain canned mushrooms; put aside. In a medium pot saute onion and garlic in ½ cup of the butter. Add bouillon, tomato paste and black pepper. Bring to boiling point, reduce heat, cover and simmer 10 minutes. Meanwhile, in a large skillet saute reserved mushrooms until golden in remaining 1 cup butter; set aside. Blend cornstarch with ½ cup cold water. Mix some of the hot onion mixture into cornstarch mixture. Return all to pot; cook until clear and thickened, stirring. Strain sauce; return to pot. Add sauteed mushrooms and Marsala to sauce. Bring to boiling point and serve over steak, meat loaf, etc.

MUSHROOM BISCUITS
YIELD: 9 dozen
INGREDIENTS:

Fresh mushrooms	3 lb.
or	
Canned mushroom stems & pieces	2 cans (1 lb. ea.)

The recipe for Colonial Capped Ham Steaks in preceding color page, uses ingredients first purchased when the cracker barrel was a prominent feature in the country store including the crackers which make the dressing atop the ham. Cranberry juice, brown sugar, sweet potatoes, pecans, marjoram and all-spice are other ingredient ideas borrowed from early larder shelves.

Butter or margarine	4 tbsp.
Onion, finely chopped	1½ cups
Thyme, ground	1½ tsp.
White pepper, ground	½ tsp.
Biscuit mix	3 lb.
Milk	1 qt.

METHOD:
Rinse, pat dry and coarsely chop fresh mushrooms (makes about four and half quarts) or drain canned mushrooms. Heat butter in a large skillet. Add mushrooms and onion and saute for 5 minutes, or until mushrooms are golden brown. Sprinkle with thyme and white pepper. Cool slightly. Blend mushroom mixture into biscuit mix. Add milk and stir until well mixed. Drop by the tablespoon onto greased cookie sheets 2-in. apart. Bake in preheated hot oven (450°F) 12 minutes or until nicely browned. Serve with chicken, meat or fish.

SWEET-SOUR SAUERKRAUT RELISH
Stephenson's Apple Farm Restaurant
YIELD: 1 gallon
INGREDIENTS:

Apples (chopped medium)	4 cups
Sauerkraut (drained)	8 cups
Celery, chopped	2 cups
Onion, chopped	1 cup
Red bell peppers, chopped	1 cup
Green bell peppers, chopped	1 cup
Mustard seed	4 tsp.
Celery seed	2 tsp.
Cider Vinegar	2 cups
Sugar	2 cups

METHOD:
Boil until the cider vinegar and sugar become thick. Pour syrup while hot over above fruit and vegetable mixture. Cover tightly and put in refrigerator for 24 hours before using.

CRACKER PUDDING
Groff's Farm, Mount Joy, Pa.
YIELD: 60 servings
INGREDIENTS:

Milk	4 qt.
Eggs, separated	8
Sugar	2⅔ cups
Salted crackers, broken	8 cups
Sweet coconut, grated	8 cups
Vanilla	4 tsp.

METHOD:
Beat egg yolks with sugar. Bring eggs and milk to boil. Gradually add broken crackers and add coconut stirring until thickened. Fold in stiffly beaten egg whites and vanilla. Serve as a side dish with meat.

TAVERN GOULASH
Salem Tavern Dining Rooms
YIELD: 24 servings
INGREDIENTS:

Onions, chopped	6 large
Butter	3 tbsp.
Oil	3 tbsp.
Veal, cubed	3 lb.
Beef, cubed	3 lb.
Pork, cubed	1½ lb.
Coarse black pepper	2 tbsp.
Hungarian paprika	8 tbsp.
Sauerkraut	1 #10 can
Beef broth	1 qt.
Beer, dark	1 qt.
Caraway seeds	6 tbsp.
Sugar, brown	2 tbsp.
Sour cream	1½ qt.

METHOD:
Wilt onions in butter and oil. Add combined meats and brown, stirring. Add remaining ingredients, except sour cream. Cook slowly 2 to 2½ hours. Stir in sour cream, heat thoroughly and serve, liberally sprinkled with chopped parsley and accompanied by buttered noodles.

Eighteenth-Century Dining

Christiana Campbell's Tavern

THIS was one of *George Washington's* favorite eating Places. Reopened after 200 Years, it offers delicious Food and colorful Surroundings which make Dining at *Campbell's* a "must" in *Williamsburg*. It features fresh Seafood from the *Chesapeake Bay*, charcoal-broiled Steaks, and superb southern Spoonbread. Beverage Specialties include several international Coffees, fine Wines, and *Black Velvet* Cocktails. Luncheon 12 to 2:30; Dinner 6 to 8:30.

King's Arms Tavern

FAMOUS for its colonial and southern Foods served in an eighteenth-century Setting. Enjoy fine Meals here as did *Thomas Jefferson* and *Patrick Henry*. Dine by Candlelight, using three-foot-square Damask Napkins and relive the Days when Dining was a gracious Experience. *Virginia* Ham, fried Chicken, Mutton Chops, Peanut Soup, *Sally Lunn* Bread, and a choice Selection of Wines are among the delicacies served by Waiters in colorful Costumes. Light Luncheons are featured 12 to 2:30; Dinner is served from 6 to 8.

Chowning's Tavern

ENJOY traditional Tavern Gaiety and good Food in this picturesque eighteenth-century Alehouse. Specialties include *Brunswick* Stew, *Welsh* Rabbit, Pecan Waffles, fine Ale, and *Michelob* Beer from oaken Kegs at the Wicket Bar. *Chowning's* also features Steaks, charcoal broiled in the Garden during the Evening. Open from Noon to 10:30 P.M.

Luncheon Reservations are not necessary at these Restaurants. Evening Reservations are suggested for *King's Arms Tavern* and *Christiana Campbell's Tavern*. They may be made in Person or by calling CApital 9-1700.

The Charm of Country/Colonial

Above, as simple and satisfying as a Shaker design is Gingerbread, a favorite dessert of our founding fathers. Bring it up to date with a new recipe using yams which keep the cake moist, but by all means maintain the tradition by serving fragrant, spicy Gingerbread warm with whipped cream or a not-too-sweet topping.

There were many miles of hard going between inns for our early travelers, but often as not there was a steaming kettle of soup awaitin' at the stop-off. Thick bean soup, hearty chowders or invigorating Pepper Pot, shown top right.

Early Yankee kitchens were filled with the tantalizing aromas of molasses cookies, fruit pies, baked beans and brown bread. If a peddler stopped by to show milady or an innkeeper his wares and exchange the latest gossip, he might be invited to sit down at the table and sample a bowl of freshly baked cobbler, like the one shown bottom right, made with a favorite Yankee cookie, the Fig Newton.

Country/Colonial

A COUNTRY KITCHEN SPICE CHART

How to use this chart: These are suggestions for bringing new variety to "old favorite" dishes through the addition of a new spice or two. Basically, this is a flavor compatibility chart, designed to indicate flavors that enhance or contrast deliciously with various foods. Amounts are left to your taste and experimentation. In many cases you may only want to introduce a hint of flavor difference, but in all these ideas there is the promise of distinction—that touch that puts your name on the dish. All of these suggestions can be used with convenience food products as well as when you are cooking from scratch.

STARTERS	SOUPS	MEATS	POULTRY	SEAFOOD	VEG'T'BLES	RELISHES	DESSERTS
TOMATO JUICE Crumbled Basil Leaves and Celery Salt.	CLAM CHOWDER Crumbled Thyme Leaves.	BEEF STEW Stick Cinnamon and Ground Nutmeg.	SIMMERED CHICKEN Marjoram Leaves, Onion Salt, Parsley Flakes, and Ground Mace.	CRABMEAT Ground Nutmeg (in sauce).	BAKED POTATOES Dried Shallots (in sour cream).	CRANBERRY RELISH Mixed Pickling Spice.	APPLE PIE Caraway Seed (in crust).
MELON BALLS Mint Flakes and Ground Ginger.	SPLIT PEA Dill Weed.	CHILI CON CARNE Chili Powder and Instant Onion and Garlic Powders.	ROAST DUCK W/ORANGE Curry, Powder, Ground Ginger, and Instant Onion and Garlic Powders.	POACHED FISH Fennel Seed, Bay Leaves (in liquid).	CREAMED SPINACH Onion and Celery Salts plus Ground Nutmeg.	APPLE-SAUCE Ground Cinnamon and Ground Ginger.	BLUEBERRY PIE Ground Allspice (in filling).
FRUIT COCKTAIL Stick Cinnamon, Whole Cloves and Ground Mace.	CREAM OF TOMATO Poultry Seasoning, Sweet Pepper Flakes and Ground Nutmeg.	MEAT BALLS Instant Garlic Powder and Ground Cumin Seed.	BARBECUED CHICKEN Barbecue Spice and Onion and Garlic Salts.	TUNA FISH SALAD Ground Turmeric and Celery Flakes.	STIR FRIED KERN. CORN Paprika, Instant Onion Powder and Ground Black Pepper.	PICKLED MUSHR'MS. Instant Minced Onion, Instant Garlic Powder, Fennel Seed, and Thyme Leaves.	CHERRY PIE Ground Mace (in filling).
CHOPPED CHICKEN LIVERS Instant Garlic Powder and Ground Black Pepper.	CREAM OF MUSHROOM Ground Coriander Seed.	LAMB STEW Crumbled Rosemary Leaves and Mixed Vegetable Flakes.	TURKEY STUFFING Poultry Seasoning, Sesame Seed and Sweet Pepper Flakes.	BOILED LOBSTER Curry Powder (in butter).	BUTTERED BROCCOLI Crumbled Tarragon Leaves.	SPICED PEACHES Ground Ginger, with Clove-studding.	AMBROSIA Mint Flakes and Ground Nutmeg (in juice).
RASPB'RY SHRUB Ground Allspice.	ONION Ground Marjoram.	PORK ROAST Mixed Pickling Spice (in a stock-based marinade).	LEMON CHICKEN Parsley Flakes, Ground White Pepper and Onion Flakes.	FRIED SCALLOPS Seasoned, or Flavor Salt (in breading).	GRILLED TOMATOES Crumbled Oregano Leaves, Ground Black Pepper and Instant Onion Powder.	PICKLED BEETS Dill Seed and Onion Flakes.	STRAWB'RY WHIP Ground Cinnamon and Ground Nutmeg.
GRAPE-FRUIT Ground Cardamon (in brown sugar).	CORN CHOWDER Chili Powder and Mixed Vegetable Flakes.	HAM STEAK Ground Cinnamon and Ground Cloves; top with Sesame Seeds.	ROAST GOOSE Stuff with Caraway-flavored Sauerkraut.	BAKED FISH Basil Leaves, Ground Black Pepper and Saffron (in tomato sauce).	GREEN BEANS Ground Savory.	PINEAPPLE PICKLE Anise Seed.	CHEESE-CAKE Poppy Seed (in filling).
SEAFOOD COCKTAIL Curry Powder (in a tomato-mayonnaise sauce).	OYSTER STEW Ground Allspice.	FLANK STEAK Powdered Mustard, Ground Savory and Ground Black Pepper.	CHICKEN PIE Instant Minced Onion and Garlic, plus Ground Turmeric.	SHRIMP Shrimp Spice or Crab Boil (in cooking water).	COLE SLAW Poppy Seed (in dressing).	TOMATO Celery Seeds and Powdered Mustard.	CUSTARD Ground Nutmeg and Ground Allspice.
APPLE JUICE Stick Cinnamon.	BEAN Ground Ginger.	ROAST VEAL Instant Onion and Garlic Powders, Ground Ginger, and Tarragon Leaves.	CHICKEN CROQUETS Celery Salt and Ground Nutmeg.	BROILED FISH Paprika and Onion Salt, (sprinkled liberally).	CUCUMBERS Dill Seed, Ground Oregano and Ground Black Pepper (in sweetened vinegar).	PICKLED WATER-MELON RIND Apple or Pumpkin Pie Spice.	BREAD PUDDING Pumpkin Pie Spice.

Succeeding with Country/Colonial Themes

An atmosphere that offers a change from the everyday must be created, if a dining-out experience is to capture the interest of American patrons. Experts stress that escape is a primary factor in any formula for eating out success today. In underscoring this belief, Arthur Morgan, AID affirms, "Going out to be 'entertained' at dinner will continue to be one of the good American reasons for eating out."

The early days of America or the remembered tales of happy farm life conjured up by Colonial and Country settings have the added appeal of nostalgia when selected as themes for dining out.

An historic building, the history of a locale, rural activities or the preservation of national customs by a rural group—any one of these may contain the theme for a unique food service.

That historic buildings can successfully dominate the development of the setting and menu is underlined by the Salem Tavern Dining Rooms, Winston-Salem, N. C., the Colonial Inn, Concord, Mass., Emily Shaw's Inn in Pound Ridge, N. Y. or the three dining rooms of the Williamsburg, Va. restoration.

The historic importance of the area is stressed at Lenape Inn. It is reached from Philadelphia over a one-time stage coach route along winding roads, a destination for travelers who seek "to dine on the banks of the historic Brandywine." The lure is a return to romantic quaintness. Increasing patronage proves that the 15 miles from Wilmington or the 25 from Philadelphia is no deterrent.

Moselem Springs Inn, between Reading and Kutztown, draws on its historic location too. Purchased from the Commonwealth of Pennsylvania, the land changed hands four times before the hotel was erected in 1852 on what was then an important trade route from Philadelphia to the West.

A reputation for fine food and hospitality was established from the outset as the Inn drew a dozen or more Conestoga wagons nightly. Often more guests than beds, old records show. Today's dining rooms at the Moselem Springs Inn display design reminders of its historic role in Pennsylvania's development; a menu, representative of the Inn's fine food heritage, completes the scene.

The fruits of an apple orchard, inspiration for Stephenson's Apple Farm Restaurant near Kansas City, Mo. or the spaciousness of the converted barn at Angus Barn, Raleigh, N. C. provide foundations for highly effective country dining experiences.

Country/Colonial

An added dimension for rural Americana comes when it is combined with a national heritage of colorful food and customs. The popularity of eating places capitalizing on the food heritage of the Pennsylvania Dutch proves this. The dimension may be Scandinavian, as at Jul's, Rock Falls, Ill. with its exceptional smorgasbord, or German, as in the several family-style dining rooms of Iowa's Amana Colonies. The favorite foods of Cornish miners, served in rooms restored from early Welsh dwellings, give another world flavor to Pendarvis House near Spring Green, Wis.

A pleasant retreat to the past, achieved by whatever path, draws patrons in increasing numbers to food service/lodging operations today.

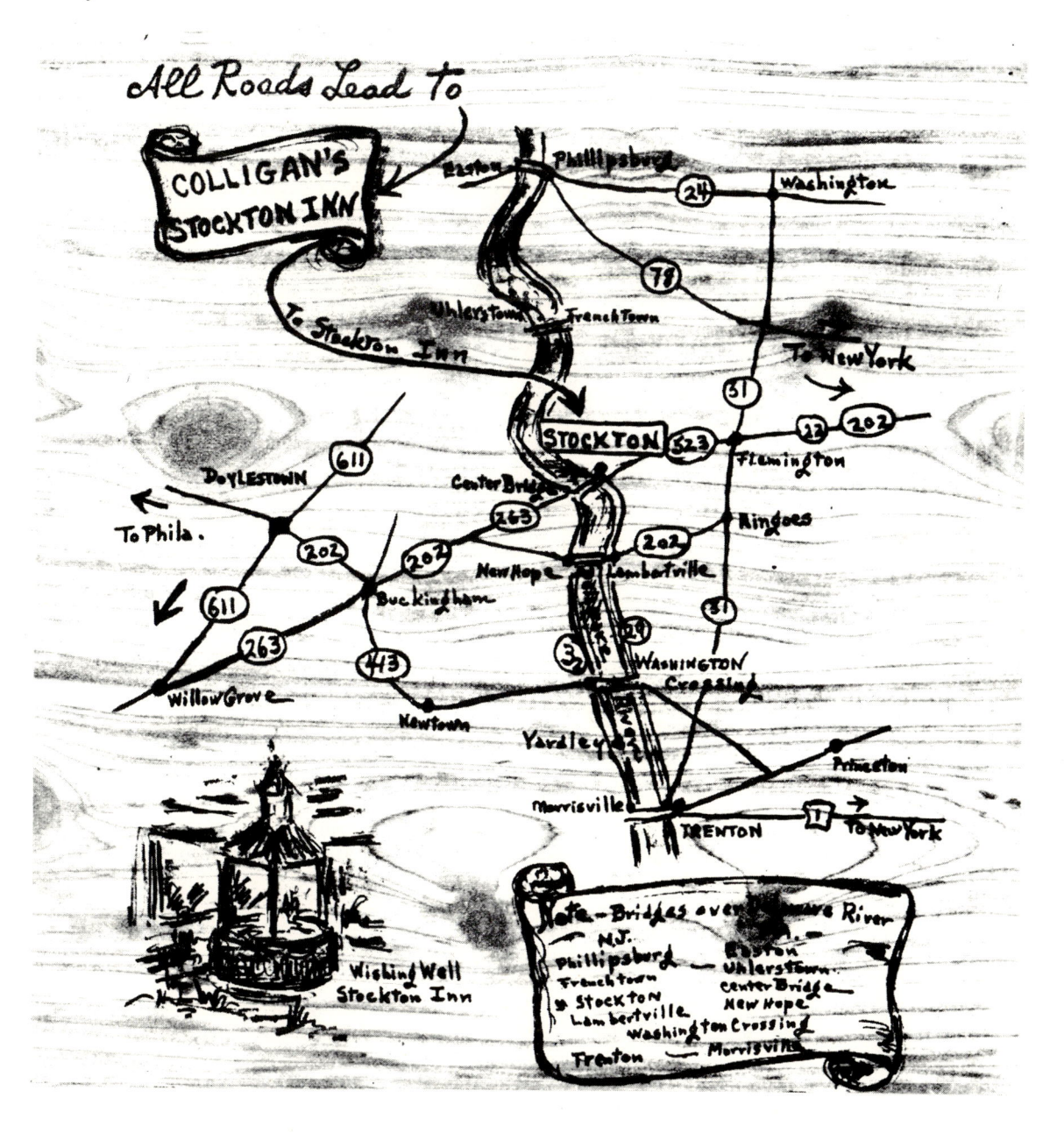

Historic Appeals For Modern Diners

Although American society continues to be characterized as mobile and largely rootless, a counter concentration on preserving the past is developing among a growing segment of the population. Almost every community has its organization devoted to searching out and saving historic buildings or even well designed buildings from an earlier day.

The efforts of these organizations can uncover sites for food service/lodging operations that have unique appeal. Since the work of preservationists is of general interest, and usually well publicized, public anticipation is well developed long before the opening day.

GROWING ACCEPTANCE FOR ATMOSPHERE BASED ON THE SIMPLE LIFE

Food service/lodging in historical settings, with its option to patrons of "dropping out" for an hour or so in surroundings styled for a slower-paced period, becomes increasingly inviting as the turmoil of today continues. Salem Tavern Dining Rooms, Old Salem, Winston-Salem, N. C., is a profitable example of the way in which cooperating with preservation efforts can establish the theme for a successful food service.

In 1950, a non-profit corporation, Old Salem, Inc. was organized to preserve and restore the historic area known as Old Salem. These efforts resulted in the re-creation both of the outward appearance and the atmosphere of an 18th and early 19th century Moravian congregation town.

Salem had been founded in 1766 by a group of Pennsylvania Moravians and rapidly grew as a trading center and as the center of Moravian religious activity. Moravian settlers had early established a reputation for delicious foods and baked items. Family celebrations were marked by the serving of Love Feast Buns and Moravian Sugar Cake. At Christmas, special spicy cookies were traditional.

In describing Moravian food contributions to American cuisine, The American Heritage Cookbook reports, "In Old Salem, North Carolina love feasts were celebrated at least five times a year: at New Year's, during Lent, at Christmas, and on August 13 and November 13 (two special Moravian feast days). In 1783, when the community celebrated the Fourth of July for the first time, the observance included a love feast."

The area now known as Old Salem flourished as a Moravian community from 1766 until about 1830. It was a planned com-

Country/Colonial

munity with buildings constructed flush to the walks and clustered around a central square.

One of the first requisites of a trading center in Colonial days was a tavern to care for travelers; thus Salem Tavern was constructed soon after the town's founding. As the Salem Tavern brochure states:

In their plans for the town of Salem, the 18th century Moravians assigned a high priority to their tavern. For Salem was to be a trading center in what was then rugged back country. It was essential that there be a lodging place both for passing travelers and for traders who would come to Salem to buy the wares of the skilled Moravian craftsmen. Moreover, Salem was to be operated as a congregation town in which the church would direct the town's economic as well as its religious affairs. A tavern, the practical-minded Brethren agreed, could generate income to help defray community expenses.

From the beginning, the congregation elders laid down strict rules for the operation of Salem Tavern. Guests must be treated "with kindness and cordiality," and "served with wholesome and plentiful food." Beds, windows, crockery and utensils were to be "clean and in good order." Soon the reputation of the well-run Tavern spread, and travelers often journeyed extra miles to reach its homelike comforts.

On January 31, 1784, fire destroyed the half-timber Tavern building. But the Tavern had proved to be so important to Salem that five days later the ruins were cleared, and immediately a new building was started—this one of brick. This 1784 Tavern, which has been designated a Registered National Historic Landmark, still stands and is one of the major exhibit buildings in Old Salem.

Under the watchful eye of the Salem elders, the Tavern continued to offer good food and warm hospitality throughout the late 18th and early 19th centuries. By 1805 all of the available space in the brick Tavern had been converted to accommodate the many travelers who wished to stop there. So in 1816 a weather-boarded, 2-story, 8-room building just north of the Tavern was constructed to take care of the overflow of Tavern guests. It is this adjacent building, now restored, that houses the Salem Tavern Dining Rooms. In the restoration, detailed descriptions of the house as found in the records kept by the early Moravians have been followed closely.

Restoration efforts, started in 1950, had proceeded by 1967 to a point where it became feasible to provide dining facilities for the visitors to Old Salem. The initial planning for the food service operation was guided by two purposes:
(1) To provide facilities within the historic area of Old Salem where visitors and residents of the community could be served a good meal in pleasant surroundings;
(2) To add another dimension to the interpretation of 18th and early 19th century life as exemplified by the Old Salem restoration effort.

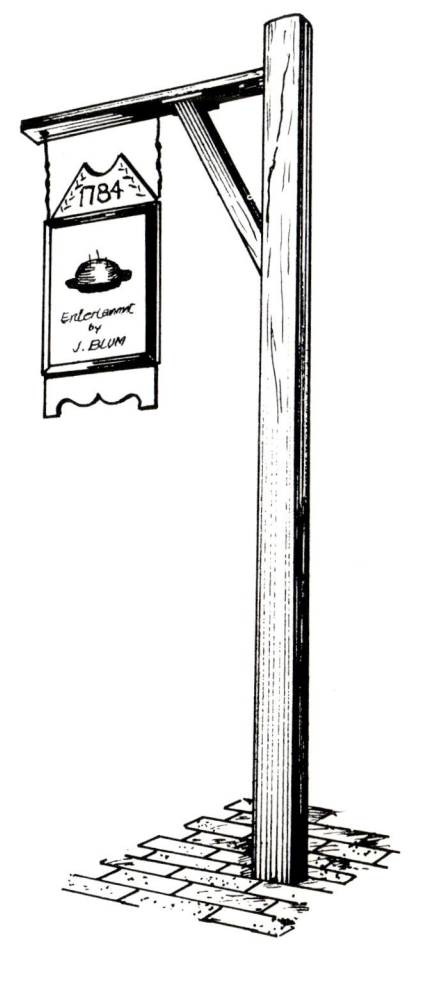

Visitors to Old Salem, who would be expected to patronize the dining rooms, vary widely in age, educational background and income level. They include teachers, antiquarians, families on vacation, retired couples, professional people, secretaries, housewives, top-ranking government officials and industrialists.

Local patrons cover much the same range. The operation was therefore, planned to provide quality food in a pleasant atmosphere at prices which would be judged reasonable in terms of the overall experience offered. The range of prices also allows for anticipated differences in income levels. Luncheons are available from $1.25 to $2.75 and dinners, from $3.65 to $6.25.

The design for the renovation of the Tavern annex was based on the idea of making those areas that would be seen by the patrons as true to the 1816 period as possible. A design goal of equal importance was developing as practical an arrangement as possible for the kitchen and serving facilities.

To these ends, the exterior of the two-story, weatherboarded structure was restored to its 1816 appearance, as shown in illustrations preserved from those days.

On the interior, the design of the hallways and staircase of the original building was retained. Six of the building's original eight rooms (three on each floor) were restored as dining rooms; four of the dining rooms have fireplaces. The remaining two rooms (one on each floor) were converted into serving pantries and concealed from public view.

Preservation of an historic building does have built-in limitations which must be recognized in the initial planning. Basic in all cases, as at Salem Tavern Dining Rooms, is special concern with fire prevention. The historical importance of the structure led to the use of cement slab to separate the basement kitchen from the restored structure above it.

The cost per seat at the Salem Tavern Dining Rooms is admittedly higher because of the added expense of the historical restoration of the building itself, the necessity of placing the kitchen in a basement and the need for certain costly aesthetic features required to protect the historical appearance of the building.

When an existing building must be used to provide modern food service, ingenious solutions are often required to control operating costs.

One special concession to preservation of the setting was the underground ducting of the kitchen hood exhaust to a point approximately 100 ft. away from the building. This was dictated by the belief that no appendage should be permitted to mar the external historical appearance of the building.

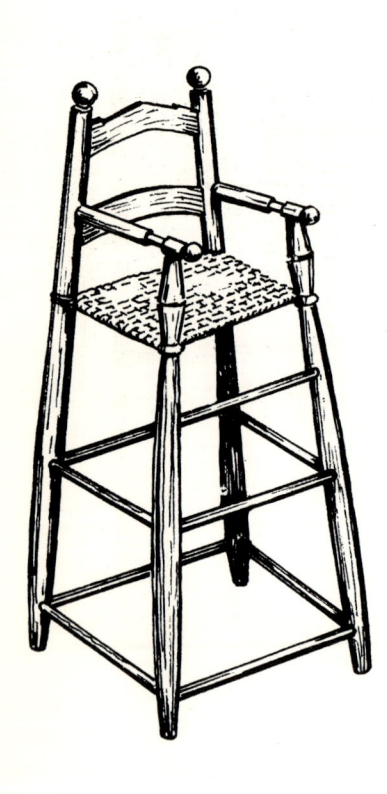

Both the building and the operation of the Salem Tavern Dining Rooms were planned to offer the patron not only good food but also the enriching experience of dining in an atmosphere of another time in history. Dining was to be kept on the same unique level as any other experience enjoyed while visiting other parts of the Old Salem restoration. To this end, in many instances, economy and practicality of operation, were knowingly sacrificed.

A basement level kitchen was one such compromise with practicality. The only area for a kitchen of sufficient size was in the basement. The area to be occupied by the kitchen had to be further enlarged by extending it outward under the front and rear porches of the building and under the front sidewalk. The sloping ramp for delivery access to the kitchen had to be semi-concealed to conform with the architectural requirements of the restoration.

Moravian dishes, Germanic in origin, were to be featured items on Salem Tavern Dining Rooms menus. The 1816 recipes were first researched for authenticity, then the historic menu items were reworked to fit into modern operations. In this area of operation, every advantage was taken of cost cutting, layout and labor-saving equipment.

One of the requirements in the design of the kitchen was the incorporation of equipment that could be utilized to take advantage of the convenience food trend. Pre-preparation and pre-fabrication procedures would be applied to the scheduled Moravian food specialities.

Among items of equipment selected to further this goal were a convection oven, a micro-wave oven, a vertical cutter/mixer, a self-

WINKLER BAKERY—This structure, erected in 1800, was built by John Gottlob Krause, the best of the Salem master builders. It takes its name from Christian Winkler, a Swiss-born Moravian who came to Salem from Lititz, Pa., in 1807 to operate the town bakery. His descendants continued to operate a bakery in the building until well into the 20th century. The upper floors of the bakery provided living quarters for the baker's family. In the restored building, early baking methods are demonstrated, using some of the original Winkler family recipes. A small retail shop at this site now sells Moravian baked goods prepared in the kitchens of the Salem Tavern Dining Rooms.

contained steam cooking center and adequate freezer storage. With this equipment, certain Moravian food items featured on the menu are effectively prepared in advance, portioned and frozen for future use. They can be quickly reconstituted from the frozen state as needed.

Because the supporting menu items, such as soups, salads, beverages and desserts originate in the service pantry, a complete meal price is offered to simplify control. Desserts at lunch are an exception and priced separately. In order to simplify entree preparation and service, a limited menu is used. Typical is this luncheon menu:

Food is brought from the kitchen to a serving pantry on each floor by dumbwaiters, one for each floor. Dishes from both floors are returned to the kitchen by a third dumbwaiter, located separately from the dumbwaiters that transport food.

Plans for the future will incorporate, in favorable weather, table service to a landscaped outdoor courtyard. It can easily be provided through a direct cellar entranceway from kitchen to courtyard.

The kitchen has been designed to handle 86 seats in the six dining rooms, approximately 20 seats on porches and the approximately 60 additional seats planned for the future in the courtyard patio. This totals 166 seats.

Included in the kitchen is a small bakery preparation area to service both the restaurant and a small retail bakery. The Winkler Bakery, located a few yards north on Main Street, has been restored to its original 18th century appearance and demonstrations of early Moravian baking are regularly scheduled there.

A small retail shop at the Winkler Bakery is supplied by the Salem Tavern Dining Room kitchen. Some of the items featured are cookies, cakes, breads, cream puffs, pies and tortes. These are prepared in limited quantities at present.

The physical design of the restaurant requires that waiters and waitresses work out of a service pantry on each serving floor. An attendant is stationed in each pantry to load and unload kitchen dumbwaiters, assemble orders, make coffee, etc.

As many food items as possible are served directly from the pantry. Designated for pantry service are most appetizers, soups, salads, beverages, cold desserts, draft beer and wine.

The main entree and accompanying vegetables come from the kitchen via the dumbwaiter. Guests are offered a triple selection of vegetables by the waiter who serves the day's choices from special "family style" vegetable dishes.

Draft beer service is provided from a two keg storage unit in the kitchen that feeds to a two-head dispenser mounted on top of the ice machine in the first floor pantry. Beer service to the second floor requires the waiter or waitress either to come to the first floor pantry to obtain it or to procure the beer via the dumbwaiter.

TUESDAY LUNCH

Corn Chowder	$ .85
Oyster-Mushroom Pie	2.50
Kaldomar	1.75
Sandwich der Tag	1.25
Cabbage Salad	Tavern Bread
Winklers Cream Puffs	
Rice Pudding with Rasberry Sauce	.40
Apple Dumpling	Orange Gustav
Coffee Tea Milk	Cider

Draft Beer
Wine: bottle
half bottle
glass

Country/Colonial

Because of the distance between the kitchen and the dining rooms,—a common problem for restaurants installed in existing buildings—particular stress has been placed on arrangements that will insure the serving of "hot foods hot". Many casserole-type dishes are featured. These retain heat well and can be portioned in the kitchen, covered and sent to the dining room to be served at the table.

All plated hot entrees are covered with heated banquet plate covers. Hot plates and covers are maintained in the kitchen in a warming cabinet or under heat lamps. Cold plates are held at optimum temperatures in a drawer under the salad-sandwich unit and in a reach-in refrigerator. (See drawing of pantry, page 32.)

Orders from the dining rooms are sent to the kitchen via a gravity feed order tube. This consists of two 2-in. plastic pipes installed along the outer wall of the dumbwaiter, with the pipe from each serving floor terminating in a receiving box at the chef's station. Three-in. lengths of 1-in. plastic rubber tubing serve as transmission vehicles.

A waiter, upon taking an order, writes it in duplicate on a two-part check. He retains the hard copy for his own use and later presentation to the guest. The duplicate is rolled up and placed in the 3-in. piece of plastic, then dropped through the transmission tube to the kitchen.

A dull thud announces its arrival in the kitchen. Check colors differ for each floor, making it easy for the chef to match order to destination. An intercom system also connects each pantry with the kitchen.

While luncheon and dinner menus feature Moravian specialties developed from 18th century recipes, established American favorites are also available to guests. Offered for lunch are such American menu staples as Chicken Pie and Chopped Sirloin Steak, each accompanied by a green salad. Conventional dinner items include Strip Sirloin Steak, Rib Eye Steak, Double Loin Lamb Chops with a repeat of the Chicken Pie and Chopped Sirloin Steak and Green Salad.

(For pictures and descriptions of dining interiors at Salem Tavern Dining Rooms, see pages 12 and 13.)

Directional markers on major highways inside the city point the way to the Old Salem Reception Center, where information may be obtained. The Tavern is located on Main Street in Old Salem, one block south of Salem Square.

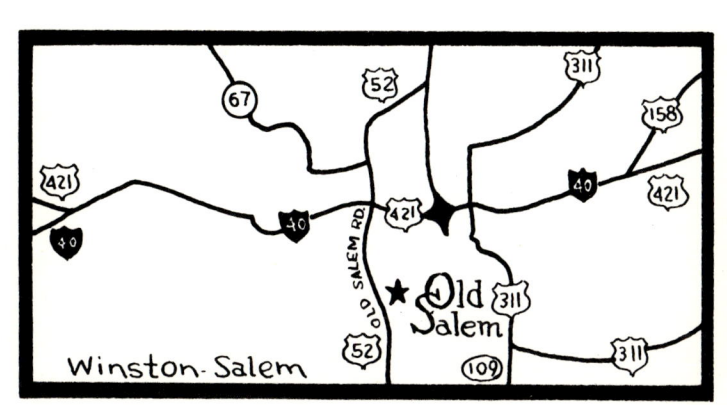

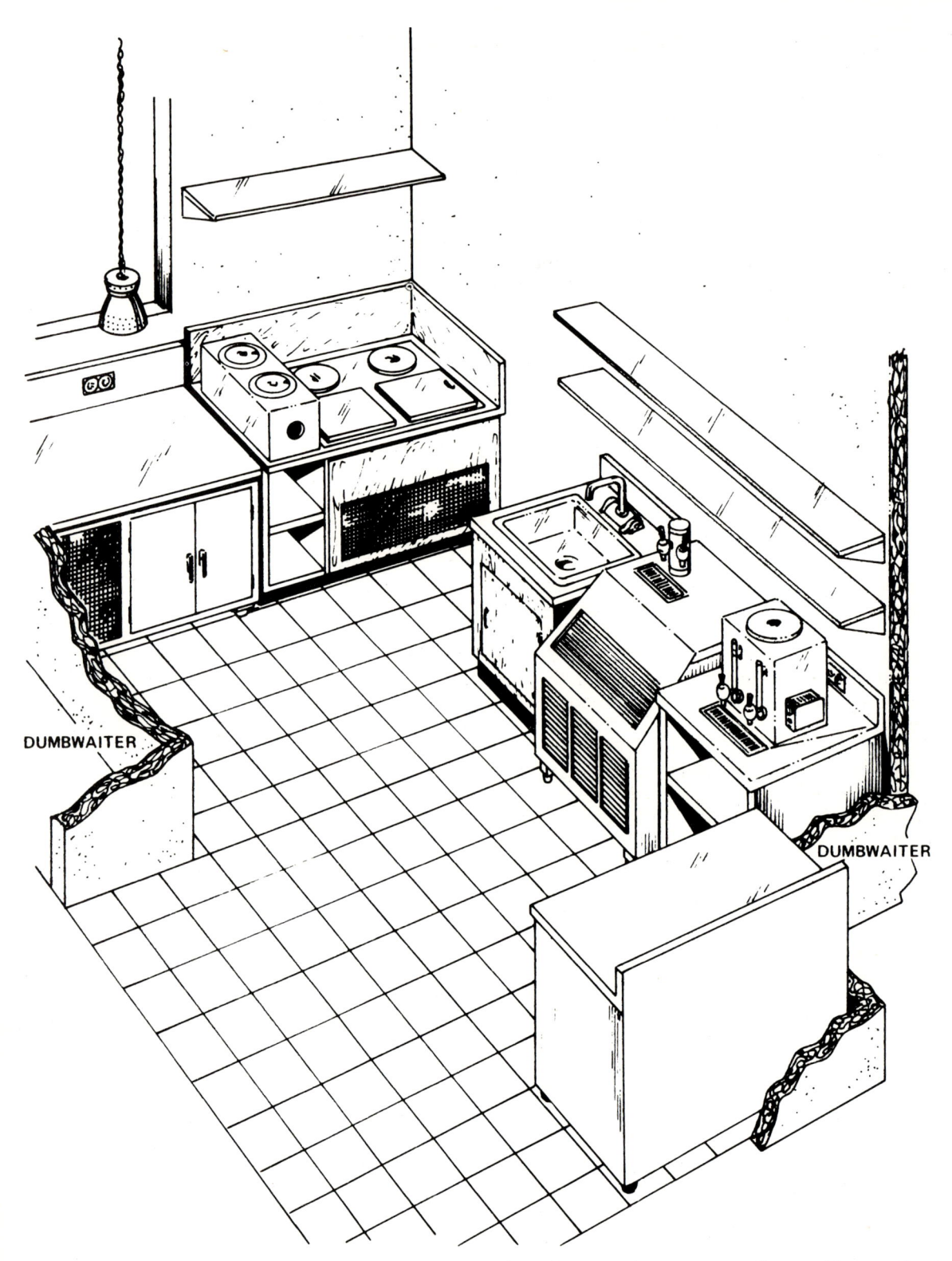

An attendant is stationed in each pantry at Salem Tavern Dining Rooms to load and unload dumbwaiters, assemble orders, make coffee. As many food items as possible are served from pantry.

Keep Patrons Coming Back to the Farm

"Over the river and through the woods to Stephenson's Farm we go"—that has been a theme phrase with many Kansas Citians for nearly a quarter century. Stephenson's Apple Farm Restaurant is the place they choose to celebrate birthdays, anniversaries and other special occasions, or to entertain relative and friends from out of town.

The location has been in the Stephenson family since 1870 when the grandfather of the current owners, Leslie and Loyd Stephenson, developed an orchard and vegetable gardens there. When recent plans for remodeling and expansion were being made, the special problems created by a country location were recognized.

Although Stephenson's took reservations, many people came without them. If they drove out and there was no space for them, there was no other place nearby for them to go. Guests could not be counted on to continue to come if they thought they would not be able to get in.

The guests who arrive at a country establishment after a drive are especially appreciative of such Stephenson arrangements as:

1. Large parking areas on the site, located at the sides and rear of the building, that give guests (and employees too) "off-highway, off-street" parking. Areas for guests and employees are separate. A parking lot watchman patrols the area during the evening hours and all day Sunday, assuring that cars will remain undisturbed.

2. The spacious entrance lobby that prevents waiting guests from feeling that they are "lined up" for a table. The old cider barrel, complete with wooden spigot and a supply of paper cups alongside is a welcoming gesture in the lobby too.

3. A reservation routine that permits the arriving guest to verify his reservation with the hostess on duty at a desk on a low platform in the upper right hand corner of the lobby. There is a checkroom just across the lobby where hats and coats may be left.

If there is a short wait before the guest can be seated, he can either help himself from the cider keg or he may cross to right of the lobby and enter the area designed as an old country store. Here he may browse among the quaint and varied items for sale until called for his table.

Should he prefer a cocktail before dinner, a short flight of nearby stairs will take him to the entrance of the Cider Mill Lounge.

When a table is ready, he will be called over the public address system and after returning to the lobby downstairs, he will be taken to his table.

His table may be in any one of eight dining rooms, each created to be a separate dining experience. On the ground level the choice is between The Parlor, The Cupboard, The Larder, The Back Porch or The Back Yard. On the second floor he will find The Quilt Room, The Attic Room and the Closet.

In its earlier years, when Stephenson's Apple Farm Restaurant was a one-room facility with 40 seats, decor was, of necessity, of secondary importance. The emphasis had to be on the preparing and serving of quality foods; the country location, surrounded by apple trees and farm, was depended upon to supply any atmosphere or image. However, even in those days the owners were aware of the value of interior design in creating atmosphere.

As youngsters growing up on the farm, the Stephenson brothers noticed the strong appeal that the country had for city people. Visitors who came seemed to love getting away from the city; made a point of bringing their children out and letting them romp through the orchard. City people seemed to revel in the rustic, the quaint, the old-fashioned, the feeling that the clock was turned back.

As the food service operation expanded, the rural theme expanded with it. Stephenson's Apple Farm Restaurant became the place to go for "a spell in the country". Guests clearly appreciated the chance to enjoy a return to rural pleasures.

Because this was so, when time came to update their country location, it was quickly decided to keep the atmosphere rural. Selected to keynote the theme were the words: apples, rural, rustic, farm, quaint early Missouri.

Since extensive remodeling and additions had to be made that would alter familiar physical arrangements, the owners and decorators agreed that it was essential to preserve the rural farm theme and the country atmosphere. They must recreate the same things in design and decor that combined to make up the image guests identified with Stephenson's. Keeping in mind the apples—rural—rustic—quaintness theme, the owners and decorators worked out a total plan with results that clearly demonstrate its success.

All furnishings, accessories, even basic materials used (in walls and draperies, for example) were selected primarily on the basis of their contribution to the atmosphere to be established.

Authenticity was a primary goal wherever feasible; when not feasible, the appearance of authenticity was substituted. In applying this theory in the Cider Mill Lounge, the cocktail area, a truly authentic old cider press was installed in a theme-setting position in the center of the room; however, the apparently old cider keg with wooden spigot placed in the entrance lobby is, for practical reasons, a sturdy modern product with every appearance of authenticity. Both items are assets to the development of the rural theme.

Country/Colonial

Unusual pieces of furniture are for the most part authentic. Their authenticity makes an important contribution to the believability of the interiors.

Among outstanding pieces of furniture contributing impact to the interiors are: massive mahogany sideboard in The Parlor Room which came out of the old Armour Mansion in Kansas City, dating back to the 1800's when meat packing was a major Kansas City industry; the prairie era farming tools displayed in the entrance lobby; the antique iron cookstove on The Back Porch; the quilts that cover two walls in The Quilt Room in the upstairs dining area; the big antique showcase in the Country Store. Equally conversation-provoking are the many small pieces from earlier times displayed for maximum effectiveness on walls and shelves throughout the establishment.

The placement of the eight different dining rooms, carefully separated from each other, and the selection of distinctive decor for each one, offers guests a chance for varied experiences in the same establishment.

To assure that guests would feel relaxed and at ease, the rule in room planning was for small areas with their greater feeling of intimacy to be created by room separation. The pleasure of guests in not feeling hemmed in by a great number of other diners, as they would be if seated in a large dining area, offers operating advantages too.

When business is slow, Stephenson's can close a room or even two, for those hours, yet guests do not know they are not in use. In the small separate areas, noise is controlled more easily; there are fewer service personnel needed, consequently there is less movement in the room that must be shut out of the guest's awareness. When a room must be cleaned, or requires a decorating change, it can be closed off, again without patrons being aware of the activity.

Although varied dining destinations are available for Stephenson's patrons, it is not unusual for regular diners to select one room as their favorite and request it whenever they make reservations.

Throughout the eight dining rooms, warm colors were chosen in preference to the hot or cool colors. Blue and green, usually cool tones, were used only in their richer shades; also in use were browns, oranges and amber and, for a brighter note, ruby red.

Wood was used extensively on walls and in furnishings and brings its own value into the color schemes. In many cases it was used in its natural shades; where staining was necessary, natural wood tones were used.

Walls of the entrance lobby are covered with boards from a tobacco barn that was blown down in a tornado. The wood was used just as it was, its soft greenish-gray color derived from age and weather.

The brick-colored tile laid in a brick pattern for the floors of the entrance lobby and the Country Store has inherent color value for the total scheme of these areas.

The carpeting in the Quilt, Attic and Closet Rooms was made especially for Stephenson's and was woven to resemble an old-fashioned hooked rug. The colors in it are red, blue, amber, green and black. The same colors were picked up in other furnishings used as accents. Tablecloths used in these rooms are blue and white designed in a quilt pattern; water goblets and tumblers used on the tables are of blue, green, amber and ruby red.

In the Closet Room, the colors of the carpeting are picked up on false closet doors built into the walls.

Walls in these three rooms are of wood paneling stained a medium walnut. The folding doors that divide the rooms match the walls. The Attic has paneled walls only from the floor to just above the table line; the upper part of the walls is washable wall covering in a neutral beige tone and is patterned to look like homespun cloth.

The Parlor Room (on the ground level) uses only two colors in its more formal scheme. Ruby red and pale ivory. The carpeting is ruby red in a solid color. All wood trim is painted pale ivory. A delicate wood fronts a small balcony that runs around three walls of the room.

From the balcony down to the floor the walls are covered with an ivory wall coating in a linen pattern. From the balcony up to the top of the walls, the wall covering is ruby red paper with a textured vertical stripe.

Booths in the Parlor are upholstered in ruby red covering which has a velvety finish. Chairs are upholstered in a tapestry patterned fabric in ruby red and ivory. Underneath the balcony a plate shelf holds a display of red and white china in an early Willow pattern. On the walls along the balconies, quaint "family portraits" of long ago are hung and lit by picture lights.

The Larder and The Cupboard both use the warm tones of brown, rust and orange in their color scheme. The Larder walls are of knotty pine; walls in The Cupboard are of finished pine (knot-free) from the floor to slightly above the table line. The walls above the table line are papered in a Pennsylvania Dutch pattern on a beige background. The curtains in the room are of deeper beige with a floral design that blends with the wallpaper.

Accessories of copper, pewter, brass and wrought iron are used in both rooms. There are also pictures of antique guns, still lifes of fruits, and similar subject matter; all are framed in soft pine. As accessories in The Larder, strings of peppers, onions, sausages, and other farm products hang on the walls and large sacks of onions and potatoes are stored overhead under the eaves and above the rough hewn rafters.

The Back Porch has a wooden floor, dark-stained and unvarnished. The walls are covered with exterior house shingles which have been stained and treated to look discolored and worn from age and weather. Pots of geraniums hanging from the eaves of The Porch add a bright note of color and a visual divider between The Porch and The Yard. Colorful seed posters, outsize old straw hats are notes of color on the gray shingled walls. More warmth is introduced with pieces of bright brass and copper and unusual pottery in bright colors arranged in small wooden hutches placed to break wall expanses.

The flagstone patterned slate floor in The Back Yard has an inherent color value that contributes to the overall effectiveness of the room. Decorative highlights in the room combine: an unpainted wooden picket fence covering three walls; a bright line of color behind the five foot fence created with hollyhocks and sunflowers in bloom; walls of dark brown, rough wood; apple tree branches bearing bright red fruit that hangs over the fence into the dining room at several points among the hollyhocks and sunflowers. A small apple tree in the center of the room is a focal point.

Although The Back Porch and The Back Yard share the same entrance and are not separated by a solid divider or a wall, the completely different interior design and decoration of the two rooms gives each of them an entirely individual identity. The division of the rooms was effected by a simple back porch railing with potted plants in baskets hanging from the eaves of the porch above the railing. This arrangement partially screens one area from the other and yet permits the diners in each room interesting glimpses of the room beyond.

Each of the eight dining rooms, through its interior design, has been given an individual identity corresponding to its name. Lighting fixtures were selected to harmonize with these identities.

The Parlor has brass chandeliers with white globes, bringing back recollections of days when gas lighting was in vogue; The Cupboard has hanging fixtures of wrought iron, reproductions of candle light fixtures which have flame shaped bulbs.

In rooms that are without hanging fixtures, ceiling illumination is provided by flat round fixtures set flush with the ceiling. In rooms that are open raftered, such as The Larder and the entrance lobby, the high, open ceiling area is illuminated by indirect lighting at the top of the walls.

All ceiling illuminations is on a dimmer system; individual area control allows lighting in each room to be adjusted to any desired level. Rooms are evenly lit as the dimmer balances ceiling lighting with all other lighting in the room, both on the walls and at the tables. All wall accessories are softly lit by picture lights; candles or small lamps are used on tables.

The Stephensons believe that the proper lighting effect can encourage relaxed, leisurely dining. They wanted the total lighting effect in all dining rooms and guest areas to be soft and filtered. All areas are adequately and fully lighted and any harsh brightness, dark shadows or sudden light changes from one area to another have been eliminated.

The three dining areas on the upper level, The Quilt Room, The Attic Room and The Closet, were designed for use as banquet areas as well as for regular dining. The Stephensons wanted a banquet set-up that could be used to complement their everyday business so room arrangements had to be flexible.

Because patronage is especially high on weekends, and at all times during June, July and August, no banquets can be scheduled during those periods. The rest of the time banqueters are welcome, and numerous.

To permit easy shifting from regular to banquet service the three rooms are in a straight line. Folding doors between them allow for speedy division of the space or enlarging it to provide for large groups. The folding doors also make it possible to have regular diners in part of the space and the rest set aside for a group dinner.

The rooms with banquet potential are located so they can be reached from the parking area without coming into the main entrance lobby. There a large group of patrons would serve as a bottle neck. At the entrance from the parking lot to the rooms, there is a foyer with telephone, checkroom and rest rooms. This foyer is only used when the rooms are booked for banquets and private parties; at other times it is closed off behind a door.

Two added attractions at Stephensons that offer both practical and aesthetic value are the Country Store and the Old Wine and Fruit cellar. The Country Store is right off the lobby. It is a colorful interior of wooden shelves holding: home-made preserves and food products, gift items and curios; an antique showcase with a glass top and front reveals a variety of small items and oddments; large wooden barrels full of items for sale: a display of old-fashioned dolls with painted china heads; an antique brass scale hanging above the old wood-topped store counter; door stops in the guise of plump calico hens; stick candy in every imaginable flavor in glass jars. All these and many more quaint and interesting accessories are designed to produce in the viewer a feeling of having stepped back in time.

The practical value of the Country Store is demonstrated by its sales of Stephenson's own label apple butter, jams, jellies, preserves and relishes. The sales more than pay for the space. It's an advertising aid, too, as guests make purchases both for their own use and to send as gifts to all parts of the country.

Although not a profit-maker like the Country Store, another enhancer of Stephenson's rural theme is the Old Wine and Fruit Cel-

Country/Colonial

lar. On the way to and from the ground floor dining areas, guests walk through this low-ceilinged, L-shaped passageway (originally the actual area used for the family's winter fruit storage). Shelves lined with glass jars of colorful fruits, vegetables, preserves and relishes offer an appealing vista to passing guests.

Contents of the jars are all prepared and put up in canning facilities located on the second floor of the new addition and entirely separate from the food service operation. Beneath the shelves of jars, half-opened wooden bins display real potatoes, onions, turnips and sweet potatoes.

Along the opposite wall of the cellar passageway, wine racks present their multi-hued bottles in orderly rows; storage cupboards beneath the racks give the promise of hidden reserves. They are, in fact, actual cupboards used for storage of wines and liquors to be dispensed from the service bar just around the corner.

Rambling country structures often present twin safety problems: fire and falls. At Stephenson's, special precautions have been taken to control both:

To prevent the spread of fire, fireproof materials were used between old and new structures. Walls are of cement block and/or brick. All openings between new and old structures have fire doors which close automatically at a specific degree of temperature. This shutting off of one part from another would allow an orderly evacuation of each part if it became necessary. Fire doors are easily operated manually should the automatic temperature controlled device fail to function.

Slight differences in ground level between the hall approaches to dining areas and the various dining rooms were adjusted by ramps rather than a step or steps. The cocktail lounge, which is reached on two sides by stairways, does not open on either side directly on to a stairway. It opens on one side to a hallway which leads to the stairway; on the other side it opens into a small foyer which must be passed through before the stairway is reached.

The proper complement of sweets and sours is an important consideration in planning the entrees for a Pennsylvania Dutch meal. Pictured here are some of the specialties served at Groff's Farm near Mount Joy, Pa. While tradition stipulates 7 sweets and 7 sours, the ratio at Groff's often varies. The selection is based on what Mrs. Betty Groff feels is the best combination of the dishes scheduled for the meal. The compartmented dish in the center displays several of the relishes prepared in Groff's kitchens from old Pennsylvania Dutch recipes.

Old Country Customs Add to Rural Charm

Capturing the unique character of a region as background for a food service operation has paid off in many parts of America. National groups that have settled in one area and continued to observe the festivals and serve the foods of their original country can be the source of an unusual dining experience for Americans of different backgrounds.

A Pennsylvania Dutch farm home restaurant, lauded by such popular food authorities as Craig Claiborne and James Beard, is drawing a larger clientele each year through word-of-mouth advertising only.

The restaurant is operated by Betty and Abram Groff near Mount Joy, a small town in Lancaster County, Pa. in what is actually their home in the center of a 90-acre dairy farm. The restaurant came into their lives early when the Groffs demonstrated unusual skill in providing food for sizable groups.

Mrs. Groff explains that it is a custom in the Mennonite faith, of which they are members, for a young pair of newlyweds to entertain all the uncles and aunts and cousins at dinner in their home once they are settled down. Family groups the newlywed Groffs entertained included as many as 32.

About the time the young Groffs had satisfactorily demonstrated their ability to prepare meals in quantity proportions, a motel operator asked Mrs. Groff's father, Clarence N. Herr, if he knew anyone who could serve meals to bus loads of passengers arriving 42 at a time. Herr, it should be noted, is a Lancaster County figure in his own right, growing Persian melons and other choice products, and smoking hams that are in great demand.

Herr asked Betty if she'd be interested in the bus feeding, "If you can cook for 32 uncles and aunts, your worst critics," she mused, "why couldn't you cook for 42 people that never tasted Pennsylvania Dutch cooking before?" And so the Groffs took on the assignment.

The well fed bus travelers spread the word. Mrs. Groff received postcards asking for reservations, addressed, "To the Mennonite Cook in Mount Joy" and in other ways. Since the postmaster was a neighbor, she got the mail and made the reservations.

The Groff's now may handle as few as two persons in an evening, or as many as hundreds in a day at their Pennsylvania Dutch Feasting Board. All meals are on a reservation basis. Largest number for a seated full dinner thus far is 85, all in the downstairs of their

"COOK ALREADY LIKE THE DEUTSCH"

spacious stone home. Largest crowd has been 200 for a wedding buffet.

Here's the way they handle things...

"Every day I do all the baking of the cakes, the pies, the puddings and the roasts," says Betty.

"All the fruit cup is made every day."

"Mrs. Erma Engle comes in one hour before serving time, prepares the vegetables, debones the chicken, and stays at the stove all the way through dinner. She is in charge of the kitchen, cooking from then on until the end of the evening."

"The girls come in one hour before serving. They set up the tables and see that the relishes and all are put on the table. They do the waitressing. They are neighborhood girls, all wearing white uniforms."

"Since we live in our own home, the tables are all taken down at the end of the meal and it looks like a home during the day. All the tables we use are there."

"Abe and I do the hosting. Abe does all the carving, using knives from my Dad's butcher shop. He also helps manage the kitchen."

The Groffs freeze their own corn and sugar peas, and buy the very best of other frozen vegetables. They cook to order, not boiling any vegetable over three minutes.

They have a total of 10 burners on two electric stoves, with four electric ovens. Mrs. Groff has only one commercial range, with two ovens. One power failure hit them after Craig Claiborne had written about them in the New York Times. They carried their vegetables to a neighbor's for cooking. Now they can hook up to a generator, if necessary.

"We're learning as we go," Betty continues. "We have an electric dish washer which does a tray in three minutes. We have designed the tables in the kitchen so we can serve 50 people in an hour and a half. That's one tourist bus coming in and sitting down, and getting out with an allowance of 20 minutes to set the tables with the same china."

"On busy Saturdays we serve at 12, 2,4 and 6:30—all busloads of 50 at a time—that's what you call pushing it.

"We have Christmas reservations in April. We serve any time from noon on, if they reserve for it."

Among the largest factors in the couple's success is one that the Groffs provide in their personal hospitality. Betty is a lively young woman who can supply a running commentary on Pennsylvania Dutch food, customs, bringing up children and innumerable

Country/Colonial

other topics that delight her guests. Abe is a little quieter, but he is knowledgeable about farming, food and the Lancaster County scene.

Another factor, which Betty will discuss readily, is that "we use butter like it's going out of style". Since they run a dairy farm with 34 head of livestock, they push dairy products.

The plenitude of the bounding board is another. There is no dearth of food. All the famous Pennsylvania Dutch delicacies are spread out in lavish, eye-appealing and taste-pleasing array. And chocolate cake is first on the menu.

The unfolding mysteries of the meal hold many diners rapturously spellbound. They not only pitch into the many foods they find on the table, but watch the girls expectantly as they emerge from the kitchen with new servings. And part of the training Betty gives her girls is that they whisk out smiling; even if there is an occasional flurry or mishap in the kitchen, no waitress shows it to the diners.

"I think the intriguing thing about Pennsylvania Dutch cooking is mostly that you use fresh vegetables," Betty adds. "I do not believe in overcooking anything."

Sugar peas, for instance, get a once-over boil. No soggy peas for Betty. Sugar peas are peculiar to the region, although not exclusively a Pennsylvania vegetable. New brides have been known to try to remove the pods when they cook them the first time. When cooked by a skilled hand, they are incomparable.

"We can all our own relishes," Betty reveals further. "We canned over 500 quarts of melon last year. These came from my Dad's farm. We make 100 quarts of chow chow at a time. It may last three months. If we'd sell it in bottles, diners would buy a lot. Sometimes we sell 15 of my Dad's hickory-smoked hams in a day."

Betty, who was a secretary and bookkeeper before marriage, keeps the books. Abe runs the farm, which could be a fulltime occupation in itself in a county known for the high production of its fertile fields. A retired man answers the telephone, books parties, writes orders and grocery lists—and makes fruit cups and chops celery: the two Groff sons and foster son get to meet many of the guests.

Staff complement at peak is two in the kitchen and five waitresses, with Abe and Betty—and they can handle 60 at a time, or if they're all in the same party, 80 guests can be served. Betty serves on fine china, some of which is ceramic ironstone she fired in her own kiln.

The house is Early American, built of native limestone. Colorful surroundings are evident from the time guests enter the farm lane. Gardens are planted in Pennsylvania Dutch flower favorites—petunias, geraniums and red roses ("If the horse doesn't chew them all off," Betty adds). A trout pond provides trout—which diners may catch if they wish, for cooking while they wait.

"THE SWEETS AND SOURS"

"PUT RED SUGAR ON THE COOKIES FOR PRETTY"

Built around 1756, the home has 11 large rooms. It was restored in 1955-56. One of the most attractive features is a fireplace, built like one from a Pennsylvania Dutch farmhouse in the Metropolitan Museum of Art in New York. The one in the "Met" may have come originally from her house, Betty thinks. The house has the original oak and pine floors, walls of alabaster and lime wash—German door latches.

Some of the favorite foods at Groff's include Chicken a la Stoltzfus, which is an Amish wedding chicken; spiced Persian melon; cauliflower with cheese; old-fashioned chocolate cake; chicken and corn soup, one of the dishes for which Claiborne published the recipe; and shoo fly pie (wet), which James Beard found so enjoyable.

The "seven sweets and sours" are traditional accompaniments to a Pennsylvania Dutch meal. At Groffs these "own-canned" relishes include spiced Persian melon, pickled watermelon rind, chow chow, string beans, carrots, celery, corn, cucumbers, cranberry sauce, apple sauce and sweet pickle sticks but guests are seldom restricted to seven choices.

Drawn here are dishes as arranged on the other half of the table at Groff's farm as pictured on page 7.

Design Approach to Country/Colonial

Artifacts abound for the development of either Colonial or Country motif. This abundance can be a hazard since when choices are not sufficiently restrained clutter rather than calm develops as the design impression.

The advantages of a careful approach to Colonial decor are summed up in this quote from a visitor to Emily Shaw's Inn, Pound Ridge, N. Y. "...a completely delightful experience. By day, the sunlight plays on the surrounding trees, by night, the landscape is illumined by hidden spotlights turning the surrounding countryside into a land of enchantment.

"The attractive, rambling frame house which houses the Inn is more than 175 years old, and although over the years many changes and additions have been made within and without, the original charm of the building has been carefully retained. It now offers six dining rooms to receive guests for luncheon and dinner—rooms which are spread over two levels of the Inn and each of which manages to have a charm of its own."

Entry is through a narrow hall which leads to a spacious lounge where, when meeting friends, guests may wait in comfort. To the right is an inviting room, paneled and beamed with mellow old barn woods. Table cloths are a delicate ice blue and napkins are twisted in slim tapers, rising high from the goblets on each table.

Oil paintings are spaced at wide intervals along the walls and, at the far end of the room, floor to ceiling windows offer an inviting view of the terraces, gardens and woodlands beyond.

At the Colonial Inn, Concord, Mass., the sign welcoming patrons is the first of the many image-building decor elements to be encountered. Furnishings as carefully selected as the food is prepared, complete the pleasure of guests dining in the sunny dining room at this Colonial Inn overlooking the Village Green.

Approximately 300 guests can be seated in the four, large, connected dining rooms. Separate function rooms can handle up to 125 people. Cocktails are served in the Village Forge Lounge, decorated with interest-evoking pieces of Americana.

At Moselem Springs Inn, Kutztown, Pa., characteristic Colonial touches surround the fireplace in the Golden Eagle Room. The warmth of flames burning brightly on cold nights draw patrons to admire the wood mantel set high against the mellow old brick of the fireplace.

On the mantel a distinctive old wood clock and several pewter items are attractively placed. Pewter is also an effective decor element in the Early American bar where a row of pewter mugs on hooks lines a shingled overhang. The mugs, owned by members of the Moselem Springs Inn Noggin Club, each bear the name of the owner on the bottom.

This part of the Inn was once a long narrow general store and postoffice. The rich dark leathers, grained wood and large brick and stone open hearth were selected to convey a sense of calm and stability.

Pieces of Blue Willow Ware, the china of the Inn's early days, are the focal point of the decor in the Blue Willow Room. Plates and platters are arranged over the fireplace in the room which is decorated in complimentary blue and white.

Capitalizing on another bit of decorative innovation that was recorded in Moselem Springs Inn history, the owners installed gas lamps on the many pillars along the Inn's porches. The first location in the area to replace kerosene lamps with a compressed gas lighting system, the Inn in the early days had visitors from miles around who came to see the "new fangled lamps." The modern replicas, still gas burning, are an attractive reminder of the Inn's traditional interest in new trends.

Extra authority can be claimed for decisions about country decor at Stephenson's Apple Farm Restaurant, Kansas City, Mo. Evolved against 25 years of expansion in a rural setting, the elements selected had to satisfy three sets of requirements. While costs and maintenance factors were essential considerations, suitability to the overall plan of country image dictated certain limitations in style.

How this was worked out has been described by the owners: Basic furnishings, such as tables and chairs for dining areas, cocktail lounge seating, lobby seating, floor covering, wall covering and all other such fundamentals which would receive almost continual use and would require regular and frequent maintenance procedures were carefully evaluated. How would they stand up under the necessary shampooing, scrubbing, vacuuming, brushing and wiping? When a choice had to be made between two chair coverings and there was a preference for one but the other would soil less easily or stand up better under many shampooings, the more practical choice was made.

Carpeting, which was used in all but one or two areas, is all of synthetic fiber with rubber backing for practical maintenance. Wood was selected for many furnishings—sturdily built and hard finished to withstand much handling. Upholstery, on the other hand, was used sparingly throughout. The booths and chairs in the Parlor Room were upholstered because the desired effect of old-time elegance and propriety could not be obtained without it.

The only other upholstered furnishings are booths in one dining room where a vinyl material was used that can be easily cleaned with a damp cloth and soap. It was selected in a thickness that would

Country/Colonial

endure hard wear. All other coverings or padding for seats and backs of chairs are either separate pieces or removable so that when they become soiled or worn they may be easily cleaned or replaced.

In a few instances, the decorative value of furnishings selected did outweigh the cost, maintenance and wearability factors. The high ladder-backed, rush-bottomed chairs used as seating on The Back Porch are genuinely old and handmade. While not excessively fragile, the seats are woven and will certainly not be as lasting as wood or a similar hard substance since they are made of reeds. However, the effect gained and the attention they have received has offset the disadvantages.

The many and varied accessories chosen to enhance Stephenson's country motif were either actual antiques or of an age, condition or appearance to suggest antiquity. Genuine antiques, if unusual and of more than ordinary value, were reserved for display only. Some sturdier ones, however, are in regular use.

Using antiques is not necessarily an impractical procedure, the Stephensons point out. Antiques, especially those from rural areas, are generally of good material, well-made and serviceable. Marks that appear on them seem to be the natural result of years of usage and, as a rule, only add to the value of the article.

This is the unique advantage in an interior design plan that incorporates the display or use of antiques or articles from years gone by: whether standing idle as a display or when put into use and performing some daily service, the article advances in value simply as it gains in age.

Antiques do create extra housekeeping chores. Pictures, small items on display, wall hutches, shelves must be kept polished, straightened, and dust free. Their contribution to the effectiveness of the overall plan can override this cost.

Another approach to country decor was taken by Angus Barn, Raleigh N. C. Their authentic barn projects a rural image complete from animals in the barnyard to hayracks used as dividers in the dining room.

Among the elements used to lend an authentic touch to the interior design are brick flooring and old wood paneling. Other elements used such as the spinning wheel, stuffed hens and butter churn might seem maintenance-costly selections since they would normally be dust catchers requiring frequent care. However, the five acres of grass that surrounds Angus Barn holds the dust problem to a minimum.

"Historic" Moselem Springs Inn
Since 1852

Where Your Ancestors Wined and Dined

On the Crossing of 222 and 662 — Between Reading and Allentown, Pa.

Friendly hospitality and good food await you at "Historic" Moselem Springs Inn. The Inn has been a famous Pennsylvania eating place since 1852.

Today, too, it holds for its guests all of the charm and reputation for fine food it has had for more than a century.

The main dining area, the Presidential Room, has the Colonial charm and calm grace that typifies the period. The name is a carry-over from a dining room in the Inn when it first opened.

The Blue Willow Room, in days past, served as a combination sitting and waiting room, and the blue Willow Ware crockery used then has been successfully carried over as the motif for this charming room.

The Golden Eagle room, with its rich, dark leathers, grained woods, and brick open-hearth provide a calm sturdiness for the tavern which is located there.

Gifts, skillfully hand-made by local area craftsmen, can be purchased at the "Korner Kupboard," our new gift shop, located in the basement. Browsers are always welcome to this latest addition to the Inn complex.

Travelers passing through are welcome to enjoy "Dinner at the Springs" with the many local guests who come to dine amid the historic atmosphere.

We are sure you will find this landmark of hospitality and good food a most enjoyable dining experience.

The Innkeeper
Madeline I. Stoudt

Closed Monday. Tuesday through Saturday - 11 A.M. to 11 P.M.
Sunday - 11 A.M. to 7 P.M. Holidays - 11 A.M. to 8 P.M.
While reservations are not required, they are advisable.
Telephone - Fleetwood 944-8213

Getting the Word to Country/Colonial Patrons

Effective promotion is needed to keep Colonial and Country theme dining places operating at capacity. Enlarging on the background of the basic theme for potential or in-house guests is a sure way to whet interest in the establishment.

A favorite way to pass along this information is via the menu. A moment of reading just before or just after menu choices have been made establishes the mood. The guest thus fits more easily into the setting, is conditioned from the start to respond to the atmosphere that has been created for his enjoyment.

On the back of the handwritten menu at Emily Shaw's Inn, Pound Ridge, N. Y., patrons find a History of the Inn:

"Emily Shaw's Inn was opened as a restaurant in 1939. Prior to that time, it enjoyed a long and varied history which included being a grocery store, local post office, private home and a stop-over Inn for travelers between New York, Danbury and points north. The incomplete records of the Inn have been traced back 182 years and it is believed that the building is one of the earliest pre-revolutionary structures in Pound Ridge.

"An interesting fact, which few people realize, is that the Hessian mercenaries of the British Army went through this town during the American Revolution in July 1779, destroying all of the buildings but three, one of which was the Inn."

The Colonial Inn at Concord, Mass. uses red, white and blue for its recounting of the Inn's history. A menu tied with gold cord carries comprehensive data in blue printing with red headings on the white back cover:

"Early Inns
"Undoubtedly the first inn built in the original American Colonies was the Jamestown Inn in Virginia, built in 1607. The story of our early inns runs parallel with the development of our nation. William Penn used the facilities of the Blue Anchor Inn while working on the plans for the city of Philadelphia. The Boston Tea Party was hatched at The Hancock Tavern in Boston. The British occupied the Wright Tavern, across the green, on April 19th, 1775—that famous day of 'a shot heard round the world'.

"The early inns were primitive affairs according to our modern standards, but perhaps they were cozier. Beds could have as many as five occupants, but they were not permitted to wear boots under the covers.

"The Colonial Inn

"In 1716, Captain James Minot, A. M., a soldier and physician, built the oldest part of the Inn. He left the house to his son, James, Jr., a Lieutenant Colonel serving in the French and Indian War, who was also a Justice of Peace and a Representative and member of the Royal Governor's Council. A later descendant of the family and owner, Timothy Minot, Jr., a physician, attended the wounded on April 19, 1775, when the 'shot heard round the world' was fired. Prior to the event the central part of the Inn was built and used as a provincial storehouse during the Revolutionary War.

"In 1789, Deacon John White acquired the central section which he maintained as a variety store, residing in one end of it. The Deacon was noted for his fondness for children to whom he presented books as gifts; equally notable was his strictness of the observance of the Sabbath, (he was known to have stopped travelers on the highway passing his door, berating them for unnecessary Sunday traveling.)

"In 1799, John Thoreau, sailor and merchant, grandfather of Henry Thoreau, the famous naturalist-author, purchased and lived in that part of the Inn which houses the office and the main sitting room, (Thoreau Room). Henry Thoreau's family lived here while he studied at Harvard.

"In 1839 it was sold to Daniel Shattuck, who had bought the store from Deacon White 18 years previously. In 1850 the store was made over into a dwelling and was occupied by a series of families until 1885 when it was transformed into a boarding house. Later the three buildings were operated as a small hotel called the Thoreau House. In the meantime, various owners added to and rebuilt the Inn to fit their

Country/Colonial

own needs. The Inn probably assumed its present appearance about the turn of the century when at that time a Mr. and Mrs. Abrams ran it under the name of Colonial Inn.

"In 1947 the Inn was purchased by the Grimes family. To accommodate the changing demands the Inn has been completely renovated, air conditioned and redecorated, ever mindful of The Inn's traditional atmosphere. In 1961 a complete new wing was added boasting motor-inn conveniences and comforts. This addition brings the total number of rooms to 60, including several housekeeping apartments."

The country theme at Stephenson's Apple Farm Restaurant near Kansas City is focused on an apple image. In explanation, their menus carry this description:

"A Little About the Apple Farm Restaurant
"Stephenson's orchards were planted by the family over a half century ago. Since that time these orchards, located in the heart of the rich Jackson County apple country, have grown and matured into one of the largest and most productive in the Mid-West. There are now more than 400 acres of orchards including apples, peaches, plums and strawberries. Part of the original building was where the apples were stored while waiting to be sold. This apple storage area we made into the Cellar Room. That is the reason for the thick walls and low ceilings. The cider press and the grading and packing buildings are located three miles south of the restaurant down old Lees Summit Road.

"Stephenson's Apple Farm Restaurant had its beginning in the little one room stone building at the side of Lees Summit Road where for many years Stephenson's sold their fruit to folks traveling between Independence and Lees Summit. Old timers still remember the little stone building at the edge of the orchard, which, they say, was regarded as a half-way point between Independence and Lees Summit. Back in 1926 when Hi-way 40 was constructed, it cut across Lees Summit Road right at Stephenson's and so the old building was abandoned for the present fruit and berry store just east of the restaurant on Hi-way 40. But the original old stone building still stands. It remains as the superstructure of the first dining room—the Apple Room.

"The Stephenson family like most early Missouri people has always smoked meat, made apple butter and canned their own fruit and vegetables. And so in the mid-forties when Loyd and Les, the twin Stephenson brothers, decided to reopen the old stone building as a restaurant it seemed only natural to call their restaurant the Apple Farm and to serve old-fashioned hickory smoked meats, apple butter and sweet apple cider prepared in the unique manner they had known from boyhood.

"On April 16, 1946, Stephenson's Apple Farm Restaurant was born. The first day 38 people came to dine and the number has continued to grow ever since. Stephenson's Orchard originally consisted of the home orchard here. Norman Stephenson, the oldest son, joined our father in the orchard business in 1935 and since that time five orchards have been planted at Blue Springs, Grain Valley, Sibley and Lees Summit. In 1951 the Barn Room was added, then in 1955 the Pantry Room and a new kitchen were constructed. Again in 1959 the restaurant was expanded to include the Country Store Room.

"Loyd and Les join the young men and women who are serving you in welcoming you to Stephenson's."

The apple image predominates in all Stephenson's promotion, including their large sign. Apples are even used as decorations painted on the outside of their catering vehicles. Over the years there have been many special promotions for the apple theme, a natural, of course, their very successful "Miss Apple Queen" contest.

A special book "Stephenson's Apple Farm Restaurant Receipts" is sold in their Country Store. It contains nearly 75 recipes, many for home size service of Stephenson's best known specials. A full-page ad for the restaurant, giving location and phone number of the country food service, appears at the front of the book and is followed by this opening note from owners Les and Loyd Stephenson:

"For many years guests have asked us to share some of our favorite recipes. Some are heirlooms that have changed little during the passing years. Others have been developed and altered as we have grown.

"At long last, we have gathered this collection of favorites to share with our friends and guests. We hope you will enjoy serving them in your home as much as we have enjoyed serving them to you in our restaurant and at our special parties.

"Our recipe for hickory smoked meats is not included because, being done in our huge smoke ovens, we can't duplicate the method for you on a small scale. But you will find the recipe for our barbecue sauce which we use in preparing our smoked meats.

"It has always been our goal to serve the finest

Country/Colonial

food and give the finest service. In true farm style we use plenty of fresh butter and cream, fresh fruits and vegetables and our portions are generous. We really follow our recipes exactly, measuring exactly and baking exactly as directed. For best results, we hope that you will, too.

"Good luck and happy cooking.   Les & Loyd."

Open Hearth And Oven

BAKED CHICKEN 'N' BUTTER AND CREAM
(Makes 3 to 4 servings)

½ cup Flour
1½ teaspoons Salt
½ teaspoon Paprika
¼ teaspoon Pepper
1 cut-up Frying Chicken
¼ cup Butter
1½ cups hot Water
½ cup Nonfat Dry Milk Powder

always on our menu.

Dip chicken into water. Coat with mixture of flour and seasonings. Put skin side down into 13x9x2-inch baking pan. Dot with butter. Bake at 350° for 30 minutes. Mix water, milk powder. Pour around chicken. Bake 1¼ hours more, or until chicken is tender.

HAM ROULADES
(Makes 6 servings)

Sauce:
2 tablespoons Butter
¼ cup Flour
¼ teaspoon Salt
1 cup hot Milk
½ cup grated Swiss Cheese

Roulades:
½ cup Tomato Sauce
6 thin slices Ready-To-Eat Ham
¼ cup Evaporated Milk
¼ cup grated Swiss Cheese
2 tablespoons Butter

Sauce: Melt butter over low heat. Stir in flour, salt to make smooth paste. Remove from heat. Stir in milk gradually until smooth. Add cheese. Stir over low heat to melt. Cool.
Roulades: Pour tomato sauce into 10x6x2-inch baking pan. Roll about 2 spoonsful of cheese sauce in each ham slice. Put folded side down on tomato sauce. Blend evaporated milk into rest of cheese sauce. Pour over ham. Sprinkle with cheese. Dot with butter. Bake at 350° about 15 minutes, or until hot and bubbly.

Located between Reading and Allentown, Pa. on crossing of 222 & 662 where your ancestors wined and dined.

Promoting the location of the food service/lodging operation, especially if it's a bit off the beaten track, is especially important. The maps that follow, as well as those on pages 25 and 31, illustrate ways of effectively making sure that the world does beat a path to your door.

The signboards gaily presented on the cover of a Moselem Springs Inn brochure are also helpful in impressing its not-too-far-from-Philadelphia location on the prospective patrons' minds.

While the map locating the Salem Tavern Dining Rooms, Winston-Salem, N. C. is a part of a brochure designed for mailing, the Glockenspiel, Kutztown, Pa. map is presented on a table tent. The table tent also outlines the restaurant's reservation policy on the side opposite the map:

"Even though reservations are not required they are desired, particularly on Saturday nights, Sundays and holidays.

"We can best accommodate groups of six or more with a reservation. We try to schedule these reservations so that no waiting period occurs, but if it should, it will not exceed twenty minutes. These reservations are honored for twenty minutes in case of late arrival.

"You are never late for a reservation until you are more than 20 minutes late.

"We also beg you to allow us to be 20 minutes late with your reservations.

"If you request a preferred location we will do everything possible to seat you there, however we cannot guarantee it on Saturday nights, Sundays and and Holidays because of the constant flow of guests.

"The quality of the food we do guarantee every time you visit us.

"Reservations made from 12:00 or 12:30 on Sundays and Holidays are ready upon arrival.

"Parties who arrive without reservations are seated as soon as possible in order of arrival.

"Please bear with us under these arrangements. We show no preference or favoritism to any group. We do everything possible to please all of our guests.

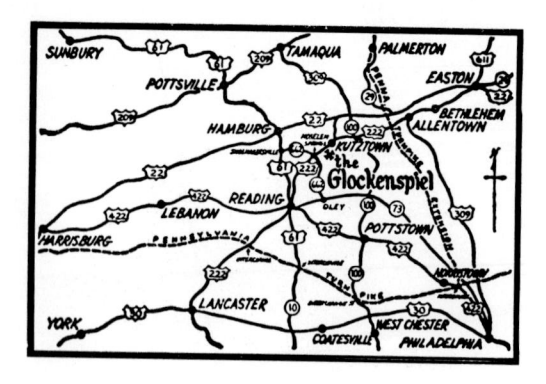

Country/Colonial

"When mailing your reservations PLEASE INCLUDE YOUR TELEPHONE NUMBER. Thank you! OUR telephone number is 215-944-8211.

* * *

"WHEN YOU ARE ASKED
'Did you enjoy your meal?'
...the management is NOT seeking a compliment. It is our check to determine your feelings, and to help us keep dining at the Glockenspiel truly an 'Adventure in Good Eating'."

A carefully worded description of the hospitality available at the end of a drive into the country can be inserted into tour guides or in newspaper advertising. On page 48, the material describing Moselem Springs Inn, between Reading and Allentown, Pa., is an excellent example of this type of advertisement, which also gives clear directions for reaching the Inn.

"There being no place
Like this place
Near this place
This must be the place"

This introduction to Kimberton (Pa.) Tavern's mailing brochure is translated into driving directions that appear in eye-catching red and white against the pale blue of the first class mailing piece. Other pages of the brochure show pictures in color of the Inn's exterior and charming 18th century interiors. The brochure uses as its focal point this description of the Tavern's development:

"Kimberton was named after a Quaker, Emmor Kimber. Friend Kimber opened an exclusive girls' school in 1796, the official name of the school was The French Creek Seminary for Females. Only half of the school remains today diagonally across from the Country House.

"The original Inn was built to house the parents who visited their daughters and was a boarding house for 50 years until the school closed.

"Friend Kimber was openly active in the Underground Railway. Stories are handed down about the silent acceptance of Mr. Kimber's excursions at night in a farm wagon carrying escaped slaves under sacks of potatoes to Norristown. His dedication to the cause was such that he willingly sacrificed his fortune and the esteem of his neighbors.

"The present owners, Mr. and Mrs. Leon Slobodzian, have been the innkeepers since 1946. Though many changes have been made, they always keep in mind the history surrounding the area and strive to retain the Colonial atmosphere."

Special atmosphere dining, when it's successful in providing patrons with a sense of escape to another time or era, calls for sending word to the folks back home. Postcards picturing the inn or restaurant, outside or inside, or the food specialties on its menu get wide distribution. They can create a constantly widening circle of patrons.

An interestingly written description that accompanies an appropriate illustration in color on a postcard is good advertising, especially when it is sent with a confirming message about lodging or eating pleasure. Patrons often also keep such picture cards as reminders of places they want to return to or recommend to traveling friends.

At Colligan's Stockton (N. J.) Inn, an unusual double postcard pictures two inviting interiors and a set-in photograph of their wishing well. When folded and fastened together, the outside of the card displays a map of highways leading to Colligan's. With the map goes information about the establishment, assurance of ample parking, the Inn's address and phone number as well as space for the customary message.

A series of five postcards available at the Kimberton Tavern "The Country House" covers these appeals: (1) An aerial photograph of the Inn in its peaceful leafy setting. (2) A close-up of the mill wheel, duck pond and small wooden bridge over the brook that are a picturesque attraction on the grounds of the Inn. (3) A photograph from the interior of the dining room showing the pond area as viewed by diners. (4) An interior photograph showing attractively set tables near a roaring wood fire blazing in a large fireplace—"A dining room for all seasons". The array of Early American pieces pictured on the mantel over the fireplace would be a special attraction for antique buffs. (5) An irresistible color photograph of Chicken on the Plank as served only at "The Kimberton Country House". The dish is unusual, colorful and photogenic—a small whole roasted bird nested in a bordure of mashed potatoes, red cabbage, baby lima beans and sauteed carrots. The glass of wine and small loaf of fresh baked bread pictured beside the planked entree make their own points about the special features of Kimberton Tavern cuisine.

Country/Colonial

> *Autumn Splendor Comes To Kimberton*
> particularly picturesque at this colorful time of year, the Kimberton Tavern invites you to a nostalgic retreat to the good life of yesteryears. Situated in historic Chester County, no other area offer as splendor a setting, for a lovely new dining room overlooks our duck pond and water-wheel mill house, which displays a magnificent display of colorful fall flowers. We hope you'll come soon and suggest that it be early in the week, when our staff can gracefully serve you. Open daily for dinner from 4 p.m., Sunday from 1 to 7 p.m., Closed Monday.
> *NOW SERVING LUNCHEON DAILY FROM NOON*
> **Kimberton Tavern**
> "The Country House"
> Just of Route 113, Kimberton, Pa. 215/933-8148

The changes of the seasons can be described in advertising to offer a new reason for visits to a country inn. This newspaper advertisement, developed by Kimberton Tavern, uses the seasonal approach to attract patrons from Philadelphia, a 45-mile drive away.

The Colonial Inn, Concord, Mass., has selected three effective approaches to use in advertising its operation's special claims. Since 1716, The Colonial Inn has provided a haven for hungry and tired travelers. Located just 18 miles from downtown Boston, and 8 miles from the Mass. Turnpike, The Colonial Inn has seven charming function rooms and 60 modern bedrooms complete with TV, airconditioning and direct dial telephones.

The Inn enjoys an excellent reputation not only for its food and charm but also for its accommodations. Located in historic Concord, it is only minutes away from major Massachusetts highways and downtown Boston. It does a large lunch and dinner business all year around. It also has separate function rooms that can handle up to 125 people for private social or business events.

The dining room decorated in Colonial style, consists of four large connected rooms where approximately three hundred people can be seated at one time.

To bring these advantages to the attention of potential guests, campaigns in the Wall Street Journal and the New Yorker magazine have centered on appeals designed to attract various segments of their anticipated market; see illustrations AA, page 68.

Another series (see illustrations BB, page 69) injects humor into descriptions of the same appeals.

Loring Grimes, owner-innkeeper, himself becomes the focal point in one series (see illustrations CC, page 69) written with a light touch.

However the information is presented, it concentrates on emphasizing the same basics: the unique surroundings, good food and service that the Colonial Inn can provide. This is the message that all Colonial and Country Inns must convey to attract prospective patrons and hold repeat business.

SPECIAL ATMOSPHERE THEMES FOR FOODSERVICE

Dear Anne,

I'm writing this from the Colonial Inn Concord, Mass. It's the place your brother recommended. I checked in yesterday, and it's very relaxing after those other impersonal motels I've been stopping at. Tonight I had a marvelous dinner in the Inn's dining room. I love New England cooking anyway, but this was really superb. The Inn is very homey and charming. Maybe when I get back from this sales trip, we could leave the children with Mother and come back to the Colonial Inn all by ourselves. You deserve a change.

Love Jim

The Colonial Inn
on the green – CONCORD, MASSACHUSETTS
Loring N. Grimes, Innkeeper (617) 369-9200

Dear Miss Walker,

I'm having a wonderful vacation and putting work completely out of my mind. The Colonial Inn in Concord has been the highlight of my trip, and I want you to thank your sister's friend for recommending it. In fact, it would be a good spot for our spring sales meeting. It has all the facilities, and it's reasonable – but let's not talk shop. The food is great, *real* New England cooking for a change. (Incidentally, don't let everyone go haywire on lunch hours while I'm away.) I'm getting to be quite a history buff, and this Inn has quite a story of its own ... which I won't go into because I've already kept you from your work too long.

A.W.T.

have you done about th
count?

The Colonial Inn
on the green – CONCORD, MASSACHUSETTS
Grimes, Innkeeper (617) 3

Dear Children,

I know I haven't written you since your father and I started our trip, but it's been hectic. Yesterday, we arrived at the Colonial Inn in Concord. It's so relaxing here, and they couldn't be nicer. It's like stepping back into the past, except it's a lot more comfortable. We might even spend a couple of extra days here. Our room is air-conditioned and has color TV, which I'm sure will interest Bobbie. It's nice to see some places still cater to their guests. I know you're going to think this sounds conceited, but this is the first place we've stayed where the cooking is better than mine. I'm sending you a menu so you can all be jealous of your parents' second honeymoon.

Love, Mother

The Colonial Inn
on the green – CONCORD, MASSACHUSETTS

Dear Tommy,

I am writing this from Concord, Mass., which is where a lot of history went on. We got here yesterday, and Mom says we won't be leaving for awhile. Partly because she wants to see all these old places where historical people lived, but mostly because Aunt Clara loves the food at the Colonial Inn – that's where we're staying. It's real cool here; we even got a color TV in the room. The Inn looks like a movie set, but Mom says it's authentic. Food's good too. Dad says he loves Concord, but he spends most of his time in the dining room downstairs. Well, I gotta go because today we visit some dumb old house where a bunch of girls lived.

YOUR FRIEND, BOBBY

The Colonial Inn
on the green – CONCORD, MASSACHUSETTS
Loring N. Grimes, Innkeeper (617) 369-9200

Dear Cindy,

Can you imagine? I was actually standing in the very room where Emerson lived! I mean, can you imagine? Concord, Mass., is really divine, really. And we're staying at the most charming Inn you ever saw. It's called the Colonial Inn, and it is (colonial, I mean). It's authentic, except for the rooms. They all have color television and air-conditioning. They didn't have those in the old days, you know. The Innkeeper, Loring Grimes, is handsome ... mmm! And the food! You remember how I stuffed myself at Angela's party? Well, that was nothing compared to the way I gorged myself on lobster tonight. I just can't tell you. You simply must jet up here. It's really top drawer.

Gretchen (who else?)

The Colonial Inn
on the green – CONCORD, MASSACHUSETTS
Loring N. Grimes, Innkeeper (617) 369-9200

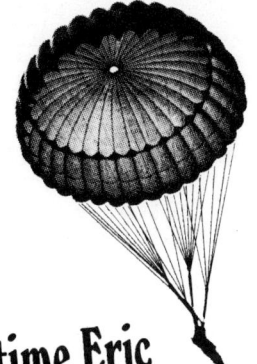

Country/Colonial

Every time Eric is looking for a place to stay
he drops in at the Colonial Inn.

Eric likes the kind of prompt hospitality that never leaves him hanging. The 60 modern bedrooms and cordial atmosphere bring him down our way often. Why not chute over yourself for a Flintlock or two in the Village Forge Lounge, stay for dinner, or stay the night?
We'll be watching for you.

The Colonial Inn
on the green — CONCORD, MASSACHUSETTS
Loring N. Grimes, Innkeeper (617) 369-9200

BB

Every time Miss Abigail has a coming out party,
it's at the Colonial Inn.

(She's been coming out every week for thirty five years.) Discerning swingers like Abby find the Colonial Inn the perfect place for a quiet soiree. We have an authentic colonial atmosphere, but there's none of the puritan left. Think of us when you're planning a great time for a lively group...two function rooms...And of course the Village Forge Lounge. Why don't you come out?

The Colonial Inn
on the green — CONCORD, MASSACHUSETTS
Loring N. Grimes, Innkeeper (617) 369-9200

Barge In On Cap'n Grimes!

If you do his crew will go overboard to see that your food and lodging are first-rate. Function rooms are also ship-shape for that banquet or meeting. Join the mutiny against so-called "modern" quarters and sign on at the original Colonial Inn. Always on deck is Owner-Skipper Loring Grimes, who really prefers reservations.

The Colonial Inn
on the green — CONCORD, MASSACHUSETTS
Loring Grimes, Innkeeper (617) 369-9200

CC

It's 'Over There' For Mr. Grimes.

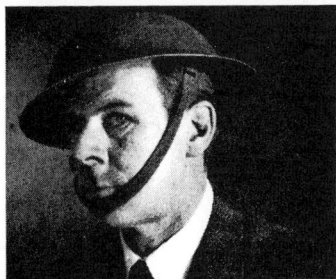

When clubs and companies start planning functions, they often say, "let's have it over there at the Colonial in Concord". Veteran innkeeper that he is, Mr. Grimes offers superb service, top cuisine, and a wide choice of rooms in this unique 250-year-old Inn. Why not give him a call at HQ?

The Colonial Inn
on the green — CONCORD, MASSACHUSETTS
Loring Grimes, Innkeeper (617) 369-9200

Menus that Meld with Country/Colonial Interiors

Menu planners must resist the temptation to be too "country" or too "historical" when selecting the dishes they count on to be reputation-building for a special atmosphere dining room.

Compatibility with contemporary tastes is the measure required for sound construction of a menu made up of theme dishes. Lack of public acceptance has caused marrow puddings, stewed carp and broiled eels to be dropped from the menu at Chowning's Tavern, one of the dining rooms in the Williamsburg restoration. However, Welsh Rabbit and Brunswick Stew remain high volume items in the same restaurant.

It is also true that the loaded tables with their eat-til-you-burst potential, although anticipated by Americans of the early days, would be wasted on their descendants today. Even at family style dining tables today, restaurant patrons expect to encounter platter portions pretty well tailored to reasonable appetites.

Calorie counting is a game nearly everyone plays now at some time or another in his life, so although the appearance of country abundance is one of the recognized appeals of country dining, actual amounts of food served are most acceptable when fairly closely related to a guest's capacity.

In Country/Colonial dining rooms, the most successful menu approach seems to be the highlighting of a theme-setting dish or two among a larger selection of more modern favorites.

The Original Planked Salmon Steak Kimberton, prepared in the "fisherman style of years ago", continues to create menu conversation at Kimberton (Pa.) Tavern. Among the more modern seafood dishes listed with it are Lobster Thermidor, De Luxe Crabmeat Imperial, Alaskan King Crab en Casserole, Shrimp Italiene.

Another item on Kimberton's menu seldom encountered elsewhere is Kimberton's Own Famous Snapper Soup. This thick rich snapper soup is made from the meat of the snapping turtle. It can be flavored with sherry to suit individual tastes.

Yankee Pot Roast of Beef is a down-to-earth touch for a menu that also presents Kimberton Chateaubriand with Fresh Vegetables Jardiniere—a generous portion of center cut filet mignon, fresh mushroom caps and french fried onion rings. Other popular contemporary broiled offerings: Hickory Smoked Ham Steak, Spring Lamb Chops, Filet Mignon and Prime Sirloin Steak.

Country/Colonial

A fresh baked loaf of bread for at-table slicing and garden fresh vegetables are country tavern lures credited with building repeat patronage at Kimberton's.

One patron-building description of New England food service recites these entrees to be considered in menu preparation:

"Any Traveler to Boston should give himself the pleasure of trying some New England dishes, especially seafood. Fish cakes go with baked beans and brown bread on Saturday night. New England clam chowder and fish chowder, made with salt pork and rich milk, win admirers from every region. Cape scallops, tiny morsels of shellfish, broiled in butter, are an Event; they're harvested just for a couple of months in late fall; after the season, they'll be frozen (but still good). Oysters, clams, sea scallops, swordfish, halibut, haddock, all come fresh from New England waters.

"The culinary climax, for those from inland areas, will be lobster. They can order it broiled, or boiled if taught how to tackle shell and claws with nutcracker and pick. The timid, or lazy, can settle for baked stuffed, saute, Newburg or Thermidor.

"Then there's the boiled dinner of corned beef, cabbage, potatoes, onions and turnips, served with mustard pickles and horse-radish which, as true Yankees say, 'stays by you'.

"As for desserts, you can't go wrong on pie, especially blueberry. 'Boston Cream Pie' is a cake. Indian pudding, which dates back to the Indians, is really a pudding made of corn meal, molasses, milk and spices, baked slowly for hours. Every restaurant which serves Indian pudding has its own recipe, in every degree of thickness and spiciness."

Emily Shaw's Inn

The New England note is introduced with Daily Specials on the menu at Concord's Colonial Inn in Mass. A recent menu lists these:

Monday	COLONIAL BEEF PIE
Tuesday	OLD-FASHIONED TURKEY PIE
Wednesday	BAKED COUNTRY SMOKED HAM
Thursday	NEW ENGLAND BOILED DINNER
Friday	BOILED BOSTON SCHROD
Saturday	NEW ENGLAND BAKED BEANS
Sunday	ROAST STUFFED FARM FRESH TURKEY

At Salem Tavern Dining Rooms in Winston-Salem, N. C. all menus carry a prominently placed notation to the effect that while many dishes are a heritage from the area's historic past, Strip Sirloin Steak, Rib Eye Steak, Double Loin Lamb Chops, Chicken Pie and Chopped Sirloin Steak are ALWAYS AVAILABLE.

Lasting impressions can be made on tired travelers when they step into the gracious food world created by some New England country inns. It may be a gesture as simple as placing tart, red apples on bedside tables at Treadway Inn's Publick House, Sturbridge, Mass.

SPECIAL ATMOSPHERE THEMES FOR FOODSERVICE

Or, it may be that guests will remember the unmistakable flavor of fresh fruits as at the tables at John Hancock House, Hancock, N. H., where the garden yields produce for pickles, relishes, mincemeat as well as blueberries, raspberries and strawberries.

Coventry Forge Inn specialties are given a French interpretation although the dishes are of regional origin. Best sellers at this Pottstown, Pa. Inn are Sauteed Chicken Coventry Forge, Roe-Stuffed Shad and Soft Shell Crab.

Hearty New England fare characterizes food service at the many Treadway Inns. Their Lobster Pie and Indian Pudding have long since proved themselves as patron pleasers.

Cobb's Mill by the Waterfall, Weston, Conn. has had success with a buffet featured on Thursday evenings. To carry on this established New England tradition, waiters attired in black trousers with

More often than not, Country/Colonial dining is a "whole family" experience. Gifts for good behaviour, place mats or booklets to color, special napkins—all these help to make meals a pleasure for every member of the party. The menu with read-to-me or read-it-yourself information also helps span time between ordering and food arrival. This children's menu from Stephenson's Apple Farm Restaurant near Kansas City was put together with the special thought for children's happiness that is always a "grabber" for parents.

KIDS PLATES

HENNY PENNY
2 pieces baked or hickory smoked chicken. Hot bread.
9 dimes and 2 nickels

CHICKEN LITTLE
1 piece baked chicken, baked potato or french fries. Hot bread.
2 quarters and 5 nickels

MOM!
If you like, we will be glad to just bring you an empty plate so that you may share some of your dinner with your child.

CHILDREN'
$1.

SMOKEY WOKEY – ¼ hickory in the world – smoked over

THE SPECIALITY (

THREE LITTLE PIGS – Hickory s hickory & apple wood. Picl

PIGGY WIGGY – A hickory entirely different flavor in

PORKY PIG – ½ center cut rea with honey sauce.

LITTLE RED HEN – ¼ baked Tender and delicious.

FISHY WISHY – Fried jumbo tasty. Served with a spec

Above dinners include your frozen – or marshmallow salac milk – coke – iced tea or cider.

Country/Colonial

bright red coats, served dishes from a wide selection of New England specialties.

Country foods with an irresistible aura are so numerous that holding a menu to reasonable lengths is the menu planner's chief problem. At Stephenson's Apple Farm Restaurant near Kansas City, they've concentrated on hickory or apple-wood barbecued ham, chicken and ribs, charcoal broiled steaks, hot bread with apple butter, pickles and relishes and such dessert choices as apple dumplings, hot apple pie with brandy sauce or hickory nut pie.

Specials at other country inns range from crisp crusted chicken pie, fried chicken, sizzling ham slices, raw spinach salad, macaroni and cheese, country style ham and eggs with American fried potatoes and dollar pancakes, corn chowder, stuffed yellow squash, candied parsnips, corn muffins, fresh rhubarb pie, apple brown betty rich chocolate and angel food cakes.

S DINNERS
50

smoked chicken. Finest chicken hickory & apple wood.

OF THE HOUSE

moked ribs really cooked over up and eat with your fingers.

smoked pork chop. This is an pork chops.

l hickory smoked ham — served

chicken in butter and cream.

shrimp. They are large and ial shrimp sauce on the side.

choice of the following tossed — l, baked or french fried potatoes,

HEY KIDS

Don't forget the cider barrel at the entrance.

It is filled with sweet pure cold apple cider made here on the farm from red ripe juicy apples and squeezed in our big press.

You may have all you like, that is, as long as your parents don't object.

Sweet cider is very good for you. In fact, you can drink it in the morning for breakfast instead of orange juice. So on the way out get a cup, turn the wooden spigot and have another drink of HEALTH.

The value of a special menu in promoting group business is generally recognized. Using Colonial or Country as the theme with items featured that fit well into regular production schedules can be highly salable in all kinds of food service operations.

The recently published American Heritage Cookbook, American Heritage Publishing Company, Inc., has collected "500 Great Traditional and Historic Menus" many of which readily lend themselves to adaptation for modern menus, both daily and special.

The historic specialties of Early America as well as happily remembered items of farm fare can be produced coast to coast as the ingredients needed are now available either in convenience form or fresh by air.

For the menu maker who wants to introduce a special occasion Early American menu, a collection of background ideas and authentic dishes like this list researched by ARA Services for use as a special occasion dinner in the many operations they manage for hospitals, schools and employee food services is a good way to start.

AN AMERICAN HERITAGE MENU

APPETIZERS
  VEGETABLE RELISHES WITH DIPPING SAUCE
  OYSTERS ON THE HALF SHELL "He was a brave man that first eat an oyster."
  Jonathan Swift
  CHOPPED CHICKEN LIVER AND EGGS, NEW YORK STYLE

SOUPS
  CHILLED LOVE APPLE Recalls that day in 1830, when Salem, N. J. townsfolk watched in awe as Robert Gibbon Johnson calmly ate a deadly poisonous (or so they thought) tomato. When he survived, people began to grow love apples for food, rather than as ornamental plants.

  CLAM BISQUE
  FRESH VEGETABLE

FISH
  LOBSTER NEWBURG Originally created and named for Delmonico patron Ben Wenberg, the name was changed from Lobster Wenberg to Lobster Newburg. The switch came when the gentleman fell from grace during a brawl in the main dining room.
  POMPANO PONTCHARTRAIN
    AMANDINE "As delicious as the less criminal forms of sin."
  Mark Twain

Country/Colonial

MEATS

   RIVERBOAT BEEF ROAST

   HAM STEAKS BAKED IN MAPLE SYRUP — Virginians made ham into one of the chief culinary glories of our country. Rubbed with salt, pepper and sugar, hung over hickory fire in the smoke house, ham was considered at its peak after a year and a half of curing.

   ROAST TURKEY, THANKSGIVING STYLE

   COUNTRY CAPTAIN — The recipe first appeared in print (as far as we know) around 1828, in the "New Cookery Book" by Miss Eliza Leslie. Coastal Georgians claim the dish although Miss Leslie believed it to be East Indian in origin.

   PAN FRIED PORTERHOUSE STEAK WITH MUSHROOM CAPS, SARATOGA POTATOES — Saratoga potatoes, now known as potato chips, were created at Saratoga Springs, the nineteenth century spa. Guests ate so many of these crisp offerings that it was said crowds at the resort sounded like the wind rustling dried leaves.

VEGETABLES

   NEW POTATOES WITH FRESH DILL

   BABY CARROTS WITH RAISINS

   PLANTATION STRINGBEANS

   FIESTA CORN PUDDING —
> "And those who came resolved to be Englishmen
> Gone to the world's end, but English every one,
> And they ate the white corn-kernels, parched in the sun,
> And they knew it not, but they'd not be English again."
>
>   Stephen Vincent Benet

SALADS

   CAESAR SALAD — California's contribution dates only from 1945, but has since gained nationwide popularity, completely deserved.

   MARY RANDOLPH'S TOMATO SALAD — Recipe from "The Virginia Housewife" by Mrs. Randolph. First published in 1824.

   CUCUMBERS IN SOUR CREAM

   TRAY OF PRESERVES & RELISHES — Spiced Peaches, Watermelon Rind Pickle, Corn Relish, Vegetable Cottage Cheese, Apple Butter, Blackberry Jam

BREADS

   EGG BREAD, SOUTHERN STYLE — Washington's daily breakfast after he retired to Mount Vernon was corn bread, honey and coffee, according to a house guest's diary.

   PHILADELPHIA STICKY BUNS

   PARKER HOUSE ROLLS — In 1855, Harvey Parker opened a restaurant in Boston. The soft hot rolls served there have since become immortal.

DESSERTS

APPLE TARTS WITH CHEDDAR CHEESE OR WHIPPED CREAM

CHOCOLATE SPICE CAKE — "No where is the stomach of the traveller or visitor put in constant peril as among the cake-inventive housewives and daughters of New England."
Charles Latrobe, 1836. Note with relief this is a cherished <u>Southern</u> recipe.

PRALINE SUNDAE — The ice cream Sundae evolved from the wicked ice cream soda, to circumvent a local law prohibiting the sale of "stimulating beverages" on Sunday.

MUSK MELON WITH VANILLA ICE CREAM — One of America's first recipes for ice cream was transcribed by Thomas Jefferson. The Monticello recipe used vanilla bean, eggs and plenty of heavy cream.

PUMPKIN MOUSSE

STRAWBERRY SHORTCAKE WITH RICH BISCUITS — Captain John Smith found growing wild in Virginia "fine and beautiful Strawberries, foure times bigger and better than ours in England."

ICED WATERMELON — "When one has tasted it, he knows what Angels eat." — Mark Twain

BEVERAGES

BUTTERMILK, ICY COLD — "Buttermilk will flow like water", if prohibition is revived.

SWEET MILK
ICED TEA WITH MINT
HOT COFFEE, REAL CREAM

"IT'S BETTER TO DIE EATING THAN FIGHTING"
Pennsylvania Dutch Proverb

Drawing on the background they put together for their Adventures in Dining series, ARA Services suggested this menu combination for sit-down service:

Chilled Love Apple Soup
Ham Steak Baked in Maple Syrup
New Potatoes with Fresh Dill   Plantation String Beans
Cucumbers in Sour Cream
Tray of Relishes and Preserves
Egg Bread, Southern Style
Apple Tarts   Cheddar Cheese
Hot Coffee Real Cream

The decorating and promotion ideas for Country/Colonial dinners are as numerous as the groups that can be interested in them so even those food service operations not committed totally to either theme can work out decor elements and attention-getting promotions for a special dining event based on either theme. The recipe collection on pages 77 to 97 contains operation-tested quantity recipes for use in constructing Colonial and Country menus, either for theme operations or special events.

Appetizers

PENNSYLVANIA DUTCH APPETIZER TRAY
YIELD: 25 servings
INGREDIENTS:

Frankfurters, quartered	25 (about 3 lb.)
Whole Cloves	
Wine Vinegar	2 cups
Salad Oil	1 cup
Garlic	2 cloves
Salt and Pepper	
Sauerkraut, drained	1 (6-lb. 3-oz.) can
Sour Cream	2 cups
Onions, chopped	1 cup
Celery Seed	2 tsp.
Beets, diced, cooked or canned	1 qt.
Onions, chopped	½ cup
Prepared Horseradish	1 tbsp.
Mayonnaise	½ cup
Potato Salad	
Dill Pickles	
Cucumber Slices	
Cottage Cheese and Chives	

METHOD:
Cook frankfurters in boiling water 10 minutes; drain and cool. Stud with cloves.

Combine vinegar and oil; beat well. Add frankfurters, garlic, salt, pepper. Chill 1 hr.

Meanwhile, to half of kraut, add cream, 1 cup onions and celery seed; mix well and chill.

To remaining kraut, add beets and ½ cup onions. Combine horseradish and mayonnaise; mix well. Add to kraut-beet mixture; mix well. Chill.

Arrange frankfurters and kraut mixture on tray. Surround with remaining ingredients. Serve with rye bread, pumpernickel bread, an assortment of cheeses.

Soup

CREAM OF CHICKEN SOUP
YIELD: 90 5-oz. portions
INGREDIENTS:

Chicken Fat	1 lb.
Flour, all-purpose	1½ lb.
Chicken Stock	3 gal.
Cream (18-20%)	1 gal.
Salt	4 tbsp.
Chicken, cooked, finely chopped	8 oz.
Rice, cooked	8 oz.
Parsley, minced	1 bunch
Food Coloring, yellow	Few drops

METHOD:
Melt chicken fat, add flour gradually. Blend well. Cook on low heat for approximately 10 minutes or until mixture is smooth, stirring all the time. Add hot chicken broth and heated cream. Simmer for approximately 45 minutes. Add yellow food coloring and salt and stir in well. Combine minced chicken, rice and parsley and add to soup just before serving.

CREAM OF FRESH VEGETABLE SOUP
YIELD: 12 gal. making 192 8-oz. portions
INGREDIENTS:

Beef Stock, hot	7 gal.
Tomatoes, canned	2 No. 10 cans
Celery, chopped	5 lb.
Onions, chopped	5 lb.
Carrots, julienned	7 lb.
Milk	4 gal.
Thickening (roux)	3 lb.
Worcestershire Sauce	2 tbsp.
Parsley, chopped	2 oz.
Celery Salt	2 tsp.
Nutmeg	2 tsp.
Salt and Pepper	To season

METHOD:
Add fresh vegetables and canned tomatoes to hot beef stock. Cook over medium heat 1½ hr. Make a cream sauce using the roux and milk. Remove stock mixture from heat. Add the hot cream sauce and seasonings. Keep hot over hot water.

NEW ENGLAND CLAM CHOWDER
YIELD: 100 8-oz. portions
INGREDIENTS:

Milk, scalded)	2 gal.
Cream, light, heated)	2 qt.
or	
Milk, scalded	2½ gal.
Salt Pork, cubed, ¼ in.	1 lb. 4 oz.
Onions, A.P., chopped	2 lb.
Flour, all-purpose	1 lb. 4 oz.
Potatoes, A.P., cooked cubed	8 lb.
Clams, canned, No. 5 finely chopped	6
Salt and Pepper	To season

METHOD:
Cook salt pork slowly until fat begins to fry out. Add onions and cook until pork is crisp and onions are tender. Blend in the flour stirring well. Add scalded milk, and cook until mixture is slightly thickened. Add chopped clams, clam liquor, cooked potatoes, salt and pepper. Heat to boiling point, stirring occasionally. Taste for seasoning. When cream is used, add it heated just before serving.

PEPPER-POT SOUP

YIELD: 24 servings

INGREDIENTS:		TEST SIZE
Chicken Bouillon Cubes	18	6
Boiling Water	4½ qt.	6 cups
Bay Leaves	3	1
Salt	1 tbsp.	1 tsp.
Ground Black Pepper	2 tsp.	¾ tsp.
Dried Thyme Leaves	½ tsp.	1/8 tsp.
Honeycomb Tripe	3 lb.	1 lb.
Bacon	½ lb.	4 slices
Onion, chopped	1½ cups	½ cup
Green Pepper, diced	3 cups	1 cup
Celery Stalks, sliced	6 stalks	2
Potatoes, pared, cubed	1½ qt.	2 cups
All-Purpose Flour	¾ cup	¼ cup
Light Cream	1½ cups	½ cup
Saltine Crackers		

METHOD:

Dissolve bouillon cubes in water. Add next five ingredients. Bring to boil; skim surface; then simmer, covered, 1¼ hours.

Cook bacon until crisp; drain and crumble. In bacon fat, saute onion, green pepper and celery until onion is transparent. Add with potatoes and crumbled bacon to soup. Simmer, covered, 30 minutes, or until meat and vegetables are tender. Beat together flour and cream. Stir into soup. Simmer about 10 minutes, or until flavors are blended. Serve 1¼ cup servings with saltine crackers.

OLD-FASHIONED POTATO SOUP

YIELD: 25 gal. making 400 8-oz. portions

INGREDIENTS:	
Beef Stock	12½ gal.
Onions, ground fine	3 lb.
Potatoes, raw, ground fine	12½ lb.
Potatoes, cut in pieces as for stew	12½ lb.
Cream Sauce	12½ gal.
Salt and Pepper	To season
Nutmeg	To season
Celery Salt	To season

METHOD:

Add onions and all of the potatoes to the beef stock, and cook until pieces of potato are soft. (The potatoes may all be ground if desired, but leaving half of the potatoes in large pieces gives the soup more character and body.)

Add 3 gal. chipped ice to the beef stock mixture. (When chipped ice is added to the stock before adding the cream sauce, the soup will not curdle or separate while standing on the steamtable. This practice can be used for other cream soups, and greatly assists in keeping the soup smooth.)

Add cream sauce which should be warm rather than piping hot. Add seasonings and bring the soup to a rolling boil.

OXTAIL SOUP

The oxtail joints form part of the service and are served in the soup. This makes oxtail soup the only one that is also served with a knife and fork.

YIELD: 18 portions of 8-oz. soup and 2 oxtail joints each

INGREDIENTS

Oxtail, 3½ lb. each	2 (36 joints)
Flour	2 oz.
Butter	3 oz.
Bouillon Stock	1 gal.
Carrots, small cubes	1 lb.
Onions, small cubes	1 lb.
Leeks, small cubes	½ cup
Celery, diced, small	6 oz.
Barley	1 lb.
Tomato Puree	1 pt.
Worcestershire Sauce	1 tbsp.
Salt and Pepper	To season
Cayenne	A dash
Parsley, snipped	1/3 cup
Sherry Wine	8 oz.
Brandy	2 oz.

METHOD:

Cut oxtails into small pieces. Place in hot oven (400°F.) to brown well. Transfer joints to saucepan. Add butter and flour. Place on top of range, and cook until flour is brown. Add bouillon stock. Bring to a boil. Add vegetables and barley. Simmer 2 hours. Add tomato puree, worcestershire sauce, salt, pepper, cayenne and parsley. Simmer 10 minutes. Before serving, add sherry wine and brandy. Blend well. Serve 2 oxtail joints with each individual serving of the soup.

NAVY BEAN SOUP

YIELD: 15 gal. making 240 8-oz. portions

INGREDIENTS:	
Navy Beans	15 lb.
Stock, ham or beef	10 gal.
Ham, chopped	4 lb.
Bacon Dripping (optional)	1 pt.
Onions, minced	3 lb.
Carrots, minced	3 lb.
Monosodium Glutamate	2 tbsp.
Tomatoes, canned	5 No. 10 cans
Tomato Catsup	1 pt.
Prepared Mustard	1 pt.
Salt	To season

METHOD:

Soak navy beans overnight in water to cover. Drain. Cook in fresh water to cover until done. Puree beans using water in which they were cooked. Press canned tomatoes through a coarse sieve, and add with other ingredients to pureed beans. Simmer gently 2 to 3 hours.

CORN CHOWDER

YIELD: 12 gal. making 156 6-oz. portions
INGREDIENTS

Salt Pork, diced ½ in.	1 lb.
Onions, diced, fine	1 lb.
Flour, all-purpose	2 lb.
Corn, cream-style	3 No. 10 cans
Milk	9 gal.
Potatoes, E.P., raw, diced	14 lb.
Worcestershire Sauce	2 oz.
Salt and Pepper	To season

METHOD:

Saute the salt pork until light brown and crisp. Remove from pan. Saute onions in hot pork fat until tender but not brown. Add flour. Stir well to make a roux. Add salt pork. Combine corn and milk and bring to boiling point. Add roux, stirring constantly. Add raw diced potatoes, worcestershire sauce, and season with salt and pepper. Simmer slowly, stirring frequently, for approximately 30 minutes.

WISCONSIN CHEESE SOUP

YIELD: 2½ gal. making 50 6-oz. portions
INGREDIENTS:

Celery, diced fine	3 cups
Carrots, diced fine	3 cups
Onions, diced fine	1½ cups
Stock	6 qt.
Butter	1½ cups
Flour	1½ cups
Sharp Cheese, diced	1½ qt.
Milk, hot	1½ gal.
Baking Soda	¾ tsp.
Paprika	1½ tsp.
Cornstarch	½ cup
Sugar	3 tbsp.
Salt	4½ tbsp.
Milk, cold	¾ cup (approx.)
Worcestershire Sauce	2 tbsp.
Parsley, chopped	To garnish

METHOD:

Cook celery, carrots and onions 10 minutes in 2 qt. of the stock. Add the remaining 4 qt. stock and enough water to bring the stock up to the original 6 qt. Melt butter and blend in flour to make a roux. Cook 10 minutes. Gradually add stock and vegetables to the roux, stirring to make a smooth sauce. Add diced sharp cheese. Cook very slowly until cheese is blended into the sauce.

In meantime, heat milk. Combine baking soda, paprika, cornstarch, sugar and salt. Add enough cold milk to make a thin paste. Add with the worcestershire sauce to the cheese mixture. Stir in the hot milk. Bring to simmering point. Taste for seasoning. Serve sprinkled with chopped parsley.

NOTE: To prevent curdling, exercise care in the choice of cheese used in this recipe.

Entrees

BEEF KIDNEY STEW

YIELD: 25 8-oz. portions
INGREDIENTS:

Beef Kidneys	10 lb.
Margarine	8 oz.
Onions, minced	½ cup
Carrots, sliced thin	1½ cup
Tomatoes, canned	2½ cup
Barley	¼ cup
Salt	2 tsp.
Pepper	1/8 tsp.
Monosodium Glutamate	2 tsp.
Flour	½ cup
Water	

METHOD:

Wash kidneys. Remove outer membrane. Split kidneys, and cut in ¼ in. slices. Snip out fat and tubes with scissors. Soak in salted water 30 minutes. Drain well.

Saute in margarine 10 minutes, turning frequently. Add the next 7 ingredients, and simmer 30 minutes. Combine flour with enough water to make a paste. Add to kidney mixture. Blend well.

Simmer slowly 30 minutes, stirring occasionally. Taste and adjust seasonings, if necessary.

Serve garnished with chopped parsley.

STUFFED LAMB PATTIES

YIELD: 24 portions
INGREDIENTS:

Lamb Meat, lean, ground	6 lb.
Pepper	½ tsp.
Salt	1 oz.
Marjoram or Rosemary	1 tsp.
Bread Crumbs	3 oz.
Eggs, beaten	5
Milk	½ cup
Tomatoes	3 lb. (approx.)
Onions, sweet	2 lb. (approx.)

METHOD:

Combine the first 7 ingredients and mix well until thoroughly blended.

Dip into 48 mounds using a No. 16 scoop. Make each mound into a thin patty.

Place a thin slice each of tomato and onion on 24 of the patties. Cover with the remaining patties. Press edges together.

Broil on grill approximately 10 minutes on each side.

Serve on piping hot plates with french fried potatoes and buttered peas seasoned with fresh mint.

BEEF LOAF WITH SAUCE TOPPING
YIELD: 32 servings
INGREDIENTS:

Lean Beef, ground	5 lb.
Lean Pork, ground	1¼ lb.
Bread Crumbs	½ lb.
Eggs, beaten	8
Milk	1¼ qt.
Salt	2 tbsp.
Pepper	¼ tsp.
Onion, chopped fine	1 cup
Sauce for Topping	
Vinegar	2 cups
Worcestershire Sauce	¼ cup
Chili Powder	¼ cup

METHOD:
Combine meat with all other ingredients. Mix well. Shape in loaves in oiled baking pans.
Cover with sauce. Bake 1½ to 2 hours at 350°F.

BRAISED LAMB SHANKS WITH MIXED VEGETABLE GRAVY
YIELD: 25 portions of 1 lamb shank, 3 oz. mixed vegetable gravy.
INGREDIENTS:

Lamb Shanks, average weight per shank, 12 oz.	25
Bacon Fat	4 oz.
Lemons	4
Water	1½ gal.
Salt	1 oz.
Pepper	1 tbsp.
Carrots, chopped fine	4 lb.
Onions, chopped fine	4 lb.
Celery, diced	4 lb.
Roux	2 cups

METHOD:
Wipe lamb shanks and brown on all sides in hot bacon fat.
Squeeze lemons. Add lemon juice, water, salt and pepper. Simmer slowly 1 hour. Add finely chopped carrots, onions and celery. Simmer slowly 45 minutes longer.
Add roux and cook until gravy thickens.

LAMB STEW WITH DUMPLINGS
YIELD: 14 lb., 25 (approx.) 8-oz. portions
INGREDIENTS:

Lamb, lean, cut in 1 in. cubes	7 lb. 8 oz.
Salt and Pepper	To season
Meat Stock	To cover
Carrots, small, whole	2 lb. 8 oz.
Potatoes, small, whole	2 lb.
Green Peas	2 lb.

METHOD:
Sprinkle meat with salt and pepper. Braise in oven. When meat is brown, add enough meat stock to cover it. Cook slowly in oven 1½ hr.
Remove from oven, and transfer to kettle on top of stove or to steam-jacketed kettle.
Add raw potatoes and continue cooking. When potatoes are nearly done, add the whole onions and carrots which have been cooked in boiling salted water and drained.
Season with salt and pepper to taste.
Just before serving add cooked peas.
Serve with fluffy dumplings. Sprinkle with chopped parsley. Note: When unable to get small baby carrots, cut off tip end of larger ones, and use only these tips. (Use remainder of the carrots for other purposes.)
When small new potatoes are not in season, use potato balls, cut with a french cutter.

DUMPLINGS FOR LAMB STEW
YIELD: 5 lb. making 50 portions
INGREDIENTS:

Flour, Bread	2 lb. 4 oz.
Baking Powder	5 tbsp.
Salt	1 tbsp.
Eggs	8
Milk	3 cups
Butter, melted	½ cup

METHOD:
Sift together the flour, baking powder and salt. Combine beaten eggs and milk, and pour slowly into the dry ingredients. Mix lightly. Do not use power mixer. Add melted butter, and work it into mixture gently. Do not overmix, but combine thoroughly. Drop by spoonfuls into hot chicken stock. Cover while cooking.

HAM LOAF WITH CURRANT SAUCE
YIELD: 200 4-oz. portions
INGREDIENTS:

Ham, smoked, E.P., ground	24 lb.
Veal, E.P., ground	12 lb.
Pork, E.P., lean, ground	12 lb.
Cornflakes	3 gal.
Onions, chopped	1 qt.
Green Peppers, chopped	2 cups
Pimientoes, chopped fine	2 cups
Parsley, chopped	2 bunches
Nutmeg	4 tbsp.
Salt and Pepper	To season
Eggs, beaten	48
Milk	1½ gal.
Currant Sauce	
Currant Jelly, 13 oz. jars	12
Prepared Mustard, small jars	12

METHOD:
Combine all ingredients for Ham Loaf and blend thoroughly. Pack mixture in greased loaf pans.
Place in bakepans with hot water. Cover and

Country/Colonial

cook in a 300°F. oven 1½ hr.

Uncover and cook until Ham Loaves are browned.

In meantime combine currant jelly and prepared mustard. Stir over hot water until jelly is melted and ingredients are blended. Serve with the Ham Loaves.

VEAL FRICASSEE
YIELD: 2 gal., making 36 7 oz. portions
INGREDIENTS:

Leg of Veal	10 lb.
Carrots, large pieces	12 oz.
Onions, whole or large pieces	12 oz.
Bouquet garni	
Celery Stalk, cubed	1
Peppercorns	3
Bay Leaf	1
Whole Cloves	3
Thyme	½ tsp.
Parsley Sprig	1
Salt	1½ tbsp.
Chicken Broth or water	1½ gal. approx.
Fricassee Sauce	
Chicken Fat	1 cup
Flour	1½ cups
Stock from Veal	1 gal.
Cream, 18 per cent	1 pt.
Egg Yolks, beaten	6
Salt and Pepper	To season

METHOD:
Cut veal in 1 in. cubes. Cover with cold water. Bring to a boil. Drain off water to remove any scum. Cover with chicken stock or cold water.

Tie bouquet garni in cheesecloth bag and add with carrots, onions and salt to the veal.

Bring to boiling point and simmer gently until meat is tender. Remove carrots, onions and bouquet garni.

Drain stock from meat to make the sauce. There should be 1 gal.

Make a roux of the chicken fat and the flour. Gradually add the veal stock, stirring constantly. Then add the cream. Cook until sauce thickens.

Beat egg yolks. Pour over some of the hot sauce, and add to the remainder of the sauce.

Season with salt and pepper. Cook only a few minutes longer.

Arrange veal cubes over rice or noodles in serving dish and strain hot sauce over them.

NOTE:
For Fricassee of Veal Shortcake, use 4 lb. veal for each gal. and 1 pint green peas. Serve over hot baking powder biscuit halves.

CAPPED HAM STEAKS
(see picture, page 18)
YIELD: 24 servings

INGREDIENTS:		TEST SIZE
Cracker meal, medium grind	1 lb.	4 oz.
Dried Marjoram Leaves	2 tsp.	½ tsp.
Ground Allspice	1 tsp.	¼ tsp.
Canned Sweet Potatoes, drained, cut into small pieces	1 qt.	1 can (8½-oz,)
Onion, chopped	1 cup	¼ cup
Butter or Margarine, melted	1¼ cups	1/3 cup
Ham Steaks (4 ounce portions)	6 lb.	1½ lb.
Light Brown Sugar, firmly packed	2 cups	½ cup
Cornstarch	6 tbsp.	1½ tbsp.
Grated Orange Rind	¼ cup	1 tbsp.
Ground Cloves	½ tsp.	1/8 tsp.
Cranberry Juice Cocktail	2¼ cups	½ cup
Orange Juice	2¼ cups	½ cup
Lemon Juice	¼ cup	1 tbsp.
Pecans, chopped	1 cup	¼ cup

METHOD:
Combine first three ingredients; add sweet potatoes; toss lightly. Saute onion in butter or margarine until golden. Mix with cracker meal mixture. Pile on ham in baking pan. Bake in a preheated moderate oven (350°F.) 30 to 35 minutes. Meanwhile combine next seven ingredients. Stirring, bring to boil; cook until thickened. Stir in pecans. Serve ¼ cup over each portion of ham.

CRANBERRY GLAZED HAM
YIELD: 20-24 servings (approx.)
INGREDIENTS:

Smoked Ham	1 (8 to 10 lb.)
Cloves, long-stemmed	2 doz.
Jellied Cranberry Sauce	1 lb. can
Brown Sugar	½ cup

METHOD:
Bake ham according to manufacturer's directions. One-half hour before end of baking time, remove from oven. Score fat with sharp knife, stud with cloves, return to baking pan. (Any fat that has collected in bottom of pan should be poured off before placing ham back in pan.) Crush cranberry sauce with a fork; combine crushed cranberry sauce and brown sugar. Spread ½ of mixture over ham. Bake one half hour longer, basting occasionally. Heat remaining cranberry mixture to serve.

VEAL PASTIES

YIELD: 25 portions, 1 pasty each
INGREDIENTS:

Onions, E.P. chopped	6 oz.
Butter or Shortening	4 tbsp.
Veal, cooked, diced	4 lb.
Parsley, chopped fine	2 tbsp.
Salt	1 tbsp.
Pepper	1 tsp.
Monosodium Glutamate	½ tsp.
Chili Sauce	½ cup
Potatoes, cooked, diced	4 oz.
White Turnips, cooked, diced	4 oz.
Brown Gravy	1 qt.
Pie Dough	

METHOD:
Saute onions in butter until limp but not brown. Combine all ingredients. Blend well. (Turnips and potatoes are optional.)

Roll pastry in individual circles approx. 6 in. in diameter. Place 2 tbsp. or 3 tbsp. of the meat mixture in the center of the lower half of circle. Wet edges of pastry. Fold over to form turnover and crimp edges.

Bake in a hot oven (450°F.) until pastry is cooked—approx. 12 to 15 minutes.

Serve with some of the Brown Gravy poured over the pasty with an underlining of a bouquet of vegetables.

O'BRIEN'S FAMOUS COUNTRY SAUSAGE
O'Brien's, Waverly, New York

This is the recipe for the country sausage for which O'Brien's are famous. The hogs—200 to 300 of them—are raised on the O'Brien farm, and slaughtered when they weigh 180 lb. All hams, shoulders and loins go into the famous O'Brien lean sausage which shows little shrinkage when cooked. The bacon is honey-cured and hickory-smoked in the farm smokehouse. The lard is rendered for use in the restaurant. Regardless of the number of pounds of pork that are to be made into sausages, the O'Brien's never make up the recipe in a larger quantity than is given here.

In the restaurant, the sausage is served in 5 oz. patties. It is also retailed in tubs at the food counter.

YIELD: 31 lb.
INGREDIENTS:

Lean Pork	20 lb.
Fat and Lean Pork	10 lb.
Special Seasoning	10 oz.
Sugar	3 oz.
Salt	2 oz.
Cardamom	1/3 oz.
Sage	4 tbsp.

METHOD:
Grind meat, and add other ingredients. Blend well. Mold into 5 oz. patties.

HAM A LA KING

YIELD: 50 6-oz. portions
INGREDIENTS:

Ham, cooked, diced	6 lb.
Green Peppers, ¼ in. cubes	1 lb.
Mushrooms, fresh, sliced	2 lb.
or	
Mushrooms, canned, sliced	1½ lb.
Butter or Shortening	4 oz.
Paprika	¼ tsp.
Sherry Wine	6 oz.
Cream Sauce (medium)	1½ gal.
Pimientoes, chopped	6 oz.

METHOD:
Cut ham in ½ in. pieces. Saute green peppers and mushrooms in butter or shortening. Do not brown.

Blend in the paprika. Add sherry wine and cubed ham. Cover and remove from the direct heat. Let stand 5 minutes for the sherry wine flavor to permeate all ingredients.

Strain Cream Sauce over ham mixture. Add pimientoes and mix gently.

Heat thoroughly. Taste for seasoning, and adjust, if necessary. Serve on toast points in casserole or on plate.

CREAM SAUCE (MEDIUM)

YIELD: 1½ gal.
INGREDIENTS:

Fat	12 oz.
Flour, all-purpose	1 lb. 2 oz.
Milk	1½ gal.
Salt	1½ tbsp.
Pepper, white	½ tsp.

METHOD:
Melt fat. Add flour. Blend with wire whip until smooth. Add hot milk gradually, stirring constantly.

Simmer gently 20 to 30 minutes, stirring frequently. Add salt and pepper. Blend well.

SCHNITZ UN'KNEPP— TAVERN ADAPTATION
Salem Tavern Dining Rooms

YIELD: 24 servings
INGREDIENTS:

Dried Sweet Apples	6 cups
Smoked Ham	6 lb.
Brown Sugar	6 tbsp.
Noodles	1 lb.

METHOD:
Cover apples. Let soak 2 hours. (If home dried, soak over night.) Cook ham in simmering water 2 hours for tenderizing. Drain ham and cook apples in part of stock to which the brown sugar has been added. Simmer for ¾ of an hour.

Cook noodles in rest of ham stock until tender. Make layer of noodles, apples and ham. Repeat till pan is full. Bake 20 min. at 350°F.

Country/Colonial

BAKED PORK CHOPS STUFFED WITH APPLE AND ONION DRESSING

YIELD: 50 1-chop portions
INGREDIENTS:

<u>Apple and Onion Stuffing</u>

Salt Pork, finely chopped	4 oz.
Celery, finely chopped	2 cups
Onions, finely chopped	1 cup
Apples, tart, coarsely chopped	1½ qt.
Bread Crumbs	5 cups
Eggs, slightly beaten	2
Salt	1 tbsp.
Monosodium Glutamate	½ tsp.
Thyme, powdered	¼ tsp.
Stock or Milk, if necessary	
Pork Chops, cut 1 in. thick	50
Pork Fat Trimmings, rendered	1 cup
Salt	1 tbsp.
Black Pepper	½ tsp.
Monosodium Glutamate	2 tsp.

METHOD:
Render salt pork. Saute celery and onions in the fat until soft. Cool.

Combine all ingredients for the stuffing. The fat, apples and eggs should provide enough moisture to blend mixture together. If not, add a little stock or milk.

Wipe pork chops with damp cloth. Cut halfway through each chop from fat to bone making a pocket for the stuffing. Stuff loosely with apple-onion mixture. Pin to keep stuffing in place.

Sprinkle seasonings over stuffed chops. Brown chops on both sides in hot fat. Place in roasting pan in a 350°F. oven. Cook 45 to 60 minutes, or until chops are tender.

POACHED EGGS AMERICAN

YIELD: 1 portion
INGREDIENTS:

Idaho Potato, baked, large	1
Egg, poached	1
Cheddar Cheese Rarebit	2 oz.
Whipped Cream	2 tsp.
Parsley	1 bunch

METHOD:
Cut 1 in. slice from top of large baked potato. Scoop out potato. Do not break skin. Combine mashed potato with Cheddar Cheese Rarebit. Blend well. Refill potato. Top with poached egg. Cover with whipped cream and glaze. Serve with Fried Parsley.

To prepare parsley:
Wash and dry parsley. Fry in oil for a few seconds. Drain. Sprinkle with salt. Serve on napkin next to the potato.

CHICKEN LOAF
*The Frances Virginia Tea Room,
Atlanta, Ga.*

YIELD: 28 portions cut from 12-by 20-by 2-1/8 in. pan
INGREDIENTS:

Onions, diced	1 cup
Celery, diced	1 cup
Mushrooms, sliced	3 cups
Butter or Margarine	6 tbsp.
Chicken, cooked, diced	1½ lb.
Eggs, beaten	5
Milk	1 qt.
Chicken Broth	1½ qt.
Salt and Pepper	To season
Bread Crumbs	1½ qt.
Butter or Margarine, melted	¾ cup

METHOD:
Saute onions, celery and mushrooms in 6 tbsp. butter. Beat eggs. Add milk and chicken broth, then the sauteed vegetables and chicken. Fold in the bread crumbs. Taste. Add salt and pepper. Pour into a greased steamtable pan. Top with melted butter. Bake in a 350°F. oven 1 hr. or until set. Serve with Giblet Gravy or Mushroom Sauce.

BREAST OF CAPON
Colligan's Stockton Inn

YIELD: 20 servings
INGREDIENTS:

Breast of Capon (8 oz. ea.)	20
Butter	½ lb.
Wild Rice	4 cups
Cling Peach Halves	20
Maraschino Cherries	20
Coconut, shredded	1 cup
Peach Juice	1 cup
Dry Red Wine	2 cups
Bay Leaves	2
Salt, Pepper, Cloves, Brown Sugar	
Espagnole Sauce	3 qt.

METHOD:
Preheat frying pan, sprinkle salt and pepper over floured capon; saute for 20 minutes. Remove from heat. Add red wine to frying pan, reduce to one-third, pour in sauce espagnole, peach juice, bay leaves, cloves, brown sugar. Simmer for 15 minutes, season to taste. Place peach filled with cherry in pan and broil with brandy under salamander flame.

Boil wild rice in chicken stock. Place cooked wild rice on plate, top with capon, pour sauce over capon.

Serve with glazed peach and sprinkle with roasted coconut.

CHICKEN POT PIE

YIELD: 6 gal. making 100 6-oz. portions
INGREDIENTS:

Stewing Chicken, 5-lb. ea.	
A.P. market dressed	8
or	
Chicken Meat, cooked	12 lb.
Chicken Broth	3 gal.
Dough:	
Flour, all-purpose	5 lb.
Shortening	4½ cups
Salt	2 tbsp.
Eggs, medium-size	8
Milk and Water, half of each	4½-5 cups

METHOD:
Simmer prepared stewing chicken in salted water until tender. Cool in broth; remove, and save broth. Remove meat from bones. Dice in ¾-in. cubes. Refrigerate until ready to use. Make dough by working flour, shortening and salt to a fine crumb. Beat eggs slightly and add to milk and water, then to flour mixture. (Dough should be of the consistency of pie dough.) Roll dough very thin on a well-floured board. Cut dough in 2-in. diamond-shaped pieces. In meantime, bring chicken broth to a boil. Add dough diamonds, piece by piece. Simmer until dough is tender and thoroughly cooked. Add chicken cubes. Heat well. Taste. If necessary, season with salt and pepper. If mixture is too thin, add a small amount of flour paste.

NOTE:
The chicken may be cooked and cubed the day prior to use, and kept refrigerated.

PECKETT'S ON SUGAR HILL SEAFOOD CASSEROLE

Peckett's on Sugar Hill, Franconia, N. H.
YIELD: 25 portions
INGREDIENTS:

Scallops	1½ lb.
Scallop Liquor	1-2 cups
Fresh Crab Meat	1½ lb.
Fresh Lobster Meat, diced	2 lb.
Butter	4 oz.
Flour	1 cup
Milk	3 qt.
Heavy Cream	2 cups
Sherry	1 cup
Salt and Pepper	To season
Cheese, grated	2 cups
Bread Crumbs	2½ cups
Butter	4 oz.

METHOD:
Put scallops in pan with barely enough cold water to cover. Bring to boiling point; reduce heat, simmer 2 minutes. Remove from heat. Drain scallops. Reserve liquor. Remove any small pieces of shell from the fresh crab meat. Boil lobster for the time prescribed according to weight. Remove flesh from shell and cut in large pieces. Make cream sauce with the butter, flour, milk and scallop liquor. When thoroughly cooked, add the heavy cream. (Important not to add the cream till now.)

Add lobster, scallops and crab meat to the sauce. Season with salt and pepper. Add sherry. Place mixture in buttered baking dish or in individual casserole dishes. Sprinkle top with grated cheese. Top with bread crumbs. Dot over with butter. Sprinkle with paprika. Bake in 350°F. oven until cheese is melted and crumbs are brown—about 30 minutes.

NEW ENGLAND CRAB MEAT BAKE

YIELD: 4-6 servings
INGREDIENTS:

Chopped Frozen Spinach, cooked and drained	1 pkg.
Flour	1 tbsp.
Cottage Cheese, drained	1½ cups
7-oz. can Crab Meat	1
Lemon Juice	1 tbsp.
Small Onion, minced	1
Tomato Paste, 6-oz. can	1
Provolone Cheese, shredded	1 cup
Salt	½ tsp.
Pepper	Dash
Grated Nutmeg	¼ tsp.

METHOD:
Place spinach in buttered casserole dish; stir in flour. Top with cottage cheese; then crab meat; sprinkle lemon juice over crab meat. Mix onion, tomato paste, cheese, salt, pepper and nutmeg; spoon over top of casserole. Bake in preheated 350°F. oven, 15 minutes.

LOBSTER A LA NEWBURG

YIELD: 2 12-oz. portions
INGREDIENTS:

Maine Lobster, cooked, 1¼ lb. each	2
Butter	4 tbsp.
Sherry	¼ cup
Heavy Cream	1 cup
Egg Yolks, slightly beaten	3
Salt	To season
Pepper	To season

METHOD:
Remove cooked meat from lobster shell. Cut meat in good-sized pieces. Melt butter in heavy skillet. Add lobster and cook until the lobster turns the butter a bright red. Combine cream

Country/Colonial

and slightly-beaten egg yolks. Cook in double boiler or in small steam-jacketed kettle until thickened. Add lobster meat, sherry wine, and seasoning. Allow to stand over very low heat 5 minutes for lobster flavor to penetrate the sauce.

Serve in lobster shells, toast baskets, patty shells, or on toast in individual flat casseroles.
NOTE: The lobster meat from the 2½ lb. lobster will weigh approximately 14 oz.

BAKED LOBSTER PIE
The Treadway Inn, North Falmouth, Cape Cod
YIELD: 20 6-oz. portions
INGREDIENTS:

Butter	9 oz.
Flour, Unsifted	13 oz.
Milk	5 qt.
Lobster Meat, cooked	4½ lb.
Butter	4 oz.
Paprika	2 oz.
Salt	1½ oz.
Sherry	8 oz.
Topping	
Bread Crumbs, fine	2½ lb.
Potato Chips, crushed	3 oz.
Paprika	2½ oz.
Parmesan Cheese, grated	2 oz.
Sherry	3 oz.

METHOD:
Make a roux using the 9 oz. butter and the 13 oz. flour. Add roux to the 5 qt. scalded milk, stirring constantly. Bring to a boil, and boil 3 minutes. Clean lobster meat and cut it in ¾ in. pieces. Saute in 4 oz. butter. Add paprika and sherry wine. Strain cream sauce through a china cap into the lobster mixture. Blend lightly. Combine bread crumbs, potato chips, paprika, parmesan cheese, and sherry wine. Place 6 oz. of lobster newburg in individual greased casseroles. Cover with bread mixture topping. Bake in a 300°F. oven 10 minutes.

Vegetables

CHEDDAR PIPPIN
YIELD: 48 servings
INGREDIENTS:

Butter	½ cup
Cheddar Cheese, grated	8 lb.
Beer	1 qt.
Tomato Sauce (8 oz. can)	1
Horseradish, prepared	¼ cup
Garlic Powder	2 tsp.

METHOD:
Melt butter and cheese in double boiler over hot water. As cheese begins to melt, gradually stir in mixture of beer, tomato sauce, horseradish and garlic powder. Cook only until smooth and hot. Serve over toast, ham or vegetables.

BEETS IN SOUR CREAM
YIELD: 25 portions, 3 beets ea.
INGREDIENTS:

Butter or Margarine	1 lb.
Flour	8 oz.
Beet Juice plus water	2 qt.
Vinegar	1 qt.
Sugar, granulated	6 tbsp.
Salt	3 tbsp.
Pepper	1/8 tsp.
Sour Cream, thick	1 qt.
Whole Beets, canned, small	2 No. 10 cans

METHOD:
Make a roux of the butter and flour. When well blended gradually add the beet juice and water. Stir until smooth. Add vinegar, sugar, salt and pepper. Cook over low heat until mixture is clear and thick. Add sour cream. Pour over small whole beets and heat thoroughly.

CORN SOUFFLE PUDDING
YIELD: 50 5½-oz. portions
INGREDIENTS:

Corn, whole kernel yellow	2 No. 10 cans
Sugar, granulated	1¼ cups
Flour, all-purpose	1¼ cups
Salt	1-2/3 tbsp.
Milk	1¼ qts.
Egg Yolks	15
Egg Whites	15
Baking Powder, double-acting	5 tbsp.

METHOD:
Drain corn, and grind it through the fine knife of the food chopper. Save any liquid that comes from corn during grinding, and add to ground corn. Combine dry ingredients, and add to ground corn. Beat egg yolks until thick and lemon colored. Combine with milk, and add to corn. Carefully fold in the stiffly beaten egg whites. Butter individual casserole dishes, and fill two-thirds full. Set in shallow pan of hot water. Bake in 350°F. oven until puffed, light brown, and set—approximately 30 minutes.

Serve in casserole with sprig of parsley stuck in the top.
NOTE:
This recipe was adapted from one made in Iowa in which dried sweet corn was used. Do not substitute cream-style corn, or leave the corn in whole kernels or you will get an entirely different product. The distinguishing characteristic flavor of this Corn Souffle or Pudding is obtained by putting the whole kernels through the food chopper and saving every drop of the thick, rich juice that accumulates when the corn is ground. This is not a true souffle. It is not meant to be as light and fluffy as a cheese souffle. It is delicious with baked ham.

DUTCH GREEN BEANS
YIELD: 4 gal. pan making 100 3-oz. portions of this popular vegetable
INGREDIENTS:

Green Beans, canned	4 No. 10 cans
Onions, chopped	1 pt.
Bacon, cooked and chopped	20 slices
Vinegar	1 pt.
Bacon Fat	1 cup

METHOD:
Cook bacon. Cool and chop into fine pieces. Cook onions in a little of the bacon fat. Place beans in steam kettle or steamer and heat thoroughly. Add bacon, bacon fat, onions, and vinegar. Heat to boiling point. Reduce steam, and serve.

PIQUANT POTATOES
YIELD: 50 4-oz. portions
INGREDIENTS:

Potatoes, E.P., peeled	10 lb.
Salt	2 tbsp.
White Sauce	1 qt.
Mayonnaise	1 qt.
Onions, chopped fine	1 lb.

METHOD:
Cut potatoes evenly in ½ in. cubes. Cook in boiling salted water until tender but not soft. Add minced onions when potatoes are almost cooked. Mix the white sauce with the mayonnaise. Combine drained cooked potatoes and onions with the sauce.

Place in a large greased baking pan or in individual baking dishes. Place in hot oven (400°F.) to brown before serving.

NOTE:
If the mayonnaise is not very flavorful, it will be necessary to add more mustard, lemon juice and seasonings to it before combining it with the white sauce.

LYONNAISE CARROTS
Toll House, Whitman, Mass.
YIELD: 50 3-oz. portions
INGREDIENTS:

Carrots, E.P.	8 lb.
Water	2 qt.
Salt	4½ tbsp.
Onions, E.P., sliced	2 lb.
Butter	1 lb.
Salt and Pepper	To season

METHOD:
Wash and scrape carrots and cut in slices. Cook in boiling salted water until tender—approximately 35 to 45 minutes. Drain. Combine cooked carrots and sliced onions.

Saute vegetables lightly in butter in frying pan until onions are tender but not brown. Season with salt and pepper.

STUFFED YELLOW SQUASH
Gold's of Nebraska, Lincoln, Neb.
YIELD: 24 portions, 1 squash each
INGREDIENTS:

Yellow Squash	24
Butter, melted	6 tbsp.
Bread Crumbs, fine	3 cups
Onion, minced	¼ cup
Parsley, minced	3 tbsp.
Salt	3 tsp.
White Pepper	¾ tsp.
Eggs	3

METHOD:
Parboil squash in boiling salted water until tender but not soft. Cool. Cut slice lengthwise off top of squash leaving the stem whole. Carefully scoop out the pulp from the center.

Stir crumbs into melted butter. Set aside 4 tbsp. crumbs for topping. Combine other 5 ingredients with crumbs, blend. Mix together the mashed pulp and bread crumb mixture. Refill squash shells with crumb-squash mixture.

Sprinkle approximately ½ tsp. reserved crumbs on top of each squash. Just before serving place in a 400°F. oven until crumbs are evenly browned and squash thoroughly heated.

CAULIFLOWER AND CHEESE CASSEROLE
The John Hancock House, Hancock, N. H.
YIELD: 8-10 servings
INGREDIENTS:

Cauliflower (large)	1 head or
Frozen Cauliflower, 2-lb. package	1
Butter	3 tbsp.
Flour	3 tbsp.
Evaporated Milk (2-3 cups)	1 can
Water	½ cup
Parmesan Cheese, grated	½ cup
Salt	½ tsp.
Pepper	dash
Egg Yolks	2
Bread Crumbs, toasted	½ cup
Butter, melted	¼ cup

METHOD:
Cook cauliflower, separate into flowerets, in salted boiling water until just tender, still white and firm. Melt butter and add flour. Mix well. Add evaporated milk and water and cook until smooth and thick, stirring constantly. Add the parmesan cheese, salt and pepper. Add several spoonfuls of sauce to egg yolks, blend, then combine with remaining sauce. Pour over cauliflower in buttered casserole. Sprinkle cheddar cheese and bread crumbs over top, drizzle with melted butter. Bake uncovered at 350°F. 30 minutes until brown.

Country/Colonial

HOT COLE SLAW
YIELD: 25 ½-cup portions
INGREDIENTS:

Cabbage, shredded	8 lb.
Bay Leaves	3
Cloves, whole	4
Bacon Fat	1 lb.
Stock	1 pt.
Sugar, granulated	5/8 cup
Vinegar, cider	1½ cups
Apples, raw, peeled, diced	2 qt.
Salt	4½ tbsp.
Pepper	2 tsp.

METHOD:
Shred cabbage. Tie bay leaves and cloves in a gauze bag. Melt bacon fat, and add stock, cabbage and sugar. Cook 8 minutes. Add vinegar and cook 5 minutes. Add diced apples, salt and pepper. Cook 10 minutes. Remove spice bag and serve.

EGGPLANT FRITTERS
YIELD: 24 fritters
INGREDIENTS:

Eggplant, A.P.	10 lb.

Batter

Flour, all-purpose	1 lb.
Baking Powder	2 tbsp.
Eggs, beaten	3
Salt	2/3 tsp.
Milk	1 pt.
Shortening, melted	3 tbsp.

METHOD:
Choose thick, chunky eggplant. Peel and cut in uniform slices ½ in. thick. Dry slices.

Make batter by combining the remaining ingredients. Mix batter until smooth. (Add additional milk if too thick.) Dip eggplant slices in batter. Drain.

Fry in deep fat at 375°F. 7 minutes or until a golden brown. Serve immediately while hot and crisp.

CANDIED PARSNIPS
YIELD: 8 portions from 10- by 10-in. pan
INGREDIENTS:

Parsnips, A.P.	1½ lb.
Butter or Margarine, melted	2 tbsp.
Salt	¼ tsp.
Cinnamon Imperials	¼ cup
Bread Crumbs, buttered	2 tbsp.

METHOD:
Peel, core and cut washed parsnips into strips approximately 2½ to 3 in. long and ½ in. thick. Steam parsnips approximately 10 min.—or until fairly tender.

Place steamed parsnips in half-size steamtable pan. Sprinkle with melted butter or margarine, salt, and cinnamon imperials. Dust with bread crumbs. Bake in a 400°F. oven 30 min.—until cinnamon imperials are melted and bread crumbs are well browned.

NOTE: Candied Parsnips should be fairly dry. Do not allow parsnips to float in excess fat or juice. Do not reuse syrup from one pan to make a second pan.

GLAZED ONIONS
YIELD: 25 servings
INGREDIENTS:

Butter, or Margarine	¾ cup
Sugar	½ cup
Water	1 cup
Onions	1 No. 10 can

METHOD:
Combine butter, sugar and water in a heavy kettle. Simmer until blended. Add drained onions and cook, stirring, until brown.

Salads

CABBAGE SALAD
YIELD: 6 lb., 14 oz. making 36 No. 12-scoop portions
INGREDIENTS:

Cabbage, shredded	4½ lb., E.P.
Salt	2½ tbsp.
Sugar, granulated	3 tbsp.
Mixed Dressing*	1 qt. (2 lb., 2-2/3 oz.)

METHOD:
Have ingredients in readiness. Mix in relays during serving period. It is better not to mix too much at one time.

*Mixed Dressing
YIELD: 3 qts. (6 lb., 8 oz.)

Cooked Dressing	2 qt.
Mayonnaise	1 qt.

CHICKEN AND PINEAPPLE SALAD
YIELD: 2 gal. making 32 8-oz. portions
INGREDIENTS:

Cubed Stewing Chicken	1 gal.
Green Onions, thinly sliced	4 bunches
Mayonnaise	1 qt.
Pineapple Chunks, chilled	½ gal.
Diced Celery, chilled	½ gal.
Lettuce Cups	32 (only)
Paprika	

METHOD:
Stew chickens the day before, and leave overnight in broth in refrigerator. Cube chicken, and slice or dice onions, tops and all, if green. Combine chicken, onions and mayonnaise. Allow to marinate in refrigerator for two or three hrs. Just before serving, add the canned, drained and chilled pineapple chunks and celery to the chicken mixture. Serve in crisp lettuce cups that have been dusted with paprika. Garnish with deviled eggs and radish roses.

SPECIAL SALAD BOWL GREENS
YIELD: 38 portions
INGREDIENTS:

Head Lettuce Hearts	1½ gals.
Watercress	1 qt.
Escarole	2 qt.
Romaine	2 qt.
Endive	3 qt.
Spinach	2 qt.
Radishes, sliced thin	1 pt.
Tomatoes, cut ¾ in. cubes	1½ qts.
Salt	2 tbsp.
Salad Bowl Dressing	3 cups

METHOD:
Cut leafy vegetables into pieces approximately 1½ in. long. Wash carefully. Drain well. Chill thoroughly. Mix all ingredients together. Do not add salad dressing until ready to use.

NOTE:
Prepare the greens for the bowl the day before, and put them into large cans with tight lids to chill and crisp in refrigerator overnight. As needed, mix greens, add tomatoes and salad dressing.

SALAD BOWL GARLIC DRESSING
YIELD: 1 gal.
INGREDIENTS:

Salad Oil	3 qt.
Vinegar	3 cups
Salt	¾ cup
Sugar	1¼ cup
Pepper	1 tbsp.
Crushed Garlic	4 cloves

METHOD:
Mix all ingredients together. Let stand overnight to season. Stir or shake each time before using.

HAM SALAD
YIELD: 2½ qts. making 30 No. 16-scoop portions or 20 No. 12-scoop portions
INGREDIENTS:

Ham, diced, ½-in. cubes	3 lb.
Celery, diced ¼ in.	1 lb.
Mayonnaise	2 cups
Salt	To taste
Pepper	To taste
Lemon Juice	2 tbsp.

METHOD:
Add lemon juice, salt, and pepper to mayonnaise. Combine celery and ham, and add seasoned mayonnaise. Serve in lettuce cup; garnish with tomato wedges or slices, and parsley.

NOTE:
This Ham Salad may be used in numerous varieties of cold plate combinations, or served a la carte. Assorted finger sandwiches, hot cheese roll, garlic bread, or potato chips are some of the accompaniments frequently served with this type of salad.

JELLIED FRUIT SALAD
YIELD: 6 gals. or 240 portions
INGREDIENTS:

Plain Gelatin	1 lb.
Cold Water	1 gal.
Hot Water	1 gal.
Sugar, granulated	2 lb.
Salt	1 tbsp. plus 1 tsp.
Pineapple Juice	1 gal.
Orange Juice	1 gal.
Lemon Juice	1¼ qt.
Other Fruit Juices	3 cups
Peaches, No. 10	1 can
Pears, No. 10	1 can
Pineapple, crushed, or	2½ qt.
Grapes, seeded	3 qt.

METHOD:
Soak gelatin and cold water for 10 minutes. Add hot water, sugar and salt and stir until dissolved. Cool. Stir gelatin mixture occasionally until partially set. This process can be hastened by placing kettle in a large dish pan of crushed ice. Have canned pears and peaches well drained cut into ¾ in. cubes, and chilled. Drain crushed pineapple and add to rest of fruit. Add fruit to gelatin mixture, and stir to evenly distribute the fruit. Pour into 6 long pans (12-in. by 20-in., 1 gal. in each pan). Chill until well congealed. Cut 40 orders to the pan.

NOTE:
Canned fruit cocktail can be substituted for the more expensive canned fruits, or to save time in cutting up the larger fruits. Drain juice from cocktail, and use in place of some of the other fruit juice.

LOBSTER SALAD
YIELD: 2 portions
INGREDIENTS:

Lobster, fresh, boiled	2 lbs. (A.P.)
Lettuce, medium-sized head	½ head
Mayonnaise	½ cup
Capers	1 tbsp.
Eggs, hard-boiled, cut in half	4 halves
Lemon, cut in sixths	1 (only)

METHOD:
Remove meat from a 2-lb. boiled and chilled lobster, being careful to keep meat in as large pieces as possible. Line an attractive serving bowl with lettuce leaves, and build up center with seasoned, tossed salad greens. Add lobster meat, having it come well above the rim of the bowl. Top with mayonnaise dotted with capers or serve dressing on the side. For dramatic serving, serve bowl of salad on platter with border of lettuce leaves, garnished with lemon wedges, scalloped egg halves, parsley or watercress. Garnish with the head, tail, and claws of the lobster shell.

KIDNEY BEAN SALAD
(Schensul's Cafeteria, Kalamazoo, Mich.)
YIELD: 40 5-oz. portions
INGREDIENTS:

Large Kidney Beans, No. 10 can	2 cans
Fresh Ground Pepper	1 tsp.
Onion, grated	½ cup
Celery, cut in rings	3 qts.
Pimientoes, chopped	1 cup
Sweet Pickles, sliced	2 cups
American Cheese, cut in ¾ in. by ½ in. cubes	¾ lb.
Mayonnaise	2 cups
Salt	2 tbsp.

METHOD:
Drain and rinse kidney beans in cold water. Drain again thoroughly. Grind pepper; grate onion; cut celery in fine rings. Slowly and carefully mix together all ingredients except the cheese. Serve on nest of salad greens. Top each salad with cubes of cheese.

POTATO SALAD
(Chicago Bar Association)
YIELD: 60 4½-oz. portions
INGREDIENTS:

Potatoes, cooked, diced ½ in. cubes	15 lb., A.P.
Onions, grated	1/3 cup (6 tbsp. approx.)
Pimiento, chopped	3 tbsp.
Parsley, chopped	4½ tbsp.
Mixed Pickles, chopped	¾ cup
Sugar	1½ tbsp.
Vinegar	3 tbsp.
Mayonnaise	3 qt.
Salt	½ cup
Eggs, hard cooked, diced	9 (only)

METHOD:
Cook potatoes, cool and dice. Combine all ingredients. Mix lightly. Let stand to season one hour before serving.

WINTER SALAD
(New York State College of Home Economics, Cornell University, N.Y.)
YIELD: 35 No. 12 scoop portions
INGREDIENTS:

Parsnips, shredded	3 qt.
Celery, diced	1½ qt.
Onions, sliced thin	1 qt.
Stuffed Olives, sliced	1 cup
French Dressing	½ cup
Mayonnaise	To moisten

METHOD:
Marinate vegetables with mayonnaise, and let stand 10 minutes. Add olives and french dressing just before serving. Garnish.

COOKED VEGETABLE SALAD BOWL
YIELD: 25 1-cup portions
INGREDIENTS:

Cooked Mixed Vegetables—carrots, peas, limas, green beans—equal parts of each	1 gal.
Celery	2 qt.
Worcestershire Sauce	1 tbsp.
Salt	2 tbsp.
Pepper	1 tsp.
Grated Onion	¼ cup
Mayonnaise	1½ cups
Roquefort or Blue Cheese, crumbled	2 lb.
Tomatoes, medium size, cut in eigths	10 (only)

METHOD:
Line chilled salad bowl with lettuce leaves. Add 1 cup tossed mixed greens which have been mixed with garlic french dressing. Add 1 cup mixed vegetables which have been combined with mayonnaise and seasonings. Sprinkle 3 tbsp. crumbled roquefort or blue cheese over top of salad. Garnish with tomato wedges—3 to a salad.
NOTE:
The cooked vegetables may be varied. Cut asparagus may be substituted for green peas and beans; kidney beans for limas, etc.

CRANBERRY GELATIN SALAD
(N.Y. State College of Home Economics, Cornell University, N.Y.)
YIELD: 2 Medium Size Pans
INGREDIENTS:

Gelatin	4 oz.
Cold Water	3 qt.
Cranberries	4 lb.
Celery Rings	1 qt.
Sugar, granulated	4 lb.
Nuts, chopped	1½ cups (6 oz.)
Oranges, sectioned	4 (only)

METHOD:
Soften gelatin by sprinkling it over a little cold water—about 1½ cups. Cook cranberries with remaining water until they break open; add sugar and cook 2 minutes longer. Remove from fire; add softened gelatin, and stir until dissolved. Place mixture in pans to chill. When partially set, add other ingredients.
VARIATIONS:
Add one tart apple and ½ cup crushed pineapple per pan. Set in individual ring molds.

WILTED LETTUCE SALAD

YIELD: 50 2-oz. portions
INGREDIENTS:

Lettuce, outside leaves	7 lbs.
Hot Sweet-Sour Sauce (See recipe, p. 98)	1 qt.

METHOD:
Wash leaves and cut or tear in strips about 1 in. in width. Pour hot sweet-sour sauce over the lettuce. Serve immediately.

Note: This is an excellent way to use the coarse outside leaves of lettuce.

MOLDED APPLE, DATE AND NUT SALAD

YIELD: 1 long counter pan (cut 7 x 4), 28 servings
INGREDIENTS:

Strawberry Gelatin	¾ pkg. (18 oz.)
Boiling Water	1½ qts.
Cold Water	1½ qts.
Delicious Apples, peeled, diced in ½-in. cubes	2½ qts.
Dates, cut in quarters	1 cup
Walnuts, chopped coarsely	1 cup

METHOD:
Dissolve gelatin in boiling water, and add cold water. Pour into large counter pan. Let partially set. Add apples and dates. Sprinkle nuts on top of mixture. Let set. Cut into 28 portions. Serve on head lettuce leaf on 6 inch plate. Garnish with one tsp. whipped cream in rosette at corner of salad.

CHICKEN AND FRESH VEGETABLE SALAD

YIELD: 16 ¾-cup portions or 18 2/3-cup portions
INGREDIENTS:

Chicken or Turkey, diced 1/2-5/8 in. pieces	2 lb.
Celery, raw, diced 1/4-3/8 in. pieces	4 oz.
Carrots, raw, cut 1/8 in. thick, and ½ in. long julienne strips	3 oz.
Green Beans, julienne strips, ¾ in. long, cooked	2 cups
Peas, cooked	2 cups
Salt	1-1/3 tbsp.
Combination Dressing	3 cups

METHOD:
Cook slivered green beans and green peas in boiling salted water until barely tender—beans, 5-6 minutes; peas, 2-3 minutes. Drain and plunge directly into ice water to cool thoroughly. Drain well.

Add well drained raw celery, carrots, green beans and peas to the diced chicken. Add salt and combination dressing. Mix lightly to combine. Chill thoroughly before service. Serve individual salads in large crisp lettuce cup. Top salad with 1 tbsp. of salad dressing, and several sliced stuffed olives.

Breadstuff

CRANBERRY LOAF

YIELD: 10 1-lb. loaves
INGREDIENTS:

Flour, all-purpose, sifted	10 cups
Salt	2½ tsp.
Baking Powder	3 tbsp. plus 1 tsp.
Soda	2½ tsp.
Sugar	5 cups
Frozen Cranberries, defrosted	7½ cups
Nuts, chopped	2½ cups
Eggs, beaten	5
Butter, melted	5 tsp.
Water, hot	3½ tbsp.
Orange Juice	2½ cups
Orange Rind, grated	From 5 oranges

METHOD:
Sift together the first 4 ingredients. Add sugar, cut cranberries and chopped nuts. To the beaten eggs, add the melted butter, hot water, orange juice and rind. Add all at once the egg mixture to the dry ingredients. Stir only until ingredients are blended but do not attempt to make a smooth batter. Place in well-greased loaf pans. Bake in a 325°F. oven 1 hour.

PRUNE CORN BREAD

Johnstown Inn, Johnstown N.Y.
YIELD: 1 loaf
INGREDIENTS:

Flour, sifted	1 cup
Baking Powder	4 tsp.
Salt	½ tsp.
Sugar, granulated, fine	3 tbsp.
Yellow Cornmeal	1 cup
Egg	1
Shortening, melted	2 tbsp.
Milk	1 cup
Prunes, cooked, pitted, and chopped	¾ cup

METHOD:
Sift together the flour, baking powder, salt and sugar. Add yellow cornmeal. Combine egg and milk and add to flour mixture. Stir in melted shortening. Blend well. Add chopped cooked prunes, and mix well. Pour into greased loaf tin. Bake in a 375°F. oven approximately 30 min. or until loaf in cooked.

PASTRY BISCUITS

INGREDIENTS:

Flour	1 cup
Shortening	½ cup
Salt	1 tsp.
Ice Water	1 tbsp.

METHOD:
Cut shortening into flour and salt. Work mixture until it forms fine crumbs. Add water and form into dough. Roll out ¼ in. thick and cut into 2-in. diamond shapes. Prick tops with a fork. Bake on cookie sheet 15 minutes at 350°F.

Cakes

HOT MILK SPONGE CAKE

"An extremely versatile cake that goes deliciously well with fruit for shortcake, or frosted for layer cakes."

YIELD: 2 sheet cakes, 12½- by 18- by 2-in. making 64 portions or 10 layers, 10-in. diameter for 5 layer cakes making 60 portions.

INGREDIENTS:

Milk	1 qt.
Butter	8 oz.
Sugar	8 cups
Eggs, whole	16 (only)
Salt	2 tsp.
Vanilla	2 tsp.
Cake Flour, sifted	8 cups
Baking Powder, double-acting	4 tbsp.

METHOD:
Scald milk, and melt butter in hot milk. On high speed of mixer, beat the eggs. At low speed, add sugar, salt and vanilla. Sift baking powder with the flour and add to egg mixture.

Add hot milk with butter. Beat only until milk is blended into mixture. Avoid overbeating.

Pour into well greased and floured baking pans. Bake in moderate oven (350°F.) 25 to 30 minutes.

ANGEL FOOD CAKE DE LUXE

YIELD: 4 cakes 10- by 4-in. diameter making 56 portions.

INGREDIENTS:

Flour, cake, sifted	1 qt.
Confectioners Sugar, sifted	1½ qt.
Egg Whites	1½ qt.
Cream of Tartar	2 tbsp.
Salt	1-1/3 tbsp.
Vanilla Extract	1 tbsp.
Almond Extract	2 tsp.
Granulated Sugar, sifted	1 qt.

METHOD:
Sift flour and confectioners sugar together 3 times. Set aside. In the bowl of the power mixer, place egg whites, cream of tartar, salt, vanilla and almond extract. Beat with wire whip on very low speed until mixture is foamy. Add granulated sugar, 2 tbsp. at a time, and continue beating until meringue holds fairly stiff peaks. Gradually sift the flour-sugar mixture over the meringue, and gently fold it into the meringue. Do not overmix. Immediately scale approximately 2 lb. of batter into each ungreased tube pan, 10 in. diameter. Gently cut through batter with knife. Bake in a 350°F. oven 35 to 45 minutes, or until cake springs back when pressed with the finger. Invert pan until cake is cold.

HARVEST MOON LIGHT FRUIT CAKE
(Holland's of Rochester, Rochester, Minn.)

YIELD: 104 lb.
INGREDIENTS:

Butter	3 lb.
Vegetable Shortening	2 lb.
Sugar, granulated	9 lb.
Salt	3 oz.
Rum or Brandy Flavoring	4 oz.
Whole Eggs	7 lb.
Honey (or Invert Sugar)	3 lb.
Water	4 lb.
Flour, all-purpose	10 lb.
Walnuts	6 lb.
Pecans	4 lb.
Candied Peel and Fruit Mix	30 lb.
Dates, pitted, cut in halves	6 lb.
Maraschino Cherries, whole or broken	12 lb.
Candied Pineapple, diced	8 lb.

METHOD:
Cream together the first five ingredients. Add unbeaten eggs, and mix until mixture is light. Add honey and water; mix well. Mix fruit and nuts with a little of the flour and blend well together. Gradually add flour to shortening-egg mixture, and mix until smooth. Add fruits and nuts mixing only until evenly distributed throughout mixture.

Scale into greased and paper-lined 1 or 2 lb. loaf tins.

Bake in 275°F. oven for 2 to 3 hours or until done. Have pan of water in oven when baking cake to supply moisture.

ROSY SPICE LAYER CAKE WITH CREAM CHEESE ICING

(The Anna Maude Cafeteria, Oklahoma City, Okla.)
YIELD: 17 lb., 2 oz. batter; 8 2-layer cakes.
Size pan 9¼ in. by 1½ in.

INGREDIENTS:

Butter	2 cups
Vegetable Shortening	2 cups
Whole Eggs	16 (only)
Sugar	10-2/3 cups
Cake Flour, sifted	16 cups
Baking Powder, double-acting	5-1/3 tbsp.
Allspice	2-2/3 tbsp.
Cinnamon	2-2/3 tbsp.
Soda	2 tsp.
Pecans, chopped	8 cups
Raisins, cut up	8 cups
Tomato Soup, canned	2 qt.

METHOD:
Cream shortening on second speed of mixer. Add sugar gradually, mixing constantly.

Add unbeaten eggs, one at a time. Beat 1 minute after each addition.

Sift together the flour, baking powder, spices and soda. Stir nuts and raisins into the flour.

Add flour mixture alternately with the tomato soup to the shortening mixture. Mix only until smooth. Avoid overmixing.

Scale 1 lb., 2 oz. into each greased layer tin lined with waxed paper.

Bake in moderate oven (350°F.) 25-30 min.

When cool, put layers together with Cream Cheese Icing, and frost the top of cakes.

Cream Cheese Icing:

Cream Cheese	1 lb. 8 oz.
Milk	1 cup
Vanilla	1-1/3 tbsp.
Powdered Sugar, sifted	16 cups
Salt	Few grains

METHOD:
Blend cream cheese, milk, vanilla and salt until soft and smooth. Add sugar gradually, beating well.

Spread between layers of Rosy Spice Cake, and on top of each cake.

BAKED CHERRY PECAN TORTE WITH CHERRY SAUCE

YIELD: 24 portions

INGREDIENTS:

Cherries, fresh or frozen, pitted	1 qt. (4 cups)
Pastry Flour, sifted	2 cups
Sugar	2½ cups
Eggs, whole	2 (only)
Butter, melted	2 tbsp.
Salt	½ tsp.
Baking Soda	1 tsp.
Cinnamon	2 tsp.
Almond Extract	2 tsp.
Pecans, chopped	1 cup

METHOD:
Beat eggs, and gradually add sugar. Blend until sugar is dissolved. Sift together the flour, salt, soda, cinnamon, and add to egg mixture. Beat until well blended. Add melted butter and flavoring.

Fold in the cherries.

Turn mixture into well greased and floured baking pan, sprinkle chopped nuts over top. Bake in 350°F. oven 45 minutes.

Cherry Sauce:

Cherry juice	1 pt. (2 cups)
Water	
Sugar	To sweeten
Cornstarch	2 tbsp.
Salt	¼ tsp.
Almond Extract	4 drops
Butter	2 tbsp.
Whipping Cream	½ cup

METHOD:
Combine sugar, cornstarch and salt; mix with small amount of cold liquid. Add to remaining liquid which has been heated, stirring all the time.

Cook until mixture thickens and all trace of raw starch disappears.

Taste for sweetness and add sugar as needed. Add butter. Remove from heat. Add flavoring. Whip cream.

Serve Torte warm or cold, topped with whipped cream with Cherry Sauce over all.

NOTE:
A few drops of red vegetable coloring may be added to the sauce to enhance its red color.

Puddings

PERSIMMON PUDDING

L. S. Ayres & Co., Indianapolis
YIELD: 1 pan, 14- by 9½- by 2½-in., cut 6 by 4 making 48 pieces for 24 portions.

INGREDIENTS:

Eggs	8
Graham Cracker Crumbs	3¾ cups
Baking Powder	2½ tsp.
Sugar	2½ cups
Milk, whole	2½ cups
Persimmon Pulp	3 cups
Butter, melted	5 oz.
Salt	¼ tsp.

METHOD:
Beat eggs until very light. Roll graham cracker crumbs fine. Add baking powder and sugar to the crumbs. Add dry ingredients alternately with the milk to the persimmon pulp. Add beaten eggs, melted butter and salt. Pour into lightly greased baking pan. Bake in a 350°F. oven 1 hour. Serve with Hard Sauce.

Country/Colonial

APPLE CRISP WITH BLACK WALNUTS AND COCONUT
YIELD: 29 lb. 8 oz., 200 2½-oz. portions
Size of Pan: 12 by 18 in. (6 pans)
INGREDIENTS:

Eggs, whole	6 lb.
Sugar, granulated	11 lb. 4 oz.
Flour, all-purpose, sifted	4 lb.
Baking Powder	8 oz.
Salt	2 tbsp.
Apples, shredded	8 lb.
Black Walnuts, chopped	2 lb. 8 oz.
Coconut	1 lb. 12 oz.
Vanilla Extract	7 oz.

METHOD:
Beat eggs until light and lemon-colored. Gradually add sugar and beat until dissolved. Sift flour, salt and baking powder, and gradually add to egg mixture.

Blend thoroughly. Add apples, nuts and vanilla. Scale approximately 4½ lb. into each greased and floured bake pan.

Top with shredded coconut. Bake in a 350° oven 45 to 60 minutes. Serve warm or cold, topped with a mound of ice cream or with whipped cream.

STEAMED CHOCOLATE PUDDING
YIELD: 38 portions
INGREDIENTS:

Flour, all-purpose sifted	2 cups
Milk	3¼ qt.
Butter or Margarine	1 cup
Sugar	4½ cups
Crumbs, bread	2 gal.
Eggs	8 (only) medium
Cocoa	2 cups
Vanilla	2 tbsp.
Baking Powder	4 tbsp.
Salt	¼ tsp.

METHOD:
Cream butter and sugar. Add beaten eggs.

Combine bread crumbs and cocoa, and add to the first mixture. Sift baking powder and salt with the flour, and add alternately with the milk. Add vanilla.

Steam in greased, covered containers 1 hour. Serve with Foamy, Hard, Custard, Chocolate, or Marshmallow Sauce.

BAKING POWDER SHORTCAKE BISCUITS
YIELD: 100 biscuits or 7½ lb. dough
INGREDIENTS:

Flour, pastry, unsifted	3 qt.
Sugar, granulated	1¾ cups
Salt	1½ tbsp.
Baking Powder	½ cup
Shortening	1¾ cups
Eggs	¾ cup
Milk	3 cups

METHOD:
Sift together the flour, sugar, salt and baking powder. Add shortening and blend well. Beat eggs and combine with some of the milk, and add to flour mixture. Use additional milk to make as soft a dough as can be handled. Turn on to a lightly floured board, and knead lightly. Roll dough ½ in. thick. Cut biscuits with doughnut cutter. Place on top of fruit mixture in pans. Bake in a 425°F. oven approximately 25 minutes.

OLD-FASHIONED BAKED RICE PUDDING
YIELD: 25 portions
INGREDIENTS:

Rice, uncooked, regular	2¾ cups
Milk, scalded	7½ qt.
Raisins, seedless	15 oz.
Salt	2/3 tsp.
Sugar	15 oz.
Butter	2 tbsp.
Cinnamon Bark	2 pieces, 1 in. long

METHOD:
Wash rice and add to scalded milk.

Bake in slow oven at 300°F. As brown skin forms, fold under and lift rice from bottom of pan gently. Do this several times during the cooking process.

When rice is almost tender, add sugar, raisins, salt and cinnamon. Continue baking until rice is thoroughly cooked.

Approximate cooking time is 1½ to 2½ hours.
NOTE:
It is essential to keep this pudding at a low temperature to prevent scorching.

APPLE BROWN BETTY

YIELD: 25 4-oz. portions
INGREDIENTS:

Apples, frozen	1 gal.
Water, warm	½ cup
Nutmeg	1 tbsp.
Salt	½ tsp.
Sugar	3 cups
Butter, melted	¼ cup

Topping:

Bread Crumbs	3 cups
Cinnamon	2 tsp.
Salt	½ tsp.
Butter, melted	½ cup

METHOD:
Combine the first 6 ingredients. Place mixture in greased baking pans. Combine all ingredients for topping and spread over top of apples.

Bake in 350°F. oven 45 to 60 minutes. Serve with whipped cream.

BAKED INDIAN PUDDING
Colonial Inn

YIELD: 8 portions
INGREDIENTS:

Milk	1 qt.
Yellow Coarse Corn Meal	¼ cup
Molasses	½ cup
Egg	1
Butter or Margarine	2 oz.
Sugar	½ cup
Cinnamon	1 tsp.

METHOD:
Combine milk, corn meal and molasses and boil for about 15 minutes. Beat egg, together with butter, sugar and cinnamon. Mix all ingredients together and pour into a baking pan. Bake in 350°F. oven for 1½ hours. Stir every 20 min. Top each serving with vanilla ice cream.

BAKED PRUNE WHIP

YIELD: 56 portions
INGREDIENTS:

Prunes, cooked, pitted, chopped	2 qt.
Sugar	2 lb.
Egg Whites	3 cups
Lemon Juice	6 tbsp.
Salt	2 tsp.

METHOD:
Put all ingredients in mixing bowl, and beat until stiff enough to form peaks, but not dry.

Spread mixture into 2 ungreased pans, 12½ in. by 20½ in., and place in pans containing ½ in. hot water.

Bake at 325°F., 60 to 70 minutes, or until inserted knife comes out clean.

Remove pudding from hot water. Allow to cool and to set before cutting into squares 3 in. by 3 in.

Serve with Custard Sauce.

CLEAR RASPBERRY TAPICOCA
The Indian Trail, Winnetka, Ill.

YIELD: 20 to 22 4-oz. portions
INGREDIENTS:

Raspberry Juice, strained	2½ qt.
Quick Tapioca	1 cup
Sugar	To sweeten
Salt	¼ tsp.
Lemon Juice, fresh	2 tsp.
Whipped Cream	

METHOD:
Combine raspberry juice and tapioca and cook a few minutes. Add sugar—the amount will depend on the sweetness of the raspberry juice. Add salt and lemon juice.

Serve 4 oz. in sherbet glasses alternating the Raspberry Tapioca with whipped cream.

BREAD PUDDING

YIELD: 1½ gal. making 48 ½-cup servings
INGREDIENTS:

Bread, day old	1½ gal.
Eggs, whole	16 (only)
Sugar, granulated	1 qt.
Salt	2 tsp.
Butter or Margarine	1½ cups
Milk	1½ gal.
Nutmeg, ground	1 tsp
Lemon Rind, grated	2 tbsp.
Raisins	2½ cups

METHOD:
Cut day-old bread into ½ in. cubes. Place in greased baking pan. Beat eggs slightly, and add salt and sugar.

Heat butter or margarine in milk until melted. Add to egg mixture gradually, stirring constantly.

Add nutmeg, grated lemon rind, raisins. Blend. Pour over bread. Bake in pan of hot water in 350°F. oven for about 1 hour.

Stir twice during first half hour of baking. Pudding is done when a knife inserted in center comes out clean. Serve warm or cold with whipped cream or Lemon Sauce.

Bread Pudding Variations:
1. Vanilla Bread Pudding: Omit nutmeg, grated lemon rind, and raisins from recipe. Add 2 tbsp. vanilla.
2. Chocolate Bread Pudding: Omit nutmeg, grated lemon rind and raisins from recipe. Add 12 oz. unsweetened chocolate. Melt chocolate in milk before adding milk to egg mixture.
3. Jelly Bread Pudding: Use Vanilla Bread Pudding recipe. Dot with jelly before baking.
4. Meringue Bread Pudding: Use Vanilla Bread Pudding recipe. Spread meringue on top of baked Bread Pudding. Bake until meringue is a golden brown.
5. Honey Bread Pudding: Substitute 2-2/3 cups honey for sugar in Vanilla variation. Stir honey into eggs.

Country/Colonial

Pies

LEMON CHIFFON PIE
(Forum Cafeterias of America Inc.
Kansas City, Mo.)

"Our Lemon Chiffon Pie is one of the most popular and profitable items we serve. It has been a great favorite with our customers for many years."

YIELD: 16 9-in. pies
INGREDIENTS:

Hot Water	3½ qt.
Sugar, granulated	2½ lb.
Salt	1½ oz.
Yellow Vegetable Coloring	1 tsp.
Cornstarch	1 lb.
Warm Water	1 pt.
Lemon Juice	24 oz.
Eggs, whole	12 (only)
Lemon Rind	2 oz.
Butter	4 oz.
Hot Water	1 pt.
Sugar	2¾ lb.
Cream of Tartar	2 tsp.
Egg Whites	2 lb.
Pie Shells, baked	16

METHOD:
Bring 3½ qt. hot water, 2½ lb. sugar, salt and yellow vegetable coloring to boiling point.

Dissolve cornstarch in 1 pt. warm water, and add to first mixture, stirring rapidly with wire whip. Boil until clear, stirring frequently. Remove from heat. Mix lemon juice, beaten whole eggs and lemon rind together, and add gradually to cornstarch mixture, stirring rapidly. Add butter, let mixture cool to 120°F. Bring to a boil the 1 pt. hot water, 2¾ lb. sugar and cream of tartar. Add hot syrup to egg whites which have been beaten stiff but not dry. Continue to whip on third speed of mixer about 5 minutes or until cool. Fold egg whites into lemon filling. Dip evenly into 16 baked pie shells. Place pies in 500°F. oven until golden.

MINCE-CREAMY-PECAN PIE
YIELD: One 9-in. pie.
INGREDIENTS:

Pie Crust Mix	1 stick
Mincemeat	28-oz. jar
Brown Sugar (packed)	3 tbsp.
Flour	2 tbsp.
Whipping Cream	1 cup
Pecan Halves	½ cup

METHOD:
Heat oven to 425°F. (hot). Prepare pastry for 9-in. one-crust pie. Build up high fluted edge. Spread mincemeat into prepared pie pan. Combine brown sugar and flour; add cream. Pour over mincemeat. Arrange pecans on top of pie. Bake 40 to 45 min. Cool slightly before serving.

OPEN FACE PEACH PIE
YIELD: 30 10-in. pies
INGREDIENTS:

Peaches, fresh, medium size	48 lb.
Sugar	3 lb.
Cornstarch	4 oz.
Cinnamon, ground	1 tsp.
Salt	½ tsp.
Butter (72 pats to 1 lb.)	30 pats
Pie Shells, unbaked	30

METHOD:
Wash peaches; halve and pit; do not peel. Place peaches, cut side up, in unbaked pie shells, allowing approximately 1 lb. 10 oz. for each pie.

Combine sugar, cornstarch, salt and cinnamon, and sprinkle 1 to 2 oz. over each pie. Place 1 pat butter in center of the pie.

Bake in 400°F. oven 45 minutes to 1 hour.

SOUTHERN APPLE PIE WITH RUM SAUCE
YIELD: 6 10-in. pies
INGREDIENTS:

Pastry for 6 double crusts	
Canned Apple Slices	2 No. 10 cans
Sugar	3 lb.
Margarine or Butter	6 tbsp.
Salt	¼ tsp.
Nutmeg	
Ground Cinnamon	

METHOD:
Line pans with pastry. Mix apples and sugar thoroughly. Fill pastry lined pans. Dot with margarine or butter; sprinkle with a few grains of salt. Sprinkle on spices as desired. Add top crust and seal. Crimp and glaze, if desired.
NOTE:
A solid top crust is best for this type of pie.

HONEY RUM SAUCE
INGREDIENTS:

Light Brown Sugar	2 lb.
Honey, strained	1 pt.
Salt	Few grains
Hot Water	1 cup
Margarine or Butter	2 cups
Rum	1 cup

METHOD:
Combine brown sugar, honey, salt and water in saucepan. Mix well. Add margarine or butter. Place over heat and bring slowly to a hard rolling boil. Remove from heat and cool. Add rum and mix well. Store tightly covered at room temperature.
TO SERVE:
Place a serving of pie on a flameproof plate. Using a 2-oz. ladle, pour sauce over pie. Run

under broiler until sauce bubbles. Serve at once while sauce is bubbly hot.
NOTE:
This is a wonderful way to use leftover apple pie. Day old pie is even better for this hot sauce than fresh pie.

SHOO-FLY PIE
YIELD: 20 servings
INGREDIENTS:
Crumb Portion:

Flour (sifted, all-purpose)	3 cups
Sugar (granulated, cane or beet)	1½ cups
Butter	2/3 cup
Salt	2 tsp.
Nutmeg	1 tsp.
Cloves	1 tsp.
Cinnamon	2 tsp.

Liquid Portion:

Molasses	2 cups
Corn Syrup	2 cups
Cornstarch	1 tbsp.
Milk, evaporated	2 cups
Eggs	4

METHOD:
Measure or scale crumb portion into mixer and mix to crumb consistency.
 Measure or scale all of liquid portion into container and stir well.
 Measure or scale liquid portion into 9-in. by 1½-in. unbaked pie shells.
 Place crumb portion on top of liquid which has been scaled into pie shells.
 Place in oven and bake at 425°F.

DOWN-MAINE BLUEBERRY PIE
(Toll House, Whitman, Mass.)*
YIELD: 1 9-in. pie
INGREDIENTS:

Blueberries, fresh	1 qt.
Sugar	1 cup
Water	¾ cup
Flour	2 tbsp.
Salt	¼ tsp.
Water	¼ cup
Pie Shell, baked	1

METHOD:
Pick over and wash blueberries.
 Reserve 3 cups and cook remaining blueberries with 1 cup sugar and ¾ cups water until soft.
 Make a paste of the flour, salt and ¼ cup water. Add to cooked blueberries and cook slowly until thickened.
 Add hot mixture to uncooked blueberries. Turn into baked pastry shell. Chill 3 hours. Serve topped with whipped cream or ice cream.
*Toll House Cook Book. Revised edition, 1953, published by Little Brown & Co.

SOUR CREAM-RAISIN PIE
YIELD: 4 8-in. pies
INGREDIENTS:

Sour Cream (18-20%)	2 qt.
Raisins, seeded	2 cups
Brown Sugar, packed	6 cups
Salt	1 tsp.
Eggs, whole, large	8 (only)
Cornstarch	½ cup
Lemon Juice	4 tbsp.
Nutmeg, ground	1 tsp.
Cinnamon, ground	1 tsp.
Cloves, ground	¼ tsp.
Pie Shells, unbaked	4 (only)

METHOD:
Mix cornstarch to paste with lemon juice and a little sour cream. Add beaten eggs, remainder of sour cream, brown sugar mixed with the spices, raisins and salt. Blend well. Fill pie shells.
 Bake at 450°F. 10 minutes, then at 350°F. until filling is firm and pastry is cooked.

Cookies

EARLY AMERICAN GINGER CUTOUTS
YIELD: 30 cookies
INGREDIENTS:

Sifted Flour	2¾ cups
Baking Soda	½ tsp.
Ginger	1 tsp.
Cinnamon	½ tsp.
Cloves	½ tsp.
Salt	½ tsp.
Butter	½ cup
Dark Brown Sugar, firmly packed	¼ cup
Dark Molasses	¾ cup
Egg, beaten	1
Hot Water	1 tsp.
Vinegar	1 tsp.

METHOD:
Preheat oven to 350°F.
 Sift dry ingredients together. Cream butter and sugar. Add molasses and egg, beating until smooth. Mix in sifted dry ingredients; then add water and vinegar and blend well. Chill dough two hours or overnight. Roll out on lightly floured board to ¼ in. thickness and cut with gingerbread man and animal cooky cutters. Place on cookie sheet and bake about 15 minutes. When cooled, decorate with various butter frostings.

Country/Colonial

DATE-FILLED OATMEAL COOKIES
YIELD: 6 lb. dough or 7 doz. cookies
INGREDIENTS:

Margarine	1 lb. 8 oz.
Salt	2 tsp.
Sugar, brown	1 lb. 4 oz.
Water, warm	1½ cups
Soda	½ tsp.
Oats, rolled, quick	1 lb. 4 oz.
Flour, cake, sifted	1 lb. 8 oz.
Baking Powder (Tartrate)	1½ tsp.
Date Filling	5 lb. 8 oz.

METHOD:
Cream margarine with salt on No. 2 speed of mixer until fluffy, 3-4 minutes. Add sugar gradually turning to No. 1 speed. When all sugar is added, beat for 3-4 minutes on No. 2 speed.

Dissolve soda in warm water, and add to shortening and the sugar mixture. Add rolled oats immediately, combining well.

Sift together flour and baking powder, and fold into the mixture on No. 1 speed. Blend well. Remove from mixer.

Place dough in refrigerator to chill.

Roll into sheets 3/8 to ¼ inch thick, using as little flour as possible. Cut into rounds with a 2½ inch cutter. Place rounds of dough on greased baking sheet.

Dip 1 oz. date filling onto center of each round of dough. Place another round of dough over filling, press edges to bottom firmly.

Bake in a 375°F. oven 10 to 12 minutes.

DATE FILLING FOR COOKIES OR CAKE
YIELD: 3 lb. 8 oz. Filling for 4½ doz. cookies or filling for 7 8½-in. cakes.
INGREDIENTS:

Dates, pitted, diced, chopped	2 lb.
Sugar, granulated	12 oz.
Salt (variable)	1 tsp.
Water, cold	2¼ cups
Lemon Rind, grated	1 tsp.
Orange Rind, grated	1 tsp.
Orange Juice	¼ cup
Lemon Juice	1 tbsp.

METHOD:
Combine dates, sugar, salt, cold water and grated rind. Bring to slow boil stirring constantly. Continue cooking over low heat until mixture is thick, and of right consistency to spread, stirring occasionally to prevent sticking. Remove from heat. Add juices, beating well to combine. Use 1 oz. for filling in Date-Filled Oatmeal Cookies.
NOTE:
Spread 8 oz. mixture on an 8½ in. layer cake, when using as cake filling.

CARROT COOKIES WITH ORANGE ICING
YIELD: 5 doz. (approximately)
INGREDIENTS:

Butter	1 cup
Sugar	¾ cup
Whole Eggs	2 (only)
Carrots, cooked, mashed	1 cup
Flour, all-purpose, sifted	2 cups
Baking Powder, double-acting	1 tsp.
Vanilla	1 tsp.
Salt	¼ tsp.

METHOD:
Cream butter and sugar. Add one unbeaten egg at a time, and beat between each addition. Add mashed carrots. Sift flour, baking powder, and salt, and add to shortening mixture. Mix well; add vanilla. Drop on greased baking sheet, and bake at 375°F. for 10-12 minutes. When cool, ice with Orange Icing.

ORANGE ICING
INGREDIENTS:

Powdered Sugar	1 lb.
Orange Juice	½ cup
Orange Rind	1

METHOD:
Sift powdered sugar, add orange rind and orange juice. Mix until smooth and of proper consistency. Dip cookies in frosting, then place on rack to dry.

FUDGE SQUARES OR BARS
(Department of Institution Management, Kansas State College, Manhattan, Kan.)
YIELD: 180 servings
INGREDIENTS:

Eggs, whole	36 (only)
Sugar, granulated	6 lb.
Butter, melted	3 cups
Shortening, melted	3 cups
Chocolate, melted	24 squares
Vanilla	1 tbsp.
Cake Flour, sifted	2 lb. 4 oz.
Baking Powder	2 tbsp.
Pecans, chopped	2 lb.
Salt	1½ tsp.

METHOD:
Beat eggs; add sugar gradually and continue beating until sugar is dissolved. Add melted butter and shortening, melted chocolate and vanilla, and beat until thoroughly mixed. Sift together the flour, baking powder, and salt, and gradually add to first mixture. Add chopped pecans. Spread on 3 oiled baking sheets. Bake in moderate oven (350°F.) 25 to 30 minutes. When cool frost with Chocolate Butter Frosting. Cut in squares or bars.

SWEET-SOUR DRESSING
YIELD: 3 gallons
INGREDIENTS:

Water	1 gal.
Vinegar	2½ gal.
Sugar, granulated	1 gal.
Bacon Fat	1 qt.
Flour	4½ cups
Diced Bacon	4½ lb.
Pepper	½ tsp.
Salt	2 tsp.

METHOD:
Cook bacon until crisp. Remove bacon slices from pan. Make paste by adding flour to hot bacon fat. Heat water, vinegar, sugar and seasonings. Add to flour and fat mixture. Cook until mixture thickens. Add finely chopped crisp bacon.

BIBLIOGRAPHY

OLE—Mexican, Spanish, Latin, South American

Spanish
Beene, Gerrie and King, Lourdes. Dining in Spain: A Guide to Spanish Cooking with Recipes from Its Most Distinguished Restaurants. Rutland, Vt.: Charles E. Tuttle Co., 1969.
De Aznar, M. P. and Froud, Nina. Home Book of Spanish Cookery, 2nd ed. Levittown, N. Y.: Transatlantic Arts, Inc., 1969.
Garcia, Clarita. Clarita's Cocina: Great Traditional Recipes from a Spanish Kitchen. New York: Doubleday, 1970.
Hatheway, Maruja. Authentic Spanish Cooking. New York: Paperback Library, 1969.
Hilgarth, Mary. Spanish Cookery. New York: Drake Publishers, 1971.
Norman, Barbara. Spanish Cookbook. New York: Atheneum, 1966.
Waldo, Myra. Flavor of Spain. New York: Macmillan, 1965.
Wason, Betty. Art of Spanish Cooking. New York: Doubleday, 1963.
Zelayeta, Elena. Elena's Famous Mexican and Spanish Recipes. New York: Prentice-Hall, Inc., 1961.

Mexican
Aaron, Van and Salom, Georgine S. Art of Mexican Cooking. New York: Doubleday, 1965.
Alvarez, Luisa M. and Mulvey, Ruth W. Good Food from Mexico. New York: Macmillan, 1962.
Booth, George C. Food and Drink of Mexico. Los Angeles, Calif.: Ritchie, Ward, Press, 1964.
Curry, Mary M. World of Mexican Cooking. Los Angeles, Calif.: Nash Publishing, 1971.
Ferguson, Erna. Mexican Cookbook. New York: Doubleday, 1967.
Ortiz, Elizabeth L. Complete Book of Mexican Cooking. Philadelphia, Pa.: M. Evans, 1967.
Stone, Idella P. Thirty Mexican Menus. Los Angeles, Calif.: Ritchie, Ward, Press, 1971.
Sunset Editors. Sunset Mexican Cook Book. Menlo Park, Calif.: Lane Magazine and Book Co., 1969.
Young, Alice E. and Stephenson, Patricia P. Discovering Mexican Cooking, rev. ed. San Antonio, Texas: Naylor, 1968.
Zelayeta, Elena. Elena's Secrets of Mexican Cooking. New York: Doubleday, 1968.

Latin American
De Brissiere, P. Caribbean Cookery. New York: Saphrograph.
Kaufman, William, ed. Recipes from the Caribbean and Latin America. New York: Dell, 1969.
Leonard, Jonathan N. Latin American Cooking. (Foods of the World Ser.) New York: Time-Life, 1968.
Valldejuli, Carmen A. Art of Caribbean Cookery. rev. ed. New York: Doubleday
Waldo, Myra. Flavor of Spain. New York: Macmillan, 1970.

South American
De Andrade, Margarette, Brazilian Cookery: Traditional and Modern. Rutland, Vt.: C. E. Tuttle, 1965.

Ole Decor
Byne, Arthur and Stopley, M. Spanish Interiors and Furniture. New York: Dover, 1970.
Enciso, Jorge. Design Motifs of Ancient Mexico. New York: Dover, 1947

NAUTICAL—Fish, Seafood

Alberson, Sarah. Blue Sea Cookbook. New York: Hastings House Publishers, Inc., 1968.
Beard, James. James Beard's Fish Cookery. Boston: Little, Brown & Co., 1954.
Better Homes and Gardens, ed. Fish and Seafood. Des Moines, Iowa: Better Homes and Gardens Press, 1971.
Brown, Helen E. Shrimp and Other Shellfish Recipes. Los Angeles, Calif.: Ritchie, Ward, Press, 1966.
Chekenian, Jane and Meyer, Monica. Shellfish Cookery. New York: Macmillan, 1971.

De Gouy, Louis P. Gold Cook Book. Fifteenth Anniversary Printing. Philadelphia, Pa.: Chilton Books, 1970.
Escoffier, A. Escoffier Cook Book, rev. ed. New York: Crown Publishers, Inc., 1953.
Frederick, J. George. Long Island Seafood Cook Book. New York: Corner, 1971.
Given, Meta. Meta Given's Modern Encyclopedia of Cooking. 2 vols. rev. ed. Wright, Mary L. ed. New York: Doubleday, 1955
Hawkins, Arthur. Complete Seafood Cookbook. Englewood Cliffs, N. J.: Prentice-Hall, Inc., 1970.
Kaufman, William J. Fish and Shellfish Cookbook. New York: Doubelday, 1968.
McMaster, Gary J. International Trout and Salmon Cookbook. Cranbury, N. J.: Barnes, A. S. and Co., Inc., 1970.
Miloradovich, Milo. Art of Fish Cookery, rev. ed. New York: Doubleday, 1970.
Morris, Dan and Morris, Inez. First and Last Word on Fish Cookery. New York: Bobbs, 1971.
Sarvis, Shirley and Calvello, Tony. Crab and Abalone: West Coast Ways with Fish and Shellfish. New York: Bobbs, 1968.
Simon, Andre L. Lobsters, Crabs, Etc. Hackensack, N. J.: Wehman Bros., 1957.
World's Fifty Best Fish Recipes. New York: Herder and Herder, 1970.
Worth, Helen. Shrimp Cookery. New York: Citadel Press, 1971.
Zachary, Hugh. Beachcombers Handbook of Seafood Cookery. Winston-Salem, N. C.: Blair, 1970.

COUNTRY/COLONIAL—Farm Style, Early American

Booth, Letha and Dutton, Joan P. Williamsburg Cookbook. New York: Holt, Rinehart & Winston, 1971.
Bowers, Lessie. Plantation Recipes. New York: Speller, Robert & Sons, 1959.
Brown, Dale. American Cooking: The Northwest (Foods of the World Ser.) New York: Time-Life, 1971.
Cannon, Poppy and Brooks, Patricia. President's Cookbook: Practical Recipes from George Washington to the Present. New York: Funk & Wagnalls, 1970.
Clark, Morton G. Wide, Wide World of Texas Cooking. New York: Funk & Wagnalls, 1970.
Cleveland, Bess A. Alaskan Cookbook. Berkeley, Calif.: Howell-North Books, 1960.
Coulter, Ellis M. ed. Confederate Receipt Book: A Compilation of Over One Hundred Receipts Adapted to the Times. Athens, Georgia: University of Georgia Press, 1960.
Dull, S. R. Southern Cooking. rev. ed. New York: Grosset & Dunlap, 1968.
Eastlake, Martha. Rattlesnake Under Glass: A Roundup of Authentic Western Recipes. New York: Simon and Schuster, 1965.
Hansen, Barbara J. Cooking California Style. New York: Macmillan, 1971.
Hearn, Lafcadio. Lafcadio Hearn's Creole Cook Book. Gretna, La.: Pelican, 1968.
Killeen, Jacqueline. One Hundred and One Secrets of California Chefs. San Francisco: 101 Productions, 1969.
Kimball, Jeffe and Anderson, Jean. Art of American Indian Cooking. New York: Doubleday, 1965.
Land, Mary. Louisiana Cookery. Baton Rouge, La.: Claitors, 1965.
Mendes, Helen. Soul Food Cooking: An African Legacy. New York: Macmillan, 1970.
Perl, Lila. Red-Flannel Hash and Shoo-Fly Pie: American Regional Foods and Festivals. New York: World Pub., 1965.
Roberson, John and Roberson, Marie. Famous American Recipes. New York: Macmillan, 1965.
Sarvis, Shirley and Calvello, Tony. Crab and Abalone: West Coast Ways with Fish and Shellfish: New York: Bobbs, 1968.
Stanforth, Deirde. New Orleans Restaurant Cookbook. New York: Doubleday, 1967.

Country/Colonial Decor

Chapman, Suzanne E. Early American Design Motifs. New York: Dover.
Ormsbee, Thomas. Field Guide to Early American Furniture. New York: Little, 1951.
Sabine, Ellen S. Early American Decorative Patterns. New York: Van Nostrand Reinhold, 1962.

INDEX TO RECIPES

OLE—Mexican, Spanish, Latin, South American

Albondigas (California Beef Ball Soup)	61
Alcachofas a la Espanola (Artichokes Spanish Style)	62
Arroz con Pollo	64
Avocado Half-Shells with Salsa Verde	75
Beef Steak Strips, Spicy	63
Beef Stew a la Bogotana (with cumin seed)	73
Beef Tacos	72
Budin de Chocolate (Mexican Chocolate Pudding)	78
Burritos	70
Camarones en Frio (Pickled Party Shrimp)	60
Cherries Dulce Borracha (Sweet Cherry Kabobs)	78
Chicken Cortez	71
Chiles Rellenos	71
Chili Beef, Monterey	64
Chili con Carne, Chicken	62
Chili con Carne (with beef and ham)	64
Chili con Queso, Trini's	62
Chili Pie	70
Chili Tomato Soup	61
Colombian Tossed Vegetable Salad (with cumin seed)	74
Crab, Alaska King a la Espanola	66
Crab, Alaska King Aperitivos a la Mexicana	60
Crab, Alaska King Spread	60
Crab, Alaska King Tostados con Jocoqui	70
Crab-Grapefruit Salad Espanol	74
Enchiladas	73
Enchilada Baked Pie	67
Enchiladas, Chicken	62
Enchilada con Pollo (Tortilla Chicken Casserole)	69
Enchiladas, Olive-Egg	63
Ensalada de Alaska King Crab con Salsa de Aguacate	75
Ensalada de Pera a la Vinagreta	74
Fiesta Salad	74
Flan, Spanish Caramel with Fruit	78
Frijoles Re-Fritos (Refried Beans)	70
Gazpacho on Half-Shell	61
Guacamole	60
Guacamole with Green Chili Peppers	60
Lentejas con Fruita	75
Lentil and White Bean Salad	75
Manzanas Fritas (Spanish Fried Apples)	78
Meat Loaf, Mexican	64
Mexicali Pie	69
Mexican Dogs	67
Mexican Fiesta	72
Paella	68
Pork and Eggs, Durango Spiced	66
Potatoes, Baked Stuffed Colombian Style (with cumin seed)	69
Sangria, Dry	78
Sangria, Lime	78
Sangria, Orange	78
Shrimp Boats, Mexican	60
Sole en Escabeche (Pickled Fish)	65
Sombrero Tostado, El	66
Sopa de Aguacate con Ajo (Avocado Soup with Garlic)	61
Spanish Rice	65
Steak Rolls Mexicano, Minute	63
Taco Meat Mixture	72
Tacos con Aguacate (Tacos with Avocado)	62
Tacos de Coctel y Acientunas Rellanas	72
Tamale Pie	65
Tamale Pie, al Fresco	67
Tamale Pie, au Gratin	66
Tamale Pie, Seaside	68
Tamale Steak Rolls	72
Tortilla Rolls, Chicken	67
Tostados	71
Tostados con Chorizos	63
Tostados con Pollo (Tostados with Chicken)	68

NAUTICAL—Fish, Seafood

Alaska King Crab Casserole Mantua	122
Almond Deviled Crab	123
Atun a la Marina (Tuna a la Marina)	122
Avocado Dip	116
Clam Chowder, Filene's	122
Codfish Cakes, New England	124
Court Bouillon	122
Crab Cakes	124
Crab Casserole de Luxe	123
Crab Meat au Gratin	123
Cucumber Sauce	115
Fillets, Low-Cal, Curried	144
Fillets, Sea Green Delight	144
Fillets, Slender Spicy	144
Fillets, Sunshine	126
Fishkabobs, Hogate's Broiled	126
Fish and Chips Batter, Old English	125
Fish Chowder, Manhattan	124
Fish Fillets, Gourmet	144
Fish Florentine	125
Fish Portions in Wine Sauce	125
Fish Steaks, Breaded Chinese Style	125
Fish Sticks with Hot Tartar Sauce	128
Fish Sticks Parmigiana	128
Flounder, Baked Stuffed	127
Flounder, Fillet of, with Dill Stuffing	127
Flounder, Stuffed, Seven Seas	127
Frog Legs a l'Americaine	127
Frog Legs Manier	127
Green Goddess Dressing for Seafood Cocktails	116
Haddock Fillets, Baked in Spanish Sauce	126
Halibut, Baked with Alaska King Crab Dressing, Tomato Sauce	129
Halibut Florentine in Casserole	130
Halibut, Grilled Oriental	129
Halibut, Polynesian, North Pacific	129
Halibut, Poached Fillet au Gratin	129
Halibut Tokay	130
Italian Diavolo	124
Lemon-Mustard Sauce	115
Lobster and Macaroni Creamed with Sherry Wine and Cheese	131
Lobster Shell, Baked Stuffed (Lobster, Shrimp and Crab Meat au Gratin)	131
Lobster Stew	131
Oysters, Baked with Crab Meat au Gratin	133
Oysters, Bienville Sauce	133
Oyster and Corn Casserole	133
Oysters, Fried	134
Oysters, Hangtown Fry	133
Pike, Polynesian	142
Red Snapper, Baked Fillet, Fresh Florida a la Creole	128
Remoulade Sauce	115
Rock Lobster, Gourmet Stuffed	134
Rijstafel-Curry of Lobster, Shrimp, Crab Meat with Sherry and Saffron Rice Pilaw	132
Salmon, Baked Fillet, Sage Dressing	135
Salmon, Dill Sauce	135
Salmon Fiesta	135
Salmon and Macaroni, Baked	135
Sandwiches, South African Souffle	134
Sauces	114-116
Scallops au Gratin Virginia	137
Scallops, Broiled with Vermouth	137
Scallops Polynesian en Brochette Flamed with Cognac	137
Scallops Roadhouse	136
Scallops, Savory New Bedford	136
Scallops and Shrimp Imperial	137
Scallops Thermidor or Coquilles St. Jacques	136
Seafood au Gratin	130
Seafood Bisque, Island Hotel	134
Seafood Casserole, Peckett's on Sugar Hill	132
Seafood Pancakes	131
Sea-Going Dip	128
Shrimp and Seafood au Gratin in Casserole, Chef Spencer	139
Shrimp, Baked Stuffed	138
Shrimp Bean Salad	128
Shrimp Creole	139
Shrimp de Jonghe	141
Shrimp, Egg and Anchovy Salad Bowl	141
Shrimp, Fried	138
Shrimp, Gumbo	140
Shrimp in Beer O'Donnell	138
Shrimp Jambalaya	139
Shrimp Louis	140
Shrimp and Mushrooms en Casserole	140
Shrimp a la Newburg	138
Shrimp Salad, Curried	139
Shrimp, Spanish Marinated	141
Shrimp Stuffed Peppers, Creole Style	140
Slimline Shellfish Salad	145
Sole Amandine, Saute Dover	142
Sole, Chef Bertil's Fillet, a la Stockholm	142
Tartar Sauce	115
Triton's Triumph	123
Tuna Cheese Roll	143
Tuna Fish Souffle, Dayton's Baked	143
Tuna Souffle Sandwich	143

COUNTRY/COLONIAL—
Farm Style, Early American

Angel Food Cake de Luxe	227
Appetizer Tray Pennsylvania Dutch	213
Apple Brown Betty	230
Apple Crisp with Black Walnuts, Coconut	229
Apple, Date, Nut Salad, Molded	226
Apple Pie, Southern, Rum Sauce	231
Beef Kidney Stew	215
Beef Loaf, Sauce Topping	216
Beets in Sour Cream	221
Blueberry Pie, Down Maine	232
Bread Pudding	230
Cabbage Salad	223
Capon, Breast of, Colligan's Stockton Inn	219
Capon, Breast of, Colonial Inn	165
Carrot Cookies, Orange Icing	233
Carrots Lyonnaise	222
Cauliflower and Cheese Casserole	222
Cheddar Pippin	221
Cheese Pie, Beershire	165
Cheese Soup Wisconsin	215
Cherry Pecan Torte, Baked	228
Chicken and Fresh Vegetable Salad	226
Chicken Loaf	219
Chicken and Pineapple Salad	223
Chicken Pot Pie	220
Chicken Stoltzfus	165
Chocolate Pudding, Steamed	229
Clam Chowder, New England	213
Cole Slaw, Hot	223
Corn Chowder	215
Corn Souffle Pudding	221
Crab Meat Bake, New England	220
Cracker Pudding	167
Cranberry Gelatin Salad	225
Cranberry Loaf	226
Cream of Chicken Soup	213
Cream of Fresh Vegetable Soup	213
Cream Sauce (Medium)	218
Dressing, Salad Bowl, Garlic	224
Dumplings for Lamb Stew	216
Eggplant Fritters	223
Eggs, Poached American	219
Flounder, Stuffed Baked	165
Fruit Cake, Light, Harvest Moon	227
Fruit Salad, Jellied	224
Fudge Squares	233
Ginger Cut-Outs, Early American	232
Goulash, Tavern	167
Green Beans, Dutch Style	222
Greens, Special Salad Bowl	224
Ham a la King	218
Ham, Cranberry Glazed	217
Ham Loaf, Currant Sauce	216
Ham Salad	224
Ham Steaks, Capped	217
Indian Pudding, Baked	230
Kidney Bean Salad	225
Lamb Patties, Stuffed	215
Lamb Shanks Mixed Vegetable Gravy	216
Lamb Stew with Dumplings	216
Lemon Chiffon Pie	231
Lettuce Salad, Wilted	226
Lobster a la Newburg	220
Lobster Pie, Baked, Colonial Inn	165
Lobster Pie, Baked, Treadway Inn	221
Lobster Salad	224
Mince-Creamy-Pecan Pie	231
Mushroom Biscuits	167
Mushroom Steak Sauce, Lenape	167
Navy Bean Soup	214
Oatmeal Cookies, Filled	233
Onions, Glazed	223
Oxtail Soup	214
Parsnips, Candied	223
Pastry Biscuits	226
Peach Pie, Open Face	231
Pepper Pot Soup	214
Persimmon Pudding	228
Pork Chops, Baked with Apple and Onion Dressing	219
Potato Salad	225
Potato Soup, Old Fashioned	214
Potatoes, Piquant	222
Prune Corn Bread	226
Prune Whip, Baked	230
Rice Pudding, Old Fashioned Baked	229
Sauce, Honey Rum	231
Sauerkraut Relish, Sweet-Sour	167
Sausage, O'Brien's Famous Country	218
Schnitz Un'Knepp—Tavern Adaptation	218
Seafood Casserole, Peckett's on Sugar Hill	220
Shoo-Fly Pie	232
Shortcake Biscuits, Baking Powder	229
Sour Cream Raisin Pie	232
Spice Cake, Rosy Layer with Cream Cheese Icing	228
Sponge Cake, Hot Milk	227
Squash, Stuffed Yellow	222
Sweet Potatoes and Apples, Escalloped	165
Sweet-Sour Dressing	234
Tapioca, Clear Raspberry	230
Veal Fricassee	217
Veal Pasties	218
Vegetable Salad Bowl, Cooked	225
Winter Salad	225